Risk and Uncertainty in Environmental and Natural Resource Economics

Risk and Uncertainty in Environmental and Natural Resource Economics

Edited by

Justus Wesseler

Assistant Professor of Environmental and Natural Resource Economics, Wageningen University, The Netherlands

Hans-Peter Weikard

Associate Professor of Environmental and Natural Resource Economics, Wageningen University, The Netherlands

Robert D. Weaver

Professor of Agricultural Economics, Pennsylvania State University, USA

Edward Elgar

Cheltenham, UK • Northampton, MA, USA

Published by
Edward Elgar Publishing Limited
Glensanda House
Montpellier Parade
Cheltenham
Glos GL50 1UA
UK

Edward Elgar Publishing, Inc.
136 West Street
Suite 202
Northampton
Massachusetts 01060
USA

A catalogue record for this book
is available from the British Library

Library of Congress Cataloguing in Publication Data

International Conference on Risk and Uncertainty in Environmental
and Resource Economics (2002: Wageningen, Netherlands)
Risk and uncertainty in environmental and natural resource economics/
edited by Justus Wesseler, Hans-Peter Weikard, Robert D. Weaver.
p. cm.
Papers presented at the International Conference on Risk and Uncertainty in Environmental and Resource Economics, held in June 2002 in Wageningen, the Netherlands.
Includes index.
1. Environmental Economics—Congresses. 2. Natural resources—Management—Congresses. 3. Risk—Congresses. 4. Uncertainty—Congresses. I. Wesseler, Justus, 1963– . II. Weikard, Hans-Peter. III. Weaver, Robert D. IV. Title.
HC79.E5I5338 2002
333.7—dc22

2003060779

ISBN 1 84376 609 4

Printed and bound in Great Britain by MPG Books Ltd, Bodmin, Cornwall

Contents

Figures

Tables

Contributors

Jock R. Anderson, Rural Development Department, World Bank, 1818 H St Washington, DC 20433, USA.

Marcel A.P.M. van Asseldonk, Institute for Risk Management in Agriculture, Wageningen UR, Hollandseweg 1, 6706 KN Wageningen, The Netherlands.

Rossella Bargiacchi, Department of Economics, Tilburg University, PO Box 90153, 5000 LE Tilburg, The Netherlands.

Mark Dickie, Department of Economics, University of Central Florida, Orlando, FL 32826, USA.

Anthony C. Fisher, Department of Agricultural and Resource Economics, University of California at Berkeley, Berkeley, CA 94720-3310, USA.

Shirra Freeman, Department of Economics, University of Haifa, Haifa, Israel 31905.

Silke Gabbert, Environmental Systems Analysis Group, Wageningen UR, 6700 HB Wageningen, The Netherlands.

Shelby Gerking, Department of Economics, University of Central Florida, Orlando, FL 32826, USA.

Peter Golubtsov, Physics Department, Moscow State Lomonsov University, Moscow, 119899, Russia.

J. Brian Hardaker, Graduate School of Agricultural and Resource Economics, University of New England, Armidale, 2351, Australia.

Veli-Pekka Heikkinen, Varma-Sampo Mutual Pension Insurance Company, P.O. Box 1, 00098 Varma-Sampo, Helsinki, Finland.

Carolien Kroeze, Environmental Systems Analysis Group, Wageningen UR, 6700 HB Wageningen, The Netherlands.

Timo Kuosmanen, Environmental Economics and Natural Resources Group, Wageningen UR, Hollandseweg 1, 6706 KN Wageningen, The Netherlands.

Robert McKelvey, Department of Mathematical Sciences, University of Montana, Missoula, MT 59801, USA.

Kathleen Miller, Environmental and Societal Impacts Group, National Center for Atmospheric Research, P.O. Box 3000, Boulder, CO 80307, USA.

Alfons G.J.M. Oude Lansink, Farm Management Group, Wageningen UR, Hollandseweg 1, 6706 KN Wageningen, The Netherlands.

Sung Hoon Park, Department of Economics and Finance, University of Wyoming, Laramie, WY 82071-3985, USA.

Stephen C. Peck, President, Flèche, 3720 Redwood Circle, Palo Alto, CA, 94306, USA.

Anne Rozan, BETA-Theme, PEGE, Université Louis Pasteur, 61 avenue de la Forêt-Noire, 67 000, Strasbourg, France.

Jason F. Shogren, Department of Economics and Finance, University of Wyoming, Laramie, WY 82071-3985, USA.

Susanne Soretz, Department of Economics, Hannover University, Königsworther Platz 1, 30167 Hannover, Germany.

Anne Stenger, INRA, LEF (Forest Economics) Engref-INRA, 14 rue Girardet, 54042 Nancy, France.

Thomas J. Teisberg, President, Teisberg Associates, 1475 Ingleside Drive Charlottesville VA 22901, USA.

Robert D. Weaver, Department of Agricultural Economics, Penn State University, 207 D Armsby, University Park, PA 16802, USA.

Hans-Peter Weikard, Environmental Economics and Natural Resources Group, Wageningen UR, Hollandseweg 1, 6706 KN Wageningen, The Netherlands.

Justus Wesseler, Environmental Economics and Natural Resources Group, Wageningen UR, Hollandseweg 1, 6706 KN Wageningen, The Netherlands.

Marc Willinger, BETA-Theme, PEGE, Université Louis Pasteur, 61 avenue de la Forêt-Noire, 67 000, Strasbourg, France.

Naomi Zeitouni, Department of Economics, University of Haifa, Haifa, Israel 31905.

Acknowledgements

This volume presents a selection of the papers presented at the International Conference on Risk and Uncertainty in Environmental and Resource Economics held in June 2002 in Wageningen, The Netherlands. The idea for the conference emerged from discussions within the Environmental Economics and Natural Resources Group of Wageningen University. We are grateful to Ekko van Ierland for his initiative and contribution to organizing the conference and for his continuous support during the preparation of this volume. We are also grateful to all participants who contributed to making our conference a success.

We wish to thank our colleagues of the Environmental Economics and Natural Resources Group and, particularly, Wil den Hartog and Femke Ruttan for their support before and during the conference.

The chapters in this volume have been selected with the help of anonymous reviewers. We thank them for their careful reading and the many suggestions to improve the chapters.

The conference and this volume would not have been possible without the financial support from the International Human Dimensions Programme on Global Environmental Change (IHDP), the Royal Dutch Academy of Arts and Sciences (KNAW), the Dutch Organisation for Scientific Research (NWO), the European Association of Agricultural Economists (EAAE), Wageningen Institute for Environment and Climate Research (WIMEK), the Dutch Organisation for Applied Scientific Research (TNO), the Dutch Ministry of Housing, Spatial Planning and the Environment (VROM) and Mansholt Graduate School of Social Sciences (MGS). We gratefully acknowledge their support.

Finally, we would like to thank Daniel de Geus for his excellent job in preparing the camera-ready copy for this volume and the editorial staff at Edward Elgar, specifically Dymphna Evans and Matthew Pitman, for their advice and assistance in completing the book.

Justus Wesseler, Hans-Peter Weikard and Rob Weaver

1. Introduction: Approaches to Risk and Uncertainty in Environmental and Resource Economics

Justus Wesseler, Hans-Peter Weikard and Robert D. Weaver

1. INTRODUCTION

Contemporary environmental policy and natural resource management face significant challenges posed by uncertainty. Underlying systems are not known with certainty. For example, the issue of reduction of greenhouse gas emissions must be addressed before the climatic system is fully understood. Further, these systems are intrinsically stochastic, implying that both their performance and the implications of their performance are uncertain. Irreversibility of actions that may affect these systems or their performance add to the relevance of uncertainties. Irreversible investment in abatement capital and potentially irreversible climate impacts require careful deliberation. Similarly, the threat of biodiversity loss calls for decisions, which will inevitably be based on very limited information about species and ecosystems.

Risk and uncertainty is a feature of economic systems for which economists have analytical tools to support decision making. However, our complex world poses ample challenges and opportunities to improve these tools. The chapters in this volume explore some of the complexities of decision making under risk and uncertainty in environmental and natural resource economics and irreversibilities. The book is divided into three parts. Part I comprises chapters that underline the importance of a variety of types of uncertainty and irreversibility. Part II explores implications for economic development and environmental policies. Part III looks at natural resource management problems of the private sector.

2. IMPORTANCE OF ENVIRONMENTAL RISK AND UNCERTAINTY

Climate change poses an important case that has become popular as a context for the testing and development of tools for decision making. Climate change policies address long-term impacts of temperature changes where magnitude and geographic distribution of temperature change are uncertain. Moreover, for any given scenario of temperature change an assessment of impacts remains speculative. In Chapter 2, Anthony Fisher surveys the recent literature with a focus on irreversibility and the possibility of catastrophic impacts.

Another important environmental issue is irreversible changes in biodiversity. In Chapter 3, Hans-Peter Weikard analyses intertemporal nature conservation strategies. Species loss is considered to be irreversible. Therefore, species protection constitutes a delay of an irreversible investment that may be beneficial if new information improves decision making. This benefit from a delay of an irreversible investment has been called 'quasi-option value' by Arrow and Fisher (1974). As we can learn about the value of ecosystems and species only if they are protected to ensure their survival, Weikard uses a model of endogenous learning to study optimal conservation paths.

Shirra Freeman and Naomi Zeitouni (Chapter 4) look at the optimal development under irreversibility and uncertainty. They assume that benefits from development are certain, though environmental consequences from development are uncertain and irreversible. They differentiate between two important models, one where the drift rate of the uncertain environmental consequences changes due to development and one where development results in a jump of the uncertain environmental implications but the variance of the uncertainty remains the same. The two models lead to different results about the optimal level of development that motivates the need for empirical representation of environmental change in economic models.

3. IMPLICATIONS FOR ECONOMIC DEVELOPMENT AND ENVIRONMENTAL POLICIES

Policy responses to environmental risk and uncertainty are the main theme of Part II. Risk policies are incentive systems which are designed to change individual responses to risk. Chapters 5 and 6 analyse how strategic interaction affects policy design in the face of risk. Sung Hoon Park and Jason Shogren analyse a public–private environmental conflict where a national park is a public good for a citizen group and a private good for a group of firms who want to extract its timber resources. In Park and Shogren's model, the environmental risk is endogenous in the sense that it is 'created' by the contest over property rights. In Chapter 6, Robert McKelvey, Kathleen Miller and Peter Golubtsov study the impact of an external environmental risk on strategic behaviour in a fisheries model. They show how increasing risk can lead to the breakdown of an efficient agreement resulting in a fish war. The model provides interesting insights into a recent case of a Canadian–US Pacific salmon fishery harvesting dispute.

Environmental risks, in particular global and potentially catastrophic risks, are often viewed as requiring precautionary actions. In Chapter 7, Rossella Bargiacchi discusses implications of the precautionary principle for climate change policies. Precaution is defined as placement of more weight on worse-case outcomes in decision making. Bargiacchi uses rank-dependent utility theory as a tool to analyse climate change scenarios. The findings are ambiguous. In some cases precaution does not imply lower levels of pollution.

In Chapter 8, Susanne Soretz studies pollution and abatement in an endogenous growth model with uncertain environmental damages. The model is used to analyse abatement decisions and (fiscal and environmental) policy instruments: income taxation, consumption taxation and subsidies for abatement investments. A main driving force in the model is households' savings behaviour as they take precautionary actions in the face of environmental risks.

Stephen Peck and Thomas Teisberg (Chapter 9) take on the question of how market-oriented methods can be used to manage environmental effects of private sector decisions. In particular, they consider the problem-setting of CO_2 emission management policy. While standards have typically been recognized as a policy response to uncertain effects, the design of standards is problematic when regulating a heterogeneous population of polluters with a pollution process in which stocks accumulate, though also naturally degrade. Peck and Teisberg consider the potential of emission permits that are tradable though for which 'where and when' flexibility is allowed. They consider the extension of such policies to allow for specification of a terminal year that brackets a time period or life for the permit. Allowing for natural depreciation of pollution stock, the permit system would induce increased pollution as the time between the emission and the terminal date increases. The flexibility that results can be interpreted as providing a hedge with respect to environmental uncertainty such as the rate of natural degradation.

The nature of decision-maker response to risk is a crucial feature of the choice problem that underlies private and public sector management of the environmental effects. In Chapter 10, Jock Anderson and Brian Hardaker take on the question of how both the extent and type of risk response influence policy. They review alternative conceptual measures of risk aversion and argue that, for policy formulation purposes, the moderate levels of risk aversion observed across economic agents motivate use of subjective expected utility methods that reflect such moderate levels of risk aversion.

An important aspect of environmental and natural resource policy formulation in a setting characterized by uncertainty and irreversibility is the complexity of processes involved. This complexity strongly motivates the need for multidisciplinary consideration of processes involved. Within this context, the utility of simple, highly abstract models begins to wilt. Silke Gabbert and Carolien Kroeze motivate the role and consider the usefulness of integrated assessment models (IAMs). In Chapter 11, they begin by motivating the need for the IAM approach and present a generalized definition of IAMs. They review within a useful typology the state of uncertainty analysis in IAMs, noting recent applications available in the literature. This primer on the concept and utility of uncertainty analysis in IAMs is then given life by a useful discussion of how so-called 'frameworks' for uncertainty analysis might be applied in the case of IAMs for atmospheric acidification.

4. PRIVATE SECTOR RESPONSE

The private sector faces two important problems in environmental and natural resources management. One is to optimally allocate resources under uncertainty and the other is to safeguard against environmental risks. Veli-Pekka Heikkinen and Timo Kuosmanen (Chapter 12) look at the optimal use of a natural resource under price uncertainty by analysing the forest harvesting problem from a stochastic dominance point of view. A portfolio consisting of four mixed forest stands and the average index of the Helsinki stock exchange are analysed for their efficiency. The holder of the portfolio has the option of harvesting the forest and buying the index or waiting before selling the forest. Using second-order stochastic dominance (SSD) the authors analyse whether it would be efficient to sell some of the forest. The main problem with SSD in this case is the identification of the optimal portfolio among the almost infinite set of possibilities. Using a non-parametric approach developed by Kuosmanen, the authors are able to identify the efficient portfolio. They compare the results with the mean variance approach but do not find major differences.

The private sector can safeguard against risky and uncertain environmental conditions using insurance-related financial instruments such as weather derivatives. These risk-transfer instruments are linked to specific events; contracts are written against defined outcomes. The motivation for shifting risks by means of objective indices is that problems posed by the presence of systemic risks and asymmetric information that manifest as moral hazard and adverse selection. Marcel van Asseldonk and Alfons Oude Lansink (Chapter 13) analyse the possibility of private protection against environmental risk by hedging based on weather-related index insurance. Their application considers hedging temperature exposure by greenhouse horticultural firms. A derivative contract is found to reduce profit volatility, but substantial heterogeneity in its performance was found across firms.

The environment and natural resources both affect and are impacted by private sector production processes and household consumption activities. When the environment affects economic outcomes that have both private and public value, a role for public policy may emerge. In Chapter 14, Mark Dickie and Shelby Gerking consider this general problem, focusing on the determinants of mitigation expenditures by households to manage the risk of skin cancer. They present a single-period household model of parental expenditure decisions to protect themselves and their children from skin cancer. The theoretic model motivates an empirical model that is estimated using survey data. Results are used to quantify the determinants of beliefs with respect to risk of skin cancer, to estimate willingness to pay (WTP) for risk mitigation products, and to compute the parent indifference map between parental versus child risk. While attitudes and family characteristics are incorporated as determinants of perceived risk, risk is specified as mitigated by use of a purchased good. Perceived risk to children is specified as conditional on perceived risk to parents. The survey method used provides an example of the current state of the art for risk valuation. Results illustrate the importance of intra-household aspects of risk and risk-related behaviour.

Similarly, one role of public policies is to provide information about environmental risks. This information role is especially important in the area of food safety when food safety risks can result in high private and public costs. In Chapter 15, Anne Rozan, Anne Stenger and Marc Willinger report the results of a food safety valuation experiment. Subjects were asked to state 'values' for food products (apples, potatoes and bread). They were also asked if they wanted to participate in markets to purchase these products. Those who accepted were asked to make an offer (bid) based on the Becker–De Groot–Marschak procedure. The objective of the experiment was to assess the subjects' WTP for food safety with respect to heavy metal content by comparing their values/bids for uncontrolled and their values/bids for controlled (labelled) products. Furthermore they compare the subjects' values/bids before and after information about heavy metal content of products was provided. Information was shown to lead to a significant increase in the valuation of labelled products. At the same time the valuation of unlabelled products decreases but not in a significant way. The results clearly identify a demand for information about food safety and support the public sector role in providing the information.

In sum, economic processes allocate scarce resources while interacting with the environment. Managing these processes under risk and uncertainty to improve the environment and the economy is a challenge that is taken up in this book. The chapters in this volume provide a useful perspective on progress towards improved management in reaction to this challenge.

REFERENCE

Arrow, K.J. and A.C. Fisher (1974), 'Environmental preservation, uncertainty and irreversibility', *Quarterly Journal of Economics*, **88**, 312–19.

PART I

Importance of Environmental Risk and Uncertainty

2. Irreversibilities and Catastrophic Risks in Climate Change

Anthony C. Fisher

1. INTRODUCTION

Much has been written over the past decade about policy options for dealing with anticipated climate change, including a range of theoretical and applied studies by academic economists. Some of these studies address the questions of what is an appropriate mechanism for coordinating international efforts to control emissions of greenhouse gases and what are the prospects for achieving control through negotiation or bargaining (see, for example, Hoel 1997). Another line of research, and the one pursued in this chapter, focuses on the questions of how soon, and how stringently, should we control emissions. Often – though not explicitly in this chapter – this takes the form of an analysis of the optimal level and trajectory of carbon taxes (see, for example, Peck and Teisberg 1992).

Although there are exceptions, discussed below, it seems fair to say that the implications for policy of uncertainty about future climate changes coupled with rigidities or irreversibilities in physical and economic systems have not been adequately analyzed. What is the nature of the uncertainty? First, it is uncertain how much the global mean temperature will increase over, say, the next 100 years – to say nothing of the more distant future. Second, impacts of a given increase are not definitely known. According to climate scientists, there is some probability, perhaps small, of catastrophic impact. For example, disintegration of the West Antarctic Ice Sheet would result in a rise in sea level of 5–6 meters. Recent research seems to suggest that more rapid (than anticipated) melting is going on in some parts of the ice shelf supporting the ice sheet, but it is not clear what is happening overall (Chang 2002). Although a 'meltdown' is by no means certain, and may even be unlikely, at least over the next several hundred years, there is a non–negligible probability that it will occur.

Another factor complicating a policy choice is the presence of rigidities, or irreversibilities, in both physical and economic systems. The irreversibilities in the context of climate policy are of two kinds. Investment in controlling emissions, for example, by accumulating a stock of capital in nuclear or renewable energy production, or more energy-efficient buildings, cars, and appliances, is irreversible in the sense that the capital is 'sunk'. Once the investment has been made, the resulting stock of capital is ordinarily not easily converted to consumption or other forms of capital, should one or another of these changes be desired at some future date, when the durable capital has not yet completely depreciated. On the climate side, the accumulation of greenhouse gases is more or less irreversible. Of course, there is 'depreciation' here too as carbon dioxide is removed from the atmosphere by terrestrial vegetation or by the oceans. But this is a long process, and some fraction of emissions will in fact remain in the atmosphere for 1000 years and beyond (Maier-Reimer and Hasselman 1987; Schultz and Kasting 1997; Joos et al. 1999). Further, impacts of even a relatively short-lived pulse may be long-lived or irreversible. This would be true of the catastrophic impacts, such as disintegration of the West Antarctic Ice Sheet, or regional climate changes that resulted in significant loss of biodiversity.

This chapter considers the question: what are the implications for the timing of climate policy of various scenarios involving combinations of these uncertainties and irreversibilities? That is, the focus is on the question posed earlier, of how soon, and how stringently, should we control greenhouse gas emissions, but with special reference to the implications of relevant uncertainties and irreversibilities.

The next section discusses uncertainty and irreversibility more generally in the context of environmental problems. Under what circumstances are they significant, and what are the implications for policy? The discussion here leads to the concept of option value, which arises in a setting characterized by both irreversibility and the prospect of resolving or reducing uncertainty with the passage of time. This option value is exactly analogous to the value of a financial option but, as will be indicated, has a history of independent development in environmental economics. The third section returns the focus to the climate problem, considering the nature of climate irreversibilities, discounting in the context of climate change, and results from the rather sparse literature here. Since the review suggests that not all questions regarding the timing of climate policy are adequately addressed in the literature, the fourth section sketches in non-technical terms a simple two-period model of the optimal level of first-period investment in control of greenhouse gas emissions that in my judgment takes appropriate account of relevant uncertainties and irreversibilities. A concluding section summarizes the main points.

2. UNCERTAINTY, IRREVERSIBILITY, AND OPTION VALUE IN ENVIRONMENTAL ECONOMICS

Uncertainty is of course a well-understood fact of economic life and often plays a role in decisions about the allocation of resources, including those of the natural environment. Economic models usually assume that the decision maker does the best he/she can, subject to what is known, or expected, about future costs and benefits of any given course of action. An interesting question arises, however, concerning timing. Clearly, if a decision, say about whether to go ahead with a development project in a natural environment, has to be made today, it has to be based on the expected values of benefits and costs, perhaps adjusted or discounted to reflect the risk preferences of the decision maker or of those in whose name the decision is made. But suppose that the decision can be deferred, say until next year. Why would one want to do this? If additional information about future costs and benefits were forthcoming, perhaps resolving the uncertainty, presumably a better decision can be made – one that reflects a more accurate view of the advantages and disadvantages of going forward. Of course, deferring the decision comes at a cost: the forgone returns from the project over the time the decision has been deferred, which needs to be balanced against the benefit of the improved decision.

In a problem of this type, the option to postpone the irreversible investment decision until better information about future costs and benefits is available, rather than being constrained to make the decision right away, has a value: option value. This is the basic result of Arrow and Fisher (1974) and Henry (1974) in the environmental economics literature. Note that the option has value only because the decision maker is assumed to learn about future returns by waiting. If this were not the case, nothing would be gained by postponing a decision on whether or not to go ahead with the project. Option value has also been identified with the value of information (Conrad 1980). This is correct but only in a qualified sense. The information about future costs and benefits is valuable only because the decision maker is assumed to have the flexibility to postpone the decision about the investment. Option value can thus be considered a conditional value of information – the value of information conditional on retaining the option to either make the investment or not make it (Hanemann 1989). It is worth noting also the parallel to finance. The option to postpone the investment decision is analogous to a call option on a share of stock. It confers the right to exercise the option to invest at a given price (the cost of the investment) to receive an asset (the project, say a dam for the production of hydroelectric power) that will yield a stream of uncertain future returns.

The dam construction example may be a bit dated. Today, the major environmental issues, at least on a global scale, are probably loss of biodiversity and climate change. Here, too, irreversibility seems to be significant in motivating concern. With respect to biodiversity, much of the concern is for endangered species. But, even if the survival of a particular species is not at issue, biological impacts can be very difficult to reverse over any time span that is meaningful for human societies. The clear-cutting of a climax forest species, for example, removes the results of an ecological succession that may represent centuries of natural processes. Further regeneration may not lead to the original configuration even after many more centuries. Opportunistic species, such as hardy grasses, may come in and preempt the niche otherwise filled, eventually, by the climax species (Albers and Goldbach 2000). With respect to climate change, relevant rigidities or irreversibilities are discussed in the next section.

3. THE CLIMATE PROBLEM

As noted in the introduction, the problem of how soon, and how stringently, we should control greenhouse gas emissions is characterized by both uncertainties and irreversibilities. The uncertainties have to do with both the degree of warming to be expected and the potential impacts. The irreversibilities are on both the climate and the investment (in emission control) sides. Does the basic result on option value, or what might be called the 'irreversibility effect' in environmental decisions, such as those discussed in the preceding section, provide any information about the timing of climate policy? Since it seems plausible to assume that additional information about the nature and impacts of climate change will be forthcoming over time, all of the conditions for the result to go through are in place, so the answer is yes – but. The 'but' refers to the presence, in this problem, of two conflicting sources of irreversibility or inflexibility: on the one side, sunk capital (to reduce greenhouse gas emissions), and on the other, a not-fully-degradable stock of greenhouse gases in the atmosphere and possibly irreversible impacts. The difficulty is that these cut in opposite directions. Therefore, it is not clear whether the conditions of the problem imply that investment in control ought to be slowed, while waiting for information needed to make a better decision, or that investment should come sooner to preserve the option to protect ourselves from impacts that may be revealed in the future as serious or even catastrophic.

It may be appropriate to characterize a debate that has sprung up over this dilemma as pitting mainly economists on the side of waiting to invest until better information is available and mainly natural scientists on the side of doing more now to forestall what they see as potentially serious impacts. Of course, this is something of a stereotype and does not fit everyone. In the remainder of this section, the concept of irreversibility as it applies to the climate problem is considered and some of the major contributions by economists who have developed models of the timing of climate policy that explicitly take account of uncertainty and irreversibility are reviewed.

3.1 Irreversibility and Climate Change

It seems useful to say a bit more about irreversibility in this context, as the relevant natural science is perhaps not well known to economists and thus not yet adequately incorporated in economic models that deal with climate change. In the introduction it is acknowledged that the accumulation of greenhouse gases in the atmosphere is not truly irreversible since, though emissions in any period cannot be negative, the resulting accumulation is subject to natural decay over time. Typically, in economic models, such as the well-known and widely-used DICE (Dynamic Integrated Climate/Economy) model, developed by Nordhaus (1993, 1994), the process of accumulation and decay is represented in a single equation, in which the accumulation, or stock, of CO_2, the main greenhouse gas, in a period (a decade in DICE) is equal to some fraction of emissions in the preceding period plus some other fraction (one minus the rate of decay over the decade) of the stock in the preceding period. The process continues unchanged over time, implying that the atmospheric concentration of CO_2 returns to its current level in about 300 years and to the preindustrial level within 1000 years. Yet, as at least a couple of recent contributions by natural scientists have pointed out, this is not likely. The difficulty is that, after relatively rapid mixing, over a few decades, of the atmosphere with the surface ocean, further removal of CO_2 from the atmosphere depends on mixing of the surface ocean with the deep ocean – a much slower process (Joos et al. 1999). According to one calculation, after 1000 years, CO_2 concentrations will still be well over twice the current level and nearly three times the preindustrial level and will remain elevated for several thousand years (Schultz and Kasting 1997).

The point about long-run concentrations in fact appeared in the climate science literature over a decade earlier (Maier-Reimer and Hasselman 1987) and is incorporated in at least two insightful and important economic analyses, by Azar and Sterner (1996), who calculate the impact on estimates of the damages from global warming, and by Farzin and Tahvonen (1996), who derive the implications for the optimal trajectory of carbon taxes. The most recent version of the DICE model (Nordhaus and Boyer 2000) also takes account of the criticism of the representation of the carbon cycle in the earlier version. The one-equation model of carbon decay in the atmosphere is replaced by a three-equation, three-medium, model designed to represent the relatively slow exchange between the surface or upper ocean layer and the deep ocean. It turns out that this makes very little difference to the simulated optimal trajectory of rates of emissions control, but this result appears to depend on the way in which damages beyond the next few decades are discounted, as discussed below.

Clearly, long-run concentrations – and also long-run or irreversible impacts, such as would result from the large-scale melting of the Antarctic ice sheets – only matter if the discount rate used in evaluating a program of emissions control is sufficiently low that damages occurring or persisting several hundred and, indeed, several thousand years in the future matter to those who will be making the decisions about investment in control today. Azar and Sterner show that a change in the earlier version of the DICE model representation of the carbon cycle, so that it more accurately reflects long-run atmospheric concentrations, as in Maier-Reimer and Hasselman, does not make much difference to the optimal rate of emission control. This is because long-run damages are so heavily discounted – just as in the new version of the DICE model with the modified carbon cycle. In turn, this raises the question of what is the appropriate discount rate (or, more generally, discounting procedure) for dealing with environmental problems, such as global warming, or management of the nuclear fuel cycle, characterized by very long-lived consequences.

3.2 Discounting in the Context of Climate Change

The discount rate is ordinarily given, in growth models in the tradition of Ramsey (1928), by the sum of the rate of pure time preference, or the utility discount rate, and the growth discount rate, where the latter is given by the elasticity of the marginal utility of consumption times the rate of change in consumption. The growth discount rate reflects the assumption that a given increment in consumption will be worth less in the future when everyone is richer. This is also the formulation in the DICE model, which is a growth model joined to a climate model.

An important feature of this formulation is that it implies that, as the rate of growth in consumption changes, the discount rate changes. In particular, if the rate of growth in consumption declines, so does the discount rate. This is reflected in the DICE simulations, in which total factor productivity is assumed to be increasing, but at a decreasing rate, yielding a social discount rate that decreases from 5.9 per cent in 1995 to 4.4 per cent in 2075 (Nordhaus 1994, p. 91). Since the utility discount rate is, however, assumed to be 3 per cent, this is a lower bound for the social discount rate. Azar and Sterner put forward a number of arguments in favor of a zero or near-zero *social* rate of time preference even though market data may suggest a non-zero private rate. Both they and Dasgupta (2000) are also considerably more pessimistic than Nordhaus about prospects for continued growth in consumption at anything like the rates observed over the past few decades, especially when prospects for long-term environmental degradation, and loss of ecosystem services, are taken into account. This last point is important. Suppose, as a result of global warming and, perhaps, other changes having an adverse impact on ecosystem services, consumption at some future date actually declines. Then the growth discount rate would become negative. If the utility discount rate were close to zero, the social rate of discount would also become negative. In this scenario, the value of future damages would be amplified, not reduced, by discounting. In the DICE model, the discount rate starts fairly high, and does not decline very much, in part because of the constant positive rate of time preference. Consequently, damages in the more distant future are given very little weight. Azar and Sterner (1996, p. 181) show that, even assuming continued, though declining, growth in consumption over a time horizon of 300 years, but alternative lower rates of time preference, the marginal cost of CO_2 emissions would rise from \$13 per ton, at a time preference or utility discount rate of 3 per cent, to \$32 at 1 per cent, to \$75 at 0.1 per cent, and finally to \$85 at 0 per cent.

A quite different approach to discounting in the context of the climate problem, rooted explicitly in uncertainty, is put forward by Weitzman (1998). Interestingly, it points in the same direction, namely, declining – in this case dramatically declining – discount rates over time. Weitzman begins by observing that there is at any time – say the present – a wide distribution of beliefs, even among the 'experts', about the social discount rate, based on differences in beliefs about rates of time preference, future growth, the impact of environmental degradation or other externalities, and so on. Representing the distribution of beliefs explicitly by a probability distribution, Weitzman shows that the implied social discount rate, an aggregation of the individual beliefs, declines over time because increasingly greater present-value weight is placed on stated or observed low discount rates. High discount rates are relatively less important over time because their present value is progressively reduced relative to that of the low discount rates. Eventually, the only rate that counts is the minimum rate.

To see how this works, let us consider a simple example. Suppose there are just two 'observations' on the discount rate, $r_1 = 0.01$ and $r_2 = 0.10$, each with a probability or weight of 0.5. The present discounted value of one euro, received in period t, will be:

$$V(t) = 0.5(1/1{+}0.01)^t + 0.5(1/1{+}0.10)^t.$$

For $t = 1$,

$$V(1) = 0.5(1/1.01) + 0.5(1/1.10) = 0.5(0.990) + 0.5(0.909) = 0.495 + 0.455$$
$$= 0.950.$$

For $t = 10$,

$$V(10) = 0.5(1/1.01)^{10} + 0.5(1/1.10)^{10} = 0.5(0.905) + 0.5(0.385)$$
$$= 0.453 + 0.193 = 0.646.$$

For $t = 100$,

$$V(100) = 0.5(1/1.01)^{100} + 0.5(1/1.10)^{100} = 0.5(0.370) + 0.5(0) = 0.185.$$

The implied effective discount rates are, respectively, 0.053, 0.044, and 0.017. The contribution of the higher rate to the effective rate at any time is progressively reduced over time. In this example, the effective rate at $t = 1$ (0.053) is approximately a simple average of the low rate (0.01) and the high rate (0.10). By $t = 100$, the effective rate (0.017) has fallen most of the way to the low rate.

In subsequent work, Weitzman (2001) specifies a particular probability distribution for discount rates, the gamma distribution, characterized by a single peak, with the left tail cut off at zero and the right tail asymptotically approaching the x-axis, and shows it to be consistent with the results of a survey of the stated beliefs of a large sample of academic economists. The implied social discount rate starts off at the mean value of the distribution and declines monotonically towards zero. On the basis of the mean and variance of the sample, and a couple of other numerical assumptions, the discount rate starts off at 4 per cent and remains there through years 1–5 (what Weitzman calls the 'immediate future'), falls to 3 per cent for years 6–25 (the 'near future'), to 2 per cent for years 26–75 (the 'medium future'), to 1 per cent for years 76–300 (the 'distant future'), and finally to zero beyond 300 years (the 'far-distant future').

Where does this leave us? In my view, a strong case can be made for some form of hyperbolic discounting, that is, a discount rate that declines over time, as opposed to the more familiar exponential discounting, where decisions with very long time horizons (and potentially very serious consequences) are considered. Both the modified Ramsey and the Weitzman approaches point in this direction, and in my view both are persuasive. Of course the practical difficulty remains: how do we determine the hyperbolic function? This is however in any event a difficulty, even in the exponential case (how do we determine the constant rate?). I would simply take the position that hyperbolic discounting in some form merits serious consideration in the context of climate change.

3.3 The Literature on Climate Change, Uncertainty, and Irreversibility: Approaches and Results

Granted, then, that irreversibilities matter – they can be serious, and they cannot be discounted away – what does the literature reveal about the implications for the timing of climate policy of the apparently conflicting or opposing irreversibilities? Surprisingly, perhaps, results here tend to downplay the importance of the climate irreversibilities relative to the investment irreversibility. The opposing effects were first recognized and jointly analyzed by Kolstad (1996a) in a two-period model of irreversibilities in stock externalities. (A stock externality is an externality that, like some forms of pollution, accumulates – and, perhaps, decays – over time.) Kolstad asks the question, how does the prospect of better second-period information about the consequences of the externality, in his example the damages from global warming, affect the desired level of first-period investment in abatement capital? Emissions are assumed to be non-negative, and the degree of capital 'sunkness' and the decay rate of the stock of greenhouse gases are fixed. He finds that, if learning is proceeding slowly enough, compared with the rates of pollution decay and capital depreciation, learning makes no difference. If, on the other hand, learning is significant, either or both of the irreversibilities can affect the desired level of first-period emissions in opposite directions. Which dominates depends on the relative magnitudes of the decay and depreciation rates and on expectations about damages.

In a second paper, a multiperiod numerical simulation of optimal investment in control of greenhouse gas emissions based on the DICE model, extended to include both the capital-stock irreversibility and a parametric representation of the rate of learning, Kolstad (1996b) finds a significant impact associated with the capital-stock irreversibility but not with the emissions irreversibility. The reason, essentially, is that in his parameterization of the model, the non-negativity restriction on emissions is never binding. Too little investment in emissions control in the early periods can be compensated by a bit more investment in later periods. There is no scenario in which it would be optimal to emit negatively in the future to correct for emitting too much today.

This is consistent with the main result in Ulph and Ulph (1997), a two-period model of global warming, irreversibility, and learning in which there is no explicit representation of investment in abatement, but, as in Kolstad, emissions are restricted to being non-negative, the decay rate of the stock of greenhouse gases is fixed, and there is learning about damages. A sufficient condition for there to be an irreversibility effect, that is, for first-period emissions with learning to be less than first-period emissions with no learning, is that the non-negativity restriction is binding in the no-learning case. Ulph and Ulph also provide a multiperiod numerical simulation. For a variety of scenarios, they find very little difference between first-period emissions with learning and without. In one case, characterized by a low discount rate and substantial uncertainty, emissions with learning are greater. Since there is no explicit capital-stock irreversibility in the model or the simulation, it is not clear what is driving this somewhat counterintuitive result and no explanation is provided by the authors.

Results with much the same flavor as Kolstad's are obtained in a recent theoretical analysis of irreversibilities in environmental policy more generally (that is, not just in climate policy though this certainly fits the framework) by Pindyck (2000). Pindyck's work also draws on concepts and methods in option-pricing theory as developed in the literature on finance. He represents the uncertainties about both the future costs and benefits of reduced environmental degradation, as could be accomplished by an investment in pollution control, and the future evolution of the environment itself, as particular stochastic processes (geometric Brownian motions in which the percentage rate of change in each of the values is a random walk with drift, that is, with a trend). This seems fairly plausible, since one characteristic of the process is that the variance increases with the passage of time, and it also accommodates a positive trend, or a negative trend, or no trend.

Pindyck too recognizes the opposing irreversibilities. He asks the question, given the opposing biases in a decision, say to invest in control of greenhouse gas emissions, is it possible to draw any general conclusions? Interestingly, the answer is 'yes' though this does depend on some assumptions. One is that the decision can be deferred; information about the evolving environmental impacts and values accrues over time and can lead to a better decision. Why make an irreversible investment in reducing emissions today if waiting a little while will reveal with greater certainty what the outcome will be? Waiting entails a cost, the forgone benefits from the investment during the waiting period, but this may be much less than the benefits from the better decision that results. Of course, the same argument applies on the other side: better to protect the environment from irreversible damage now since it can be 'unprotected' if new information suggests that the damage, though irreversible, will be minor. What Pindyck shows is that an increase in uncertainty, whether over future costs and benefits of environmental protection or over the behavior of the environment, leads to a higher threshold for policy adoption. Policy adoption involves a sunk cost associated with a reduction in the entire trajectory of future emissions whereas waiting involves only continued emissions over the waiting period.

As Pindyck notes, this result depends on the extent to which the policy is, indeed, irreversible. It is important to note also that it implicitly assumes that emissions over the period do not increase the risk of a catastrophic impact.

To sum up, the sense one gets from the rather sparse economic literature that considers the implications for the timing of climate policy of uncertainty and irreversibility is that these cut in the direction of slowing or reducing investment in control of greenhouse gas emissions rather than speeding or increasing it. The reason for this result, which must appear counterintuitive to many climate scientists and, perhaps, also to policy makers and to the general public is that, given the assumptions or parameter values built into the models, there is relatively little cost to holding off on investment while waiting to learn of the benefit. The climate irreversibility, though recognized, does not play much of a role in driving current decisions on controlling emissions.

4. CLIMATE CHANGE, IRREVERSIBILITY, AND ENDOGENOUS RISK

A model which yields a somewhat different result, more in line with the non-economist's intuition, has been put forward by Fisher and Narain (2002). Recall that a key (implicit) assumption driving Pindyck's results is that emissions in a given time period do not lead to an increase in the probability of a catastrophic impact at some point in the future – or the next period, in a two-period model. By contrast, Fisher and Narain explicitly assume that there is some probability of a catastrophic impact, and moreover that the probability may be positively related to the level of greenhouse gas concentrations in the atmosphere, or in other words, that the probability is endogenous to the model. It is worth emphasizing that nothing in the model says that a catastrophic impact is likely. It may be very unlikely. It is assumed only that there is a (possibly very small) non-zero probability that some such event will occur, and that the probability may be related to concentrations of greenhouse gases.

The key features of the model are: two discrete time periods (think of present and future); sunk or irreversible investment in controlling emissions; non-degradable or irreversible stocks of greenhouse gases; risk of catastrophic damages; and future learning about the nature of damages. Learning is fixed, in the sense that the decision maker is assumed to learn, by the start of the second period, whether a climate event – say, a 5°F rise in global mean temperature – has occurred and, if it has, the nature of the impact, high damage or low. The model then studies how the desired level of first-period investment varies with the nature of the risk of catastrophic impact, that is, whether the risk is endogenous or not. Also considered is how investment is affected by the degree of sunkness of the resulting capital stock and by the degree of non-degradability of the stock of gases.

The formal objective is to choose investment and consumption in each period to maximize the sum of benefits, or utility, over both periods. Since the agent learns about second-period damages at the start of the second period, the optimization problem is solved through backwards induction. This entails first choosing the optimal level of investment in the second period when the returns are known. The second-period choice yields in the first period an expected continuation value, expected second-period returns given that second-period investment is optimally chosen. The problem then boils down to choosing the level of first-period investment given both first-period returns and the expected continuation value.

The main result is:

1. The optimal level of first period investment when the risk of catastrophic impact is endogenous is greater than the optimal level when the risk is exogenous.

Additional results are:

2. Investment in the first period is a decreasing function of the degree of sunkness of capital for both types of risk. In other words, the more difficult or expensive it is to 'disinvest', the less investment there should be in the first period. This result however holds only for the case in which the coefficient of intertemporal substitution (of consumption) is greater than one – as in the conventional specification of summed costs and benefits over time.
3. Analytically it is not possible to show how investment in the first period is affected by the rate of decay of the stock of greenhouse gases.
4. In a numerical model (a version of the two-period model with functional forms and parameters taken from the DICE model), investment in the first period is a decreasing function of the rate of decay. Alternatively, the less degradable the stock, the greater is optimal first-period investment. The effect is stronger for endogenous risk.

5. CONCLUSIONS

This chapter has considered the question of how the timing of climate policy (that is, the timing of investment in reductions in greenhouse gas emissions) is affected by uncertainties and irreversibilities. The uncertainties are about both the degree of warming and potential impacts. Irreversibilities are manifested in both physical systems (emissions cannot be negative, impacts may be very long lasting or impossible to undo) and economic systems (capital embodied in nuclear or renewable energy production facilities or energy-efficient buildings is sunk, that is, cannot be readily converted to other uses).

A review of the environmental economics literature yields a key result: where a problem is characterized by (i) uncertainty about future costs and benefits of the alternatives under consideration, (ii) prospects for resolving the uncertainty with the passage of time, and (iii) irreversibility of one of the alternatives, an extra value, an option value, is attached to the reversible alternative(s). Put differently, an irreversible decision or action has to clear a higher hurdle to pass a benefit/cost test.

Application to the climate problem is not straightforward since there are two opposing irreversibilities that cut in different directions. The sparse economics literature to date on this problem suggests that the investment irreversibility is more important than the climate irreversibility and the investment irreversibility cuts in the direction of slowing investment in reducing greenhouse gas emissions. As the models are formulated, there is relatively little cost, in the form of future damage from current emissions, to holding off on investment while waiting to learn what damage will occur.

A new model differs primarily in an assumption that there is some probability of high damage, or catastrophic impact, and that this probability may be positively related to the level or concentration of greenhouse gases in the atmosphere. The main result is that optimal first-period investment is greater when the probability is related to the concentration than when it is not.

REFERENCES

Albers, H.J. and M.J. Goldbach (2000), 'Irreversible ecosystem change, species competition, and shifting cultivation', *Resource and Energy Economics*, **22** (3), 261–80.

Arrow, K.J. and A.C. Fisher (1974), 'Environmental preservation, uncertainty, and irreversibility', *Quarterly Journal of Economics*, **88** (1), 312–19.

Azar, C. and T. Sterner (1996), 'Discounting and distributional considerations in the context of global warming', *Ecological Economics*, **19**, 169–84.

Chang, K. (2002), 'The melting (freezing) of Antarctica', *New York Times*, 2 April.

Conrad, J.M. (1980), 'Quasi-option value and the expected value of information,' *Quarterly Journal of Economics*, **95**, 813–20.

Dasgupta, P. (2000), 'Discounting: why and how?', Tenth Annual Conference of the European Association of Environmental and Resource Economists, Rethymonon, Crete (30 June–2 July).

Farzin, Y. and O. Tahvonen (1996), 'Global carbon cycle and the optimal time path of a carbon tax', *Oxford Economic Papers*, **48**, 515–36.

Fisher, A.C. and U. Narain (2002), 'Global warming, endogenous risk, and irreversibility', Working Paper No. 908 Revised, Department of Agricultural and Resource Economics, University of California at Berkeley.

Hanemann, W.M. (1989), 'Information and the concept of option value', *Journal of Environmental Economics and Management*, **16**, 23–37.

Henry, C. (1974), 'Investment decisions under uncertainty: the irreversibility effect', *American Economic Review*, **64**, 1006–12.

Hoel, M. (1997), 'Coordination of environmental policy for transboundary environmental problems', *Journal of Public Economics*, **66**, 199–224.

Joos, F., G. Müller-Fürstenberger and G. Stephan (1999), 'Correcting the carbon cycle representation: how important is it for the economics of climate change?', *Environmental Modeling and Assessment*, **4**, 133–40.

Kolstad, C.D. (1996a), 'Fundamental irreversibilities in stock externalities', *Journal of Public Economics*, **60**, 221–33.

Kolstad, C.D. (1996b), 'Learning and stock effects in environmental regulations: the case of greenhouse gas emissions', *Journal of Environmental Economics and Management*, **31**, 1–18.

Maier-Reimer, E. and K. Hasselman (1987), 'Transport and storage of CO_2 in the ocean: an inorganic ocean-circulation carbon cycle model', *Climate Dynamics*, **2**, 63–90.

Nordhaus, W.D. (1993), 'Rolling the "DICE": an optimal transition path for controlling greenhouse gases', *Resource and Energy Economics*, **15** (1), 27–50.

Nordhaus, W.D. (1994), *Managing the Global Commons*, Cambridge, MA: MIT Press.

Nordhaus, W.D. and J. Boyer (2000), *Roll the DICE Again: Economic Models of Global Warming*, Cambridge, MA: MIT Press.

Peck, S.C. and T.J. Teisberg (1992), 'CETA: a model for carbon emissions trajectory assessment', *Energy Journal*, **13**, 55–77.

Pindyck, Robert S. (2000), 'Irreversiblities and the timing of environmental policy', *Resource and Energy Economics*, **22**, 233–59.

Ramsey, F.P. (1928), 'A mathematical theory of saving', *Economic Journal*, **38**, 543–59.

Schultz, P.A. and J.F. Kasting (1997), 'Optimal reductions in CO_2 emissions', *Energy Policy*, **25**, 491–500.

Ulph, A. and D. Ulph (1997), 'Global warming, irreversibility and learning', *Economic Journal*, **107**, 636–50.

Weitzman, M.L. (1998), 'Why the far-distant future should be discounted at its lowest possible rate', *Journal of Environmental Economics and Management*, **36** (3), 201–8.

Weitzman, M.L. (2001), 'Gamma discounting', *American Economic Review*, **91** (1), 260–71.

3. On the Quasi-Option Value of Biodiversity and Conservation

Hans-Peter Weikard

1. INTRODUCTION

Intensified agriculture, deforestation, increasing transport and a growing demand for industrial and housing areas have caused a tremendous change in land use and will continue to do so. Although many species find their niche in cultivated land and even on industrial sites, on a global scale these changes in land use tend to threaten biodiversity. Today the human-induced extinction rate of species is estimated to be between 100 and 1000 times higher than the 'natural' rate.[1] Biodiversity is essential for the functioning of ecosystems, in particular

> the formation and retention of soils and the maintenance of soil fertility via the nitrogen cycle and the activity of micro-organisms; the breakdown and recycling of organic matter by micro-organisms; provision of fresh water via the hydrological cycle, flood control via flood-plains and wetlands; insect pollination of food crops; pest control via natural predators; and the maintenance of a genetic library. (Mainwaring 2001, p. 81)

Moreover, the maintenance of biodiversity secures potential sources of food, the chances to discover useful pharmaceuticals, and the aesthetic value of nature. A major motivation for maintaining biodiversity is keeping options for the future. Since we know little about most existing species, their characteristics, their habitats and their chances of survival, a conservation decision is burdened with uncertainty. Ignorance is a strong motivation for conservation. At the current pace of biodiversity loss we do not even know what we are losing. Since the loss of species is irreversible,[2] protecting species can be seen as a delay of an irreversible investment. Such delay will be beneficial if at a later stage decisions can be based on improved information. Thus, if we can learn about ecosystems and species, there is an additional value of keeping options. This value has been called 'quasi-option value' by Arrow and Fisher (1974).[3]

A positive quasi-option value provides additional motivation for conservation and calls for a larger conservation budget. Bishop (1978) was probably the first to notice a positive quasi-option value of species protection. Also, more recently, Linddal (1993), White (1996) and Swanson (1998) have argued that traditional valuation methods will underestimate the value of conservation when conservation reduces irreversible species loss. Marwah and Zhao (2002) discuss the case of two-sided irreversibilities, where species loss is irreversible *and* land preservation efforts involve sunk costs. In this case a quasi-option value accrues to land preservation as well as to its development. Marwah and Zhao consider the case of endogenous learning, that is, the information received depends on the decision-maker's initial choice. While the literature is mainly concerned with the trade-off between conservation and other benefits, this chapter takes a different approach. We start with the assumption of a fixed conservation budget. The importance of conservation as such is not the main issue here, but rather how the quasi-option value will impact the optimal intertemporal and spatial allocation of the budget. A similar question has been addressed by Albers (1996) who examines the case of spatial and intertemporal interdependence of conservation values. However, Albers does not specifically address the issue of biodiversity loss. This chapter examines the optimal selection of reserve sites for biodiversity conservation under uncertainty and endogenous learning. The chapter contributes to the literature by developing a framework for the choice of a conservation strategy when the budget for nature conservation is limited. The findings clearly support conservation policies that increase today's conservation efforts even if this draws on tomorrow's conservation budget. Today's conservation not only keeps options open, it also helps to generate new information to improve future decision making.

For conceptual clarity the next section briefly reviews the concepts of option value and quasi-option value. Section 3 presents a simple illustrative model to account for the quasi-option value of biodiversity. Section 4 is the main section of the chapter. It presents a framework for the reserve site selection problem when the quasi-option value is accounted for. Section 5 concludes.

2. ON OPTION VALUE AND QUASI-OPTION VALUE

It is important to distinguish two different values of holding an option. First, options are valuable because they provide insurance in a world of uncertainty. Second, the possibility of learning gives rise to an additional value when decisions are irreversible, because later decisions can be based on better information. These two types of values can be clearly distinguished and have been called 'option value' and 'quasi-option value', respectively.

In environmental economics the concept of an option value has been introduced by Weisbrod (1964) in the context of uncertain demand for environmental goods. The issue is one of finding the correct welfare measure to assess public spending on environmental projects and other public goods. Following Weisbrod (1964), Cicchetti and Freeman (1971) and Schmalensee (1972) have clarified the concept; see Bishop (1982) for a survey. Their analysis reveals that the option value is essentially a risk premium. Hence, for a risk-neutral decision maker the option value will necessarily be zero. The impact of option values for biodiversity preservation is discussed by Polasky et al. (1993).

Arrow and Fisher (1974) and Henry (1974) have shown that there exists a positive value of holding options even for a risk-neutral agent when a particular decision has irreversible consequences. Arrow and Fisher have termed this value 'quasi-option value' in order to distinguish it from Weisbrod's concept. In a separate strand of literature a related concept has been introduced as 'option value'. In a famous paper, Black and Scholes (1973) have developed a theory of option pricing in financial markets. An option is the right to use or consume an asset at a suitable (later) time. The value of an option depends crucially on the additional information that will be revealed to the decision maker. Here the motive to keep an option is not insurance, but to 'wait and see' and it may be worthwhile to incur some cost to do so. Building on results from financial economics, option value has also been introduced into the theory of investment under uncertainty summarized by Dixit and Pindyck (1994).

Recently, Mensink and Requate (2003) have shown that the option value of the theory of investment under uncertainty can be decomposed into the quasi-option value of environmental economics plus a value of postponement.[4] The option value concept of environmental economics should not be confused with the option value concept of investment theory. In this chapter I adopt the terminology established in environmental economics. In the remainder of the chapter I shall discuss the quasi-option value of biodiversity and show that it may be an important determinant of cost-effective conservation policies.

3. INTRODUCING QUASI-OPTION VALUE INTO DIVERSITY THEORY

Valuing biodiversity is a complex issue. It requires, as Weitzman (1992) points out, conceptual clarity and an operational framework. Weitzman

(1992, 1998) develops a theory of diversity to facilitate decision making in conservation. He applies this theory to the case of conservation of a family of cranes using information on genetic diversity between species; see Weitzman (1993). Since genetic information is available only for few species, Weikard (2002) argues that Weitzman's framework can be made applicable to a broad class of conservation problems using information on ecosystem diversity. Weikard shows that the measurement of ecosystem diversity boils down to counting species. Hence, the model presented in what follows focuses on the ecosystem level and uses species richness, that is, the number of species, as an indicator of biodiversity.

Decision makers in nature conservation face uncertainties of various kinds. First, whether an ecosystem is safe and will maintain its features over time cannot be known with certainty. Natural or man-made disasters can alter basic conditions in such a way that an ecosystem gets lost. The best thing we can do is to use survival probabilities of ecosystems and base decisions on expected values. Weitzman (1998) analyses the solution to the maximization of the *expected* diversity-plus-species value subject to a budget constraint. We shall not repeat his analysis here. Instead, we focus on a second type of uncertainty which concerns the number of species in an ecosystem. This uncertainty is due to severely limited information. Estimates of the total number of species on earth range between 5 and 100 million.[5] Estimates of species richness for particular ecosystems are similarly burdened with uncertainty.

In a simple setting uncertainty of species richness could be dealt with in a straightforward way. In general, the *value of the diversity* of an ecosystem is assumed to be increasing in species richness. The conservation decision could be taken by simply maximizing the expected value of diversity. However, an important feature of the decision problem is that the uncertainty is (partly) resolved in the future. The fact that we may learn more about the species in an ecosystem gives rise to a quasi-option value.

Following a clearly written presentation of the quasi-option value concept by Chichilnisky and Heal (1998), we first consider the case of a single ecosystem in a two-period model. Let D be the expected diversity value of an ecosystem at the initial stage $t = 0$. At $t = 1$ it is revealed that the true diversity value is either γD or βD, $\gamma > 1$, $0 < \beta < 1$, with probabilities p and $1-p$, respectively; hence, γ is good news and β is bad news. D is considered a long-run gain with no immediate benefits at $t = 0$. Furthermore, let $c^0 \geq 0$ and $c^1 \geq 0$ be the costs of conservation at $t = 0$ and $t = 1$, respectively. Costs are assumed to be intertemporally separable. Without the possibility of learning the conservation decision must be based on current expectations concerning the value of diversity and the total cost of conservation $c = c^0 + c^1$. A decision tree is given in Figure 3.1a. The no conservation option is taken as the benchmark option where conservation costs and benefits are zero. The total expected value of conservation is given by:

$$V = p\gamma D + (1 - p)\beta D - c. \tag{3.1}$$

With learning it can be beneficial to reconsider the conservation decision at $t = 1$. Note that the decision *not to conserve* at $t = 0$ is irreversible. Also, it is obvious that the conservation decision could be settled without further reconsideration

- if it is beneficial to conserve even if there is bad news, or
- if it is not beneficial to conserve even if there is good news.

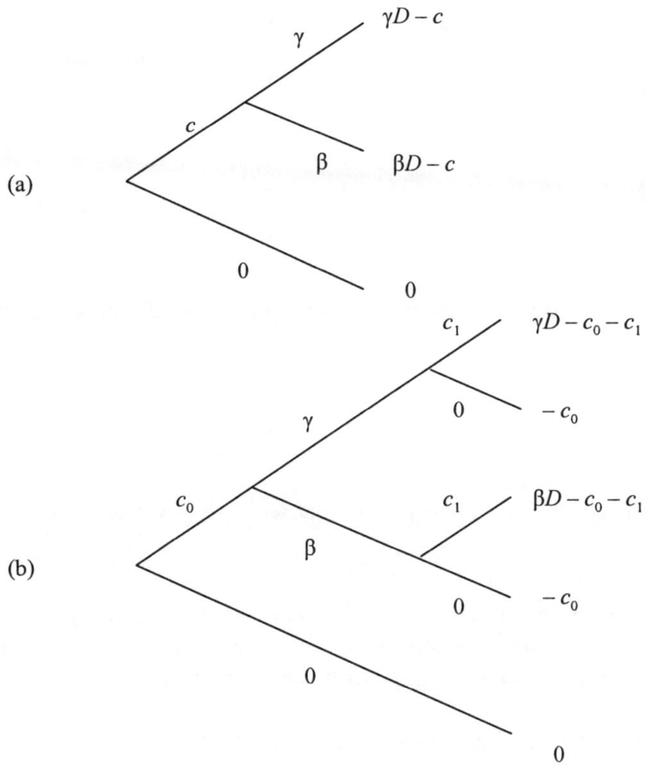

Figure 3.1 Decision trees with and without learning

Of the various possibilities the only interesting case is where $\beta D < c^1 < \gamma D$. In this case an initial decision to conserve will be changed if there is bad news; a decision tree is given in Figure 3.1b. Again, not to conserve is the benchmark option with zero conservation benefits. The expected total value of conservation at the initial stage is given by:

$$V_L = p(\gamma D - c^1) - c^0. \qquad (3.2)$$

V_L accounts for the value of future information (learning) while V does not. The quasi-option value is defined as the difference

$$V_L - V = (1 - p)(c^1 - \beta D). \qquad (3.3)$$

Keeping options for later requires an initial investment c^0. It is worthwhile to invest in conservation if c^0 is covered by the expected benefits. Without the possibility of learning the maximum acceptable initial conservation cost is:

$$\bar{c}^0 = p\gamma D + (1 - p)\beta D - c^1. \qquad (3.4)$$

With the possibility of learning, the threshold level of initial conservation costs is:

$$\bar{c}_L^0 = p\gamma D - pc^1. \qquad (3.5)$$

It is easy to check that $\bar{c}_L^0 > \bar{c}^0$ for $\beta D < c^1$. Thus we have the following proposition:

> **Proposition 1** Information about the value of an ecosystem revealed in the future increases the expected value of initial conservation (provided the option to stop the conservation effort is at all relevant).

Proposition 1 restates the results of the analysis of Arrow and Fisher (1974) and Henry (1974). The aim of the next section is to show how quasi-option values influence the optimal selection of reserve sites with regard to biodiversity protection.

The analysis in this section shows how differences in learning possibilities affect the conservation value. In the next section, the analysis focuses on the selection of reserve sites and the intertemporal allocation of a fixed conservation budget.

4. THE RESERVE SITE SELECTION PROBLEM UNDER UNCERTAINTY AND LEARNING

Consider, for illustration, a case with only two ecosystems (potential reserve sites) x, y where the expected diversity value is $D(\{x\})$ and $D(\{y\})$, respectively. As argued in Section 3, the diversity value may be captured by any strictly increasing function of the number of species in a collection of ecosystems. In what follows we make the stronger assumption that diversity value is *proportional* to the number of species (and, hence, the marginal value of diversity is constant). An ecosystem x is seen as a set of species and the diversity function $D(\{x\})$ reflects the cardinality of the set, that is, $D(\{x\})$ is the number of species in ecosystem x. Suppose now, $D(\{x\})$ is known with certainty while $D(\{y\})$ takes the values D_γ and D_β with probability p and $(1 - p)$, respectively. Assume that $D_\gamma > D(\{x\}) > D(\{y\}) > D_\beta$. Furthermore, suppose that either x or y can be saved in the long run, but not both. As $D(\{x\}) > D(\{y\})$, x should be chosen in the absence of further information. But if there is good news and $D(\{y\})$ takes the value D_γ (which happens with probability p), then preserving y is the better choice. Hence, there is a possible gain if the selection can be postponed until we learn the true $D(\{y\})$. The expected gain of waiting is $p[D_\gamma - D(\{x\})]$. Waiting, however, means that we have to conserve both ecosystems x and y at the initial stage and bear the conservation costs for both.

In the following I give a general formulation of the reserve site selection problem under uncertainty and learning and I shall analyse two example cases.

4.1 A General Framework

Consider a set of n ecosystems $E = \{1, \ldots, n\}$ existing at the initial stage. Typical elements of E, the ecosystems, are denoted x, y as before. The conservation decision is to select a subset of E, denoted E^0, which is conserved until the next stage $t = 1$. At $t = 1$ $E^1 \subseteq E^0$ is selected for subsequent conservation. At stage $t = 2$ $E^2 \subseteq E^1$ is selected, and so on. Hence, it is assumed that ecosystem loss is irreversible.

$$E \supseteq E^0 \supseteq E^1 \supseteq \ldots \tag{3.6}$$

For each ecosystem $x = 1, 2, \ldots, n$ and at each stage $t = 0, 1, \ldots$ there is a cost of conservation c_x^t. We assume there is a fixed conservation budget B. Let δ^t be the discount factor in period t, then the following budget constraint must hold:

$$B \geq \sum_{t=0}^{\infty} \delta^t \sum_{x \in E^t} c_x^t . \tag{3.7}$$

The decision-maker's objective is to find the best diversity path $\Delta = [D(E^0), D(E^1), \ldots]$. Since a summation of diversity values would lead to infinite values for a large class of infinite paths, it is convenient to rank paths using Weizsäcker's (1967) overtaking criterion. According to the overtaking criterion a path Δ weakly overtakes another path $\tilde{\Delta} = [D(\tilde{E}^0), D(\tilde{E}^1), \ldots]$ if there exists a time t^* such that for all $t > t^*$ it holds that:

$$\sum_{\tau=0}^{t} D(E^\tau) \geq \sum_{\tau=0}^{t} D(\tilde{E}^\tau) . \tag{3.8}$$

Of all paths which meet the budget constraint (3.7) the decision maker selects a path that weakly overtakes all other paths.

4.2 A Two-stage Model

For further analysis I examine a simple two-stage model. The conservation decision is to select $E^0 \subseteq E$ at $t = 0$ and to select $E^1 \subseteq E^0$ for subsequent conservation at $t = 1$. E^1 is maintained at all later times. The initial number of ecosystems is n. Let m be the number of ecosystems selected at $t = 0$ and let k be the number selected at $t = 1$, and, hence, $k \leq m \leq n$. Using the overtaking criterion the decision can be based on the long-run diversity value $D(E^1)$ without considering $D(E^0)$. Hence, the selection problem is to maximize $D(E^1)$ subject to a budget constraint. We analyse two examples which differ with regard to the initial information and the information that can be obtained through learning. In example 1 we look at distant reserve sites. We call a collection S distant from collection T if S has no species in common with T. Example 1 is the relevant case if, for example, the decision maker seeks to protect sites with unique characteristics concerning soil and climate. In example 2 we drop this assumption and allow for similarity of reserve sites.

Example 1: Selection of distant reserve sites
The following simplifying assumptions are adopted:

1. Diversity is additive, that is, for any two collections of ecosystems S, $T \subseteq E$, $S \neq T$, it holds that $D(S \cup T) = D(S) + D(T)$. Since the diversity measure D essentially counts species, this assumption is suitable for disjoint reserve sites; $S \cap T = \varnothing$.
2. We examine an extreme case of learning with almost full ignorance of all ecosystems at the initial stage. We assume that the initially expected diversity value is the same for all $x, y \in E$, that is, $D^0(\{x\}) = D^0(\{y\})$. At the later stage the true diversity value $D^1(\{x\})$ of each ecosystem x is revealed.
3. We assume that $D^1(\{x\})$ is independently drawn from an identical random distribution F with probability density function $f[D^1(\{x\})]$ defined on the interval $[\underline{D}, \bar{D}]$ for all $x \in E$.
4. Conservation costs c_x^t are the same for every $x \in E^t$, at each stage, $t = 0, 1$, but costs may differ between initial and long term conservation.
5. Furthermore, there is a fixed budget constraint

$$B \geq \sum_{x \in E^0} c_x^0 + \sum_{x \in E^1} c_x^1 = mc^0 + kc^1. \tag{3.9}$$

Now suppose that after conservation at the initial stage the remaining budget is sufficient to conserve all remaining ecosystems, that is, $B^1 = B - mc^0 \geq mc^1$. In this case, there is no choice at $t = 1$ and, hence, no gain from learning. A positive value of learning can be captured only if $m > k$. The intuition is that it may not be optimal to preserve the maximum number of ecosystems in the long run, but rather conserve more ecosystems initially to be able to make a better choice later.

We start the analysis at stage $t = 1$. At this stage the remaining budget is B^1 and there still exist m ecosystems. Since at this stage the true value of the remaining ecosystems is revealed, the cost-effective conservation policy selects k ($k \leq m$) ecosystems such that kc^1 just meets the budget constraint; thus $k = \text{Integer}(B^1/c^1)$. More precisely, the ecosystems with the k highest values will be selected out of m still existing ecosystems at stage $t = 1$.

At stage $t = 0$ the only issue is to determine how many ecosystems m should be conserved (since we have assumed that all ecosystems are equal, given the initial knowledge). In order to determine the optimal initial conservation m some additional notation is useful. Let $f_{(i,m)}(D)$ be the probability density function of the value ranked ith in an ordered set of m values independently drawn from F. Thus $f_{(1,m)}(D)$ is the probability density function of the highest value and $f_{(m,m)}(D)$ is the probability density function of the lowest value.[6] The expected diversity value of the ith-best ecosystem selected from m ecosystems is given by:

$$\mu_{(i,m)} = \int D f_{(i,m)}(D) \mathrm{d}D \,. \tag{3.10}$$

The decision problem at the initial stage is to choose the level of initial preservation m. Later the k best of m remaining ecosystems can be selected. Note that for a given budget $k = k(m)$. Initially m must be chosen to maximize

$$D(E^1) = \sum_{i=1}^{k} \mu_{(i,m)} \tag{3.11}$$

subject to the budget constraint (3.9).

In order to bring out more clearly the trade-off between initial conservation (the choice of m) and long-term conservation (the choice of k) we briefly look at the special case where $f(D^1)$ is the uniform distribution on the unit interval [0, 1]. In this case:[7]

$$\mu_{(i,m)} = \frac{m+1-i}{m+1} \,. \tag{3.12}$$

By combining (3.11) and (3.12) we obtain the expected diversity value for preserving k ecosystems at $t = 1$ which are selected from m ecosystems preserved initially:

$$D = \frac{2km - k^2 + k}{2(m+1)} \,. \tag{3.13}$$

The diversity value D can easily be tabled. Table 3.1 gives the diversity value for every possible m–k combination. Recall that irreversibility requires $k \leq m$. To exemplify the decision problem suppose now that $B \leq 12$, $c^0 = 1$ and $c^1 = 3$.

Then the feasible set is the shaded area and 11/7 is the maximum attainable diversity value. Here, instead of conserving three sites for the long run, the best option is to select six sites initially and choose two sites out of these six after their true value is revealed.

Table 3.1 Expected diversity values for different combinations of m *and* k

m \ k	1	2	3	4	5	6	7	...
1	1/2							
2	2/3	1						
3	3/4	5/4	6/4					
4	4/5	7/5	9/5	10/5				
5	5/6	9/6	12/6	14/6	15/6			
6	6/7	11/7	15/7	18/7	20/7	21/7		
7	7/8	13/8	18/8	22/8	25/8	27/8	28/8	
⋮	⋮	⋮	⋮	⋮	⋮	⋮	⋮	⋱

Note: The shaded area is the budget set: $m + 3k \leq 12$.

This analysis is sufficient to state the following proposition:

Proposition 2 Under uncertainty and learning there is a trade-off between initial conservation which generates information and the number of reserve sites conserved for the long run. Hence, it is not always optimal to conserve the largest possible number of sites for the long run.

To see that proposition 2 is not an artefact of assumption (i) that reserve sites are distant, I shall discuss a second example.

Example 2: Selection of reserve sites when sites may be similar
In example 1 we assumed that each species is unique on its site. Now we drop this assumption to allow for interdependence of the diversity value of different ecosystems. We consider a programme to conserve l species which are potentially located on n initial sites. More specifically, we adopt the following assumptions:

1. Diversity is subadditive, that is, for any two collections of ecosystems S, $T \subseteq E$, $D(S \cup T) \leq D(S) + D(T)$. Since the diversity value D is proportional

to the number of species, we assume here that the collection S might have some species in common with collection T.

2. There exist l species and n ecosystems in the initial state, however it is not known whether or not a species is present on a particular site. If a site is preserved information about its species composition will become available at the second stage.
3. Let p_j be probability that species j is present on a particular site. Since the characteristics of the sites are assumed to be unknown, we assume that p_j is the same for all sites.
4. Conservation costs c_x^t are the same for every site $x \in E^t$ at each stage, $t = 0, 1$, but costs may differ between initial and long-term conservation.

As before, there is a fixed budget constraint; see equation (3.9).

To see how learning may affect the intertemporal allocation of the budget and the selection of sites, we first calculate the expected diversity value (number of species) in a collection of ecosystems without learning D_N (N for no learning). The probability that some species j is *not* present on a particular site is $1 - p_j$. The probability that it is present on one of k_N selected sites is $1-(1-p_j)^{k_N}$. Since there are l species the expected diversity value of a selection of k_N sites (neglecting a scaling factor) is:

$$D_N = \sum_{j=1}^{l}\left[1-(1-p_j)^{k_N}\right]. \tag{3.14}$$

In the case with learning, the decision maker selects $m > k_N$ sites at the first stage of which the species composition is revealed at the second stage. Based on this information $k < k_N$ sites are selected. In general, whether or not it is worthwhile to give up some long-term conservation area $k_N - k$ for a better selection of sites depends on all parameters involved: budget and conservation costs determine k_N, the ratio c^1/c^0 reflects the cost of information, the number of species l, and the probability p_j which reflects the rarity of a species. To avoid complicated and tedious combinatorics the possibility of a positive quasi-option value is best demonstrated with a simple numerical example.

Let $k_N = 2$, $l = 3$ and $p_j = 1/4$ for $j = 1, 2, 3$. Then the benchmark value is $D_N = 3(1 - 9/16) \approx 1.31$. Suppose now that $c^1/c^0 = 2$, and hence it is possible to preserve two additional sites initially, that is, $m = 4$, at the cost of preserving one site less in the long run, that is, $k = 1$. To calculate the expected diversity value from this procedure, note that the best site of the four preselected sites will be chosen. There are four possible outcomes: (i) $D = 3$, if at least one of the four sites contains all three species. This is the case with probability $\pi_3 = 1 - (1 - p^3)^4 \approx 0.06$. (ii) $D = 2$, if at least one of the sites contains two species, but no site contains three species. This is the case with probability $\pi_2 = 1 - [3p(1 - p)^2 + (1 - p)^3]^4 - \pi_3 \approx 0.43$. (iii) $D = 1$, if the best site contains only one species. This is the case with probability $\pi_1 = [3p(1 - p)^2 + (1 - p)^3]^4 - (1 - p)^{12} \approx 0.48$. (iv) $D = 0$, if none of the sites contains any of the l target species. This is the case with probability $\pi_0 = (1 - p)^{12} \approx 0.03$.

The final step is to calculate the expected diversity value as the weighted sum $D_L = \sum_{i=0,1,2,3} i\pi_i \approx 1.52$. A comparison of this value with the benchmark value $D_N \approx 1.31$ shows that a larger conservation effort at the first stage is justified, even at the expense of reduced long run conservation. The quasi-option value is the difference $D_L - D_N \approx 0.21 > 0$.

5. CONCLUSION

This chapter contributes to the development of a framework for the choice of conservation policies under uncertainty. It is straightforward to apply the results of Arrow and Fisher (1974) and Henry (1974) to the case of biodiversity conservation. Such analysis shows that the conservation budget should be larger than the budget that seems to be optimal from the perspective of a traditional cost–benefit analysis since the latter ignores the value of future information. While this result comes as no surprise and has been mentioned in the literature (see introduction) it is interesting to look at the allocation of a conservation budget over time. This is the new contribution of this chapter. The results in this chapter are derived from a model of endogenous learning where the value of the information gained depends on the initial decision. If, as can be supposed for the case of nature protection, information comes from observation, an endogenous learning model is the only appropriate one; once a species is lost its features can no longer be observed and its potential uses will never become known. The main result from the model is that the prospect of future information gives an incentive to spend more on initial conservation even at the expense of long-run conservation. Nature conservation for species protection should start out with large areas preserved. Long-run conservation will be less extensive, but the remaining reserve sites can be more carefully selected. To fill this qualitative result with quantitative information in order to determine an optimal path of spending of the conservation budget remains, however, a challenge for future empirical research.

ACKNOWLEDGEMENTS

I would like to thank two anonymous referees for comments and Paul Mensink for stimulating discussions on an earlier version of this chapter.

NOTES

1. Tacconi and Bennett (1995, 211) quote these figures.
2. Perhaps this may change in the future if it becomes possible to store or to recover sufficient genetic information and use it to 'reconstruct' lost species.
3. See Ready (1995) for a survey.
4. Mensink and Requate (2003) have discovered a flaw in Fisher's (2000) alledged proof that quasi-option value and option value of investment theory are the same concepts.
5. See Tacconi and Bennett (1995, 211).
6. For an introduction to order statistics the reader is referred to Pitman (1993, 325 ff.). David (1970) offers a rigorous treatment of the subject.
7. Cf. David (1970, 27).

REFERENCES

Albers, H.J. (1996), 'Modeling ecological constraints on tropical forest management: spatial interdependence, irreversibility, and uncertainty', *Journal of Environmental Economics and Management*, **30**, 73–94.

Arrow, K.J. and A.C. Fisher (1974), 'Environmental preservation, uncertainty and irreversibility.' *Quarterly Journal of Economics*, **88**, 312–19.

Bishop, R.C. (1978), 'Endangered species and uncertainty: the economics of a safe minimum standard', *American Journal of Agricultural Economics*, **60**, 10–18.

Bishop, R.C. (1982), 'Option value: an exposition and extension', *Land Economics*, **58**, 1–15.

Black, F. and M. Scholes (1973), 'The pricing of options and corporate liabilities', *Journal of Political Economy*, **81**, 637–59.

Chichilnisky, G. and G. Heal (1998), 'Global environmental risks', in G. Chichilnisky, G. Heal and A. Vercelli (eds), *Sustainability: Dynamics and Uncertainty*, Dordrecht: Kluwer, pp. 23–46.

Cicchetti, C.J. and A.M. Freeman III (1971), 'Option demand and consumer surplus: further comment', *Quarterly Journal of Economics*, **85**, 528–39.

David, H.A. (1970), *Order Statistics*, New York: Wiley.

Dixit, A.K. and R.S. Pindyck (1994), *Investment under Uncertainty*, Princeton, NJ: Princeton University Press.

Fisher, A. (2000), 'Investment under uncertainty and option value in environmental economics', *Resource and Energy Economics*, **22** (3), 197–204.

Henry, C. (1974), 'Option values in the economics of irreplaceable assets', *Review of Economic Studies*, **41** (Symposium), 89–104.

Linddal, M. (1993), 'The quasi-option value from irreversible loss of biodiversity', *Scandinavian Forest Economics*, **34**, 58–73.

Mainwaring, Lynn (2001), 'Biodiversity, biocomplexity, and the economics of genetic dissimilarity', *Land Economics*, **77** (1), 79–93.

Marwah, S. and J. Zhao (2002), 'Irreversibility, uncertainty and learning in land preservation decisions', in E.C. van Ierland, H-P. Weikard and J. Wesseler (eds), *Proceedings of the International Conference on Risk and Uncertainty in Environmental and Resource Economics*, Wageningen, The Netherlands, 5–7 June 2002.

Mensink, P. and T. Requate (2003), The Dixit-Pindyck and the Arrow-Fisher-Hanemann-Henry option values are not equivalent. *Economic Working Paper 2003-09*, Department of Economics, University of Kiel.

Pitman, J. (1993), *Probability*, New York: Springer.

Polasky, S., A.R. Solow and J. Broadus (1993), 'Searching for uncertain benefits and the conservation of biological diversity', *Environmental and Resource Economics*, **3**, 171–81.

Ready, R.C. (1995), 'Environmental valuation under uncertainty', in D.W. Bromley (ed.), *The Handbook of Environmental Economics*, Oxford: Blackwell, 568–93.

Schmalensee, R. (1972), 'Option demand and consumer's surplus: valuing price changes under uncertainty', *American Economic Review*, **62**, 813-24.

Swanson, T. (1998), 'The source of genetic resource values and the reason for their management', in R.E. Evenson, D. Gollin and V. Santaniello (eds), *Agricultural Values of Plant Genetic Resources*, Wallingford, UK: CAB International, pp. 67–81.

Tacconi, Luca and Jeff Bennett (1995), 'Economic implications of intergenerational equity for biodiversity conservation', *Ecological Economics*, **12**, 209-23.

Weikard, H-P. (2002), 'Diversity functions and the value of biodiversity', *Land Economics*, **78** , 20–27.

Weisbrod, B.A. (1964), 'Collective-consumption service of individual consumptive goods', *Quarterly Journal of Economics*, **78**, 471–8.

Weitzman, M.L. (1992), 'On diversity', *Quarterly Journal of Economics,* **107**, 363–405.

Weitzman, M.L. (1993), 'What to preserve? An application of diversity theory to crane conservation', *Quarterly Journal of Economics*, **108**, 157–83.

Weitzman, M.L. (1998), 'The Noah's Ark problem', *Econometrica*, **66**, 1279–98.

Weizsäcker, C.C. von (1967), 'Lemmas for a theory of approximately optimal growth', *Review of Economic Studies*, **34**, 143–51.

White, B. (1996) 'Natural resource management: the case of heather moorland', in P Allanson and M. Whitby (eds), *The Rural Economy and the British Countryside*, London: Earthscan, pp. 62–82.

4. Optimal Environmental Development under Differing Stochastic Regimes

Shirra Freeman and Naomi Zeitouni

1. INTRODUCTION

The coexistence of high levels of uncertainty and irreversibility has long challenged environmental planners. Because knowledge about many environmental processes is incomplete and because these processes include inherently stochastic elements, the consequences of using environmental resources are often unpredictable a priori (Kolstad 1996).

This work is motivated by the need to improve environmental decision making when the planner cannot reduce the uncertainty with which he or she is faced. The best information available in these circumstances is the state of the environment, past and present and the probability distribution or stochastic evolution governing environmental change. There is no opportunity to learn about the complex processes underlying environmental change. Faced with irreversible and uncertain consequences, the planner must choose the timing and magnitude of development in order to maximize the total economic value of the use of an environmental resource. Development confers benefits in the private sphere but has public sector impacts in the form of environmental damage. The damage includes the amount of the resource used. For example, the value of an area of wilderness or wetland permanently destroyed would be measured in terms of the commercial value of extracted or harvested resources (for example, timber or fish stocks), recreation and amenity. The value also extends to the long-term impact of lost habitat on native species and impairment of systemic ecological function that existed in the preserved state. Tabulation of both benefits and costs is critical to making a decision that maximizes net social value but is often limited because of the difficulty of assessing with accuracy the value of environmental resources. This is a result of limits in our ability to evaluate non-market commodities and because of the often great uncertainty as to the nature and severity of environmental impacts. This work deals only with the latter.

The following two examples illustrate the general nature of the problem. Extensive deforestation was blamed for the disastrous flooding which occurred along the Yangtze River in 1998 and 1999. While the siltage of the river bed and shrinkage of basins such as Dongting Lake could be anticipated, the heavy rainfall and unusually warm weather which caused the melting of exceptionally heavy snowfalls of previous years were largely unpredictable. The combination of these known and stochastic events led to damage of unprecedented proportions. Moreover, even restoration could not reverse the damage in terms of loss of life, property and livelihood that was incurred. Nor would it change the necessity of de-silting the affected areas of the river to make them more flood resistant in the future (Zhang 1999).

In Northern Israel, in the early 1950s, an area of peat wetland totalling approximately 10 500 acres, including a 4 000-acre lake was drained. The objective was to clear the area for agriculture and settlement and to reduce the prevalence of mosquito-borne malaria in the region. Though massive, the project left 1 500 acres of the original ecology intact, with the result that much of the plant and animal life survived. Nevertheless, three species of plants and three species of animals gradually disappeared from the locale. Planners had been aware of the potential for some of these and other consequences when the project was undertaken, but not with certainty. In fact, the preservation of a small portion of the wetland was intended to address concerns about habitat loss. The local extinction and numerous other serious environmental costs were fully realized only 30 years after the drainage took place and most occurred gradually. During the late 1980s, the problems had become sufficiently severe that a decision to re-flood the area was taken (Chamish 1996).

In each of the above examples, the planner was faced with two types of uncertainty. The first can be reduced over time as more is learned about the nature of the environment. The second is pure stochasticity, that is uncertainty that does not change with the acquisition of information. The complex ecological interactions that underlie environmental change limit our ability to learn and understand and predict more accurately. In addition, there are elements that are purely stochastic. Extreme weather such as that involved in the Yangtze river flooding is one example. In contrast, no single event is implicated in the disappearance of species from the Hula wetland. The exact combination of processes which led to the disappearance is not fully understood. Nor is it clear why the species involved proved more vulnerable than others. Notwithstanding the fact that damage became evident after the development decision was taken, the planner, making a similar decision today would face a level of uncertainty very similar to that existing at the time of the original decision and the same decision taken today could have very different results given the unpredictability that prevails. Under these circumstances, the potential for learning is limited. This is often the situation in which planners must decide whether or not to develop. In these circumstances, the condition of the environment at a given point of time is the maximum amount of information available.

An analagous situation is found in the literature on investment and finance. The decision to buy a derivative security such as an option is based exclusively on the price of the underlying stock. Similarly, the value of an opportunity to invest in fixed capital is tied to the price of the commodity produced by the fixed capital. Market prices are inherently stochastic. Little can be learned about the future price from today's price but updating price information provides the best information about the value of the proposed investment. As in the case of environmental change, there is irreversibility. It is the sunk cost of purchasing the stock when an option is exercised or installing fixed capital (Pindyck 1991; Dixit and Pindyck 1994).

There is a large literature in environmental economics and investment that shows that when a decision has uncertain and irreversible consequences and when the decision maker can be flexible as to the timing of action, there is value to waiting in order to update information about uncertain variables. Consideration of the value of delay yields results that differ significantly from the standard net present value and cost–benefit rules. Specifically, the total expected benefits of a project must exceed its total costs. The difference between the two values is the value of delay and is known as the quasi-option value (QOV) (Arrow and Fisher 1974). It is shown to be positive or zero (Arrow and Fisher 1974; Henry 1974; Fisher and Hanemann 1987; Hanemann 1989). Therefore, the inclusion of the value of delay in analyses generally leads to more conservative resource use and investment (Arrow and Fisher 1974; Henry 1974; Fisher and Hanemann 1987; Hanemann 1989; Dixit and Pindyck 1994). The techniques of analysis use a combination of option pricing techniques, principally the contingent claims methodology and stochastic dynamic programming depending on whether the rate of discount is market determined. The real options approach (ROA) treats the opportunity to invest in fixed capital as a financial call option, offering an asset of uncertain value (the future returns to the completed project) in exchange for payment of a known sunk cost (the cost of purchase and installing the fixed capital) (Bernanke, 1983; McDonald and Siegel 1985, 1986; Pindyck 1988, 1991, 1993; Dixit and Pindyck 1994). As in the QOV approach, analysis focuses on the value to the agent of updating information; however, the source of stochasticity is price variability and the discount rate is generally market determined.

The ROA has been applied in several analyses of the timing of action in resource and environmental management. Pindyck (2000) explores implications for global climate change and attributes the reluctance of governments to undertake CO_2 abatement policies with high up-front costs and uncertain outcomes. Coggins and Ramezani (1998) prove a variation of the Arrow and Fisher result showing that the value of an 'unpriced' asset such as land can be imputed from the uncertain prices of alternative uses such as mining. Bosetti and Messina (2001) develop a model which incorporates both price and environmental uncertainty as well as two types of irreversibility, and decision rules for different levels of flexibility in land use. Several other works have explained waiting by agents in terms of stochastic fluctuations influencing decisions in energy conservation, SO_2 abatement and agriculture (Hassett and Metcalf 1992; Heberlot 1992; Thurow et al. 1997; Olmstead 1998; Mithöfer and Wesseler 2002; Tzouramani and Mattas 2002).

A number of other works also address the magnitude of action together with its timing. Pindyck (1988) presents a model of the optimal capacity of the firm. The firm's expansion is a series of optimally timed, marginal investments and much of the firm's value comes from its opportunity to add capacity. In a similar vein, Bar-Ilan and Strange (1999) and Capozza and Li (1994) distinguish between marginal and non-marginal investments by the firm and develop a model which solves for both the optimal timing and magnitude of investment. Largely absent from the literature are ROAs that address both timing and magnitude in environmental planning. Xepapadeas (1999) adds location choice to timing for investment in abatement. Other works, though not strictly in the ROA or QOV tradition, address both timing and magnitude. They focus on improved information and learning rather than updating and pure stochasticity. Kolstad (1996) develops a modified cost–benefit model of pollution reduction, in which the cost of pollution damage becomes known over time. The more rapid the accumulation of information, the lower emissions early on should be, unless the sunk costs of emission control rise with abatement. In a similar vein, Manne and Richels (1992, 1994) and Nordhaus (1994) recommend parallel implementation of policies that balance the need for improved information against the need to avoid negative consequences of global change.

In this chapter, we consider how the optimal development decision is determined by the stochastic process. The decision maker can update information on the state of the environment but does not learn in the sense that uncertainty is reduced. The source of uncertainty is stochastic environmental change and the development causes change in the stochastic process itself. Effectively, the decision maker faces two stochastic processes, one that holds prior to development and one that holds from the point of development forward. This element of endogeneity distinguishes environmental uncertainty from price variability. The price process that is the focus in the investment literature is entirely exogenous. This endogeneity creates a situation in which the optimal magnitude of development is as important as its timing. In fact because of its influence on the stochastic evolution, the magnitude of development in part determines the timing. As in the investment literature on uncertain cost (Pindyck 1993), the consequences of the action become evident only after the action has taken place.

This work's most significant result is its dependence on the underlying stochastic processes. We demonstrate using two examples that the results from the QOV and ROA do not hold universally. There are cases in which endogeneity will result in both a positive value to waiting and prescriptions for lower levels of development; equally, there are cases in which there is no value to waiting but the level of development depends on the environmental externality; in other cases stochastic change may increase the value to waiting without affecting the magnitude. The centrality of the stochastic process points to the need for improved understanding and representation of underlying ecological processes in economic modelling.

This chapter is organized as follows. Section 2 presents the framework and its solution for two different stochastic processes. It reports the planner's decision and discusses the relevance of the stochastic processes to given planning problems. The method of solution and basic results are presented. Particular attention is paid to the interaction between timing and magnitude and to the different policy prescriptions that follow from the results. The chapter concludes in Section 3 with a discussion of the model's results and directions for future research.

2. THE FRAMEWORK

In this section, two variations of the same land-use decision are presented. The first is based on a drift control process in which development causes the level of environmental sensitivity to rise. In the second, development causes a one-time jump environmental impact as a portion of the resource disappears permanently. The level of uncertainty remains unchanged in both models.

Consider the environmental planner facing the decision of whether to develop a tract of wilderness. In its undeveloped state, the area provides a range of functions including amenity, recreation, consumptive use values, habitat provision and a range of systemic ecologic functions (for example, groundwater catchment and other watershed functions). In its developed state, there is a project that confers benefits in the form of a stream of net revenues that are essentially private in nature and fully known. It also has uncertain public costs stemming from the loss of preservation benefits. These losses may be sufficiently long-lived from the perspective of the planner's time horizon to be considered irreversible.

The first model is more appropriate for the planner concerned with environmental functions that become more sensitive because of development. An example is habitat and species loss. As the number of a particular species is reduced, existence itself often becomes more sensitive and risk of extinction increases. Thus, if development results in habitat loss which significantly reduces the number of a particular species, the planner will need to consider this increased sensitivity reflected in the drift control process. In contrast, the reduction in amenity or recreation is more likely to be a one-time phenomena, more readily portrayed in the second model.

Both models consider a single environmental impact that becomes evident as soon as development occurs. The planner's objective is to balance the certain private and uncertain public aspects of the project by determining its optimal magnitude and/or starting time in order to maximize net social return. The environment exists in one of two states. State one is the preserved or undeveloped state during which all environmental changes are unrelated to the planner's decision and no private benefits to development accrue. State one exists as long as it is optimal for the planner to defer development in order to update his or her information on the quality and quantity of the resource.

Let k_t represent the value of environmental impact at time t. Positive values of k_t indicate damage to the environment. k_t's evolution is given by the Ito diffusion:

$$dk_t = \alpha k_t dt + \gamma k_t dw, \tag{4.1}$$

where, α is the rate at which damage is incurred. It reflects the sensitivity of the environment to change and the higher the value of α the more sensitive the environment. For example, rain forest ecology is far more vulnerable to clear-cutting than is deciduous forest. The latter has been shown to have the capacity for a high degree of regrowth as the source of much regeneration is the soil. In the case of the latter, it is the plant life itself that generates and recycles nutrients needed by the system. Thus once the vegetation is removed, so is the source of regrowth. γ is the instantaneous standard deviation and dw is the increment to a white noise process.

In state two, it is optimal to develop, and private benefits and environmental externalities begin to accrue. The environment remains subject to stochastic shocks and is influenced by the magnitude of development, and thus the eventual value of the environmental impact of development is not known in advance. Once begun, the project must be completed in a single stage. All non-environmental aspects of the project are known and the operation of the completed project has no environmental impact.

In both states, the evolution of the environment consists of a known time trend and a random component. Current values are known but future values are uncertain. Though information on the system's condition can be updated, uncertainty is never fully eliminated because of the persistence of the random element.

2.1 Model 1: Drift Control

Development causes a one-time jump in k_t and increase in the trend of the process. When development begins, at $t = \theta$, the trend rises from α to $\alpha + I$. That is, development creates increased sensitivity in the system.

$$dk_t = (\alpha + I)k_t dt + \gamma k_t dw, \ t \geq \theta \tag{4.2}$$

where I is the magnitude of development.

The value of the development opportunity, $F(k_\theta, I^*)$ including the opportunity to delay is given by:

$$F\left(k_\theta, I^*\right) = \max_{k_t, I} E\left[W(I)e^{-r\theta} - \left(\int_\theta^\infty k_{t|I=I^*} e^{-rt} dt - \int_\theta^\infty k_{t|I=0} e^{-rt} dt\right)\right] \tag{4.3}$$

where, I^* is the optimal level of development and $W(I)$ is the known, non-environmental net benefit of the project. Its form must satisfy the standard convexity assumptions (that is, $W'(I) > 0$ and $W''(I) < 0$); r is the social discount rate.

The incremental environmental damage resulting from development is

$$\left(\int_\theta^\infty k_{t|I=I^*} e^{-rt} dt - \int_\theta^\infty k_{t|I=0} e^{-rt} dt\right).$$

Over the period $t = [\theta, \infty]$, it is the difference between the change occurring as a consequence of development, $\int_\theta^\infty k_{t|I=I^*} e^{-rt} dt$ and the change that would have occurred if no development had been initiated, $\int_\theta^\infty k_{t|I=0} e^{-rt} dt$.

This incremental environmental cost is a public good externality and the non-environmental benefit is equivalent to a private return. In order to maximize net social return, the planner's task, through the choice of magnitude and timing of development, is to balance the certain private return with its associated risky public cost. For tractability two additional conditions must hold. First $r > \alpha$, that is the discount rate must exceed the net rate of environmental sensitivity, otherwise it is always optimal to defer development (Dixit and Pindyck 1994). Second, $\alpha > \gamma^2/2$, otherwise it is always optimal to develop immediately.

Three additional assumptions are made. First, private net benefits accrue over a finite period, the life of the development project. Second, environmental impacts last indefinitely. This reflects the fact that most projects, particularly in terms of commercial return have a finite life span before they must be replaced, refitted or abandoned. In contrast, environmental impacts are generally longer-lived. Third, the planner is assumed to be risk neutral.[1]

In the terminology of optimal stopping, k_t is the stochastic state variable, whose value determines the optimal solution; state one is the continuation region, during which the planner waits until the expected environmental impact falls to a low enough level to permit development; θ is the optimal stopping time marking the division between the continuation region and the period after development has taken place, the stopping region. At time θ the environmental impact k_θ is known to the planner. Thus, k_θ determines both θ and θ is defined as the first time that k_t achieves the critical value k_θ.

Each level of development has a corresponding level of environmental impact. The solution to the planner's problem is to identify the unique pair, k_θ and I^* that maximizes F. The critical boundary is shown to be a function of the optimal level of development, I^* and therefore, $k_\theta = k_\theta(I^*)$. The vector (k_θ, I^*) is expressed as:

$$\left(k_\theta, I^*\right) = \underset{k_t, I}{\arg\max} E\left[W(I)e^{-r\theta} - \left(\int_\theta^\infty k_{t|I=I^*} e^{-rt}\,dt - \int_\theta^\infty k_{t|I=0} e^{-rt}\,dt\right)\right] \quad (4.4)$$

The solution is achieved in two steps. First, the boundary is expressed as a set of values $k_\theta = k_\theta(I)$ which are a function of the level of development; then, the optimal level of development, I^* is determined from first-order conditions.

The solution consists of the value function at the boundary, the optimal level of development and the corresponding optimal level of environmental damage. That is the initial level of environmental impact, k_θ that permits development I^*.

In order to find the optimal magnitude of development, we will need to solve the first-order conditions from the value function, $dF\left(k_\theta, I^*\right)/dI = 0$.

To do this, it is first necessary to find an expression for the expected cumulative, incremental environmental damage,

$$E\left[\int_{\theta}^{\infty} k_{t|I=I^*} e^{-rt}\,dt - \int_{\theta}^{\infty} k_{t|I=0} e^{-rt}\,dt\right].$$

Using appropriate substitutions of equation 4.2 into the objective function, the following is obtained:

Prior to development,

$$E\left[\int_{\theta}^{\infty} k_{t|I=0} e^{-rt}\,dt\right] = \frac{k_{\theta}}{r-\alpha} e^{-r\theta} \tag{4.5}$$

After development,

$$E\left[\int_{\theta}^{\infty} k_{t|I=I^*} e^{-rt}\,dt\right] = \frac{k_{\theta}}{r-\alpha-I^*} e^{-r\theta} \tag{4.6}$$

Giving:

$$E\left[\int_{\theta}^{\infty} k_{t|I=I^*} e^{-rt}\,dt - \int_{\theta}^{\infty} k_{t|I=0} e^{-rt}\,dt\right] = \frac{I^* k_{\theta}}{(r-\alpha)\left(r-\alpha-I^*\right)} e^{-r\theta}. \tag{4.7}$$

The objective function (equation 4.3) becomes:

$$F\left(k_{\theta}, I^*\right) = \max_{k_t, I} E\left[W(I)e^{-r\theta} - \frac{I k_{\theta}}{(r-\alpha)(r-\alpha-I)} e^{-r\theta}\right]. \tag{4.8}$$

The full workout of the computations are contained in Appendix 4A1.

When size and timing are optimal, equation (4.8) is the stopping value of the problem, that is, the expected total economic value of developing I^* of the resource at time θ, when the expected level of environmental impact is k_{θ}. Since θ depends on the environmental change at the time of commencement, it remains to derive an explicit expression for k_{θ}. This is obtained as the solution to the continuation region. The full workout of the solution is found in Appendix 4A2.

Recall that the continuation region exists as long as the planner finds it more beneficial to wait for the level of environmental damage to fall before beginning development. That is, the 'private' benefit of development is outweighed by its environmental cost. Alternatively, the value of the development opportunity is greater than the value of the actual development, when the benefits of flexibility and updating information are considered. Commencement will be deferred as long as the 'capital appreciation' ($\max E[dF]$) of the opportunity exceeds the expected return from the completed project ($rFdt$).

Since, k_θ is the optimal boundary, for all $k_t > k_\theta$, it is optimal to wait and for all $k_t \leq k_\theta$, it is optimal to develop. Since F is a monotonic function of the Ito process, k_t, dF can be approximated by an Ito expansion. The identity, $rFdt = \max E[dF]$ provides the Bellman equation for the continuation region:

$$0 = rF - \alpha \frac{dF}{dk_\theta} k_\theta - \frac{1}{2}\gamma^2 \frac{d^2F}{dk_\theta^2} \tag{4.9}$$

The solution to equation (4.9) is the maximized value of the opportunity. The form:

$$F(k_t) = Ak_t^b,\ b < 0 \tag{4.10}$$

satisfies the limiting conditions that

$$\lim_{k_t \to \infty} F(k_t, I) = 0$$

and

$$\lim_{k_t \to 0} F(k_t, I) = W(I).$$

That is, the evolution of k_t is such that as the level of environmental damage rises without bound, it is expected to remain so high that it is never optimal to develop and the value of the opportunity is zero. Conversely, in the absence of the uncertain externality, the solution is the private optimum.

At the boundary, k_θ, the planner is indifferent between developing and not developing and the value of the opportunity must equal the value of actually developing (that is, the stopping value).

If the stopping value of the problem is defined as:

$$V\left(k_\theta, I^*\right) = W(I) - \frac{I^*}{(r-\alpha)\left(r-\alpha-I^*\right)} k_\theta, \tag{4.11}$$

then, for all $k_t \leq k_\theta$, $F(k_\theta, I^*) = V(k_\theta, I^*)$. This is known as the value-matching condition (Dixit and Pindyck 1994). To ensure continuity at the boundary, it is also necessary that the smooth-pasting condition hold:

$$\frac{dF\left(k_\theta, I^*\right)}{dk_\theta} = \frac{dV\left(k_\theta, I^*\right)}{dk_\theta} = \frac{I^*}{(r-\alpha)\left(r-\alpha-I^*\right)}. \tag{4.12}$$

Using $F\left(k_t\right) = Ak_v^b$, $b < 0$ and applying the value-matching and smooth-pasting conditions we obtain:

$$k_\theta = \frac{W\left(I^*\right)}{I^*}(r-\alpha)\left(r-\alpha-I^*\right)\frac{b}{b-1}. \tag{4.13}$$

Solving the differential equation (4.9) gives:

$$b = \left(-\frac{1}{\gamma^2}\right)\left[\alpha - \frac{1}{2}\gamma^2 + \sqrt{\left(\beta - \frac{1}{2}\gamma^2\right)^2 + 2\gamma^2 r}\right] < 0 \ \forall r > \alpha; \alpha > \frac{\gamma^2}{2} \tag{4.14}$$

Applying the value matching condition and differentiating $F(k_\theta, I^*)$ with respect to I gives:

$$\frac{d}{dI}F = W'\left(I^*\right) - \frac{k_\theta}{\left(r-\alpha-I^*\right)}. \tag{4.15}$$

This gives the first order condition for the optimal magnitude of development:

$$W'\left(I^*\right) = \frac{k_\theta}{\left(r-\alpha-I^*\right)^2} \geq 0 \ \ \forall k_\theta \geq 0; r-\alpha > I^* \tag{4.16}$$

Equivalently, by substituting equation 4.13 into equation 4.16 we obtain:

$$W'\left(I^*\right)=\frac{W\left(I^*\right)}{I^*}\frac{b(r-\alpha)}{(b-1)\left(r-\alpha-I^*\right)}>0 \quad \forall\, b<0; r-\alpha>I \qquad (4.17)$$

The existence of a closed form or numeric solution for I^* depends on the form of $W(I)$ and parameter values. Since, $W(I^*) > 0$ and given the convexity assumptions, the socially optimal level of development must be smaller than the private optimum. This is the standard result in the presence of negative environmental externalities.

Consideration of uncertainty and irreversibility prescribes more conservative development in terms of both magnitude and timing. Moreover, the endogeneity of I^* and its relationship to the model's parameters, in particular, $(r-\alpha)$ (That is, as long as $(r-\alpha) > I^*$, $k_\theta \geq 0$) is a unique and necessary component of the environmental application.

A brief look at the relationship between k_θ and I shows that in the region of the optimal I, where

$$W'\left(I^*\right)=\frac{W\left(I^*\right)}{I^*}\frac{b(r-\alpha)}{(b-1)\left(r-\alpha-I^*\right)},$$

changes in the boundary as the amount of development changes,

$$\frac{d}{dI}k_\theta=\left[\frac{W'(I)I-W(I)}{I^2}(r-\alpha-I)-\frac{W(I)}{I}\right](r-\alpha)\frac{b}{b-1} \qquad (4.18)$$

becomes

$$\frac{d}{dI}k_\theta=-\frac{b}{(b-1)^2}(r-\alpha)^2\frac{W(I)}{I^2}>0 \quad \forall\, r>\alpha;\, b<0, \qquad (4.19)$$

implying that the waiting period falls as the magnitude of development rises to its optimal level. It also implies that levels of development that are slightly larger than optimal may have a shorter waiting period as well.

2.2 Model 2: Brownian Motion with a Discrete Jump in k_t

In this model, development causes a single jump in the magnitude of k_t, leaving all parameters unchanged. After development, the environment evolves according to the process:

$$dk_t = \alpha\left(k_t + I\right)dt + \gamma k_t dw, \ t\forall\theta \tag{4.20}$$

In contrast to the model in Section 2.1, the trend is unchanged, however there is a rise in the level of damage that is permanent. (k_t + I) becomes the baseline level of impact and I can be thought of as the value of amenity lost when a portion of the previously preserved area is developed. Remaining preserved areas continue to provide amenity function at the same rate as before. There is simply less preserved area in existence.

The objective function (equation (4.3)) and the change in the condition of the environment in the absence of development (equation (4.5)) are unchanged. The cumulative environmental impact resulting from development corresponding to the process described in equation (4.20) is:

$$E\left[\int_{\theta}^{\infty} k_{t|I=I^*} e^{-rt} dt\right] = \left(\frac{k_\theta}{r-\alpha} - \frac{\alpha I}{r\left(r-\alpha\right)}\right) e^{-r\theta} \tag{4.21}$$

and incremental environmental impact is now given by:

$$E\left[\int_{\theta}^{\infty} k_{t|I=I^*} e^{-rt} dt - \int_{\theta}^{\infty} k_{t|I=0} e^{-rt} dt\right] = \frac{\alpha I}{r\left(r-\alpha\right)} e^{-r\theta}. \tag{4.22}$$

The objective function is rewritten as:

$$F\left(k_\theta, I^*\right) = \max_{k_t, I} E\left[W\left(I\right)e^{-r\theta} - \frac{\alpha I}{r\left(r-\alpha\right)} e^{-r\theta}\right]. \tag{4.23}$$

The absence of k_θ in the objective function makes it clear that the timing of development is not part of the solution of this model. That is, the optimal starting time is the current period regardless of the magnitude of development. The optimal solution to the magnitude of development is determined by the first-order conditions, $dF\left(I\right)/dI = 0$.

$$\frac{dF(I)}{dI} = W'(I)e^{-r\theta} - \frac{\alpha}{r(r-\alpha)}e^{-r\theta} = 0\,, \tag{4.24}$$

which is satisfied by

$$W'(I) = \frac{\alpha}{r(r-\alpha)} \tag{4.25}$$

Since the marginal private return is larger than zero, the optimal level of development must be smaller than the private optimum. Significantly, the parameter for uncertainty, γ appears nowhere in the solution. This result is fundamentally the same as the prescriptions for more conservative development policy arising from standard cost–benefit-type analyses of projects with environmental externalities.

3. DISCUSSION AND DIRECTIONS FOR ONGOING RESEARCH

In this model, two variations of a planner's land-use problem are solved using an optimal stopping framework with a single stochastic state variable, the level of environmental impact stemming from development. The variations differ in the stochastic process that characterizes environmental change after development has taken place. As a consequence, two very different policy prescriptions follow from the models' basic results.

In both cases, the optimal magnitude of development is smaller than the private optimum; however, there is a positive value to delaying implementation when development causes an increase in the level of environmental sensitivity. When development causes a jump in the level of damage but leaves other parameters unaffected, there is no value to waiting to develop.

These two results clearly outline the conditions under which the standard prescriptions of the real options and quasi-option value approaches to environmental management hold, when the decision variable directly influences the stochastic process. It also demonstrates that the standard cost-benefit policy prescription for restricting the magnitude of development may not hold when uncertainty and irreversibility are considered. Moreover, the results point to the importance of the underlying ecological/environmental processes in economic modelling. Through the two examples in this chapter, it is shown that different environmental problems must be accurately represented in order to be managed efficiently. Thus, an important area of basic research must be improving the understanding and precise representation of environmental change and improved links between modelling in environmental sciences and economics.

ACKNOWLEDGEMENTS

We thank Avner Bar-Ilan, Ishai Maoz, two anonymous referees and the editors for constructive criticism and suggestions that have been instrumental in moving this work forward.

NOTE

1. This problem assumes that the planner and society are risk neutral because the risk associated with the project is both diversifiable and spreadable. The development project is assumed to be one of a number of public finance undertakings in a diversified portfolio of projects having different expected returns and risk profiles. The 'insurance' provided by diversification limits the impact of a single adverse outcome on the portfolio as a whole. Further, there is an element of risk spreading over a large population so that an adverse result would represent only a small component of agents' total wealth. For further details on the properties of diversification and spreading, see Arrow and Lind (1970).

   Though the assumption of risk neutrality is common in QOV and ROA, consideration must nevertheless be given to the limits of diversifiability and spreadability in environmental applications. Both may be circumscribed by the potential for large, possibly catastrophic outcomes and by the non-divisibility of certain values associated with public environmental goods (for example non-use, amenity, pollution damage and so on) In such cases, the planner's and society's risk attitudes must be incorporated.

REFERENCES

Arrow, K.J. and A.C. Fisher (1974), 'Environmental preservation, uncertainty and irreversibility', *Quarterly Journal of Economics*, **88**, 312–19.

Arrow, K.J. and R. Lind (1970), 'Uncertainty and the evaluation of public investment decisions', *American Economic Review*, **60**, 364–78.

Bar-Ilan, A. and W.C. Strange (1999), 'Timing and intensity of investment', *Journal of Macroeconomics*, **21** (1), 57–77.

Bernanke, B.S. (1983), 'Irreversibility, uncertainty and cyclical investment', *Quarterly Journal of Economics*, **98**, 85–106.

Bosetti, V. and E. Messina (2001), 'Quasi option value and irreversible choices', Milan: Fondazione Eni Enrico Mattei – Economic Theory and Applications (FEEM-ETA) paper, 14.2001.

Capozza, D.R. and Y. Li (1994), 'The intensity and timing of investment: the case of land', *American Economic Review*, **84**, 889–904.

Chamish, B. (1996), 'Reflooding the Hula', *International Water Power and Dam Construction*, **6**, 32–4.

Coggins, J.S. and C.A. Ramezani (1998), 'An arbitrage-free approach to quasi-option value', *Journal of Environmental Economics and Management*, **35**, 183–90.

Dixit, A. and R.S. Pindyck (1994), *Investment under Uncertainty*, Princeton, NJ: Princeton University Press.

Fisher, A.C. and W.M. Hanemann (1987), 'Quasi-option values, some misconceptions dispelled', *Journal of Environmental Economics and Management*, **14**, 183–90.

Hanemann, W.M. (1989), 'Information and the concept of quasi-option value', *Journal of Environmental Economics and Management*, **16**, 23–36.

Hassett, K.A. and G.E. Metcalf (1992), *Energy Tax Credits and Residential Conservation Investment*, Cambridge, MA: National Bureau of Economic Research.

Heberlot, O. (1992), 'Option valuation of flexible investments: the case of environmental investments in the electric power industry', Doctoral Dissertation, Massachussetts Institute of Technology, Cambridge, MA.

Henry, C. (1974), 'Investment decisions under uncertainty: the irreversibility effect', *American Economic Review*, **64** (4), 1006–12.

Kolstad, C.D. (1996), 'Learning, irreversibilities and climate', paper presented at the seventh annual conference of the European Association of Environmental and Resource Economists, Lisbon, Portugal, 27–29 June.

Manne, A.S. and R.G. Richels. (1992), *Buying Greenhouse Insurance: The Economic Costs of CO_2 Emission Limits*, Cambridge, MA: MIT Press.

Manne, A.S. and R.G. Richels (1994), 'CO_2 hedging strategies: the impact of uncertainty upon emissions', in OECD/IEA, *The Economics of Climate Change*, Paris: Organization for Economic Cooperation and Development, pp. 59–69.

McDonald, R. and D.R. Siegel (1985), 'Investment and the valuation of firms when there is an option to shut down', *International Economic Review*, **26** (2), 331–49.

McDonald, R. and D.R. Siegel (1986), 'The value of waiting to invest', *Quarterly Journal of Economics*, **101**, 707–28.

Mithöfer, D and J. Wesseler (2002), 'When will farm-households consider planting domesticated indigenous fruit trees? A real options approach', paper presented at Conference on Risk and Uncertainty in Environmental and Resource Economics, Wageningen, The Netherlands, 5–7 June.

Nordhaus, W.D. (1994), *Managing the Global Commons: The Economics of Climate Change*, Cambridge, MA: MIT Press.

Olmstead, J.M. (1998), 'Emerging markets in water: investments in institutional and technological change', Doctoral Dissertation, University of California, Berkeley.

Pindyck, R.S. (1988), 'Irreversible investment, capacity choice and the value of the firm', *American Economic Review*, **79** (12), 969–85.

Pindyck, R.S. (1991), 'Irreversibility, uncertainty and investment', *Journal of Economic Literature*, **29**, 1110–52.

Pindyck, R.S. (1993), 'Investments of uncertain cost', *Journal of Financial Economics*, **34**, 53–76.

Pindyck, R.S. (2000), 'Irreversibilities and the timing of environmental policy', *Resource and Energy Economics*, **22**, 233–359.

Thurow, A.P., W.G. Boggess and C.B. Moss. (1997), 'An ex ante approach to modeling investment in new technology', in D. Parket and Y. Tsur (eds), *Decentralization and Coordination of Water Resources Management*, Dordrecht: Kluwer, chapter 19.

Tzouramani, I. and K. Mattas (2002), 'Employing real options methodology in environmentally friendly production systems', paper presented at Conference on

Risk and Uncertainty in Environmental and Resource Economics, Wageningen, The Netherlands, 5–7 June.
Xepapadeas, A. (1999), *Environmental Policy and Firm Behaviour: Abatement Investment and Location Decisions under Uncertainty and Irreversibility*, Cambridge, MA: National Bureau of Economic Research.
Zhang, L. (1999), 'Thematic reviews: environmental and social assessment for large dams', World Commission on Dams – United Nations Environment Programme, Nairobi, Kenya.

APPENDIX 4A1 SOLUTION TO EQUATIONS (4.5) AND (4.6)

Take expectations of both sides of equation (4.2),

$$dk_t = (\alpha + I)k_t dt + \gamma k_t dw$$

$$E[dk_t] = dE[k_t] = (\alpha + I)E[k_t] \tag{4A1.1}$$

Let $z_t = E[k_t]$ to obtain

$$dz_t = (\alpha + I)z_t \tag{4A1.2}$$

This is a simple ordinary differential equation with the solution:

$$z_t = Ce^{(\alpha + I)t} \tag{4A1.3}$$

Note that at time $t = \theta$, $k_t = k_\theta$ so that:

$$E\left[k_t \mid k_\theta, I = I^*\right] = k_\theta e^{(\alpha + I)(t-\theta)} \tag{4A1.4}$$

Integrating both sides from θ to ∞ gives:

$$E\left[\int_\theta^\infty k_{t|I=I^*} e^{-rt} dt\right] = \frac{k_\theta}{r - \alpha - I^*} e^{-r\theta} \tag{4A1.5}$$

Similarly,

$$E[k_t \mid k_\theta, I = 0] = k_\theta e^{\alpha(t-\theta)} \quad . \tag{4A1.6}$$

APPENDIX 4A2 SOLUTION TO THE OPTIMAL BOUNDARY, k_θ

Deriving Expressions for k_θ

Applying the value-matching condition to $F(k_t) = Ak_\theta^b,\ b < 0$:

$$F\left(k_\theta, I^*\right) = Ak_\theta^b = W\left(I^*\right) - \frac{I^*}{(r-\alpha)\left(r-\alpha-I^*\right)}k_\theta, \qquad (4A2.1)$$

and dividing through by the smooth-pasting conditions and rearranging gives:

$$k_\theta = \frac{W\left(I^*\right)}{I^*}(r-\alpha)\left(r-\alpha-I^*\right)\frac{b}{b-1}. \qquad (4A2.2)$$

Solution to b

Equation (4.1) is used to solve the Ito expansion of F from the continuation region:

$$0 = rF - \alpha\frac{dF}{dk_\theta}k_\theta - \frac{1}{2}\gamma^2\frac{d^2F}{dk_\theta^2} = r - \left(\alpha - \tfrac{1}{2}\gamma^2\right)b - \tfrac{1}{2}\gamma^2 b^2. \qquad (4A2.3)$$

Solving for the negative root of the quadratic equation:

$$b = \left(-\frac{1}{\gamma^2}\right)\left(\alpha - \frac{1}{2}\gamma^2 + \sqrt{\left(\beta - \frac{1}{2}\gamma^2\right)^2 + 2\gamma^2 r}\right) < 0 \ \ \forall r > \alpha; \alpha > \frac{\gamma^2}{2}. \qquad (4A2.4)$$

Proof of $b < 0$

It is sufficient to show that,

$$\left[\alpha - \frac{1}{2}\gamma^2 + \sqrt{\left(\beta - \frac{1}{2}\gamma^2\right)^2 + 2\gamma^2 r}\right] > 0. \qquad (4A2.5)$$

Square both sides of (4A2.5) and rearrange:

a. $$\left(\alpha-\frac{1}{2}\gamma^2\right)^2<\left(\beta-\frac{1}{2}\gamma^2\right)^2+2\gamma^2 r$$

$\leftrightarrow$

b. $$\alpha-\frac{1}{2}\gamma^2<\sqrt{\left(\beta-\frac{1}{2}\gamma^2\right)^2+2\gamma^2 r}$$

and since

c. $$\sqrt{\left(\beta-\frac{1}{2}\gamma^2\right)^2+2\gamma^2 r}>0$$

QED.

PART II

Implications for Economic Development and Environmental Policies

5. Public–Private Environmental Conflicts

Sung Hoon Park and Jason F. Shogren

1. INTRODUCTION

The United States Supreme Court recently reinforced an old idea that private citizens have legal standing in the enforcement of federal laws.[1] Most major US federal environmental regulations have codified this legal standing through citizen suit provisions (for example Clean Air Act, Clean Water Act, and Endangered Species Act; see Miller 1987; Naysnerski and Tietenberg 1992). Citizen suits do not replace the legislative process; rather they provide a means of 'realistic access to legislatures so that the theoretical processes of democracy can be made to work more effectively in practice' (Sax 1970, p. 11). Citizen suits created a venue for rational environmental conflicts between developers and conservationists, each expending scarce resources to increase the odds that their side wins the contest (see Settle et al. 2001).

The economic theory of environmental conflict has examined the efficiency consequences of a citizen group and firms competing over a risky prize defined as either a private good or a public good, but not both (for example, Baik 1993; Baik and Shogren 1994; Heyes 1997; Hurley and Shogren 1997; Katz et al. 1990). In reality, however, many environmental conflicts involve a prize that is a *private good* for the firms but a *public good* for the citizen group. An illustrative example is the case over the New World Mine Project in the Beartooth Mountains near Yellowstone National Park. In the mid-1990s, miners estimated that they could remove $1 billion worth of gold, silver and copper from deposits missed by earlier prospectors. Securing the rights to develop the mine under the General Mining Act of 1872 generates a rival and excludable private good that accrues to the owners and investors. Environmental citizen groups like the Greater Yellowstone Coalition countered that the New World Mine would threaten wildlife, ecosystem services, water quality, and the tranquility of the wilderness area. Preventing the development of the mine through the Endangered Species Act (via grizzly bear habitat on the mine site) provides the public benefits of species protection that are non-rival and non-excludable, accruing to the entire nation. Other public–private conflicts include the debate over the potential oil reserves in the 20-million-acre Arctic National Wildlife Refuge (ANWR) in Alaska; the mineral assets in the 1.9-million-acre Grand Staircase-Escalante National Monument in Utah, and the natural gas supplies in the 600,000-acre Jack Morrow Hills in the Red Desert, Wyoming.

These disputes can be characterized as *public–private environmental conflicts*. Herein we explore the effort levels and efficiency consequences of a public–private environmental conflict, with and without asymmetric reimbursement rules. Building on Baik and Shogren (1994), our public–private conflict model assumes a citizen group fights to preserve access to the public goods provided by, say an old-growth forest. A syndicate of firms fight for access to the timber, which is a private good shared among them based on their pre-assigned sharing rule. For the citizen group, forest preservation is a public good. All citizens share the use and non-use benefits the forest provides through recreation, biological diversity, and carbon sequestration. For the firms, development is a private good. Once one firm fells trees and develops a housing tract, for instance, fewer acres now are available for development by others. These firms share the private benefits given the competitive sharing rule they choose.

Our results suggest that double free-riding can exist in the conflict–the hungriest citizen fights for the public good as the other citizens free ride; each firm free rides off the others' efforts given an effort-independent sharing rule.[2] The regulator considers two elements: each group's probability-of-winning function depends on the relative magnitude of reimbursement and the sharing rule; and efficiency depends on the relative valuation of the prize. We also examine the consequences when a regulator sets policy through the degree of asymmetric reimbursement which affects the odds of the conflict. If the firms have more legal ability, a fair-minded regulator might increase the reimbursement level to maintain equality of strength, for any given sharing rule. Finally, we consider how the number of firms affects the contest efficiency.

2. A PUBLIC–PRIVATE CONFLICT MODEL

Consider a conflict between two groups, C and F, who compete to win a prize by expending observable and irreversible efforts with reimbursement. Group C, the *citizen group*, consists of n risk-neutral players; group F, the firms, consists of m risk-neutral players. Define x_{ik} as the irreversible effort level spent by player k in group C or F, where $i \in (c, f)$. Let X_c and X_f be the effort level spent by all players in group C or group F, in which

$$X_c = \sum_{i=1}^{n} x_{ci} \text{ , } X_f = \sum_{j=1}^{m} x_{fj} \text{ .}$$

Following the contest literature let the probability-of-winning functions for groups *C* and *F* be represented by the logit functions:

$$P_c = \frac{X_c}{X_c + X_f} \text{ and } P_f = \frac{X_f}{X_c + X_f},$$

which are continuous and concave in own effort.

2.1 The Citizen Group

Assume that citizens value the prize differently. Let v_{ci} represent the valuation of player *i* in group *C*, such that

$$V_c = \sum_{i=1}^{n} v_{ci} \text{ .}$$

Assume that $v_1 > v_{ch} > 0$ for $h = 2,\ldots, n$ with group *C*. Since each player has his or her own subjective valuation of the prize, he or she chooses their effort levels independently. All information is common knowledge.

Let the expected payoff of player *i* in group *C* be written as $\Pi_{ci} = P_c v_{ci} - x_{ci}$. Given the effort levels of all players, the equilibrium level of effort, x_{ci}^*, is obtained from:

Max $\Pi_{ci} = P_c v_{ci} - x_{ci}$
s.t. $x_{ci} \geq 0$

where the first-order condition is:

$$\frac{X_f}{(X_c + X_f)^2} v_{ci} - 1 = 0. \qquad (5.1)$$

The second-order sufficient condition is satisfied since Π_{ci} is strictly concave in x_{ci}.

As shown by Baik (1993), given *F*'s equilibrium effort level, X_f^*, group *C*'s equilibrium effort level is neither greater nor less than group *C*'s player-1 best response, $X^*_c\{1\}$. This means that total citizen group effort equals the effort of the player in the group who values the prize the most–the *hungriest* *citizen player*. This implies that $x_{c1}^* = X^*_c\{1\}$, and $x_{ch}^* = 0$ for $h = 2, \ldots, n_c$ if $v_{c1} > v_{c2}$ (see Baik 1993).

2.2 The Group of Firms

Define the group of firms, F, as a competitive-share group (Baik and Shogren 1995). Assume that (i) group F acts as a single player competing with group C to win the prize; (ii) each member of the firm group chooses its effort non-cooperatively; and (iii) each member competes within the group to earn a larger share of the rent, provided the group wins, based on an exogenous sharing rule. The expected payoff of firm j in group F is $\Pi_{fj} = P_f(\sigma_{fj}G) - x_{fj}$, where G is the fixed private good prize, and

$$\sigma_{fj} = \delta\frac{x_{fj}}{X_f} + (1-\delta)\frac{1}{m}$$

is the sharing rule. Define the sharing rule as the weighted sum of two elements – an effort-dependent component in which each firm's share of the private prize is set by its effort relative to total group effort (x_{fj}/X_f), and an effort independent part in which each firm shares the prize equally ($1/m$). The parameter δ sets the relative weight of the two elements. If $\delta = 1$, the sharing rule is totally effort-dependent; if $\delta = 0$, the sharing rule is totally effort-independent; and if $0 < \delta < 1$, the sharing rule is a composite of the two polar cases.

Given the effort levels of all players, the optimal level of effort x_{fj}^* is obtained from:

$$\text{Max } \Pi_{fj} = P_f(\sigma_{fj}G) - x_{fj}$$
$$\text{s.t. } x_{fj} \geq 0.$$

The first-order condition for an interior optimum is:

$$G\frac{\delta(m-1)+1}{m}\frac{\partial P_f}{\partial X_f} + G\delta\frac{X_f - x_{fj}}{(X_c + X_f)^2} - 1 = 0 \tag{5.2}$$

The firm's marginal gross payoff,

$$G\frac{\delta(m-1)+1}{m}\frac{\partial P_f}{\partial X_f} + G\delta\frac{X_f - x_{fj}}{(X_c + X_f)^2},$$

decreases in its effort level, x_{fj}, which implies the second-order condition is satisfied.[3]

At the symmetric Nash equilibrium, $x_{f1} = \ldots = x_{fm}$ and $X_c + X_f = x_{c1} + mx_{fj}$. Using expressions (5.1) and (5.2), we obtain:

$$x_{fj}(x_{c1}) = \frac{G\delta(m-1) - 2mx_{c1} + \sqrt{G^2\delta^2(m-1)^2 + 4mGx_{c1}}}{2m^2}, \tag{5.3}$$

$$X_f(X_c) = \frac{G\delta(m-1) - 2mx_{c1} + \sqrt{G^2\delta^2(m-1)^2 + 4mGx_{c1}}}{2m} \tag{5.4}$$

and

$$x_{c1}(X_f) = X_c(X_f) = -X_f + \sqrt{v_{c1}X_f} \tag{5.5}$$

where $v_{c1} > 0$.

From equations (5.4) and (5.5), we rewrite the reaction functions, $X_f(X_c)$ and $X_c(X_f)$ as:

$X_f(X_c) = \varepsilon$, for $X_c = 0$

$X_f(X_c) = \dfrac{G\delta(m-1) - 2mX_c + \sqrt{[G\delta(m-1)]^2 + 4mGX_c}}{2m}$, for $0 < X_c \le \dfrac{G[1+\delta(m-1)]}{m}$

$X_f(X_c) = 0$, for $X_c > \dfrac{G[1+\delta(m-1)]}{m}$

and

$X_c(X_f) = \varepsilon$, for $X_f = 0$

$X_c(X_f) = -X_f + \sqrt{v_{c1}X_f}$, for $0 < X_f \le v_{c1}$

$X_c(X_f) = 0$, for $X_f > v_{c1}$.

Group effort Nash equilibrium is therefore[4]

$$(X_c^*, X_f^*) = \left\{ \frac{Gv_{c1}[1+\delta(m-1)][mv_{c1} - \delta G(m-1)]}{(mv_{c1}+G)^2}, \frac{G^2 v_{c1}[1+\delta(m-1)]^2}{(mv_{c1}+G)^2} \right\}.$$

3. EFFORT AND EFFICIENCY WITHOUT REIMBURSEMENT

Before considering environmental policy rules, we first establish how our public–private model fits into the general contest literature. We define our model in three ways: establish a comparative baseline by defining a benchmark model that links our public–private model to the private–private conflict case; show how effort dependence in the firm groups' sharing rule tips the conflict toward them; and explore the comparative statics on how changes in the conflict structure affect two measures of social welfare.

3.1 A Benchmark Model

We establish the link between our public–private model and the traditional private–private or public–public conflict with a benchmark model. The benchmark assumes equal total effort, $X_c^* = X_f^*$, given an effort-independent sharing rule ($\delta = 0$), and an equal valuation of hungriest citizen and the average firm ($v_{c1} = G/m$). Figure 5.1 shows the reaction function and symmetric Nash equilibrium for the benchmark (point A), and the following proposition summarizes the results.

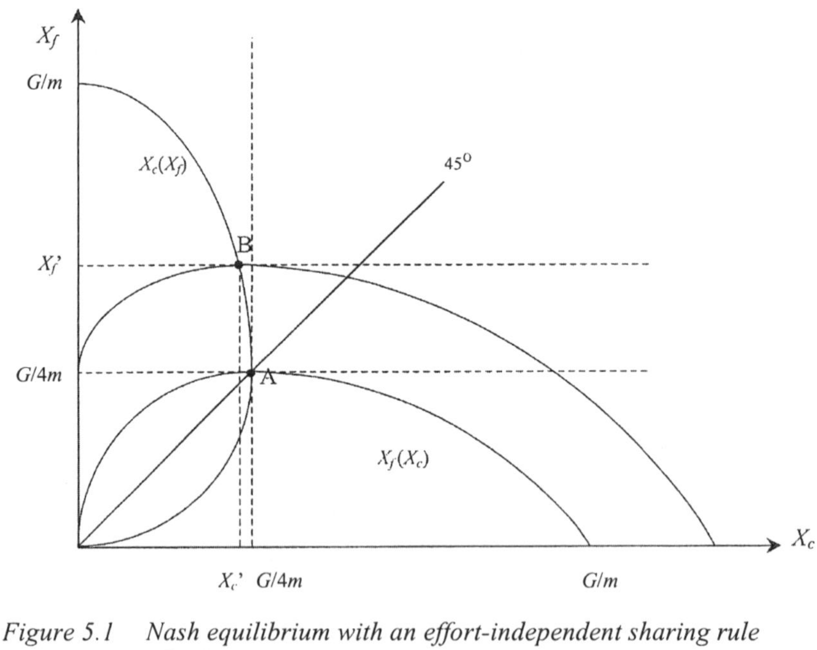

Figure 5.1 Nash equilibrium with an effort-independent sharing rule ($\delta = 0$)

Proposition 1 Assume that the comparative benchmark case has an effort-independent sharing rule ($\delta = 0$), and an equal valuation of hungriest citizen and the average firm ($v_{c1} = G/m$). The benchmark symmetric group effort Nash equilibrium is $(X_f^*, X_c^*) = (G/4m, G/4m)$, and the level of total effort equals $TE = G/2m$.[5]

A double dose of free-riding causes our players to expend fewer resources in the public–private benchmark model relative to the standard symmetric contest: $G/2m < G/2$, given $m > 1$. Free-riding occurs within the citizen group for the public good as only the hungriest citizen expends effort while the rest expend no effort. Free-riding occurs within the firm group for the private good as the effort-independent sharing rule removes all within-group competition. Players in this restricted public–private conflict are willing to waste fewer resources given the free-riding incentives. Neither the firm group nor the citizen group is the contest favorite or underdog since the odds of victory at the Nash equilibrium are 50:50. Note that if there is only one firm in the contest ($m = 1$), the Nash equilibrium and total effort are exactly the same as the standard symmetric contest model, $(X_c^*, X_f^*) = (G/4, G/4)$ and $TE = G/2$.

3.2 An Effort-dependent Sharing Rule

A firm group, however, is likely to be concerned with using whatever tool it has at its disposal to reduce within-group free-riding–to tip the conflict in their favor. In our model, the firm group uses the sharing-rule parameter, δ, to induce its members to expend more effort. Assume now that the firms' sharing rule has some degree of effort dependence, that is, $\delta > 0$. Figure 5.1 shows how the conflict changes with the new sharing rule. If $\delta > 0$, the firms' reaction function, $X_f(X_c)$ shifts up to point B, whereas the citizen group's reaction function, $X_c(X_f)$, does not change. A strictly positive δ makes the firm group the contest favorite–the firm group's chance of winning exceeds 50 per cent at the Nash equilibrium; the citizen group is the underdog.

The sharing rule, $\delta > 0$, creates two countervailing effects on total effort, $X_c^* + X_f^*$: more firm effort due to more within-group competition, and less citizen group effort because the contest is now more lopsided (see Baik and Shogren 1994). Which effect dominates? The net impact on total effort is shown by considering $\partial X_c/\partial X_f$ and $\partial(X^*_c + X^*_f)/\partial\delta$:

$$\frac{\partial X_c}{\partial X_f} = -1 + \frac{v_{c1}}{2\sqrt{v_{c1}X_f}} > -1 \qquad (5.6)$$

$$\frac{\partial\left(X_c^* + X_f^*\right)}{\partial\delta} = \frac{Gv_{c1}\left(m-1\right)}{mv_{c1} + G} > 0 \tag{5.7}$$

and

$$\frac{\partial^2\left(X_c^* + X_f^*\right)}{\partial\delta^2} = 0 \tag{5.8}$$

Expressions (5.6)–(5.8) imply that the increase in firms' effort (X_f^*) exceeds the decrease in citizen groups' effort (X_c^*). We summarize this result in the following proposition.

> **Proposition 2** Assume the sharing rule has some fraction of effort dependence, $\delta > 0$. An increase in δ causes the firm group to increase its effort and the citizen group to decrease its effort, $\partial X_c^*/\partial\delta < 0$ and $\partial X_f^*/\partial\delta > 0$ from the benchmark Nash equilibrium. The firm group is now the contest favorite – their odds of victory exceed 50 per cent at the Nash equilibrium.

Proposition 2 suggests that the firm can increase its odds of victory with a positive sharing-rule parameter. Increasing the size of the parameter induces the citizen group to cut back its effort since the contest has become more lopsided.

3.3 Efficiency

Consider now how changes in the structure of the conflict affect economic efficiency. We focus on changes in the size of the firm group (m) and the level of the sharing-rule weighting parameter (δ). Efficiency is measured both by traditional rent dissipation (*RD*) and the more general case of contest efficiency (*CE*). Following Tullock (1980), rent dissipation is the total effort expended (*TE*) by the two groups:

$$RD = TE = X_c^* + X_f^*. \tag{5.9}$$

More rent dissipation usually implies less efficiency as more resources are wasted in the fight to win the fixed prize.

When valuations differ across the prize, however, rent dissipation might not accurately reflect social efficiency. Following Hurley (1998), define contest efficiency (*CE*) as the net expected benefit of the contest – the expected benefit (*EB*) minus rent dissipation (*RD*) divided by the maximum valuation of the two groups:

$$CE = \frac{\frac{X_c^*}{X_c^* + X_f^*}V_c + \frac{X_f^*}{X_c^* + X_f^*}\sum_{j=1}^{m}\sigma_{fj}G - (X_c^* + X_f^*)}{\max(V_c, G)} \tag{5.10}$$

Contest efficiency accounts for how asymmetric values can affect efficiency – society benefits when the group with the greater value for the prize wins even if they expend more effort. Hurley showed it is possible for contest efficiency to increase even though more rent is dissipated.

Proposition 3 summarizes how more firms (m) affect efficiency (see Appendix 5A1 for details).

Proposition 3 Assume an effort-independent sharing rule ($\delta = 0$). Consider now how an increase in the number of firms in the group, m, affects the welfare of conflict as measured by rent dissipation (*RD*) and contest efficiency (*CE*):

1. *RD*: As m increases, both X_c^* and X_f^* decrease, which implies that rent dissipation decreases.
2. *CE*: As m increases, *CE* increases provided that the citizen group has a greater value on winning than the firm group, $V_c \geq G$. Now more firms increase the odds that the citizen group wins, which would lead to greater contest efficiency. If, however, the citizen group has a lower value than the firm group, $V_c < G$, two solutions exist. First, if $V_c < G < V_c + v_{c1}$, adding more firms increases contest efficiency. In contrast, if $V_c + v_{c1} < G$, more firms leads to lower contest efficiency.

Proposition 3 illustrates the efficiency gains from adding firms to their group, assuming the effort-independent sharing rule. In general, more firms lead to more free-riding and less rent dissipation. The firms reduce effort as their numbers increase because the expected payoff of each firm falls. The citizen group C is now the favorite because additional firms reduce the share of the fixed reward, which in turn increases the free-riding within the group. The citizen group responds to the firm free riding by reducing its effort. The overall effect on contest efficiency, however, depends on the relative valuation of the prize. If the citizen group's valuation exceeds the firm group's, contest efficiency increases with additional firms–the high-value citizen group is more likely to win. But if the firms value the prize more, adding more firms can reduce contest efficiency. If the relative values are $G > V_c + v_{c1}$, more free riding between the firms reduces contest efficiency because the lower-value citizen group is the favorite.

The second set of comparative statics we consider are for the sharing-rule parameter, δ. From (5.7) with the assumption $v_{c1} = G$, more effort dependence affects rent dissipation:

$$\frac{\partial TE}{\partial \delta} = \frac{G(m-1)}{(m+1)} > 0 \text{ since } m > 1.^{6} \qquad (5.7)'$$

Figure 5.2 shows how total effort (*TE*) increase with δ for different firm group sizes. We see that more firms leads to a steeper slope for *TE*. We now break down total effort into group effects by considering how X_c^* and X_f^* change with a greater δ:[7]

$$\frac{\partial X_c^*}{\partial \delta} = \frac{G(m-1)^2(1-2\delta)}{(m+1)^2}$$

$$\left.\begin{array}{l} \text{if } 0 < \delta < \tfrac{1}{2}, \text{ then } \dfrac{\partial X_c^*}{\partial \delta} > 0 \\[2ex] \text{if } \delta = \tfrac{1}{2}, \text{ then } \dfrac{\partial X_c^*}{\partial \delta} = 0 \\[2ex] \text{if } \tfrac{1}{2} < \delta \le 1, \text{ then } \dfrac{\partial X_c^*}{\partial \delta} < 0 \end{array}\right\} \qquad (5.11)$$

$$\frac{\partial X_f^*}{\partial \delta} = \frac{2G(m-1)[1+\delta(m-1)]}{(m+1)^2} > 0.^{8} \qquad (5.12)$$

Figure 5.2 also shows that as effort dependence increases, the firm group expends more effort. In response, the citizen group fights hard at first when δ is relatively small, 0 < δ < ½. The citizen group cuts back its effort as δ becomes sufficiently large because the firms have become extra aggressive within their own group since their share of the reward depends mainly on their fraction of total effort, which is summarized below.

> **Proposition 4** The citizen group is the favorite when the effort-dependent parameter is relatively small, 0 ≤ δ < ½. The firm group become the favorite when the effort-dependent parameter becomes sufficiently large, δ > ½.

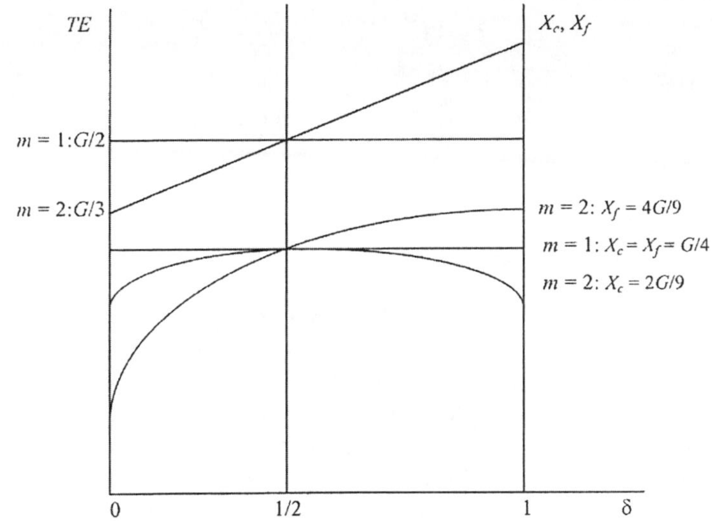

Figure 5.2 Effort levels with δ and m

Proposition 4 illustrates how the effort-dependent sharing rule causes the firm group to increase its effort as its expected payoff increases. As we approach $\delta \to ½$, both groups' effort approaches the high-effort level benchmark effort levels because the contest is becoming more evenly matched ($X_c^* = X_f^* = G/4$). At $\delta = ½$, the firm group continues to expend effort, but the citizen group (that is, the hungriest player) starts to reduce its effort because the contest is now becoming more lopsided, which increases the difference between total effort levels ($X_f^* - X_c^*$).

Contest efficiency is again complicated by the relative values of the two groups. Now $\partial CE/\partial\delta$ is written as:[9]

$$\text{At } V_c > G, \ \frac{\partial CE}{\partial\delta} = \frac{G(m-1)(G - V_c - v_{c1})}{V_c(mv_{c1} + G)} < 0 \tag{5.13}$$

$$\text{At } V_c = G, \ \frac{\partial CE}{\partial\delta} = -\frac{v_{c1}(m-1)}{(mv_{c1} + G)} < 0 \tag{5.14}$$

$$\text{At } V_c < G, \ \frac{\partial CE}{\partial\delta} = \frac{(m-1)(G - V_c - v_{c1})}{(mv_{c1} + G)} \tag{5.15}$$

$$\text{If } G > V_c + v_{c1}, \frac{\partial CE}{\partial \delta} > 0$$

$$\text{If } G < V_c + v_{c1}, \frac{\partial CE}{\partial \delta} < 0$$

$$\text{If } G = V_c + v_{c1}, \frac{\partial CE}{\partial \delta} = 0.$$

Figure 5.3a shows that when the citizen group's valuation is not less than the firm value ($V_c \geq G$), more weight on effort-dependence sharing reduces contest efficiency. The high-value citizens are less likely to win the conflict. Figure 5.3b shows the complication when the firms have the greater relative value. Again the valuation of the hungriest citizen relative to the citizen group total value sets the threshold. As δ increases, both expected benefit (*EB*) and rent dissipation (*RD*) always increases regardless of $\tilde{m}$: with $\tilde{m} > v_{c1} + V_c/v_{c1}$, both X_c and X_f increases and with $\tilde{m} < v_{c1} + V_c/v_{c1}$, X_f increases while X_c increases or decreases. If $\tilde{m} > v_{c1} + V_c/v_{c1}$, contest efficiency (*CE*), which is the difference between *EB* and *RD*, divided by maximum valuation, decreases. If $\tilde{m} < v_{c1} + V_c/v_{c1}$, *CE* increases. We summarize these results below.

Proposition 5 Consider how a change in the sharing-rule parameter affects social welfare given the relative valuations of the public good (V_c) and private good (G), for $m > 1$:

1. $V_c \geq G$: If players' effort-dependence sharing in group F is completely independent of their relative efforts ($\delta = 0$), when the number of firms increases ($m^* \rightarrow m^{**}$), *CE* increases. If players' effort-dependence sharing in group F is completely dependent of their relative efforts ($\delta = 1$), when the number of firms increases ($m^* \rightarrow m^{**}$), *CE* decreases. In addition, more weight on effort-dependence sharing reduces contest efficiency given the number of firms.
2. $V_c < G$: If $\tilde{m} > (V_c + v_{c1})/v_{c1}$, *CE* decreases. If $\tilde{m} < (V_c + v_{c1})/v_{c1}$, *CE* increases.

Proposition 5 captures the idea that for a fixed number of firms, an increase in the effort-dependence parameter (δ) increases the expected payoff of the firm group. Assuming that a pure effort-dependent sharing rule ($\delta = 1$) implies no free-riding, the sharing rule, $\sigma_{fj} = \delta x_{fj}/X_f + (1-\delta)/m$, becomes

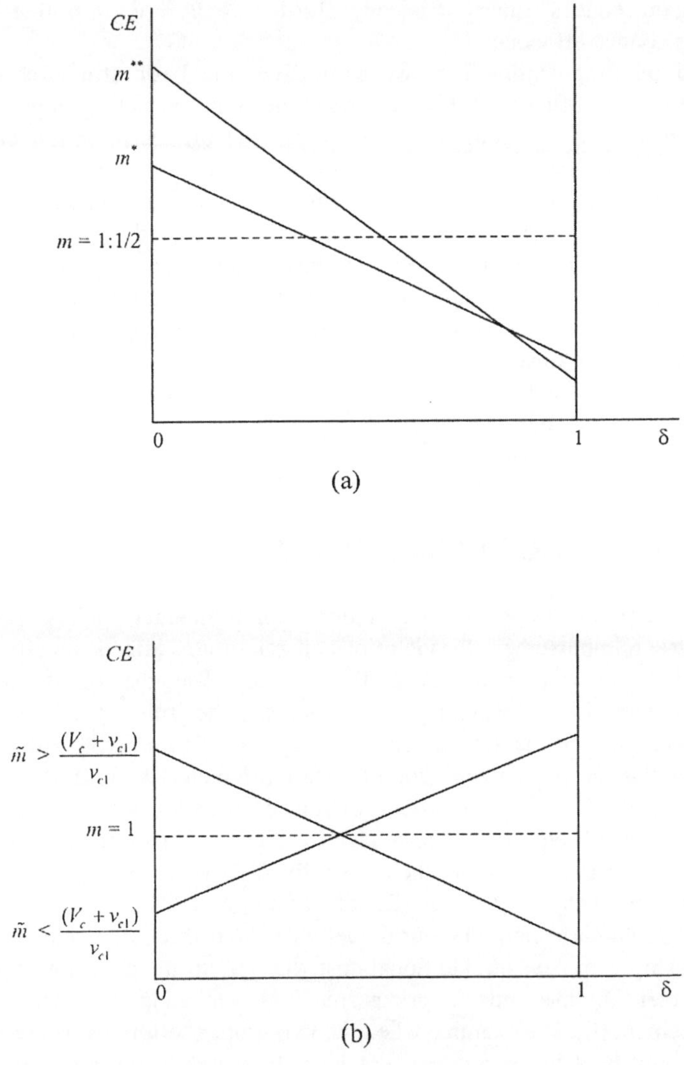

Figure 5.3 *Contest efficiency with an effort-dependent sharing rule and the number of firms: (a)*$V_c \geq G$, *(b)*$V_c < G$

$\sigma_{fj} = x_{fj}/X_f$. No firm has any incentive to free ride. Assuming that society prefers the group with the greater valuation to win the prize, we can say the following. If $V_c \geq G$, an increase in the effort-dependence parameter causes contest efficiency (*CE*) to decrease. If $V_c < G$ so that $G < V_c + v_{c1}$, less free-riding again reduces contest efficiency. But if $G > V_c + v_{c1}$, less free-riding increases contest efficiency.

Based on propositions 1–5, we summarize the basic structure of our public–private conflict model as follows. Free-riding in both groups lowers effort expended in the contest. Citizens free ride off the hungriest citizen; firms free ride off each other with an effort-independent sharing rule. Adding more firms to the group actually puts themselves at a disadvantage – citizens are the contest favorite, and firms the underdog because they free ride even more when new members join the group. Firms can reverse this disadvantage if they allow for effort dependence in their sharing rule. Now the firm group can turn itself into the favorite because free-riding no longer pays. Finally, we see that rent dissipation is only a reasonable proxy for contest efficiency if the citizen group total value exceeds or equals the firms' valuation. But if firm valuation exceeds the citizen group value, rent dissipation can be a biased measure of contest efficiency.

4. ASYMMETRIC REIMBURSEMENT

We now consider how the US federal environmental policy rule of asymmetric reimbursement for victorious citizen groups affects the effort and efficiency of our public–private conflict model. The goal of asymmetric reimbursement is to promote citizen suits. The rule is a one-sided modification of the classic British loser-pays system. Only a losing firm group reimburses the citizen group's effort (Shavell 1982). If the citizen group loses, the firms' effort is not reimbursed. The idea behind asymmetric reimbursement of legal fees is to reduce the financial risks of these 'private attorney generals' by repaying their costs for discovery, investigation, court cost, and support staff if they win (Baik and Shogren 1994).

We add reimbursement into our model with the restriction on player j in F – each losing firm pays an additional cost $(\beta X_c/m)$ to the citizen group; and each player in the citizen group receives an additional prize with reimbursement (β). We examine when the two groups' effort levels are equal, $X_c = X_f$, and how the reimbursement level β relates to the level of effort dependence in the firms' sharing rule, δ.

4.1 Adding Asymmetric Reimbursement

With reimbursement, player i's expected payoff within the citizens group is $\Pi_{ci} = P_c(v_{ci} + \beta X_c v_{ci}/V_c) - x_{ci}$.[10] The first-order condition is

$$\frac{X_f}{(X_c+X_f)^2}(v_{ci}+\beta\frac{v_{ci}}{V_c}X_c)+\beta\frac{v_{ci}}{V_c}\frac{X_c}{(X_c+X_f)} - 1 = 0 \quad (5.16)$$

The player's expected marginal payoff,

$$\frac{X_f}{\left(X_c+X_f\right)^2}\left(v_{ci}+\beta\frac{v_{ci}}{V_c}X_c\right)+\beta\frac{v_{ci}}{V_c}\frac{X_c}{\left(X_c+X_f\right)},$$

decreases with his or her effort level, x_{ck}, for $0 < X_f < V_c/\beta$. Since $v_c < V_c/\beta$, the second-order conditions hold. Again we know that only the hungriest player expends effort, so that $x_{c1}^* = X_c^*$ (see Appendix 5A2).

The expected payoff of player j in group F is:

$$\Pi_{fj} = P_f(\sigma_{fj}G + \beta\frac{X_c}{m}) - x_{fj} - \beta\frac{X_c}{m}.$$

The corresponding first-order condition for an interior optimum is:

$$\frac{G[m\delta(X_c+X_f-x_{fj})+(1-\delta)X_c]+\beta X_c^2}{m(X_c+X_f)^2} - 1 = 0. \quad (5.17)$$

The player's marginal gross payoff decreases with his or her effort level, x_{fj}, which implies that the second-order condition for the maximum problem is satisfied.

At the symmetric Nash equilibrium, $x_{f1} = \ldots = x_{fm}$ and $X_c + X_f = x_{c1} + mx_{fj}$. Using equations (5.16) and (5.17) and given group C's equilibrium effort level, X_c^*, we obtain:[11]

$$X_f(X_c) = \frac{G\delta(m-1)-2mX_c+\sqrt{[G\delta(m-1)]^2+4mX_c(G+\beta X_c)}}{2m} \quad (5.18)$$

$$X_c(X_f) = \sqrt{\frac{v_{ci}(V_c-\beta X_f)X_f}{V_c-\beta v_{ci}}} - X_f. \quad (5.19)$$

From (5.18) and (5.19), we write the reaction functions as:

$X_f(X_c) = \varepsilon$, for $X_c = 0$

$$X_f(X_c) = \frac{G\delta(m-1) - 2mX_c + \sqrt{[G\delta(m-1)]^2 + 4mX_c(G+\beta X_c)}}{2m},$$

$$\text{for } 0 < X_c \leq \frac{G[1+\delta(m-1)]}{m-\beta}$$

$$X_f(X_c) = 0, \text{ for } X_c > \frac{G[1+\delta(m-1)]}{m-\beta}$$

$$X_c(X_f) = \varepsilon, \text{ for } X_f = 0$$

$$X_c(X_f) = \sqrt{\frac{v_{ci}(V_c - \beta X_f)X_f}{V_c - \beta v_{ci}}} - X_f, \text{ for } 0 < X_f < v_{c1}$$

$$X_c(X_f) = 0, \text{ for } X_f > v_{c1}$$

As a comparative benchmark, we see that group effort Nash equilibrium when $\delta = 0$, $mv_{c1} = G$(benchmark), and $V_c = G$ is:

$$(X_c^*, X_f^*) = \left\{ \frac{G\left[\frac{\sqrt{m(m-\beta)}}{m-\beta} - 1\right]}{2\beta}, \frac{G\left[m - \sqrt{m(m-\beta}\right]}{2m\beta} \right\}.$$ [12]

First, consider whether the effort levels with reimbursement, β, are larger than the effort levels without β. Without reimbursement, $X_c^* = G/4m$ and $X_f^* = G/4m$. With reimbursement,

$$X_c^* = \frac{G\left[\frac{\sqrt{m(m-\beta)}}{m-\beta} - 1\right]}{2\beta}$$

and

$$X_f^* = \frac{G\left[m - \sqrt{m(m-\beta)}\right]}{2m\beta}.$$

Therefore, each group Nash equilibrium with β is greater than group Nash equilibrium without β; and total effort with β is greater than the total effort without β.

At the Nash equilibrium, we know that group C is favorite and group F is underdog.

Using comparative statics and assuming $X_c \neq 0$ and $m > 1$, we know that as the sharing-rule parameter δ increases the effort of player *j* in the firm group increases.[13] Also we know that with $0 \leq \delta \leq 1$ and $X_c \neq 0$, adding more firms (*m*) causes the effort of player *j* in the firm group to decrease.

Proposition 6 Assume that the sharing rule has some effort dependence, $\delta > 0$. Now δ induces the firm group to expend more effort, regardless of the level of reimbursement. Again an increase in the group size, *m*, increases the free-riding within the firm group, regardless of the level of reimbursement.

Proposition 6 says that with asymmetric reimbursement, the effort-dependent parameter (δ) causes each firm to expend more effort since its expected payoff increases. Meanwhile, an increase in the group size (*m*) causes each firm to free ride more since its expected payoff decreases.

4.2 Sharing and Reimbursement Rules (δ versus β)

We know the firm group can use the sharing-rule parameter to increase its within-group competition, which in turn increases firm total effort and transforms the firms into the contest favorite. Firms that put more weight on effort-dependent sharing tips the contest in their favor. The question we consider now is to find the relative level of the reimbursement rule that can rebalance the power in the public–private environmental conflict, given the sharing rule. We explore the level of reimbursement, β, relative to the size of the sharing-rule parameter, δ.

Using first-order conditions, given X_c^* and X_f^*, we obtain:

$$\beta\left[\left(\frac{mv_{c1}}{V_c}-1\right)X_c^2+2m\frac{v_{c1}}{V_c}X_cX_f\right]=$$

$$G[m\delta(X_c+X_f-x_{fj})+(1-\delta)X_c]-mv_{c1}X_f \tag{5.20}$$

Since $x_{f1} = \ldots = x_{fm}$, $x_{fj} = (X_f/m)$, and given $X_c^* = X_f^*$, we obtain:

$$\beta=\left[\frac{2V_cG(m-1)}{(3mv_{c1}-V_c)X_f}\right]\delta+\frac{V_c(G-mv_{c1})}{(3mv_{c1}-V_c)X_f}. \qquad (5.21)^{14}$$

Figure 5.4a shows our benchmark case, in which $v_{c1} = G/m$ and $2V_cG(m - 1)/(3mv_{c1} - V_c) = X_f$. The 45-degree line from the origin shows the cases of equal power between the two groups given the level of reimbursement, β, and the sharing-rule parameter, δ.

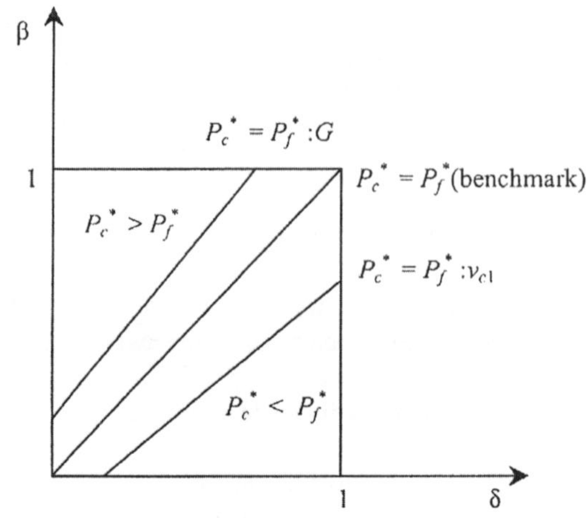

(a)

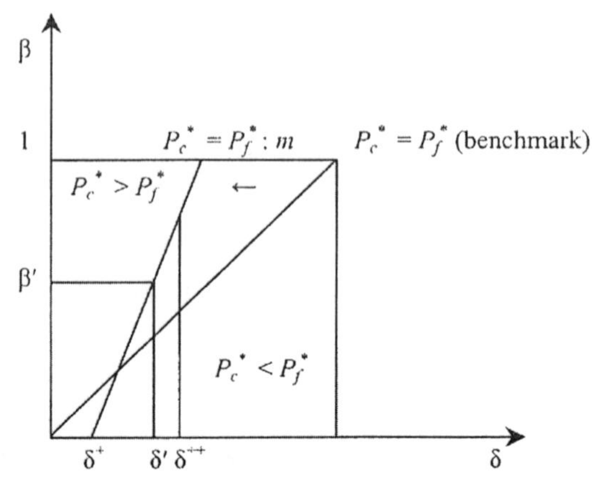

(b)

Figure 5.4 The relationship between β and δ

Now consider how the reimbursement rule should be altered to rebalance power for a set of given changes in the conflict environment. The following three propositions summarize the results for a change in the fixed rent to the firm group increases, *G*; the valuation of the hungriest citizen; and the number of firms.

> **Proposition 7** If the fixed rent of the firm group, *G*, increases, holding the sharing rule constant (δ), the firm group increases its effort and its probability-of-winning function increases, P_f^*. In these cases, a regulator must increase the level of reimbursement, β, to maintain equality of strength, for any given δ; or the firm group must decrease δ to maintain equality of strength, for any given β.

Proposition 7 says that if the fixed rent of firm group moves from $V_c = G$ such that $V_c < G$, the group's expected payoff increases. Figure 5.4a shows that the firm group increases its effort and its probability-of-winning function increases for any given δ. Efficiency increases now since society prefers that the higher-value firm group wins the conflict. In this case, promoting asymmetric reimbursement would decrease efficiency because the low-value citizen group would be more likely to win. A regulator would have to justify this asymmetric reimbursement policy on grounds other than economic efficiency (for example empowerment, constitutional right to petition).

> **Proposition 8** If the valuation of the hungriest player in the citizen group increases, v_{c1}, his or her effort increases and therefore the probability-of-winning function increases, P_c^*, even if β is fixed. When v_{c1} increases, the regulator must decrease the level of reimbursement, β, to maintain equality of strength, for any given δ; alternatively the firm group must increase δ to maintain equality of strength, for any given β.

Proposition 8 captures the idea that if the valuation of the hungriest player in the citizen group increases from $V_c = G$ to $V_c > G$, the citizen group's expected payoff increase. The hungriest player will increase his or her effort for any given β, thereby increasing his probability-of-winning function (see Figure 5.4a). Efficiency now increases since the high-value citizen group is more likely to win the conflict. The regulator can use the asymmetric reimbursement policy to reinforce this result, especially if the firm group chooses an effort-dependent sharing rule (δ > 0).

> **Proposition 9** An increase in the number of firms, *m*, has an ambiguous effect on the probability-of-winning function for the firm group, P_f^*. We can say, however, that if *m* increases when $\delta < \delta'$, then P_f^* decreases,

where δ' represents a sharing-rule threshold. This threshold distinguishes how the firm reacts to adding new members to the group. This suggests that if the sharing rule is small 'enough', an increase in the number of firms leads to more free-riding with the group. Alternatively, if m increases when $\delta > \delta'$, P_f^* increases. Therefore if δ is large 'enough', adding more firms does not increase intra-group competition, free-riding decreases, and P_f^* increases.

Proposition 9 suggests that with an effort-independent sharing rule, more firms reduce the group's probability of winning due to free-riding. More firms given an effort-dependent sharing rule, however, are less clear cut. Figure 5.4b shows that each group's probability-of-winning function depends on the relative magnitudes between reimbursement and the sharing rule, β and δ. One can find combinations of the two rules to balance out the conflict such that neither group is the favorite or the underdog.

4.3 Efficiency given Asymmetric Reimbursement

We now consider how increasing the level of reimbursement, β, affects economic efficiency. Again consider both rent dissipation and contest efficiency, $\partial TE/\partial\beta$ versus $\partial CE/\partial\beta$ with $\delta = 0$ and $mv_{c1} = G$ (benchmark).[15] We summarize this impact of greater reimbursement on rent dissipation (see Appendix 5A3).

> **Proposition 10** Asymmetric reimbursement (β) of the citizen group's effort increases the effort of both groups, thereby increasing total effort. Moreover, the reimbursement rule causes the citizen group to expend even more effort since now the group has more motivation to win the public good.

Proposition 10 captures the trap that asymmetric reimbursement imposes on the firm group – the firm group continues to expend effort even though its expected payoff is negative.[16] As the level of reimbursement increases, both groups continue to expend more effort, and the difference between effort levels ($X_c^* - X_f^*$) increases. In this case, reimbursement creates more rent dissipation.

The results for contest efficiency are summarized as follows (see Appendix 5A3).

> **Proposition 11** Consider now the welfare consequences given the relative valuations of the public good (V_c) and private good (G), for $mv_{c1} = G$:

1. $V_c \leq G$: Contest Efficiency (*CE*) decreases as the level of reimbursement increases, β. Overall, *CE* is lower than the *CE* (benchmark).
2. $V_c > G$: If the gap between V_c and G is sufficiently large ($V_c >> G$), an increase in reimbursement, β, increases *CE*. But if the valuation gap is insignificantly large ($V_c > G$), an increase in β causes *CE* to decrease.

For (1), if the firms' total valuation (G) is greater than or equal to the citizen group total valuation (V_c), Contest Efficiency (*CE*) decreases as the level of reimbursement increases, β. *CE* declines due to two reinforcing effects: first, it becomes more likely that the lower-value player wins the conflict; and second, Rent Dissipation increases – the players expend additional effort to decrease the odds that the higher-value group wins.

In (2), if the gap between V_c and G is sufficiently large ($V_c >> G$), an increase in reimbursement, β, leads to an increase in *CE*. Now *CE* increases because the benefits of increasing the odds that the higher-value group wins outweigh the costs of greater Rent Dissipation. The effect is similar to the free-rider problem. If the valuation gap is not large enough ($V_c > G$), however, increasing reimbursement reduces *CE* – now the additional rent dissipation exceeds the expected benefits from the citizen group winning.

Proposition 11 suggests that a policy of asymmetric reimbursement within this class of conflict models can be justified by contest efficiency only in the case in which the gap between V_c and G is sufficiently large ($V_c >> G$). If, however, $V_c \leq G$, or for a small gap in $V_c > G$ with a low or decreasing δ, the regulator cannot justify the reimbursement policy on efficiency grounds. Here a regulator reduces economic efficiency by using reimbursement to promote citizen suits.

5. CONCLUDING COMMENTS

Environmental conflicts set firms against citizen groups. Firms gain private benefits from developing land; citizen groups gain public benefits from conserving the same land. The firms' private gains are rival and excludable; the citizens' public gains are non-rival and non-excludable. Herein we address how a public–private environmental conflict affects effort expended and economic efficiency, with and without asymmetric reimbursement rules. Three key results emerge from our model. First, a form of double free-riding can exist in the conflict – the hungriest citizen fights for the public good as the others free ride; each firm free rides off the efforts of the others for the private good given an effort-independent sharing rule. Firms address the within-group free-riding by making the sharing rule more effort dependent.

For a fixed number of firms, more emphasis on an effort-dependent sharing reduces free-riding relative to the effort-independent case. The citizen group responds to the firms with a change in effort by the hungriest player, not with less free-riding by the rest of the group.

Second, when additional firms enter the group, the firm group's expected payoff decreases. More firms cause each firm to reduce its effort. The citizen group responds to this additional firm free-riding by also reducing its effort, thereby decreasing the overall level of rent dissipation in the conflict. Lower rent dissipation does not necessarily imply more economic efficiency, however, when the valuation of the prize differs between the groups. Measuring economic efficiency depends on the relative values assigned to the public and private good. If the citizen group values the prize more than the firm group, then more free-riding increases efficiency because it is now more likely that the high-value citizen group will win the contest.

Finally, an increase in the level of asymmetric reimbursement for the citizen group causes the firm group's expected payoff to decrease. The citizen group responds by exerting more effort, even more than the firms. The conflict now becomes increasingly lopsided in favor of the citizen group. Again the impact on economic efficiency depends on the relative valuations of the two groups – efficiency increases with reimbursement when it becomes more likely that a high-value citizen group wins. Otherwise, reimbursement can reduce efficiency. In such cases, regulators would use criteria other than economic efficiency to justify the use of the asymmetric reimbursement rule.

ACKNOWLEDGEMENTS

We thank a reviewer and Kyung Hwan Baik, Sherrill Shaffer, and Hans-Peter Weikard for their helpful comments.

NOTES

1. The Supreme Court voted 7–2 in January 2000 to preserve the right of a private citizen to sue an alleged polluter or developer for violating a federal environmental regulation (*Friends of Earth, inc. v. Laidlaw Environmental Services (TOC), Inc.* (98-822), 149 F.3d 303). Private citizens helping to enforce laws dates back over 600 years to a 1388 statute in England (Dickinson 1997). See for example Clauson (1997), Grant (1997), Leonard (1995), and Pring and Canon (1995) for discussions on the legal aspects of citizen suits in environmental policy.
2. The group of firms can eliminate within-group free-riding with a pure effort-dependent sharing rule within the non-cooperative framework.
3. The second-order conditions are satisfied since the expected returns, Π_{ci} and Π_{fj}, are strictly concave in x_{ci} and x_{fj}, or $(\partial^2\Pi_{ci}/\partial x_{ci}^2) = -[2X_f v_{ci}/(X_C + X_f)^3] < 0$ and $(\partial^2\Pi_{fj}/\partial x_{fj}^2) = -\{2G[\delta(m-1) + m\delta(X_f - x_{fj}) + 1]/(X_C + X_f)^3\} < 0$.

4. The following condition must hold, $mv_{c1} > \delta G(m-1)$, to guarantee a unique solution; see Nitzan (1991).
5. The reviewer made an excellent point. Assume that the total public benefit equals the total private benefit:

$$G = \sum_{i=1}^{n} v_{ci} \,.$$

Then

$$TE = \frac{v_{c1}}{mv_{c1} + G} G$$

is the same as in equation (5A1.1), so

$$\frac{v_{c1}}{mv_{c1} + G} G >(<) \frac{1}{2} G \text{ when } m <(>) 2 - \frac{1}{v_{c1}} G.$$

This expression implies that TE is lower than the conventional $G/2$ if $m > 1$, due to free riding on the part of firms. If $m = 1$, TE is lower provided $G > v_{c1}$, due to free riding by the citizens. If $G > v_{c1}$ and $m = 1$ (the case of one citizen and one firm), we are back to $TE = G/2$.
6. Note $\partial^2 TE/\partial\delta^2 = 0$.
7. $X_c^* = G[1+\delta(m-1)][m-\delta(m-1)]/(m+1)^2$, $X_f^* = G[1+\delta(m-1)]^2/(m+1)^2$.
8. Note $\partial^2 X_c^*/\partial\delta^2 = -2G(m-1)^2/(m+1)^2 < 0$ and $\partial^2 X_f^*/\partial\delta^2 = 2G(m-1)^2/(m+1)^2 > 0$.
9. Note $\partial^2 CE/\partial\delta^2 = 0$.
10. Each player in group C receives the additional prize with a valuation-dependent reimbursement rule if victorious. Assume that each player in group C receives the additional prize with an effort-dependent reimbursement rule if victorious. Player i's expected payoff can be rewritten as $\Pi_{ci} = P_c(v_{ci} + \beta x_{ci}) - x_{ci}$ with the first order, $X_f/(X_c + X_f)^2(v_{ci} + \beta x_{ci}) + \beta X_c/(X_c + X_f) - 1 = 0$. The sufficient condition to satisfy the second-order condition is $x_{c1} = X_c$. With this condition, we find that group C's effort level with an effort-dependent reimbursement rule is greater than group C's effort level with a valuation-dependent reimbursement rule, considering the difference of expected marginal payoff between two rules. Without the sufficient condition, we cannot guarantee a Nash equilibrium; we may face multiple Nash equilibria or we may not find any Nash equilibria.
11. Without reimbursement, β, (5.18) and (5.19) are identical to (5.4) and (5.5).
12. With $m=1$, we can obtain the same result as Baik and Shogren (1994), moreover group C is favorite. Without β, group effort Nash equilibrium is $(X_c^*, X_f^*) = (G/4m, G/4m)$.
13. The result is the same without β. See equation (5.12). Note that with $X_c \neq 0$ and $m = 1$, when δ increases the effort of player j in group F is fixed.
14. With $m > 1$, the slope is positive.
15. The comparative static on social welfare given additional firms reveals the following. Assume an effort-independent sharing rule ($\delta = 0$) and $V_c = G$. We can show how more firms, m, affects the welfare of conflict as measured by Rent Dissipation (RD) and Contest Efficiency (CE). As m increases, both X_c^* and X_f^* decrease, which implies that RD decreases. Here now the citizen group C becomes the favorite because additional firms reduce the share of the fixed reward, which in turn increases the free-riding within the group. As m increases, CE increases.
16. This is the same as the result in Baik and Shogren (1994).

REFERENCES

Baik, K.H. (1993), 'Effort levels in contests: the public-good prize case', *Economics Letters*, **41**, 363–7.

Baik, K.H. and J.F. Shogren (1994), 'Environmental conflicts with reimbursement for citizen suits', *Journal of Environmental Economics and Management*, **27**, 1–20.

Baik, K.H. and J.F. Shogren (1995), 'Competitive share group formation in rent seeking contests', *Public Choice*, **83**, 113–26.

Clauson, H.L. (1997), 'How far should the bar on citizen suits extend under Section 309 of the Clean Water Act?' (1996 Ninth Circuit Environmental Review), *Environmental Law*, **27**, 967–90.

Dickinson, D. (1997), 'Is "diligent prosecution of an action in a court" required to preempt citizen suits under the major federal environmental statutes?', *William and Mary Law Review*, **38** (4), 1545–82.

Grant II, D.S. (1997), 'Allowing citizen participation in environmental regulation: an empirical analysis of the effects of right-to-sue and right-to-know provisions of industry's toxic emissions', *Social Science Quarterly*, **78**, 859–73.

Heyes, A.G. (1997), 'Environmental regulation by private contest', *Journal of Public Economics*, **63**, 407–28.

Hurley, T.M. (1998), 'Rent dissipation and efficiency in a contest with asymmetric valuations', *Public Choice*, **94**, 289–98.

Hurley, T.M. and J.F. Shogren (1997), 'Environmental conflicts and the SLAPP', *Journal of Environmental Economics and Management,* **33**, 253–73.

Katz, E., S. Nitzan and J. Rosenberg (1990), 'Rent-seeking for pure public goods', *Public Choice*, **65**, 49–60.

Leonard, A. (1995), 'When should an administrative enforcement action preclude a citizen suit under the Clean Water Act?', *Natural Resources Journal*, **35**, 555–624.

Miller, J.G. (1987), *Citizen Suits: Private Enforcement of Federal Pollution Control Laws*, New York: Wiley Law Publications.

Naysnerski, W. and T. Tietenberg (1992), 'Private enforcement of federal environmental law', *Land Economics*, **68**, 28–48.

Nitzan, S. (1991), 'Rent-seeking with non-identical sharing rules', *Public Choice*, **71**, 43–50.

Pring, G.W. and P. Canan (1995), *SLAPPs: Getting Sued for Speaking Out*, Philadelphia: Temple University Press.

Sax, J.L. (1970), *Defending the Environment: A Strategy for Citizen Action*, New York: Alfred Knopf, Inc.

Settle, C., T. Hurley and J. Shogren (2001), 'Citizen suits', in A. Heyes (ed.), *The Law and Economics of the Environment*, Cheltenham, UK and Northampton, MA, USA: Edward Elgar, pp. 217–48.

Shavell, S. (1982), 'Suit and settlement vs. trial: a theoretical analysis under alternative methods for the allocation of legal costs', *Journal of Legal Studies*, **11** (1), 55–81.

Tullock, G. (1980), 'Efficient rent-seeking', in James M. Buchanan, Robert D. Tollison and Gordon Tullock (eds), *Toward a Theory of the Rent-Seeking Society*, College Station, TX: Texas A&M University Press, pp. 97–112.

APPENDIX 5A1

Focusing on the benchmark model ($X_c^* = X_f^*$ with $\delta = 0$), we can show:

$$TE_{\delta=0} = \frac{Gv_{c1}}{mv_{c1} + G}, \quad (5A1.1)$$

$$\frac{\partial TE_{\delta=0}}{\partial m} = -\frac{Gv_{c1}^2}{(mv_{c1} + G)^2} < 0.\text{[1]} \quad (5A1.2)$$

We can see how more firms affects group effort, $\partial X_c^* / \partial m$ and $\partial X_f^* / \partial m$, which is

$$\partial X_c^* / \partial m = G\left(1 - \frac{m}{\bar{m}}\right) \Big/ \bar{m}^2 \left(\frac{m}{\bar{m}} + 1\right)^3,$$

assuming that $v_{c1} = G/\bar{m}$. If $m > \bar{m}$, the slope is negative; if $m = \bar{m}$, it is zero; and if $m < \bar{m}$, it is positive.[2] For firms,

$$\partial X_f^* / \partial m = -2 \Big/ \bar{m}^2 \left(\frac{m}{\bar{m}} + 1\right)^3 < 0.\text{[3]}$$

Figure 5A1.1 illustrates the impact of more firms on total effort. We see that as firms increase, total effort by the firms always decreases at a decreasing rate. Citizen group total effort increases in the range of $0 < m < \bar{m}$, and then decreases with more firms. But note that the citizen group is the contest favorite at $m > \bar{m}$, citizen total effort falls with $X_c^*\big|_{m>\bar{m}} > X_f^*\big|_{m>\bar{m}}$. Meanwhile, the citizen group is the contest underdog at $m < \bar{m}$, citizen total effort increases with $X_c^*\big|_{m>\bar{m}} < X_f^*\big|_{m>\bar{m}}$.

For contest efficiency, $\partial CE/\partial m$ with $\delta = 0$, the change in social welfare depends on the relative values of the firms and citizens, V_c relative to G.

$$\text{At } V_c = G,\ CE_{\delta=0} = \frac{G + v_{c1}(m-1)}{mv_{c1} + G} \quad (5A1.3)$$

$$\text{At } V_c > G,\ CE_{\delta=0} = \frac{mv_{c1}V_C + G(G - v_{c1})}{G(mv_{c1} + G)} \quad (5A1.4)$$

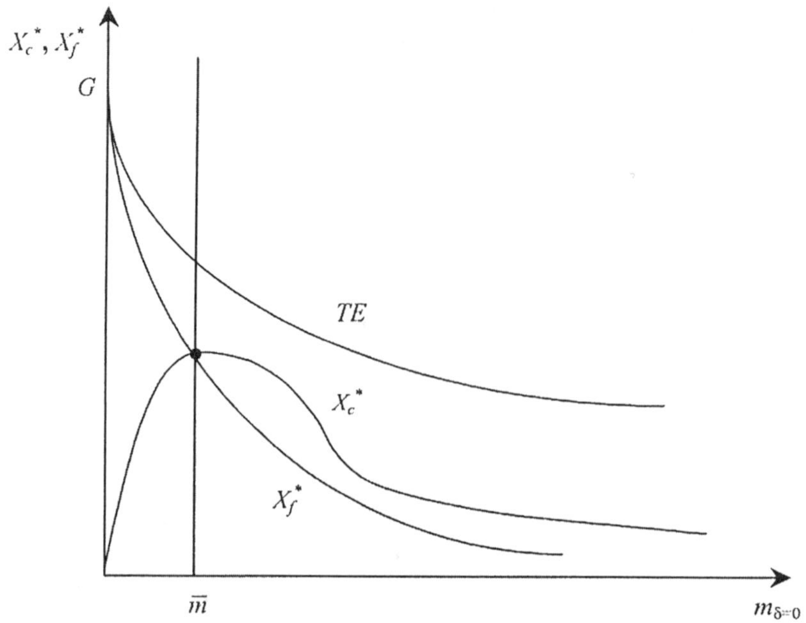

Figure 5A1.1 *Effort with the number of firms* ($m_{\delta=0}$)

$$\text{At } V_c < G,\ CE_{\delta=0} = \frac{mv_{c1}V_c + G(G - v_{c1})}{V_c(mv_{c1} + G)}. \tag{5A1.5}$$

From equations (5A1.3) and (5A1.4) and assuming $\bar{m}=1$ as the benchmark, Figure 5A1.2a illustrates the impact for when the citizen group's valuation is not less than the firms' value ($V_c \geq G$) – more firms increases contest efficiency because now citizens who have the greatest value are even more likely to win the conflict.

The story is more complicated, however, when the firm – as the underdog – values the prize more than the citizen group, $V_c < G$, as in expression (5A1.5). Figure 5A1.2b shows that contest efficiency declines in Region 1 – which contradicts the less rent dissipation result. Here *CE* falls because now it is more likely that the high-value firms will lose and total effort is decreasing. In Region 2, however, *CE* increases – which supports less rent dissipation. Now more firms lowers total effort enough to overcome the lower odds that the high-value group will win. The threshold between these two regions, $\tilde{m} = (v_{c1} + V_c)/v_{c1}$, is set by the magnitude of the hungriest citizen relative to the total valuation of the citizen group (v_{c1} versus V_c).

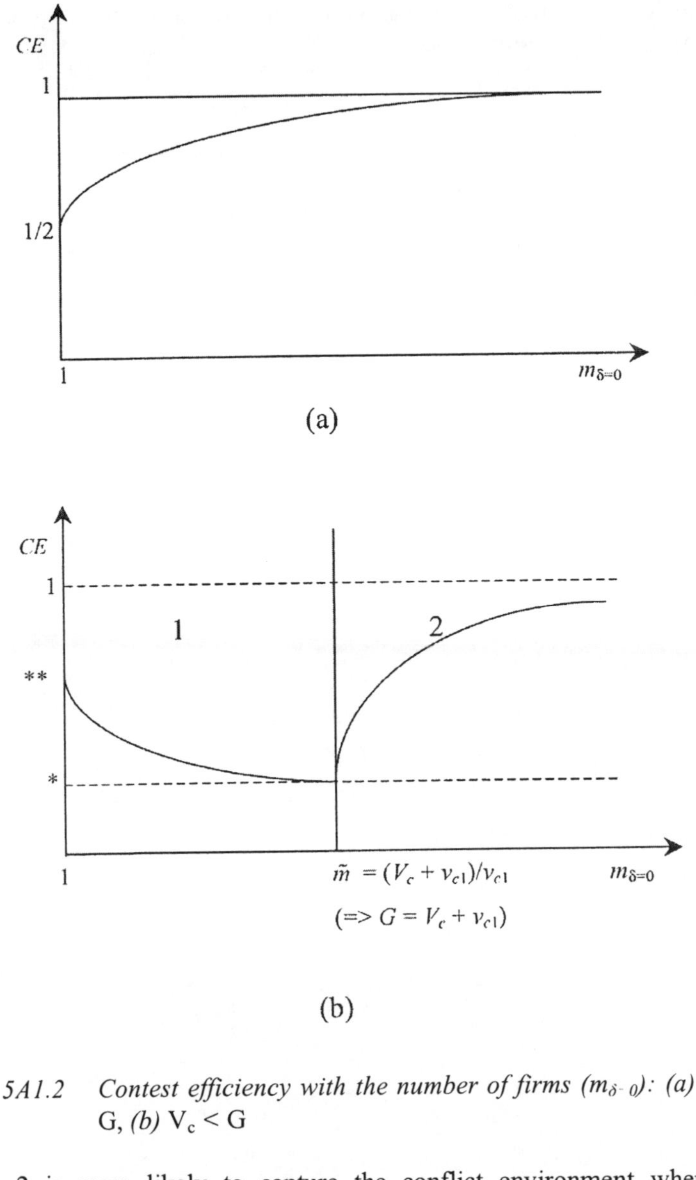

Figure 5A1.2 *Contest efficiency with the number of firms ($m_{\delta=0}$): (a)* $V_c \geq G$, *(b)* $V_c < G$

Region 2 is more likely to capture the conflict environment when the hungriest citizen's valuation dominates the citizen group – which implies that rent dissipation is a useful proxy for contest efficiency. Otherwise, if Region 1 reflects the contest, then rent dissipation does not reflect the actual social welfare consequences of adding more firms to the contest. Proposition 3 summarizes these results.

NOTES

1. Note $\partial^2 TE_{\delta=0}/\partial m^2 = 2Gv_{c1}^3/(mv_{c1}+1)^3 > 0$.
2. Note $\partial^2 X_c^*/\partial m^2 = -2G[2-(m/\bar{m})]/\bar{m}^3[(m/\bar{m})+1]^4$. At $m < 2\bar{m}$, then $\partial^2 X_c^*/\partial m^2 < 0$. At $m = 2\bar{m}$, $\partial^2 X_c^*/\partial m^2 = 0$. At $m > 2\bar{m}$, $\partial^2 X_c^*/\partial m^2 > 0$.
3. Note $\partial^2 X_f^*/\partial m^2 = 6/\bar{m}^3[(m/\bar{m})+1]^4 > 0$.

APPENDIX 5A2

Following Baik (1993), given group F's equilibrium effort level, X_f^*, the first-order condition for player i in group C is as follows:

$$\frac{X_f^*}{(X_c+X_f^*)^2}\left(v_{ci}+\beta\frac{v_{ci}}{V_c}X_c\right)+\beta\frac{v_{ci}}{V_c}\frac{X_c}{(X_c+X_f^*)}-1=0\text{, if } x_i>0.$$

Since the term

$$\frac{X_f^*}{(X_c+X_f^*)^2}\left(v_{ci}+\beta\frac{v_{ci}}{V_c}X_c\right)+\beta\frac{v_{ci}}{V_c}\frac{X_c}{(X_c+X_f^*)}$$

decreases in X_c, for $0 < X_f^* < V_c/\beta$, and the term shifts paralleled for v_{ci}, we obtain Lemma 1 for any h and k.

Lemma 1 $x_{ch} > x_{ck}$ holds if $v_{ch} > v_{ck}$
First, suppose that $X_c > x_{c1}$ holds. Since

$$\frac{X_f^*}{(X_c+X_f^*)^2}\left(v_{ci}+\beta\frac{v_{ci}}{V_c}X_c\right)+\beta\frac{v_{ci}}{V_c}\frac{X_c}{(X_c+X_f^*)}=1$$

for any i in group C if $X_c > 0$, then

$$\frac{X_f^*}{(X_c+X_f^*)^2}\left(v_{c1}+\beta\frac{v_{c1}}{V_c}X_c\right)+\beta\frac{v_{c1}}{V_c}\frac{X_c}{(X_c+X_f^*)}<1$$

for player 1 in the group, which means that $x_{c1} = 0$ and contradicts Lemma 1.

Second, suppose that $X_c = x_{c1}$ holds. Since

$$\frac{X_f^*}{(X_c+X_f^*)^2}\left(v_{c1}+\beta\frac{v_{c1}}{V_c}X_c\right)+\beta\frac{v_{c1}}{V_c}\frac{X_c}{(X_c+X_f^*)}=1 \text{ if } X_c = x_{c1} > 0,$$

then:

$$\frac{X_f^*}{(X_c+X_f^*)^2}\left(v_{ck}+\beta\frac{v_{ck}}{V_c}X_c\right)+\beta\frac{v_{ck}}{V_c}\frac{X_c}{(X_c+X_f^*)}<1$$

for player k in the group, which means that $x_{ck} = 0$, $k = 2, \ldots, n$, and satisfies Lemma 1.

APPENDIX 5A3

For rent dissipation in proposition 10, we know:

$$TE_{\delta=0} = \frac{G\sqrt{m(m-\beta)}}{2m(m-\beta)}, \quad \frac{\partial TE_{\delta=0}}{\partial\beta} = \frac{G}{4(m-\beta)\sqrt{m(m-\beta)}} > 0$$

and

$$\frac{\partial^2 TE_{\delta=0}}{\partial\beta^2} = \frac{3G}{8(m-\beta)\sqrt{m(m-\beta)}} > 0.$$

We can also show how group effort changes, X_c^* and X_f^*, with increasing β:

$$\frac{\partial X_c^*}{\partial\beta} = \frac{G[m^{1/2}(m-\beta)^{-3/2}(3\beta-2m)+2]}{4\beta^2} > 0 \qquad (5A3.1)$$

$$\frac{\partial X_f^*}{\partial\beta} = \frac{G[\beta m^{1/2}(m-\beta)^{-1/2}+2m^{1/2}(m-\beta)^{1/2}-2m]}{4m\beta^2} > 0 \qquad (5A3.2)$$

We now sign expressions (5A3.1) and (5A3.2) $\partial X_c^*/\partial\beta$ and $\partial X_f^*/\partial\beta$. From expression (5A3.1), we know the following expression holds:

$$m^{1/2}(m-\beta)^{-3/2}(3\beta-2m)+2>0. \qquad (5A3.3)$$

Define the following function: $f(\beta) = m^{1/2}(m-\beta)^{-3/2}(3\beta-2m)+2$. With the function, $f(\beta)$, we know that if $\beta = 0$, then $f(0) = 0$. We also know that the slope of the function is positive: $df(\beta)/d\beta > 0$ with the conditions, $m \geq 1$ and $0 < \beta < 1$. Therefore, (5A3.3) is satisfied, and consequently, expression (5A3.1) has a positive sign. ■

From expression (5A3.2), we know:

$$[\beta m^{1/2}(m-\beta)^{-1/2}+2m^{1/2}(m-\beta)^{1/2}-2m]>0. \qquad (5A3.4)$$

Define the following function: $g(\beta) = [\beta m^{1/2}(m-\beta)^{-1/2}+2m^{1/2}(m-\beta)^{1/2}-2m]$. With the function, $g(\beta)$, we know that if $\beta = 0$, then $g(0) = 0$. We also know that the slope of the function is positive: $dg(\beta)/d\beta > 0$ with the conditions, $m \geq 1$ and $0 < \beta < 1$. Therefore, (5A3.4) is satisfied, and consequently, expression (5A3.2) has a positive sign. ■

For contest efficiency in proposition 11, relative total valuations drive the results.

$$\text{If } V_c > G,\ \frac{\partial CE}{\partial \beta} = \frac{2m(m-\beta)(V_c - G)\sqrt{m(m-\beta)}[2(m-\sqrt{m(m-\beta)}-\beta] - \beta^2 G\sqrt{m(m-\beta)}}{4m\beta^2 V_c (m-\beta)^2}.$$

$$\text{If } V_c = G,\ \frac{\partial CE}{\partial \beta} = -\frac{1}{4m^{1/2}(m-\beta)^{3/2}} < 0\cdot$$

$$\text{If } V_c < G,$$

$$\frac{\partial CE}{\partial \beta} = \frac{2m(m-\beta)(V_c - G)\sqrt{m(m-\beta)}[2(m-\sqrt{m(m-\beta)}-\beta] - \beta^2 G\sqrt{m(m-\beta)}}{4m\beta^2 V_c (m-\beta)^2} < 0\cdot$$

When the valuation of the citizen group exceeds the firms, $V_c > G$, we know that contest efficiency depends on the following:

$$\text{If } V_c > G\left[1 + \frac{\beta^2}{2m(m-\beta)} - 2\sqrt{m(m-\beta)}\right], \text{ then } \frac{\partial CE}{\partial \beta} > 0.$$

$$\text{If } V_c = G\left[1 + \frac{\beta^2}{2m(m-\beta)} - 2\sqrt{m(m-\beta)}\right], \text{ then } \frac{\partial CE}{\partial \beta} = 0.$$

$$\text{If } V_c < G\left[1 + \frac{\beta^2}{2m(m-\beta)} - 2\sqrt{m(m-\beta)}\right], \text{ then } \frac{\partial CE}{\partial \beta} < 0.$$

6. Fish Wars Revisited: A Stochastic Incomplete-Information Harvesting Game

Robert McKelvey, Kathleen Miller and Peter Golubtsov

1. INTRODUCTION

Many of the World's marine fisheries are shared between the fleets of two or more nations. Efforts to cooperatively manage harvests are complicated by uncertainties caused by large natural variations in the abundance or migratory behavior of shared fish stocks. Cooperation may collapse if natural variations are unanticipated or misinterpreted, have asymmetrical effects on the availability of fish to the different fleets, or lead the competing parties to advocate incompatible management responses.

In this context, one might imagine that reducing uncertainty would invariably be a good thing to do, but is that necessarily the case? Are there circumstances in which more information could be harmful? Would improved scientific information make achieving a stable cooperative fishery agreement easier, or more difficult? What difference would it make if one party had information that the other did not? What type of information is likely to be most valuable or strategically the most important? Here, we attempt to explore such questions.

This study employs a spatially distributed stochastic extension of the classical 'fish-war' harvesting game model to study the instabilities inherent in cooperative management of real-world transboundary fisheries. The focus here is on instabilities due to oceanic environmental change and climatic regime shifts. This situation is illustrated by an examination, in light of the model, of the history of the long-running dispute between the United States and Canada over management of their binational Pacific salmon fishery. The mathematical structure and numerical analysis of the model are described in detail in McKelvey and Golubtsov (2002).

Here, we simulate the evolution of a binational marine fishery where the fleet managers possess only incomplete information about the stochastically evolving oceanic environment. Thereby, we can explore the ways in which imperfect and asymmetric understanding of the changing environment can influence the strategic positions of competing harvesters, and hence disrupt their efforts to achieve stable coordinated management. In particular, we compare cooperative and non-cooperative game versions incorporating a range of information structures. The simulations indicate that an increase of available information (or a reduction in its degree of asymmetry) can affect the outcome of the dynamic harvesting game, often in unexpected ways. Finally, we apply the predictions of the model to shed light on the historical difficulties of the United States and Canada in crafting stable joint management arrangements for their important binational Pacific salmon fishery.

2. THE MODEL

In the model, the fleets of two sovereign countries (denoted α and β) fish down each successive generation of a marine fish population. Specifically, the migratory fish-stock, after leaving its nursery ground and maturing, constitutes the initial 'recruitment' biomass of the fishery. This recruitment stock is distributed fractionally into sub-stocks R_α and R_β which are resident, during the harvesting season, in the home waters of countries α and β respectively. Thus:

$$R = R_\alpha + R_\beta ,$$

where:

$$R_\alpha = \theta_\alpha R \, , \; R_\beta = \theta_\beta R \, ,$$

with $\theta_\alpha + \theta_\beta = 1$. The fraction θ_ν of fish stock available to each fleet $\nu = \alpha$ or β is stochastic; in the simulations the sequence $\{\theta_\nu(t)\}$ is assumed to be independent and identically distributed (iid).

During the harvesting season, each country's fishing fleet reduces its home waters' sub-stock to a residual 'escapement' level, denoted S_α or S_β respectively. Following this harvest, the separate escapements migrate back to the nursery ground, where they combine to form the brood-stock $S = S_\alpha + S_\beta$ for the next generation. Then, following the spawn, the brood stock dies. Following the hatch, the young offspring generation eventually matures, to form the next harvest season's 'recruitment' R^+, and thereby the stock life cycle is completed. The biomass R^+ is determined by the size of its spawning stock S through a so-called 'stock-recruitment relation':

$$R^+ = F(S, a^+)\,.$$

Here a is a parameter, the 'compensation factor', which determines the size and shape characteristics of the recruitment. For each a, $F(S, a)$ is monotone increasing in S, with a single positive fixed point $K(a)$, the no-harvest 'carrying capacity' at which $F[K(a), a] = K(a)$. Schematically,

$$\begin{array}{ccccccc} & & & R_\alpha = \theta_\alpha R \rightarrow S_\alpha & & & \\ & & \nearrow & & \searrow & & \\ S^- \rightarrow & R & & & & S \rightarrow & R^+ \\ & \uparrow & \searrow & & \nearrow & & \uparrow \\ & a^- & & R_\beta = \theta_\beta R \rightarrow S_\beta & & & a \end{array}$$

This cyclic pattern then repeats. In the present application, only the stock split sequence $\{\theta(t)\}$ will be random. (The full model is much more general; see McKelvey and Golubtsov 2002.)

Depending on the value of a (denoted CompFactor in Figures 6.2–6.8, below), the stock-recruitment relation may be 'compensatory', that is concave from below, or convex in its lower range and concave in the higher ranges. (See Figure 6.1.) In the convex 'depensatory' range, the recruitment gain over the spawning stock will be small or even negative (then termed 'critical depensation'). A centrally managed monopolistic fleet (or a cooperating pair of fleets) would usually avoid driving the escapement into the depensatory region; a competitive harvest may likely do so.

The immediate payoff from the seasonal harvest to the ν-fleet (where $\nu = \alpha$ or β) is:

$$\Omega_\nu(R, S) = \int_S^R \left[p_\nu - C_\nu(x)\right] dx.$$

Here p_ν is the constant unit landings price for harvested biomass, and $C_\nu(x)$ is the unit harvest cost, which is monotone non-increasing as a function of the within-season stock level x. Note that, when $C_\nu(x)$ is decreasing, the marginal cost of harvesting increases as the stock is drawn down. This gives the fleets an immediate incentive to maintain high stock levels, with optimal current harvests and target stock levels depending on the value of the cost parameter relative to price. In a competitive fishery, each fleet will ignore the impacts of its harvests on the other fleet's harvesting costs and payoffs. Thus, the competitive-fishery stock levels typically will be lower than those prevailing when the fleets cooperate.

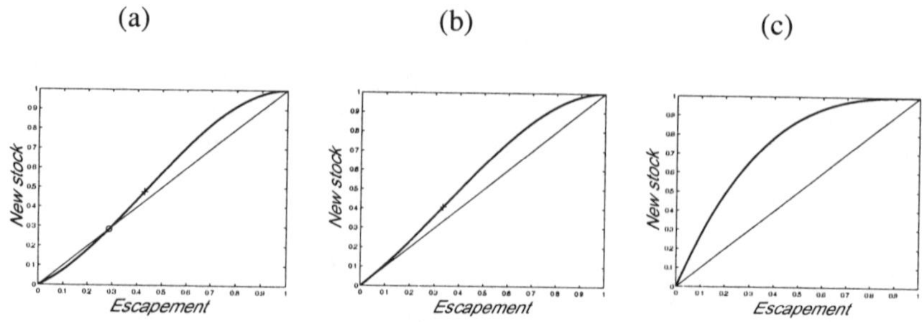

Note: 'Critical depensation' A = 0.6 (a), 'non-critical depensation' A = 1 (b), 'compensation' A = 3 (c). Circle shows critical escapement S_{crit} and cross indicates point of inflexion.

Figure 6.1 Cubic growth function

Each individual fleet is centrally managed, and chooses its current harvest escapement S_v in each harvest cycle to maximize the a priori expectation of its long-term objective function (the discounted sum of annual returns). The expectation is conditional on what the fleet currently knows of the future stochastic evolution of the fishery, and on what it can logically infer of its competitor's strategy.

Typically we shall assume that, at the beginning of each harvest season, each fleet has full knowledge of the current state of the fishery. In particular, each knows R and a, but knowledge of θ, and therefore of its own accessible sub-stock recruitment $R_v = \theta_v R$ may be incomplete. At minimum each fleet will possess only a common-knowledge a priori probability distribution of θ_v. Or one fleet (perhaps both) may possess enhanced prior knowledge (a refined probability distribution) of θ_v. Such enhanced knowledge is achieved through an imperfect observation $\tilde{\theta}_v$, and knowledge of the conditional probability distribution $p(\tilde{\theta}_v \,|\theta_v)$. In a polar case, a fleet, prior to harvest, may even know θ_v exactly. On the other hand, a posteriori, by the end of the harvest season, both fleets always will have learned the exact value θ_v (See discussion, below, of implementation of the control rule.)

We assume here risk-neutral α and β fleets. More precisely, each fleet's objective function is the (normalized) expected discounted-sum of its future payoffs, out to the infinite time horizon. (For a model with risk-averse fleets, see McKelvey and Cripe 2001.) In terms of the discount factor γ_v, and with:

$$\kappa_t = (1-\gamma)\gamma^t \text{, so that } \sum_{t=0}^{\infty} \kappa_t = 1 \text{,}$$

then:

$$V_v\left[R(0)\right] = \max_{\{S_v(t)\}} \theta_v E\left\{\sum_{t=0}^{\infty} \kappa_t \Omega_v[R_v(t), S_v(t)]\right\}$$

where:

$$R_v(t+1) = F\left[S_v(t), a\right], \text{ for } t \geq 0 \text{.}$$

Thus $V[R(0)]$ is a weighted arithmetic mean of the fleet's seasonal payoffs. The expectation is taken over the unknown future random evolution of the fishery denoted $\{S_v(t)\}$. It is conditioned on what the v fleet knows, at time $t = 0$, of the present and future states of the fishery, and on its beliefs concerning its competitor's policy. The escapement policy of the v fleet is expressed through a specification of the fraction f of the sub-stock recruitment R_v that will be left unharvested. That is,

$$S_v = f_v R_v \text{.}$$

Here f_v depends on the v fleet's knowledge of the current state of the fishery. Specifically, if the v fleet knows (R, a, $\tilde{\theta}_v$) *prior* to the harvest, but does not know θ_v until the *end* of the harvest, then its optimal policy is of the form:

$$S_v(R, a, \tilde{\theta}_v) = f_v(R, a, \tilde{\theta}_v) R_v \text{.}$$

But since in this case the fleet does not know θ_v a priori, therefore neither does it know $R_v = \theta_v R$, until the end of the harvest. Hence this harvest rule can be implemented only if an additional model refinement is made: for example that during the harvest season the migrating stock passes through the fishing ground over an extended period of time. As it does so, the fleet can control the fraction of cumulative stock that is harvested.

Note that we are assuming common knowledge of the *structure* of the game, including common knowledge of both fleets' objective functions and, prior to harvest, of current recruitment R and of the *precision* of each fleet's knowledge of the current θ_v. Hence there is no question of players' being able to learn from examining the prior play of the harvesting game. All that is of issue here is the value to each player of the environmental information that it currently *does* possess, and the expected impact (on both the fleets' payoffs and fish-stock abundance) of changes in information precision.

We are also assuming that, in a *cooperative* play of the game, the fleets share their knowledge and adopt the common objective of maximizing the expected sum of their individual payoffs. In this transferable-utility game, *if the fleets possess identical information precision*, then the total payoff to cooperation will always exceed the sum of individual payoffs under competition. Thus, an appropriate side-payment from one player to the other can always achieve a cooperative advantage for both. *However this need not be true when the competitors' information levels initially differ!*

Note finally that, in this study, we do not consider the coerced maintenance of bilateral cooperation, through trigger punishment strategies or similar 'self-enforcing mechanisms'. Deterministic studies suggest that, in transboundary fisheries, such strategies seldom will be voluntarily accepted or, if accepted, would be credible. (But see McKelvey et al. 2002.)

3. SIMULATIONS

The simulations shown here demonstrate that the payoffs to the harvesting fleets and the consequences for the resource itself are highly sensitive to the biological and environmental characteristics of the natural resource system and to the technological and economic characteristics of the fleets. They are also sensitive to the nature and timeliness of the information that the fleet managers possess when they make their harvesting decisions. It is well known that the value of information is always positive when the players cooperate. Of major importance here is that the impact of enhanced information may well be negative, both for fleets and resource, when the fleets are competing. We have organized our discussion of several striking, and sometimes unexpected, simulation results around a set of questions – questions relevant both to Pacific salmon and to other naturally fluctuating fishery resources.

In each simulation, $\theta(t) = \theta_\alpha(t)$ denotes the proportion of the run available to the α fleet during the harvest period t = 0, 1, … The sequence $\{\theta(t)\}$ consists of iid random variables, each taking on one of two possible values θ_1 and θ_2 with known fixed probabilities. A player's knowledge of the current value of θ can range from *full knowledge* (denoted 'Cur') to only *minimal knowledge* ('Min') of the prior probability distribution function (PDF) of θ.

Intermediate to these extremes are a range of levels of *partial knowledge* (through enhanced PDFs, obtained through imperfect current measurement ('Meas'), of θ.

The simulated game outcomes are displayed for a range of distinct circumstances: a *competitive* (or 'non-cooperative') fishery with a *symmetric* information structure, that is, where the fleets possess *identical* information about θ, will be designated 'Cur', 'Meas' or 'Min', respectively. If instead the game is cooperative, this designation will be preceeded by the notation 'Coop'. If the game is competitive but the information structure is *asymmetric*, then the designation is 'cur-min' or 'meas-min', and the α fleet (called fleet 1 in the figures) is understood to possess the superior level of information.

In our simulations, the stock-recruitment parameter a remains constant over time. It therefore becomes convenient to normalize the unit of biomass so that carrying capacity K, where $F(K, a) = K$, is always set at $K = 1$. Depending on the parameter a, the stock-recruitment relation may be 'compensatory', that is concave from below, or 'depensatory', that is convex in its lower range and concave in higher ranges (see Figure 6.1). In the convex depensatory range, the recruitment gain over the spawning stock will be small or even negative (denoted 'critically depensatory').

Unit market price p is taken to be constant, and the unit harvest cost functions are assumed to increase, according to $C_v(x) = c_v/x$, as the stock biomass x is depleted. If the game is *competitive*, then the harvest strategy rules, and hence the resulting steady-state stock levels, will depend on price and costs *only* through the ratio of the cost and price parameters c_v/p.

More general versions of stochastic incomplete-information fish-war models have been constructed and analyzed, with simulations carried out for a range of information structures (as reported in McKelvey and Cripe 2001; and in McKelvey and Golubtsov 2002). The simulations shown in the present report were all generated using the McKelvey–Golubtsov model, with both fleets assumed to be risk neutral. We now turn to a summary of simulated model behavior, with results organized through a series of questions.

3.1 How Does the Nature of the Stochastic Stock-recruitment Relationship Affect the Outcome of an Incomplete-information Harvesting Game?

As noted above, if the stock-recruitment relation is characterized by depensation, then there is a range over which stock size exhibits stagnant growth. It is known from deterministic fish-war models that a common-property stock externality will lead to over-harvesting, and it is evident that this effect is exacerbated by depensation. This is especially true when the common parameter ratio (c/p) is low. This effect carries over to a stochastic world, as is demonstrated in Figures 6.2–6.3. In these figures, the stochastic θ has its distribution symmetric around its mean of 0.5, so that nature treats the two fleets equitably. In addition, the unit harvesting cost function is held fixed at $c = 0.1$ while unit price varies. The contrasting results in the two figures demonstrate the striking effects of differences in the shape of the stock-recruitment function.

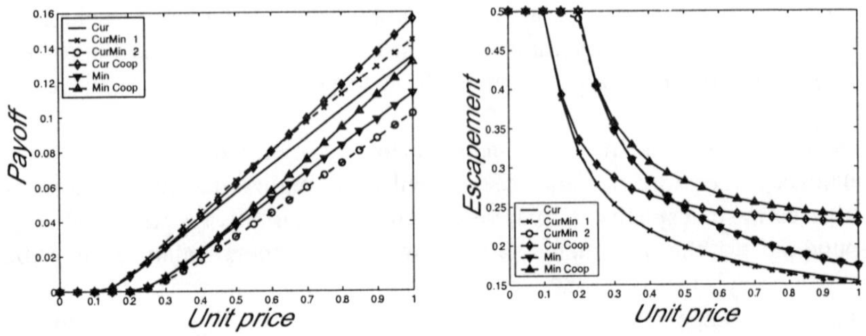

Figure 6.2 Harvesting with compensatory growth (CompFactor = 3)

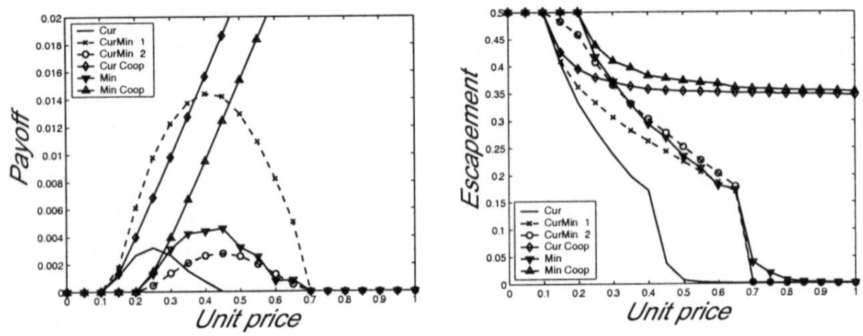

Figure 6.3 Harvesting with critical depensation (CompFactor = 0.6)

In Figure 6.2, where stock recruitment is compensatory, the effects of competitive harvest are relatively benign. While net harvest payoffs are lower with competition than with cooperation, they increase monotonically with market price p, and also with the quality of available information. In Figure 6.3, where stock recruitment displays critical depensation, competitive-fishery payoff curves are dome-shaped, so that payoffs eventually drop as market price increases. In this case, high market prices, and correspondingly high common-pool stock externalities, will depress stock levels into the depensatory low-productivity range, and may even result in extinction of the resource.

3.2 What is the Impact of Symmetrically Enhanced Information in a Competitive Fish War?

These same figures display the interplay of the common property externality with the *information structure* of each model variant. First, consider model variants where the two fleets have *identical* information. Full current information permits a fleet to fine-tune its escapements to maintain near constant escapement across its 'good' and 'bad' years. A fleet with minimal information can tune escapement with less precision. With cooperative management, additional information will enhance mean payoffs. This positive value of information can be present in a competitive fishery as well, provided that prices are sufficiently low, or the resource is sufficiently resilient (for example, compare Figures 6.2 and 6.3). Full current information can enhance a fleet's immediate harvest payoff. However, in a competitive fishery, it will exacerbate the effect of the common-stock externality, with greatest damage to future stocks and long-run payoffs occurring in the presence of depensatory growth and high prices.

3.3 What Difference Does it Make if One Party Has More Information than the Other?

Consider next, model variants involving asymmetric information. Because cooperation requires full sharing of information, asymmetric information implies competitive harvesting. In all cases, the player possessing superior information gains at the expense of the less fortunate player. Over the lower portion of the price range, the fleet possessing superior information can even reap payoffs exceeding those resulting from full cooperation. This effect becomes more pronounced as the compensation factor (CompFactor) declines (that is, a more depensatory growth function). In this range, the player with an informational advantage would never voluntarily share his or her private information with his or her competitor, unless the latter party provides a *side-payment* to buy both information and cooperation.

As price increases (while the harvesting cost function is held constant), there is a point beyond which the player possessing the superior information can gain by voluntarily sharing his or her private information in exchange for securing a cooperative agreement. The more fragile the resource (that is, the lower the value of CompFactor), the lower will be the price at which this crossover occurs. In Figure 6.2, for example, at prices above about 0.6 party

1 could gain slightly by sharing information. The incentive to share private information when prices are high is much stronger in Figure 6.3, and the crossover occurs at a price below 0.4. In that case, critical depensation causes competitive harvesting to become extremely damaging to both parties' interests as prices increase.

These simulations demonstrate a general principle, namely *that if competition rather than cooperation prevails, enhanced information can be harmful*. How harmful, depends importantly on the characteristics of the resource itself. If the shape of the stock-recruitment function makes it difficult for the resource to recover from episodes of heavy fishing pressure or entails the possibility of the stock declining to the point of extinction (depensation or even critical depensation), then information that is of high quality is likely to lead to falling payoffs and stock decline – or even to stock extinction.

3.4 How Does the Level of Stochastic Variability Affect the Game Outcome?

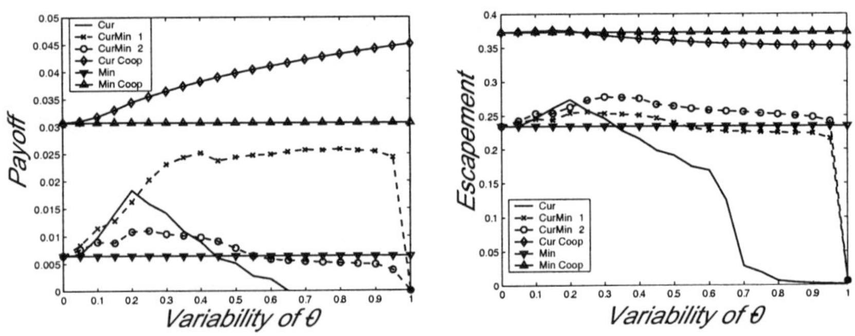

Figure 6.4 Effect of increasing environmental variability (CompFactor = 0.6)

In Figure 6.4, the distribution of θ is uniform around its mean value of 0.5, so that the fleets are treated symmetrically by nature. Maximum standard deviation is $\sigma_{max} = 0.5$, and the measurement of 'variability' on the horizontal axis is σ/σ_{max}. In the complete-information cooperative model version, the mean payoff is high, and actually increases with variability. The explanation is that cooperative management permits concentrating the seasonal harvest in that area where the stock is currently concentrated, thereby minimizing harvest costs. Cooperative management, with only minimal knowledge, cannot target harvest in this optimal way and instead will simply divide the harvest equally between the fleets. The constancy of payoff results from the simple distribution function assumed in this simulation.

When the game is competitive, complete contemporary knowledge allows each fleet manager to increase effort in those seasons when a large fraction of the stock is accessible within its stream. When the variability is large, this strategy will not be adequate to overcome the negative impact of the common property externality. As usual, this effect is most prominent when recruitment is depensatory.

3.5 What are the Effects of Changing the Quality of Information, or the Degree of Asymmetry?

Figures 6.5 and 6.6 show the same interplay between information structure, depensation, and cost–price ratio as before, but now one holds the last two fixed, while permitting the knowledge level of one or both of the fleets to range continuously across the gradations of measurement accuracy, from minimum to full. Furthermore, competitive situations are contrasted with fully cooperative ones.

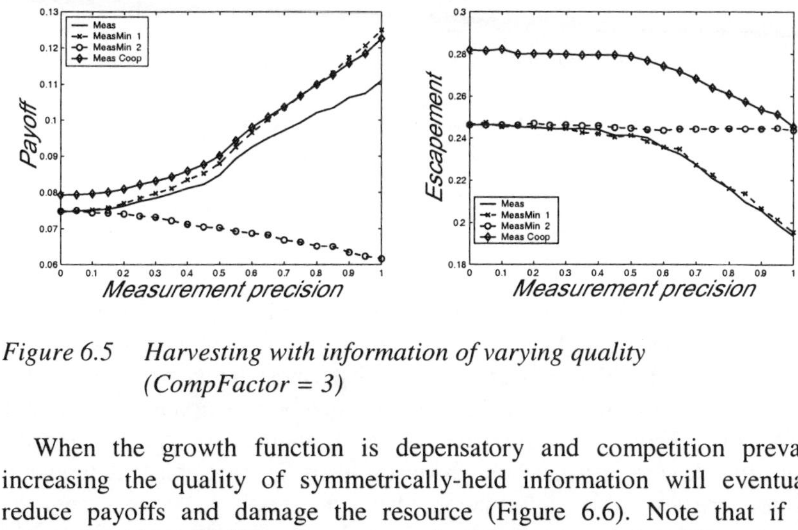

Figure 6.5 Harvesting with information of varying quality (CompFactor = 3)

When the growth function is depensatory and competition prevails, increasing the quality of symmetrically-held information will eventually reduce payoffs and damage the resource (Figure 6.6). Note that if the information is available only to party 1, that party may be able to benefit from the information and forestall a resource crash, even when the resource is quite fragile. However, payoffs would be higher with cooperation, in most instances.

Note also that, with asymmetric information, party 2 generally has more to gain by moving to cooperation than does party 1, and might agree to make a side-payment to the better-informed party to secure cooperation. In general, the effects of asymmetry in access to information appear to depend upon the type of information that is privately held, the players' harvesting costs and the shape of the stock-recruitment function. In some competitive harvesting cases, a better-informed player can gain by keeping private information secret (for example, when a high *c/p* ratio inhibits harvesting by the uninformed competitor). In other cases, the better-informed party will gain by sharing information with his or her competitor (for example, when high prices and a depensatory recruitment function combine to increase the damage that an uninformed competitor is likely to do to the stock and to future payoffs).

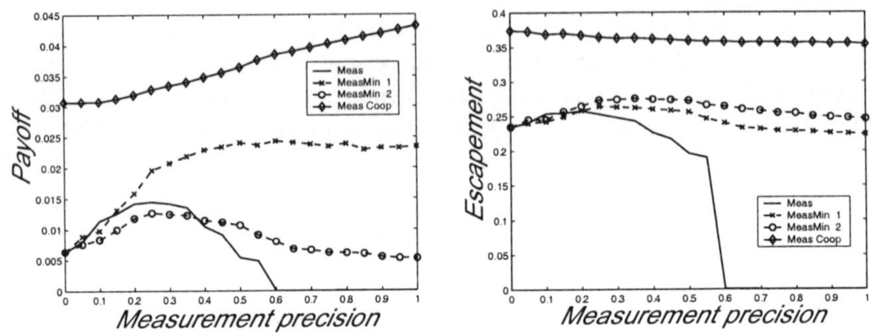

Figure 6.6 Harvesting with information of varying quality (CompFactor = 0.6)

3.6 How Does the Quality of Available Information Promote Cooperation?

These models do not explicitly address the negotiation or maintenance of cooperative agreements but, as noted above, the simulation results suggest circumstances in which cooperation would be most likely to arise and the importance of information in this context. In the simulations, cooperative payoffs invariably exceed those that could be attained by equally-informed competing harvesters. This cooperative surplus is far from constant, though it is often greatest when information levels are high. In some cases, the potential gains from cooperation are modest – as, for example, when harvesting costs are high (or the value of harvested fish is low) and the resource is characterized by compensatory growth. In other cases, competition would result in extremely low payoffs, while substantial benefits would be possible with cooperation. For example, in Figure 6.6 above, the potential cooperative surplus for equally-informed parties is large, and increases dramatically as the quality of information improves. If it is costly to negotiate and maintain agreements, it might not be worth the trouble when the resource is both resilient and lightly targeted. However, we might suppose that the parties would be more likely to undertake the cost of working out an agreement when they have more to lose by failing to cooperate. If the folk wisdom that 'it takes a crisis to force an agreement' is correct, then we might expect to see cooperative agreements arising in those cases in which competitive harvesting threatens to deplete a relatively fragile resource. Improved measurements and forecasts could play a positive role, here, by increasing the potential gains from cooperation.

3.7 What Might Be the Effect of a Climatic Regime Shift, Altering Mean θ?

One possible effect of a climatic regime shift is that the mean of the 'stock-split' PDF may change, so that the migration pattern becomes more favorable, on average, to one or the other of the players. As the mean value $\bar{\theta} = E\theta$ becomes more unbalanced, payoffs increase or decrease, always favoring the environmentally advantaged party. This holds both for cooperative and competitive harvesting. Figure 6.7a shows this phenomenon when there is full symmetric knowledge of θ, and Figure 6.7b assumes minimal knowledge. Figure 6.8 examines only competition but with knowledge asymmetries.

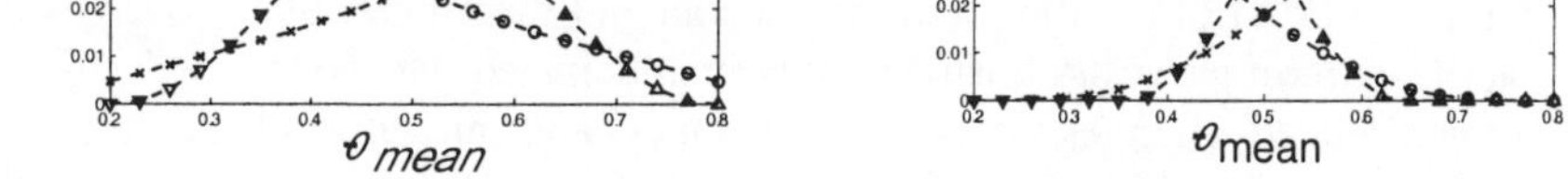

(a) Full Information

(b) Minimal Information

Figure 6.7 Effect of change in mean θ (CompFactor = 1)

An interesting point to note in Figure 6.7 is that the greater a party's natural advantage, the more he or she has to gain from cooperation. Examine, for example, the region in which the mean of θ exceeds 0.7. There, with full information, party 2 would be better off behaving competitively, while party 1, who is favored by nature, has a great deal to gain from cooperation. This situation suggests that it may be up to the advantaged party to buy the cooperation of his or her less-favored neighbor. With minimal information, the gains to the naturally advantaged player from cooperation diminish as the mean of theta becomes extremely favorable, because the disadvantaged fleet no longer plays a significant role.

Note, in Figure 6.8, that a party that is favored by nature and also possesses superior information will have a strong incentive to maintain the privacy of his or her privileged information.

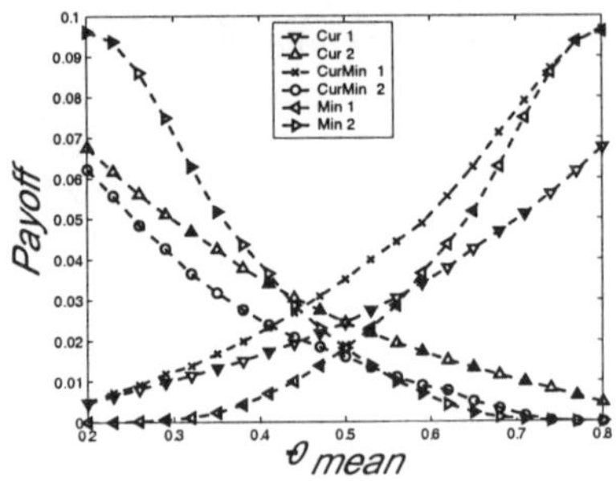

Figure 6.8 Natural asymmetry and asymmetric information (CompFactor = 1)

4. APPLICATION TO PACIFIC SALMON

A recent period of conflict between Canada and the United States over their Pacific salmon harvests illustrates how unanticipated and poorly understood climate-related changes in stock abundance and migratory behavior can contribute to the breakdown of a cooperative harvesting agreement (Miller et al. 2001). In that case, an unexpected shift to an extended period of warmer coastal waters contributed to dramatic increases in northern salmon stocks, declines in southern stocks, and a change in the migratory behavior of Fraser River sockeye that strongly favored the Canadian fleet. These changes altered the balance of power among the Treaty participants, and made it increasingly difficult to achieve the multiple objectives expressed in the language of the

Treaty. A new Pacific Salmon Agreement was signed in 1999 (US Department of State 1999), which both nations hope will prove more resilient to such stresses (Miller et al. 2001). This history provides background for our model, and allows us to examine the consistency of model predictions with real-world experience.

After spending its adult years in northern oceans, Canada's Fraser sockeye stock journeys southward to spawn. The run splits as it rounds Canada's Vancouver Island. The (normally larger) fraction, which passes seaward of the island, must pass through the Strait of Juan de Fuca, between the United States and Canada. There it is accessible to both countries' fleets. The remaining fraction stays shoreward of the island, and is accessible only to Canadian harvesters. Following harvest these substreams rejoin at the river mouth and swim upstream to spawn.

Oceanic temperatures, coastal upwelling and related physical and biological processes in the North Pacific are constantly changing, driven by the El Niño–Southern Oscillation (ENSO) and a longer-term pattern of variability, the Pacific Decadal Oscillation. This contributes to year-to-year changes in Fraser River sockeye run-size and its fractional split, which have been difficult to predict. Historically, such unanticipated changes contributed to recurring 'fish wars' between the two nations. During periods of intense competition, some individual stocks have been dangerously over-harvested. Although US/Canadian Pacific salmon management is far more complicated than our simple model, many of the events in the evolution of conflict and cooperation in this case are broadly consistent with the predictions of the model. In the case of efforts to jointly manage Fraser sockeye harvests, two periods of intense competitive harvesting stand out. The first lasted for roughly a decade prior to the signing of the 1985 Pacific Salmon Treaty, and the second during the 1993–98 dispute.

Under the 1930 Fraser River Convention, the International Pacific Salmon Fishery Commission (IPSFC) regulated harvests of the Fraser River stocks within an area designated as the 'Convention Waters'. Each nation was allocated half of the harvest (Convention 1930). When the Canadians became unhappy with the agreement, they discovered that they could circumvent the IPSFC regulations by fishing for Fraser sockeye outside of the Convention Waters. This was made increasingly possible and profitable by a change in the migratory habits of the returning Fraser sockeye. Beginning in 1977, a sudden and sustained shift in ocean conditions contributed to a marked increase in the proportion of the returning run via the northern all-Canadian route, through Johnstone Strait. In the period from 1953 to 1976, the Johnstone Strait diversion rate averaged 16.4 per cent. From 1977 through 1998, the diversion rate has averaged 48.2 per cent.

This shift strengthened Canada's hand in the negotiations leading to the 1985 Treaty. Canada clearly took advantage of unusually high diversion rates in 1978, 1980, 1981, and 1983 to concentrate harvesting efforts outside of the Convention Waters, and increase its overall share of the harvest. Referring back to our simulation of the effect of a shift in natural advantage in a competitive game, we can see that a shift in payoffs in the direction of a change in the average split is just what the model would predict.

The most striking effects of the 1977 climatic regime shift were its impacts on the relative productivity of the various salmon stocks shared by Canada and the United States. Significant warming of coastal waters was reinforced and sustained by a sequence of closely spaced ENSO–warm events from 1977 to 1998. Changes in patterns of upwelling, nutrient transport and related physical and biological processes favored salmon survival and growth in the Gulf of Alaska, while survival rates plummeted for stocks entering the marine environment along the US west coast. Alaskan salmon harvests increased nearly tenfold from fewer than 22 million salmon (of all species) in 1974 to a series of record highs, with a 1995 peak close to 218 million salmon and another high in 1999 of almost 217 million salmon. In particular, pink salmon harvests increased dramatically in southeastern Alaska, where those stocks are intermingled with Canadian salmon.

In the southern border region, the effects of the climatic regime were profoundly different. There, poor survival conditions contributed to major declines in several salmon populations. The climate-related fragile condition of those stocks can be modeled as a shift in the shape of the stock recruitment function to a lower CompFactor.[1]

Although those changes were already underway during the negotiation period for the 1985 Treaty, the linkages between climate, ocean conditions and salmon abundance were poorly understood and no one could predict how long the recent trends would last. Consequently, the negotiators of the 1985 Treaty simply ignored the potential impacts of sustained changes in salmon abundance and migratory behavior.

The 1985 Treaty created the Pacific Salmon Commission whose primary task was to develop and recommend fishing regimes based on a balancing of equity and conservation objectives as expressed in the language of the Treaty. The bargaining framework implemented in 1985 required consensus, effectively giving each party a veto, and called for frequent renegotiation of the fishing regimes, which relied heavily on the use of 'ceilings'. This approach was based on the notion that capping harvests in the intercepting fishery would allow any increase in run strength to primarily benefit the nation of origin.

The Treaty might have proved satisfactory if the shift to warmer ocean conditions had not continued. But the warming did continue and the payoffs that the Canadians and southern US interests expected from the Treaty never materialized. Instead, Alaskan interceptions of Canadian salmon increased, and Canada returned to aggressive competitive tactics with respect to its harvests of Fraser sockeye and its interceptions of other salmon stocks migrating to spawn in Washington and Oregon rivers. The latter practice was particularly damaging because the climatic shift had depressed the productivity and resilience of those stocks – a shift to a more depensatory recruitment function. The 1999 Agreement accommodates the Canadian position by further decreasing the US share of the Fraser sockeye harvest. In addition, the revised agreement provides implicit side-payments to Canada in the form of financing for research and enhancement activities through two endowment funds, funded almost entirely by the United States.[2] Most importantly, the new Agreement defines harvest shares on the basis of indices of abundance, thus limiting the parties' ability to aggressively fish 'up to the ceiling' when the resource is in a fragile state.

Pressure to resolve the Pacific salmon dispute was strongest in the south. Referring to the figures above, it can be seen that the fragile condition of those stocks meant that considerable damage could be done by continued competitive harvesting. This situation increased the potential gains from cooperation. Alaska, in contrast, remained unwilling to make concessions to secure cooperation. Given the fact that most salmon swim northwards as juveniles and follow a north-to-south route on their return migration, Alaska is in a naturally advantaged position. As Figures 6.7 and 6.8, above, demonstrate, such an advantage would lead a party to expect to receive a large share of the benefits of the fishery. Our simulations also suggest that the robust condition of Alaska's stocks would tend to reduce Alaska's expected gains from cooperation. In the end, the 1999 Agreement accommodates Alaska's position, in that Alaskan harvests will remain relatively unchanged under the new abundance-based rules.

As for the effects of information, or its absence, it is evident that when the provisions of the 1985 Treaty were negotiated, there was relatively little understanding of the potential for long-term climate-related changes in patterns of salmon production or migration. Uncertainty contributed to disagreements throughout the Treaty period. For example, interest-laden differences in estimates of interceptions were a frequent problem.[3]

In recent years, there has been a rapid accumulation of scientific research that has led to a growing understanding and awareness of the role of large-scale climatic fluctuations in driving changes in abundance and migratory behavior (Xie and Hsieh 1989; Mantua et al. 1997; Downton and Miller 1998; Beamish et al. 1999a,b). It is interesting to note that a major provision of the 1999 Agreement calls for enhanced scientific cooperation and open sharing of information (US Department of State 1999). This suggests that the parties clearly recognize the potential value of good information in a cooperative regime. While there is little publicly available information indicating that strategic withholding of data or analyses had been a common practice, the amount of attention given to the matter in the 1999 Agreement demonstrates that the parties are eager to avoid that danger.

5. POLICY IMPLICATIONS

The simulation results and case study together demonstrate the importance of adapting institutional arrangements to the inevitably limited predictability of fish-stock demographics. One management arrangement for overcoming destructive competition is, obviously, to insulate scientific assessment studies from partisan interpretation, insisting on transparency of method and findings. This can be done by making jointly funded research an integral part of a cooperative agreement or, alternatively, by relying on an impartial scientific body for stock assessments and recommended harvest levels. The Russian/Norwegian cooperative framework in the Barents Sea provides an example of the latter practice. Those nations rely on the ICES (the International Council for the Exploration of the Sea) Advisory Committee on Fishery Management for stock assessments and management advice.

However, better science alone will *not* lead automatically to more effective management, and in a competitive fishery could, in fact, hasten the demise of fragile stocks. Our findings suggest the need also for cooperative arrangements that will allow harvesting patterns to track stochastic demographic shifts more closely, by eliminating rigid quota barriers which limit national harvests by locus and scale. This might be achieved through flexible quotas, with side-payment adjustments to maintain a balance in equity. Alternatively, it might be possible to allow the national fleets to follow the movements of the stock, even across jurisdictional boundaries, while keeping total catch at optimal levels. This can be achieved by coupling fixed national shares of the TAC (total allowable catch) with a mutual access agreement allowing vessels from each nation access to the others' harvesting zone. Such an access agreement is central to the Russian/Norwegian cooperative framework in the Barents Sea, and similar agreements are used, or are under consideration, elsewhere.

The model described here represents only an initial effort to understand the problems of instability of management agreements in a relatively simple binational coastal fishery. In continuing work we hope to elaborate our modeling efforts, to deal with more complex multilateral fisheries on the high seas, still focusing on the effects of climatic fluctuations and longer-term climate change on stock dynamics and on the impacts of harvesting exploitation. The central goal of this ongoing research is an improved understanding of how to design fishery management agreements to maintain mutually beneficial multilateral cooperation, despite limited understanding of the profound changes occurring within the oceanic environment.

ACKNOWLEDGEMENTS

This project was funded by the US National Oceanic and Atmospheric Administration's Office of Global Programs through award: NOAA NA86GP02219-GC98-011, and by the US National Science Foundation through grant: DBI-9708475.

NOTES

1. Peterman (1977) discusses environmental shifts in salmon recruitment functions in relation to depensatory mortality at low population levels. In that treatment, stochastic environmental factors shift the net recruitment function up or down, changing the critical threshold at which recruitment falls below replacement.
2. The annual investment earnings on the Northern Boundary and Transboundary Rivers Restoration and Enhancement Fund (Northern Fund), and Southern Boundary Restoration and Enhancement Fund (Southern Fund) are to be used to support scientific research, habitat restoration and enhancement of wild stock production in their respective areas. The United States agreed to contribute $75 million to the Northern Fund and $65 million to the Southern Fund over a four-year period. The first installments have been made, and balance of the commitment is to be remitted in fiscal year 2003. Canada also contributed $250,000 (CND) to each of the two funds in November 2000 (PSC 2002). Since the funds (at this stage) come overwhelmingly from the United States, they can be viewed as implicit side-payments from the United States to Canada.
3. The Joint Interceptions Committee of the Pacific Salmon Commission was established to coordinate documentation of interceptions. Its few reports tended to document the wide range of uncertainty surrounding the estimates and the disparate views of the parties as to the magnitude and direction of interceptions imbalances (PSC–JIC 1993). That committee ceased issuing reports when the dispute over equitable allocation escalated.

REFERENCES

Beamish, R.J., G.A. McFarlane and J.R. King (1999a), 'Fisheries climatology: understanding decadal scale processes that naturally regulate British Columbia fish populations', in T. Parsons and P. Harrison (eds), *Fisheries Oceanography: An Integrative Approach to Fisheries Ecology and Management*, Oxford, UK: Blackwell Science Ltd., pp. 94–145.

Beamish, R.J., D.J. Noakes, G.A. McFarlane, L. Klyashtorin, V.V. Ivanov and V. Kurashov (1999b), 'The regime concept and natural trends in the production of Pacific salmon', *Canadian Journal of Fisheries and Aquatic Sciences*, **56** (3), 516–26.

Convention for the Protection, Preservation and Extension of the Sockeye Salmon Fishery in the Fraser River System, May 26, 1930, US–Can., 8 U.S.T. 1058.

Downton, M.W. and K.A. Miller (1998), 'Relationships between Alaskan salmon catch and North Pacific climate on interannual and decadal time scales', *Canadian Journal of Fisheries and Aquatic Sciences*, **55**, 2255–65.

Mantua, N.J., S.R. Hare, Y. Zhang, J.M. Wallace and R.C. Francis (1997), 'A Pacific interdecadal climate oscillation with impacts on salmon production', *Bulletin of the American Meteorological Society*, **78** (6), 1069–79.

McKelvey, R. and G. Cripe (2001), *The Split-Stream Harvesting Game II: Numerical and Simulation Studies*, National Center for Atmospheric Research Technical Report, NCAR/TN-449+STR: Part II.

McKelvey, R. and P.V. Golubtsov (2002), 'The Effects of incomplete information in stochastic common-stock harvesting games', Proceedings of ISDG2002, International Society for Dynamic Games, St. Petersburg State University, Russia, pp. 582–603.

McKelvey, R., L.K. Sandal and S.I. Steinshamn (2002), 'Regional fisheries on the high seas: the hit-and run interloper model', will appear in *International Game Theory Review*.

Miller, K.A., G.R. Munro, T.L. McDorman, R. McKelvey and P. Tyedmers (2001), 'The 1999 Pacific Salmon Agreement: A Sustainable Solution?', Canadian–American Public Policy Occasional Paper, No. 47, Canadian–American Center, University of Maine, Orono, ME.

Peterman, R.M. (1977), 'A simple mechanism that causes collapsing stability regions in exploited salmonid populations', *Journal of the Fisheries Research Board of Canada*, **34**, 1130–42.

PSC (Pacific Salmon Commission) (2002), *2000/2001 Sixteenth Annual Report*, Vancouver, BC: Pacific Salmon Commission.

PSC-JIC (Pacific Salmon Commission–Joint Interceptions Committee) (1993), *Third Report on the Parties' Estimates of Salmon Interceptions 1980–1991*, Report JIC (93)-1, Vancouver, BC: Pacific Salmon Commission.

US Department of State (1999), 'Diplomatic Note No. 0225 from Canada to the United States; reply; attached Agreement, June 30', available at: http://www.state.gov.

Xie, L. and W. Hsieh (1989), 'Predicting the return migration routes of the Fraser River sockeye salmon (*Oncorhynchus nerka*)', *Canadian Journal of Fisheries and Aquatic Sciences*, **46,** 1287–92.

7. Climate Change Scenarios and the Precautionary Principle

Rossella Bargiacchi

1. INTRODUCTION

It is well known that uncertainty regarding climate change is particularly deep and extensive. Damage may occur in a totally uncontrollable and irreversible way, after exceeding unknown threshold levels of pollution. Moreover, most of the costs of prevention of climate change have to be borne by present generations, while damage is believed to mostly affect future generations. Clearly, determination of the 'best' path of development would be controversial even if all future contingencies were known with certainty. It is therefore important that the ethical issues do not become obscured by the scientific difficulties.

The ethical guidelines for dealing with global warming and other problems related to development have been addressed by the United Nations Organization (UN). The precautionary principle, stated in the Rio '92 Declaration (UN 1992), may be read as a signal of dissatisfaction with current environmental policy practice, particularly in the face of uncertainty. Many reasons could be cited for such a failure, among them the fact that policy makers often fail in interpreting and representing the beliefs of individuals and (most of all) the scientific community. This chapter attempts to address this issue, and to provide a reasonable model for applying the precautionary principle to climate change. Towards this end, I use a somewhat different approach from that used by most of the economic literature on this topic. Many authors (for example, Nordhaus and Popp 1997; Ulph and Ulph 1997; Gollier et al. 2000) analyse the emergence and 'optimality' of conservative behaviour in the presence of varying conditions of uncertainty, learning and irreversibility. The main result emerging from this literature is that – even when irreversible damage occurs – conservative behaviour (lower emission levels) arises only under specific assumptions on the utility functions and on the distribution of risk (Heal and Kriström 2002). Another flow of literature analyses the emergence of the precautionary principle as the result of deviation from expected utility behaviour on the part of authorities that have different objectives from the maximization of collective welfare. Bouglet et al. (2002) and Chevé and Congar (2000 and 2002), fall into this category. In these contributions, the precautionary principle is either explained by or identified with the minimization of future regret (limiting the risk of a sanction). The essence of the precautionary principle, however, seems to be captured by neither of these classes of models. In my opinion, it lies in the fact that, given the special conditions that characterize the global warming issue, we should behave prudently *ex ante*, while trying to maximize collective welfare. The approach followed in this chapter, more in line with Vercelli (1995) and Henry and Henry (2002), is as follows: prudence is defined as a decision criterion, consisting in a deviation from expected utility. Given the adoption *ex ante* of such a criterion, and given a description of uncertainty based on scenarios, I derive some conclusions on the predictability of the consequences on the desired level of emissions.

Typically, information regarding climate change is made available to policy makers in the form of scenarios. Scenarios describe possible future developments of a set of variables (demographic, economic, and environmental), given assumptions on actions that might be undertaken and/or states of the world that might occur. Decisions are based on such descriptions. The idea behind this chapter is to treat scenarios as special states of the world, each representing some combination of hypotheses about interactions between climate and economy. Non-monotonic utility functions within scenarios reflect the risk of exceeding threshold levels of pollution, after which a sudden loss in utility occurs. Thus, scenarios differ from one another in the distribution of thresholds and their expected impact on utility.

The first question addressed is: what is the optimal choice of aggregate emissions and consumption when uncertainty is represented by multiple scenarios and when the precautionary principle applies? A second question is: are actual decision makers likely to pursue such optimal policies? If not, are they instead likely to pollute more or less than the optimal amount? This depends on how we think governmental decision makers behave in the face of uncertainty. The literature on decision making shows that individuals often deviate from standard definitions of rationality, even in situations where uncertainty is more straightforward than it is for climate change (Starmer 2000).

The chapter is organized as follows. Section 2 introduces the analytical set-up. In Section 2.1, I present a utility function characterized by thresholds whose location and impact are unknown and are described by probability densities. Uncertainty is the subject of Section 2.2, where I characterize scenarios and give a simplified introduction of RDU theory. Section 2.3 builds the model for choice of consumption. I derive some analytical results and illustrate the features and outcomes of performed simulations in Section 3. Finally Section 4 draws some conclusions.

2. IRREVERSIBILITY, UNCERTAINTY, AND THE PRECAUTIONARY PRINCIPLE

According to the precautionary principle, irreversibility is a sufficient prerequisite for implementing prevention measures:

> In order to protect the environment, the precautionary approach shall be widely applied by States according to their capabilities.
>
> Where there are threats of serious or irreversible damage, lack of full scientific certainty shall not be used as a reason for postponing cost-effective measures to prevent environmental degradation. (UN 1992, p. 3)

Implementation of this principle depends clearly on the framework to which it is applied: in the case of chlorofluorocarbons (CFCs), the international community agreed on banning their use (Montreal Protocol), since they were considered responsible for depleting the ozone layer of the stratosphere (with very dangerous consequences), and cheap substitutes could be introduced quickly. In the case of greenhouse gases (GHGs), a ban does not seem possible, since a fast and complete substitution of some sources of GHGs, like fossil fuels, is not economically feasible. Therefore, balancing costs and benefits, some optimal positive level of emissions should be determined, even in the presence of strong uncertainties.

Precaution, according to the Longman Dictionary of Contemporary English, is 'an action done to avoid possible danger'. Being prudent means therefore to choose among different actions, paying particular attention to their worst consequences. Such behaviour can be represented analytically by means of rank-dependent utility (RDU) models under special hypotheses, as I shall show later. Henry and Henry (2002) also make use of a similar model to discuss the precautionary principle: they argue that when the beliefs of individuals can be represented by means of non-additive probabilities, the choice of a regulator is suboptimal if it does not reflect this feature. Rank-dependent utility is a model based on non-additive beliefs, and therefore this normative argument applies.

One shortcoming of RDU is that it implies a violation of the independence axiom, which can lead to inconsistencies in choice (Machina 1989). However, more recently Ghirardato (2001) demonstrated that in the presence of unforeseen contingencies (that is, when the decision maker is aware that he or she cannot describe the problem in a complete way), non-additive beliefs can be derived without relaxing the independence axiom, considering the possibility that acts be defined not as functions but as correspondences between states of the world and consequences. This result recalls the intuition behind Vercelli (1995), who suggests that non-additive beliefs may legitimately drive choice when scientific understanding of a problem is incomplete. My personal view follows this line of reasoning, and my argument in favour of a normative use of RDU is that it reproduces prudence, and the UN recommends prudence in the face of irreversibility.

Finally, I choose to use RDU among all available models for two reasons. On the one hand, RDU is relatively tractable, since it consists of a simple transformation over cumulative probabilities, and can therefore easily be used in computer simulations just by adding a few steps to the generation of usual random variables. On the other hand, RDU is mathematically very similar to Choquet-expected utility, and includes as a limit case the minimax principle. Therefore, even if formally this model is a model of choice under risk (since it assumes an underlying probability distribution), in practice it behaves very much like models of choice under uncertainty and can easily be put in relation to them. Ideally, one would like to use a model of choice under uncertainty for the case of climate change, but it is interesting to use RDU in this framework for its pragmatic advantages, which provide the possibility of analysing quite a flexible and general model and making use of (a large number of) computer simulations at the same time.

The following section introduces a way to represent the essential features of irreversibility in a static framework, by means of thresholds in the utility function.

2.1 Thresholds

The global climate is a complex system: when a change (like pollution) occurs in one part of the system, the chain of reactions can be very sensitive to small differences in the size of the initial shock. The relation between pollution and damage can consequently present threshold values where damage increases very steeply, or even jumps up in a discontinuous way. Carpenter et al. (1999) give a relatively simple presentation of a pollution model with thresholds. The qualitative features of such a model can be considered similar to those of the climatic system.

Irreversibility in this framework means that once the threshold is crossed, a structural change in the model occurs which cannot be repaired – even if the emission level is brought back to lower levels afterwards. In other words, the choice to cross the threshold is made only once. This means that learning may not be a valuable option (Aalbers 1999), which makes a static model the most appropriate. Indeed, this chapter refers to a static model of utility maximization in the presence of thresholds, developed by Aalbers (1999). In such a framework, two independent probability densities are assumed: (1) $\pi(B)$, defined over the interval $[B_{min}; B_{max}]$, describes the location of a threshold B for GHG emissions; (2) $\theta(\alpha)$, defined on the interval [0;1], describes the fraction $(1 - \alpha)$ of consumption lost due to environmental damage, once the threshold is crossed.

If the consumption level is c, and assuming one-to-one correspondence between consumption and pollution, then the probability of crossing the threshold is $\Pr\{B \leq c\} = \Pi(c)$, where $\Pi(B)$ is the distribution function for $\pi(B)$.

Since we assume that the two variables B and α are independent of each other, their joint distribution is given by $\Omega(B,\alpha) = \Pi(B) \times \Theta(\alpha)$. Suppose the decision maker derives utility both from consumption, c, and from amenity ($a = B - c$): $U(c) = u(c) + v(a)$, where $v(a) = 0$ if $a \leq 0$ (assuming that no utility is derived from the environment if the threshold has been crossed). Once c has been chosen and when the true state of nature is $(B,\tilde{\alpha})$, utility is given by:

$$U\left[c \mid \left(\tilde{B},\tilde{\alpha}\right)\right] = \begin{cases} u(c) + v\left(\tilde{B} - c\right) & \text{if } c < \tilde{B} \\ u(\tilde{\alpha}c) & \text{if } c \geq \tilde{B}. \end{cases} \tag{7.1}$$

Therefore, a priori expected utility for each level of consumption is:

$$EU(c) = \int_{c}^{B_{max}} \left[u(c) + v(B - c)\right]\pi(B)dB + \int_{B_{min}}^{c} \left[\int_{0}^{1} u(\alpha c)\theta(\alpha)d\alpha\right]\pi(B)dB. \tag{7.2}$$

To simplify the analysis, we can assume that $u(0) = v(0) = 0$, and that $u(\alpha c) = u(\alpha)u(c)$. Substituting in (7.2), the expression for expected utility becomes:

$$EU(c) = u(c) + \int_{c}^{B_{max}} v(B - c)\pi(B)dB - l(u,\theta)u(c)\Pi(c), \tag{7.3}$$

where $l(u,\theta) = 1 - E[u(\alpha)]$ denotes the expected value in utility units of the percentage loss in consumption.

In reality, the two probability densities $\pi(B)$ and $\theta(\alpha)$ are not known, and even the most accurate analyses do not provide reliable and complete predictions about threshold values for pollution and their impact on the economy. The scientific community prefers to make use of scenario analyses, which provide projections of possible future developments for the main subsystems of interest (socioeconomic, political, and ecological), based on different probability assessments that correspond to a variety of hypotheses regarding how these systems work and how they relate to one another.

2.2 Uncertainty and the Scenario Approach

> Projected climate changes during the 21st century have the potential to lead to future large-scale and possibly irreversible changes in Earth systems resulting in impacts at continental and global scales. These possibilities are very climate scenario-dependent and a full range of plausible scenarios has not yet been evaluated. (IPCC 2001b, p. 6)

The Intergovernmental Panel on Climate Change (IPCC) works on the development of climate scenarios. Such scenarios include assumptions and predictions on both geophysical and socioeconomic factors. In particular, the latter are meant to depict possible developments for the future and to provide directions for the choice of structured sets of policies that complement one another, dealing with all dimensions of the problem. However, it is quite reasonable to think that not all these policies can be implemented simultaneously and in a coordinated way: from the point of view of one single decision unit (say, the ministry for environment of one specific country) some socioeconomic conditions are exogenously determined, beyond its own control, and substantially independent of its current decision. Therefore there is uncertainty, not only within scenarios, but also across scenarios.

Geophysical uncertainty must also be taken into account: the climate system is chaotic, which means that predictions are affected by both model uncertainty and initial conditions. To increase reliability, probability forecasts are obtained on the basis of 'multi-model, multi-initial-condition ensembles' (IPCC 2001a, p. 423). Yet, the report of Working Group I of the IPCC stresses that 'an important question is whether a multi-model ensemble made by pooling the world climate community's stock of global models adequately spans the uncertainty in our ability to represent faithfully the evolution of climate' (IPCC 2001a, p. 423).

As a result, a plurality of scenarios can be considered, which differ in their assumptions on both socioeconomic and physical parameters. Such scenarios can be treated as states of the world in a traditional decision-making problem, because they are exogenously given, while a subset of variables (here only emissions) can be considered decision variables. This is the approach taken in this chapter.

Even though I use the word 'scenario' basically as a synonym for 'state of the world', I maintain the lexical distinction, since one distinctive feature of scenarios is that they constitute a sample of possible states of the world, while decision theory requires that the set of states of the world be exhaustive and exclusive (one and only one state of the set is realized).

Characterization of scenarios

The warming effect of GHGs may be reduced by some reactions in parts of the system, which are therefore called 'negative feedbacks'. 'Negative' refers to the sign of the relative effect on the temperature, whereas it may be increased by other kinds of reactions; these are therefore called 'positive feedbacks'. The sign of a feedback is not always known – for instance, the aggregate impact of aerosols on temperature, as reported by the IPCC (2001a). We can therefore talk about several scenarios that differ in the underlying assumptions about the sign of groups of feedbacks. As already suggested, among the uncertain feedbacks we might also want to include the possible actions of parts of the human social and economic system. This is possible as long as such actions can be considered independent from the present action. Considering all possible combinations of positive/negative signs for all uncertain feedbacks, we obtain a complete and exclusive state space.

Within a scenario $s = 1, ..., S$, I assume that an assessment for the probability densities $\pi_s(B)$ and $\theta_s(\alpha)$ is given. Let us say that $s = 1$ denotes the most favourable case where all uncertain feedbacks are negative, $s = 2$ denotes a less favourable case in which some of the uncertain feedbacks are positive (and so on), until $s = S$ denotes the worst scenario in which all uncertain feedbacks are positive.

I assume that the support of the density function is the same in each scenario ($[B^s_{min}; B^s_{max}] = [B_{min}; B_{max}]$, $\forall s = 1, ..., S$). Therefore the following expected utility function represents how expected utility varies over consumption in each scenario:

$$EU_S(c) = u(c) + \int_c^{B_{max}} v(B-c)\pi_S(B)\,dB - l_S(u,\theta_S)u(c)\Pi_S(c), s = 1, ..., S. \tag{7.4}$$

The vector of expected utility values reached in each state when consumption level c is chosen $(EU_1(c), ..., EU_S(c))$ can be interpreted as a 'lottery' in which one gets $EU_1(c)$ if state 1 occurs, $EU_2(c)$ if state 2 occurs, and so on.

Choice and uncertainty

Consider the lottery $(EU_1(c), ..., EU_S(c))$, and denote $EU(c)$ as its expected utility:

$$EU(c) = \sum_{s=1}^{S} p_S EU_s(c). \tag{7.5}$$

According to traditional decision theory, individuals should choose among lotteries as if they were maximizing expected utility, for some probability distribution (p_1, …, p_S). However, in real and experimental frameworks, actual decision makers do not always seem to follow such a criterion. Evidence from experimental and field observations clearly shows that individuals deviate from expected utility maximization on many occasions, and many theories have been developed with the purpose of clarifying and predicting the patterns of actual choice in the presence of uncertainty (Starmer 2000). One possible explanation is that people transform probabilities in some systematic way, just like they do with outcomes in their utility function. We are familiar with the idea that individuals may have concave utility functions, which reflects the fact that they value differently the same change in consumption from different starting points. In the same way, they might apply a transformation on probabilities. This is the intuition behind the rank-dependent utility (RDU) theory, of which I give a short presentation hereafter. This presentation draws much from Wakker (1989), to which I refer the reader for a more precise and complete, but still intuitive, presentation of RDU theory.

For given consumption *c*, let us consider a permutation over the set of scenarios (ρ_1, …, ρ_S), such that $EU_{\rho 1}(c) \geq \ldots \geq EU_{\rho S}(c)$. For each scenario we can compute decumulative probabilities: $P_{\rho s} = p_{\rho 1} + \ldots + p_{\rho s}$. Now let $\varphi(P)$ be a non-decreasing transformation function such that $\varphi(0) = 0$ and $\varphi(1) = 1$. The RDU value of our lottery is defined as:

$$RDU(c) = \sum_{s=1}^{S} EU_{\rho_s}(c)\left[\varphi\left(P_{\rho_s}\right) - \varphi\left(P_{\rho_{s-1}}\right)\right] \tag{7.6}$$

where I abuse notation defining $P_{\rho 0} = 0$.

To understand the difference between *RDU*(*c*) and *EU*(*c*), first note that we can rewrite *EU*(*c*) as follows:

$$EU(c) = \sum_{s=1}^{S} EU_{\rho_s}(c)\left[P_{\rho_s} - P_{\rho_{s-1}}\right]. \tag{7.7}$$

Therefore, we can consider expected utility (EU) as a special case of RDU, where the transformation function is linear: $\varphi(P) = P$. Defining the decision weights

$$dw_{\rho s} = \left[P_{\rho_s} - P_{\rho_{s-1}} \right] \text{ and } dw'_{\rho s} = \left[\varphi\left(P_{\rho_s}\right) - \varphi\left(P_{\rho_{s-1}}\right) \right],$$

we see in Figure 7.1 that $dw_s \geq dw'_s$ whenever $\varphi(P_{\rho s})$ has slope not larger than 1, and $dw'_s \geq dw_s$ whenever $\varphi(P_{\rho s})$ has slope not smaller than 1. In particular, in Figure 7.1 we see that for a convex transformation function the decision weights of RDU are smaller for better outcomes and larger for worse outcomes than the decision weights for EU (remember that P, reported on the horizontal axis, are decumulative probabilities).

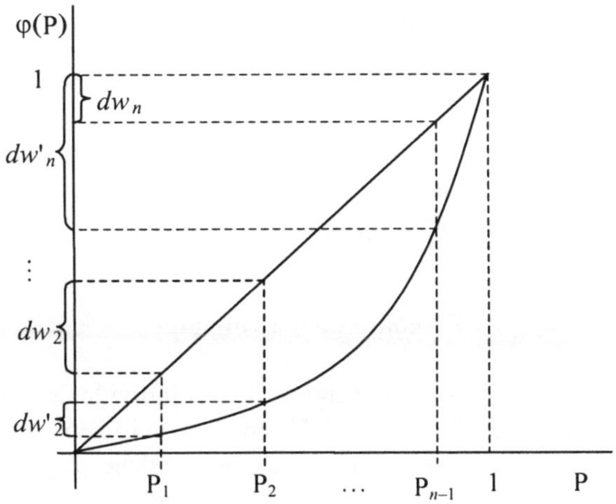

Figure 7.1 Convex transformation function and relative decision weights

RDU has been tested in experiments of choice under uncertainty, and empirical evidence (Tversky and Wakker 1995) suggests that actual weighting functions are inversely S-shaped, as is shown in Figure 7.2. The inverse S-shaped weighting functions have a very nice interpretation in terms of sensitivity to probabilistic estimates: if the weighting function is approximately linear for decumulative probabilities bounded away from the extreme values zero and one, then the slope of the linear portion of the graph represents an index of deviation from expected utility: it is one for EU maximizers, and smaller than one for RDU maximizers, as illustrated in Figure 7.2 by the dotted line with slope σ. This means that observed deviations from EU could be interpreted in terms of sensitivity to probabilistic information. The smaller σ, the more an individual deviates from EU, and the less he or she pays attention to those probabilities that are bounded away from the certainty values zero and one. Accordingly, the individual focuses more attention on the best and the worst outcomes.

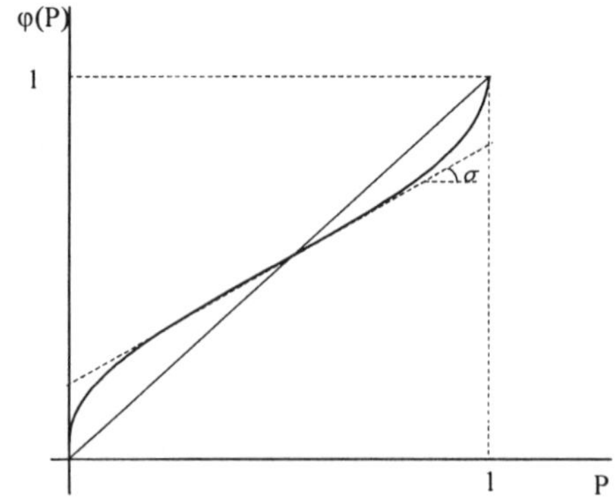

Figure 7.2 Inverse S-shaped transformation function

2.3 Implementing the Precautionary Principle

Discussing RDU gave us two insights. First, individuals do not always maximize expected utility, but RDU models with inversely S-shaped transformation functions are sometimes more adept at explaining their behaviour. This does not necessarily imply that governments also behave like that, but it raises two questions: whether they do behave in this way, and what impact this might have on their policies about climate change. Second, a hypothetical individual who maximizes RDU with a convex transformation function systematically attaches more weight to the worse outcomes, and less to the better outcomes, than an individual who maximizes EU. This may sound appealing from a normative point of view, since this kind of model seems intuitively to reproduce what we call a prudent behaviour.

It is interesting to see what would be the consequences on consumption levels if a government chose this way to implement the precautionary principle, and compare it to the two 'more realistic' situations in which the government either maximizes EU, or RDU with an inversely S-shaped transformation function. I shall refer to the last two models as 'benchmark 1' and 'benchmark 2', respectively, and I shall refer to the RDU model with convex transformation function as the 'precautionary model'.

3. RESULTS

Both benchmark 2 and the precautionary model are derived from maximization of (7.6), where only the assumptions about φ(P) change. Both models are quite complex to deal with analytically. Some results can be derived for given location densities (that is, when only expected damage varies across scenarios). In this case it is possible to prove that a convex-weight RDU maximizer always chooses a consumption (emission) level lower or equal to the level chosen by an EU maximizer. Such a result is reported in Section 3.1. For more general situations, in which both the density for the location of the threshold and the expected impact of crossing the threshold vary across scenarios, I report the results of a number of numerical simulations in Section 3.2. The experiments show that even under these more general conditions a convex-weight RDU maximizer (precautionary model) only rarely chooses higher levels of consumptions than benchmark 1. For inverse S-shaped weights (benchmark 2) no general results can be derived; simulations show, however, that optimal consumption for this model is quite often higher than for benchmark model 1.

3.1 Analytical Results

Some analytical results can be stated for the cases in which scenarios differ only in the expected impact of crossing the threshold. In this case an individual who maximizes convex-weighted RDU, which is a 'prudent' individual in my definition, will never choose a higher level of emissions when compared to an EU maximizer. This result is stated in Proposition 1, which is preceded by two preliminary results in Lemmas 1 and 2.

Lemma 1 For given $\pi(B)$, $EU_s(c) \geq EU_{s'}(c)$ $\forall c \in [0;1]$ if $l_s(u,\theta_s) \leq l_{s'}(u,\theta_{s'})$.

Proof Suppose $\pi_s(B) = \pi_{s'}(B) = \pi(B)$, and $l_s(u,\theta_s) \leq l_{s'}(u,\theta_{s'})$, then $EU_s(c) - EU_{s'}(c) = u(c)\Pi(c)[\,l_{s'}(u,\theta_{s'}) - l_s(u,\theta_s)] \geq 0$ $\forall c$.■

Lemma 2 For given $\pi(B)$, *either* $RDU(c) \geq EU(c)$ $\forall c \in [0;1]$, *or* $RDU(c) \leq EU(c)$ $\forall c \in [0;1]$, depending on probabilities of scenarios and on the transforming function. In particular, for convex weights $RDU(c) \leq EU(c)$ $\forall c \in [0;1]$.

Proof Lemma 1 ensures that the rank ordering of scenarios does not change over c. Therefore an individual who maximizes RDU applies the same weights dw_s, $s = 1, .., S$ for every c. Thus:

$$\sum_s dw_s EU_s(c) \geq \sum_s p_s EU_s(c) \Leftrightarrow$$
$$\sum_s dw_s EU_s(c') \geq \sum_s p_s EU_s(c'), \quad c,c' \in [0;1]$$

which proves the first statement. The second statement follows straightforwardly, since for convex weighting functions more weight is assigned to those states of the world for which expected utility is lower.■

Proposition 1 For given $\pi(B)$, and for convex weighting functions, an individual who maximizes RDU always chooses a level of consumption not larger than an individual who maximizes EU.

Proof Equation (7.4) implies:

$$\frac{dEU_s(c)}{dc} \geq \frac{dEU_{s'}(c)}{dc} \Leftrightarrow [\Pi(c)u'(c) + \pi(c)u(c)][l_{s'}(u,\theta_{s'}) - l_s(u,\theta_s)] \geq 0$$

that is, by Lemma 1:

$$\frac{dEU_s(c)}{dc} \geq \frac{dEU_{s'}(c)}{dc} \Leftrightarrow EU_s(c) \geq EU_{s'}(c).$$

The function that lies below has a smaller first derivative. Moreover, as already noted, it has relatively larger decisions weights in RDU than in EU. Thus it holds:

$$\frac{dRDU(c)}{dc} = \sum_s dw_s \frac{dEU_s(c)}{dc} \leq \sum_s p_s \frac{dEU_s(c)}{dc} = \frac{dEU(c)}{dc}, \forall c \in [0;1]$$

The first derivative of *RDU*(*c*) is always smaller than that of *EU*(*c*). Therefore: (i) if there is an interior global optimum both for *EU*(c) and for *RDU*(*c*), the latter must lie to the left of the former; (ii) if *EU*(*c*) has global optimum in $c = 1$, then *RDU*(*c*) has either an interior global optimum, or an optimum in $c = 0$, or in $c = 1$; (iii) if *EU*(*c*) has a global optimum in $c=0$, then *RDU*(*c*) also has a global optimum in $c = 0$, since by Lemma 2 it always lies below, and for $c = 0$ $RDU(c) = EU(c) = EU_s(c)$ $\forall s$.■

The intuition behind this result is that if the location of the threshold has the same distribution in all scenarios, the only thing that matters is the assessed impact of crossing the threshold. Within scenarios it is always true that the higher this impact, the lower the utility and its first derivative for every level of consumption. Therefore, for convex weights, *RDU*(*c*) has everywhere a smaller derivative than $EU(c)$, and it must reach the optimum at a lower or equal level of consumption.

This reasoning does not apply when scenarios also differ in the density that describes the location of the threshold, $\pi_s(B)$. In this case all sorts of situations can arise, and in some cases convex-weighted RDU leads to higher emission levels than EU. To understand the intuition behind this, consider that when consumption increases, so does the probability of crossing the threshold. But this happens at a different rate for different densities. In some 'bad' scenarios, the threshold is probably already crossed at low levels of consumption: a further increase does not lead to a big increase in the probability of crossing the threshold. In such circumstances it is better to increase consumption, in order to compensate for the environmental loss that has already occurred: the worst outcome would arise from crossing the threshold and not exploiting consumption possibilities. Depending on the other parameters of the problem, such an effect can prevail, leading a 'prudent' decision maker to choose even higher levels of consumption than a 'traditional' decision maker.

3.2 Simulation Results

In order to better understand how the model works and whether more general results can be found besides those stated in Proposition 1, I have run several simulations. To do so, I had to give some specification to the model:

1. *Probability densities for the location of the threshold* ($\pi(B)$): since the support is finite, and since I want to control the skewedness and variability of the density in order to generate various kinds of hypothetical scenarios, I used beta densities (the assumption of unimodal distributions is maintained overall in what follows); the parameters A, B for the beta distributions have been pseudo-randomly generated from a computer-based log-normal generator, so that the interval $[0;\infty]$ has been screened concentrating on more 'plausible values' for the parameters;
2. *Probability densities for the impact of crossing the threshold* ($\theta(\alpha)$): this density does not appear in the model but through the expected damage $l(u,\theta)$; I therefore used pseudo-random uniformly distributed values on the interval [0;1] to represent such expectations.
3. *Utility function*: I use a utility function of the shape $u(c) = c^b + (B - c)^a$. In simulations I always assume that $b = 1$, $a = (1/2)$.
4. *Probability of a scenario*: for most simulations I assumed two scenarios; the probability of one scenario was driven from a pseudo-random number generator that simulates a uniform distribution over [0;1]; the probability for the second scenario was of course derived by imposing $p_1 + p_2 = 1$.

5. *RDU transformation functions*: I used two types of weighting functions, one that was introduced in the decision-theory literature by Tversky and Kahneman (and that has the typically observed inverse S-shape), $\varphi(P) = P^{\gamma} \Big/ \left[P^{\gamma} + (1-P)^{\gamma}\right]^{1/\gamma}$, and a strictly convex one, $\varphi(P) = P^{1/\gamma}$; both functions are defined for $\gamma \in (0;1]$, in the simulations I tried ten values of γ ($\gamma = 0.1, 0.2, \ldots, 1$) for each combination of all other parameters.

Figure 7.3a shows an example where $S = 3$ and $A^1 = 2$ $B^1 = 3$ $l^1 = 0.5$, $A^2 = 7$ $B^2 = 6$ $l^2 = 0.2$, $A^3 = 10$ $B^3 = 10$ $l^3 = 0.3$. In Figure 7.3b the continuous line represents the expected utility function across scenarios, $EU(c)$, and c^* is the optimal choice of consumption when $p_1 = 0.3$, $p_2 = 0.5$, $p_3 = 0.2$. The dashed line instead represents the RDU expected utility function, $RDU(c)$, and c^{**} is the optimal choice of consumption when $\varphi(P) = P^{1/\gamma}$ and $\gamma = 0.4$.

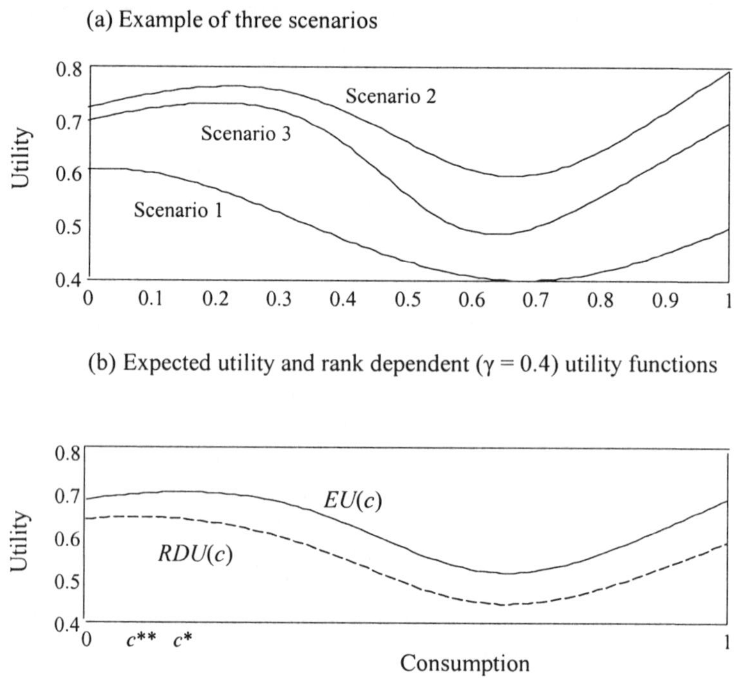

Figure 7.3 Example of three scenarios and relative cross-scenario RDU and EU functions

In this first case $c^* > c^{**}$. Figure 7.4 shows a case in which the opposite occurs.[1] This illustrates the result that no general relation between c^* and c^{**}

can easily be found. To explore this topic in more detail, I ran a number of simulations, limiting the analysis to the simple case of two scenarios. In these simulations, pseudo-random and independent values of the parameters (A, B, l) were drawn, and for each combination c^* and c^{**} were compared for γ = 0.1, 0.2, ..., 1. One hundred combinations were analysed in this way for Tversky–Kahneman weighting functions and another one hundred for convex weighting functions.

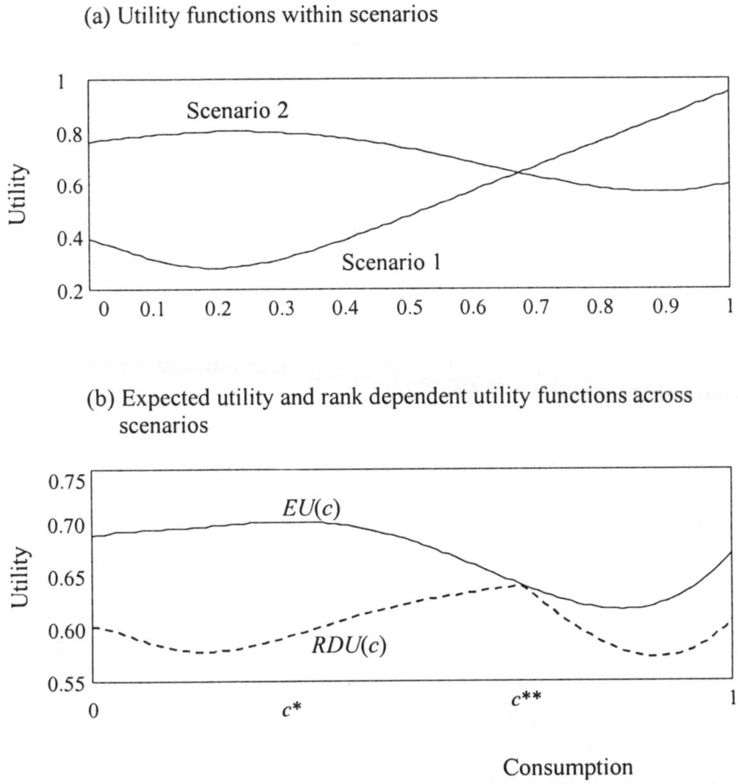

Figure 7.4 Example showing the optimum for the RDU function lying to the right of the optimum for the EU function

In the case of convex weighting functions $c^{**} > c^*$ for 12 per cent of randomly drawn parameter combinations, while in the case of Tversky–Kahneman weighting functions this percentage is 31 per cent, so we can conclude that in general it is really difficult to predict the direction of deviations from expected utility optimal values if an individual maximizes RDU. However, one can state that convex-weighted RDU maximizers only rarely choose higher levels of consumption than EU maximizers, while this is more likely for inverse S-shaped weights.

4. CONCLUSIONS

The model in this chapter aims at defining optimal choice of emission levels under special circumstances, such as thresholds in the utility function and lack of scientific knowledge about relevant aspects of the problem. The approach of the chapter has been to adopt a special decision criterion *ex ante* in order to account for the fact that the precautionary principle applies in the circumstances mentioned. I have shown that for this model results are not unequivocal, since in some cases imposing 'prudent' behaviour leads to higher levels of pollution. The reason for this result is that some model specifications make it very likely that threshold levels of pollution have already been crossed for low consumption; in these cases, if the assessed impact of climate change is not too high it is possible that the most prudent decision is indeed to compensate the loss of environmental utility with more consumption. Though the high degree of unpredictability of the results of this model is common to other models that analyse the same problem, the interpretation here is somewhat different, since it implies that a conservative use of resources is not necessarily optimal *even applying the precautionary principle ex ante*. However, it is also clear that for most parameter combinations, convex-weighted RDU (prudence) determines a lower level of emissions than the benchmark EU model, and this is always the case when scenarios differ only in the assessed impact of crossing the threshold.

Normatively, these results stress one feature of RDU: since more weight is given to the worst outcomes, a big issue is how to design the worst scenario. Making the precautionary principle operational translates then into a problem of identifying the appropriate state space, as suggested also by Henry and Henry (2002). Such a high sensitivity to the specification of the state space leaves a large degree of freedom in implementation, and it might be regarded as a shortcoming of this theory. However, it is interesting that this way of modelling actually forces the debate between economists and (climate) scientists deep into ontological aspects and away from modelling issues (such as the shape of the utility function). What really matters here are the physical parameter l (expected damage from crossing the threshold) and the distribution π (describing the location of the threshold). Indeed, there exists a tension between scientists and economists about the problem of climate change. Such a tension is obviously heightened by some communication problems between two different disciplines, but is probably more deeply rooted in diverging perceptions of 'how bad can bad be?', with respect to the consequences of climate change. If this model correctly reflects such a tension, this may turn the negative aspect of sensitivity into a positive aspect of identification of a relevant content that too often remains hidden behind sophisticated mathematics.

Finally, simulations show that there is a relevant difference between convex-weighted RDU maximizers and inverse S-shaped RDU maximizers; namely, that the latter are 'more likely' to choose higher levels of emissions than the former. This observation becomes particularly interesting if we believe that actual decision makers are inverse S-shaped RDU maximizers, as appears to be the case in experiments on individual choice under uncertainty. On the other hand, nothing can ensure that policy makers behave in the face of uncertainty in the same way as single individuals do, and the circumstances of choice about climate change have never, to my knowledge, been reproduced in laboratory experiments. This work therefore stresses the importance of testing such a hypothesis.

ACKNOWLEDGEMENTS

I wish to thank Rob Aalbers, Michela Pereira, Nicolas Treich, Peter Wakker, Aart de Zeeuw, and two anonymous referees for reading this chapter and making precious comments. My thanks also go to the participants at the economics workshop at Tilburg University, the NAKE day in Amsterdam, October 2002, and to the participants to the conference on Risk and Uncertainty in Environmental and Resource Economics at Wageningen, June 2002. Finally, I would like to express my gratitude to Jeanne Bovenberg for proofreading the manuscript. All remaining errors are mine.

NOTE

1. In this example $S = 2$ and $A^1 = 2$ $B^1 = 10$ $l^1 = 0.05$, $A^2 = 3$ $B^2 = 2$ $l^2 = 0.4$, $p_1 = 0.2$, $p_2 = 0.8$, and the weighting function is convex with $\gamma = 0.4$.

REFERENCES

Aalbers, R. (1999), 'On the implications of thresholds for economic science and environmental policy', CentER dissertation, no. 51, CentER for Economic Research, Tilburg: Tilburg University.

Bouglet, T., T. Lanzi and J.-C. Vergnaud (2002), 'The precautionary principle: an announcement of circumstance?', in E.C. van Ierland, H.P. Weikard and J. Wesseler (eds), *Proceedings of the Conference on Risk and Uncertainty in Environmental and Resource Economics*, Wageningen: Environmental Economics and Natural Resources Group of Wageningen University.

Carpenter, S.R., D. Ludwig and W.A. Brock (1999), 'Management of eutrophication for lakes subject to potentially irreversible change', *Ecological Applications*, **9**, 751–71.

Chevé, M. and R. Congar (2000), 'Optimal pollution control under imprecise environmental risk and irreversibility', *Risk, Decision and Policy*, **5**, 151–64.

Chevé, M. and R. Congar (2002), 'Managing environmental risks under scientific uncertainty and controversy', in E.C. van Ierland, H.P. Weikard and J. Wesseler (eds), *Proceedings of the Conference on Risk and Uncertainty in Environmental and Resource Economics*, Wageningen: Environmental Economics and Natural Resources Group of Wageningen University.

Ghirardato, P. (2001), 'Coping with ignorance: unforeseen contingencies and non-additive uncertainty', *Economic Theory*, **17**, 247–76.

Gollier, C., B. Jullien and N. Treich (2000), 'Scientific progress and irreversibility: an economic interpretation of the precautionary principle', *Journal of Public Economics*, **75**, 229–53.

Heal, G. and B. Kriström (2002), 'Uncertainty and Climate Change', *Environmental and Resource Economics*, **22**, 3–39.

Henry, C. and M. Henry (2002), 'Formalization and applications of the precautionary principle', *Cahier du Laboratoire d'Econometrie*, 2002-008, Paris: Ecole Polytechnique.

IPCC (2001a), *Climate Change 2001: The Scientific Basis. Contribution of Working Group I to the Third Assessment Report of The Intergovernmental Panel on Climate Change (IPCC)*, New York: Cambridge University Press.

IPCC (2001b), *Climate Change 2001: Impacts, Adaptation, and Vulnerability. Contribution of Working Group II to the Third Assessment Report of the IPCC*, New York: Cambridge University Press.

Machina, M. (1989), 'Dynamic consistency and non-expected utility models of choice under uncertainty', *Journal of Economic Literature*, **27**, 1622–68.

Nordhaus, W.D. and D. Popp (1997), 'What is the value of scientific knowledge? An application to global warming using the PRICE model', *Energy Journal*, **18**, 1–45.

Starmer, C. (2000), 'Developments in non-expected utility theory: the hunt for a descriptive theory of choice under risk', *Journal of Economic Literature*, **38**, 332–82.

Tversky A. and P. Wakker (1995), 'Risk attitudes and decision weights', *Econometrica*, **63**, 1255–80.

Ulph, A. and D. Ulph (1997), 'Global warming, irreversibility and learning', *Economic Journal*, **107**, 636–50.

UN (1992), Rio Declaration on Environment and Development, Rio de Janeiro, Brazil, available at http://www.un.org/documents/ga/conf151/aconf15126-1annex1.htm.

Vercelli, A. (1995), 'From soft uncertainty to hard environmental uncertainty', *Economie Appliquée: archives de l'Institut de Science Economique Appliquée*, **48**, 251–70.

Wakker, P. (1989), 'Transforming probabilities without violating stochastic dominance', in E.E. Roskam (ed.), *Mathematical Psychology in Progress*, Berlin: Springer, pp. 29–47.

8. Risk, Pollution Abatement and Endogenous Growth: The Impact of Perception

Susanne Soretz

1. INTRODUCTION

Within the analysis of sustainable development, ongoing growth usually is inevitably linked to environmental degradation. On the other hand, the growth process fosters abatement activities that reduce pollution. Both aspects, pollution caused by capital accumulation and reduced by abatement, are analyzed within a stochastic endogenous growth model. Households perceive pollution to be in part exogenous to individual decisions. This misperception is parameterized and can be shown to induce ambiguous effects on equilibrium growth as well as on optimal environmental policy. Risk is incorporated in the analysis, as it is an important feature of environmental problems: future environmental consequences of present actions are uncertain. Risk affects individual decisions as well as the impact of any environmental policy.

Due to misperception, decentralized growth deviates from optimal growth, and an acceleration of environmental degradation leads to counteracting growth effects. It is shown that the optimal level of pollution and optimal growth are influenced in ambiguous ways by uncertainty, depending on the degree of relative risk aversion. An optimal fiscal policy is derived consisting of income and consumption taxation as well as a subsidy on individual abatement expenditures. Due to partial individual sense of responsibility for environmental degradation, the optimal structure of fiscal policy is shown to be highly sensitive to environmental and preference parameters.

Various previous studies analyze the impact of environmental issues on the endogenous growth path, for example, Gradus and Smulders (1993), Ligthart and van der Ploeg (1994), Bovenberg and Smulders (1995), Jones and Manuelli (1995), Byrne (1997) or Stokey (1998). In these contributions two main questions are addressed. First, the papers analyze whether environmental maintenance is consistent with ongoing growth. Second, environmental policies which enable sustainable growth as an outcome of market equilibrium, are analyzed. Aghion and Howitt (1998, p. 152) summarize that 'the problem of finite, nonrenewable natural resources ... appears to be less of an obstacle to sustainable development than is the problem of environmental pollution'. As long as pollution is an inescapable byproduct of consumed goods, there is a trade-off between consumption and pollution which limits optimal growth. In the long run, optimal growth can even cease, if the environmental costs are sufficiently high (see, for example, Stokey 1998). In contrast, environmental preferences have no effect on long-run growth if there is non-polluting human capital accumulation or an abatement technology, for example as in the setting of Gradus and Smulders (1993) or Byrne (1997).

An important extension of this chapter is the formalization of the mis-perception of individual influence on pollution. The perception of pollution is parameterized and includes the case of perfect knowledge as well as the case where pollution is a pure externality. Alternatively, one could think of a partial individual sense of responsibility for environmental degradation. This market failure leads to far-reaching implications for equilibrium growth as well as optimal fiscal policy. Environmental degradation induces counteracting income and substitution effects on the equilibrium abatement ratio and growth. Due to second-order effects associated with uncertainty, equilibrium growth and the structure of optimal fiscal policy depend crucially on the underlying environmental and preference parameters. The assumption of parameterized perception relates to the setting of congestion effects within the public goods literature, for example, as used by Edwards (1990), Glomm and Ravikumar (1994) or Turnovsky and Fisher (1998).

Furthermore, uncertainty is introduced into the model. Although risk is an essential characteristic of environmental degradation, there are few contributions which focus on the impact of uncertainty on pollution and abatement in a dynamic setting. Clarke and Reed (1994) analyze the risk of an environmental catastrophe and Baranzini and Bourguignon (1995) discuss the impact of environmental decrease on the probability of survival. Reis (2001) shows that growth increases with a rise in the probability of finding a clean technology. The implications of uncertainty about future preferences for the optimal preservation of environmental assets are shown by Beltratti et al. (1998), whereas Chichilnisky and Heal (1998) focus on unknown risks. In the model presented here, pollution evolves stochastically due to an aggregate productivity shock.

The consideration of uncertainty is important, because it changes individual intertemporal decisions as well as any decision with respect to pollution and abatement. Under uncertainty, any fiscal or environmental policy affects not only expected values of economic variables but also their volatility. Hence, risk-averse individuals additionally respond to this change in uncertainty within their savings decision. The counteracting impact of fiscal policy on long-run growth under uncertainty was demonstrated first by Eaton (1981) and taken up in the endogenous growth setting, for example by Turnovsky (1993, 1995, 2000), Smith (1996), Corsetti (1997) or Clemens and Soretz (1997).

The chapter is organized as follows. After an introduction to the assumptions in Section 2, market equilibrium is derived in Section 3. The influence of (perceived) environmental degradation as well as the impact of uncertainty are analyzed. It is shown that the growth effect of pollution is ambiguous and highly sensitive to parameter settings. Optimal environmental policy, which consists of income and consumption taxation as well as a subsidy on individual abatement expenditures, is determined in Section 4. The sensitivity of expected growth with respect to environmental and preference parameters is reflected within a highly sensitive structure of optimal fiscal policy which is illustrated numerically. Section 5 gives a short summary.

2. THE MODEL

Pollution is related to the production of a single homogeneous good and can be reduced through abatement activity. Since pollution is modeled as a flow variable, I refer to pollutants which dissolve rather quickly. The pollution function recurs to Gradus and Smulders (1993) and van Marrewijk et al. (1993): the level of pollution depends on the relation between physical capital and abatement expenditure.[1]

Pollution, $P(t)$, is assumed to depend on the ratio between aggregate capital, $K(t)$, and aggregate abatement effort, $E(t)$:

$$P(t) = \left[\frac{E(t)}{K(t)}\right]^{-\alpha}, \alpha > 0. \tag{8.1}$$

In this chapter, the assumptions about pollution are extended as the perception of individual influence on aggregate pollution is parameterized. The relevant ratio between abatement and capital is perceived to depend on the ratio between aggregate abatement and aggregate capital, on the one hand, and the ratio between individual abatement activities, $e(t)$, and individual capital, $k(t)$, on the other:

$$\eta_p = \left[\frac{E(t)}{K(t)}\right]^{\delta}\left[\frac{e(t)}{k(t)}\right]^{1-\delta}, \delta \in [0,1]. \tag{8.2}$$

The perceived relation between pollution control and capital stock is denoted by η_p, where the index p refers to perception.[2] The parameter δ defines the extent to which the agents perceive pollution to be exogenous to their individual decisions about capital accumulation and abatement effort. The setting of perception in equation (8.2) relies on the formulation of congestion effects in the public goods literature (see, for example, Edwards 1990; Glomm and Ravikumar 1994). In these terms, the parameter δ could also denote the joint degree of rivalry between capital and abatement in the 'production' of pollution (see Turnovsky 1995, p. 405).

Since all agents are identical and population size is normalized to unity, individual and aggregate values are equal in equilibrium. Nevertheless, within individual optimization aggregate capital as well as aggregate abatement are given exogenously. Hence, the perception parameter δ is a measure for the consciousness of individual influence on pollution. The polar case $\delta = 0$ reflects perfect individual knowledge about pollution. On the other hand, $\delta = 1$corresponds to the case where individuals perceive pollution to be completely exogenous to individual decisions. For a perception parameter between zero and one, part of the individual influence on pollution is taken into account.

Alternatively, the degree of perception could be interpreted as the degree of responsibility for environmental concerns. Individuals with a higher sense of responsibility for the environment (lower δ) give more weight to their own activities in the determination of aggregate pollution. In spite of the infinitesimal individual influence on pollution, which results out of the assumption of a continuum of households in the economy, agents with low δ act as if they would decide about the behavior of the whole society.

Physical capital produces the homogeneous good according to the linear individual stochastic production function:

$$f[k(t)] = Ak(t)[dt + \sigma dz(t)] \tag{8.3}$$

which relates to Rebelo (1991) in the deterministic setting and to Eaton (1981) in the stochastic version.[3] A linear technology is chosen as it enables constant marginal productivity of capital without production externalities. Hence, the focus is on environmental market failures. Uncertainty is incorporated into the model through the productivity shock $dz(t)$, which is a

Wiener process with $dz \sim N(0, dt)$. Expected capital productivity is given by A.

There is a continuum of homogeneous individuals who have environmental preferences and maximize intertemporal expected utility. Environmental quality becomes relevant as pollution affects individual utility. This widely used formulation relies on the early approaches of Forster (1973) and Gruver (1976) who analyze environmental aspects within neoclassical growth models and was taken up, for example, by Smulders and Gradus (1996), Mohtadi (1996), Byrne (1997) and Stokey (1998) within the endogenous growth setting. The individuals are assumed to live infinitely long and to have additively separable preferences. Hence, intertemporal utility results in:

$$U = E_0\left\{\int_0^\infty \exp(-\rho t)u\left[c(t), P(t)\right]dt\right\} \tag{8.4}$$

with the constant rate of time preference $\rho > 0$ and the expected value conditional on time 0 information E_0.

Instantaneous utility, u, is assumed to be of the constant relative risk-aversion type:

$$u[c(t),P(t)] = \begin{cases} \dfrac{\left[c(t)P(t)^{-\gamma}\right]^{1-\varepsilon}}{1-\varepsilon} & \forall\ \varepsilon \neq 1 \\ \ln c(t) - \gamma \ln P(t), & \varepsilon = 1 \end{cases} \tag{8.5}$$

where $\gamma > 0$ denotes the environmental preference parameter and $\varepsilon > 0$ represents the degree of relative risk aversion. Smulders and Gradus (1996) show that this type of preference is the only one that allows for socially optimal steady-state growth. It combines two necessary features: a constant intertemporal elasticity of substitution and an intratemporal elasticity of substitution between consumption and pollution which is unity.

Policy consists of income and consumption taxation at the constant rates τ_y and τ_c and a constant subsidy rate on individual abatement expenditures, τ_e. The government budget results in:

$$\tau_y Akdt + \tau_c cdt = \tau_e edt\ . \tag{8.6}$$

Due to the specific structure of technology and preferences, the economy reaches the steady state without any transitional dynamics. Hence, a constant tax-transfer scheme is sufficient to realize Pareto-optimal growth. In the following section, the resulting macroeconomic equilibrium is derived. Afterwards, conditions for optimal environmental policy are determined and illustrated numerically.

3. EQUILIBRIUM GROWTH AND POLLUTION ABATEMENT

Individuals are confronted with a trade-off between consumption, capital accumulation and pollution control. Hence, they decide about consumption and individual abatement effort together with capital accumulation in order to maximize intertemporal expected utility with given initial values for physical capital and the productivity shock. Government activity as well as aggregate variables are considered exogenous throughout utility maximization and pollution is perceived to depend on individual behavior as defined in (8.2). Building on the assumptions made in the last section, capital evolves according to:

$$dk = [(1-\tau_y)Ak - (1+\tau_c)c - (1-\tau_e)e]dt + (1-\tau_y)Ak\sigma dz \tag{8.7}$$

and due to the properties of the stochastic disturbance, the variance of capital results in:

$$\sigma_k^2 = \frac{E[dk^2] - E[dk]^2}{dt} = (1-\tau_y)^2 A^2 k^2 \sigma^2 . \tag{8.8}$$

Furthermore, the additive separability of intertemporal utility leads to a time-separable specification of the value function given by $\exp(-\rho t)J[k(t)]$. According to Itô's Lemma, the stochastic Bellman equation can now be written as:[4]

$$\begin{aligned} \mathrm{B} &= \exp(-\rho t)u(c,P) - \rho\exp(-\rho t)J(k) \\ &+ \exp(-\rho t)J'(k)\frac{E[dk]}{dt} + \frac{1}{2}\exp(-\rho t)J''(k)\sigma_k^2 . \end{aligned} \tag{8.9}$$

To solve the optimization problem of the individual, maximization is done with respect to consumption, abatement and capital. Individual choice about the level of pollution control, e, is based on the formulation of perceived pollution in equations (8.1) and (8.2). Most studies which analyze the impact of pollution on growth assume that the agents neglect their individual contribution to aggregate environmental restoration completely. Hence, optimal individual abatement activity is zero. In my model, that assumption corresponds to the special case where the perception parameter is set $\delta = 1$. Nevertheless, if $\delta < 1$ applies, the agents feel at least partially responsible for their impact on pollution. There is an individual choice about abatement activity and individually optimal environmental expenditures are positive (although not Pareto optimal).

Maximization of (8.9) with respect to consumption and environmental care together with capital accumulation leads to the following necessary conditions:

$$c^{-\varepsilon}P^{-\gamma(1-\varepsilon)} \overset{!}{=} (1+\tau_c)J'(k) \tag{8.10}$$

$$\alpha\gamma(1-\delta)c^{1-\varepsilon}P^{-\gamma(1-\varepsilon)}e^{-1} \overset{!}{=} (1-\tau_e)J'(k) \tag{8.11}$$

$$\begin{aligned}&-\alpha\gamma(1-\delta)c^{1-\varepsilon}P^{-\gamma(1-\varepsilon)}k^{-1} + J'(k)\left[(1-\tau_y)A-\rho\right]\\ &+J''(k)\left[\frac{E[dk]}{dt}+(1-\tau_y)^2A^2k\sigma^2\right]+\frac{1}{2}J'''(k)\sigma_k^2 = 0.\end{aligned} \tag{8.12}$$

These conditions are derived from equations (8.1) and (8.2) which together describe private perception of pollution. Condition (8.10) in combination with (8.11) equalizes marginal utility out of consumption and abatement as perceived by the individuals. In the case of perfect anticipation of the individual influence on pollution ($\delta = 0$), static efficiency results. If $\delta < 1$, marginal utility of pollution control is underestimated and capital accumulation is accompanied by a negative externality. Condition (8.12) assures the equality of instantaneous marginal utility across time and leads to individually optimal capital accumulation.

Additionally, the transversality condition must be satisfied in order to assure feasible consumption paths:

$$\lim_{t\to\infty} E[\exp(-\rho t)J(k)] = 0. \tag{8.13}$$

With the linear technology considered here, the transversality condition is equivalent to the condition for a positive consumption ratio, if growth is Pareto optimal (see Merton 1969). As long as equilibrium growth deviates from optimal growth, only preference and technology parameters will be considered that additionally satisfy the transversality condition.

Malliaris and Brock (1982, p. 178) show that there exists a closed form solution to the system given by (8.10) to (8.12) since relative risk aversion is assumed time invariant (see equation (8.5)), the marginal product of capital is assumed to be constant (see equation (8.3)) and the variance of capital is proportional to the square of capital (see equation (8.8)). In this case, there exists a steady state with constant expected growth. The conjecture consists of the definition of a consumption ratio μ and an abatement ratio η according to:

$$\mu = \frac{c}{k} \text{ and } \eta = \frac{e}{k} \tag{8.14}$$

which are both constant in the steady state. Introducing this information into equation (8.10) leads to $J'(k) = (\mu^{-\varepsilon}\eta_{\rho}^{\alpha\gamma(1-\varepsilon)}k^{\varepsilon})/(1+\tau_c)$. Furthermore, individual and aggregate variables are equal in equilibrium, $K = k$ and $E = e$, due to the normalized population size. Combination with (8.11) and (8.12) yields the following conditions for individually optimal consumption and abatement decisions:

$$\begin{aligned}(1+\tau_c)\mu = \frac{1-\theta}{\varepsilon(1-\theta^2)+\theta^2}\{\rho/(1-\theta)+(\varepsilon-1)(1-\tau_y)A \\ -(\varepsilon-1)\left[\varepsilon(1-\theta)+\theta\right](1-\tau_y)^2A^2\sigma^2\}/2\end{aligned} \tag{8.15}$$

and

$$(1-\tau_e)\eta = \theta(1+\tau_c)\mu \, . \tag{8.16}$$

The parameters α, γ and δ appear jointly in both equations and are summarized for notational convenience within $\theta = \alpha\gamma(1-\delta)$. θ increases as environmental decay accelerates (increasing α), environmental preferences gain importance (increasing γ) or perceived responsibility for pollution rises (decreasing δ). To ensure feasibility, $\theta < 1$ is a necessary condition. In other words, environmental decay as perceived by the individuals should not be too strong. Otherwise the privately perceived marginal product of capital would become negative. Equations (8.15) and (8.16) prove that the conjectured steady state exists: consumption ratio as well as abatement ratio are indeed constant over time.

The propensity to consume (8.15) depends on the underlying parameters as well as on the fiscal instruments. Abatement is proportional to consumption (see equation (8.16)), since with the instantaneous utility function considered here, consumption and environmental quality are complementary goods ($u_{cP} < 0$) and the intratemporal elasticity of substitution between consumption and pollution is unity.

A rise of the tax rate on consumption or of the abatement subsidy leads to a decrease in equilibrium consumption and an increase in equilibrium abatement expenditures as the relative prices change. The impact of an increase in the income tax rate is ambiguous, depending on the magnitudes of income and substitution effects and will be analyzed later in more detail. Nevertheless, since consumption and abatement are complementary goods, they are influenced in the same direction by income taxation.

If environmental preferences vanish ($\gamma = 0$) or individuals neglect their individual influence on pollution completely ($\delta \to 1$), market equilibrium corresponds to the linear stochastic endogenous growth model without environmental aspects. In both cases, individual abatement activities are zero in the limit. In the first case, there is no negative impact of pollution on utility. Hence, pollution control cannot enhance utility. In the second case, individuals are not aware of their influence on disutility from pollution. Therefore, the costs are perceived to dominate the benefit from pollution control for any positive value of abatement expenditures.[5]

With the solutions (8.15) and (8.16) of individual utility maximization, the expected growth rate of the economy, φ, can be obtained from the capital accumulation equation (8.7):

$$\varphi = \frac{E[dk]}{kdt} = \frac{(1-\tau_y)A-(1+\theta)\rho}{\varepsilon(1-\theta^2)+\theta^2} + (1-\theta^2)\frac{(\varepsilon-1)\left[\varepsilon(1-\theta)+\theta\right]}{2\left[\varepsilon(1-\theta^2)+\theta^2\right]}(1-\tau_y)^2A^2\sigma^2. \tag{8.17}$$

Equilibrium expected growth can be divided in two parts. The first term of the expected growth rate (8.17) corresponds to the Keynes–Ramsey Rule of the corresponding deterministic model. The second term describes the response of a risk-averse individual to uncertainty. Equation (8.17) shows that the impact of uncertainty on growth is ambiguous and depends on the degree of relative risk aversion. In general, uncertainty has a positive income and a negative substitution effect on savings. On the one hand, an increase in risk reduces expected utility out of future income flows. Hence, savings are increased in order to compensate for this impact and to equalize expected marginal utility across time (positive income effect). On the other hand, capital accumulation gets less attractive for risk-averse individuals if uncertainty increases. There is an incentive to decrease savings (negative substitution effect).

With the linear technology considered here, the income effect dominates if the degree of relative risk aversion is above unity ($\theta > 1$). In terms of Leland (1968) or Sandmo (1970), $\theta > 1$ implies a motive for precautionary savings. That is, uncertainty leads to an increase in the equilibrium growth rate in this case. If relative risk aversion is sufficiently low ($\theta < 1$), the opposite applies and uncertainty has a negative growth effect.

Furthermore, equation (8.17) shows that neither consumption tax nor abatement subsidy has an impact on the equilibrium growth rate. Both instruments affect all time increments to the same extent and therefore do not change the intertemporal allocation. Therefore, the government can first choose the income tax rate in order to adjust capital accumulation to the optimal level. In a second step, the abatement subsidy is determined to ensure the optimal level of pollution. Finally, the consumption tax is chosen to balance the government budget. Optimal environmental policy will be discussed further in the next section.

Environmental aspects influence equilibrium growth through perceived pollution, as measured by θ. The impact is ambiguous as there are various counteracting effects which lead to a strong sensitivity of the growth effects to the degree of relative risk aversion. The effective rate of time preference and effective relative risk aversion depend on environmental parameters as was shown for the deterministic setting, for example, by Mohtadi (1996). Nevertheless, since in the model considered here individual abatement activity is included, the impact of responsibility for the environment is ambiguous: On the one hand, with increasing perceived pollution the negative impact of capital accumulation through pollution on utility is given more weight, saving gets less attractive and equilibrium growth tends to fall, on the other hand, a rise in perceived environmental decay increases the incentive for individual abatement activities.

In order to enhance the ability for future pollution control, capital accumulation tends to be increased to have easier access to abatement goods in the future. Smulders and Gradus (1996) analyze the same counteracting income and substitution effects of pollution on growth within the deterministic setting where pollution is a productive input and causes disutility.

In the model considered here, the growth impact of perceived pollution is quite complex as second-order effects due to uncertainty have to be taken into account. Figure 8.1 shows that the overall growth effect of perceived environmental degradation depends on the relation between the degree of relative risk aversion and the pollution impact measured by the composed parameter θ. The relevant parameters were set as follows: the productivity parameter $A = 0.25$, the standard deviation of the productivity shock $\sigma = 0.01$, the rate of time preference $\rho = 0.03$ and the income tax rate $\tau_y = 0.3$.

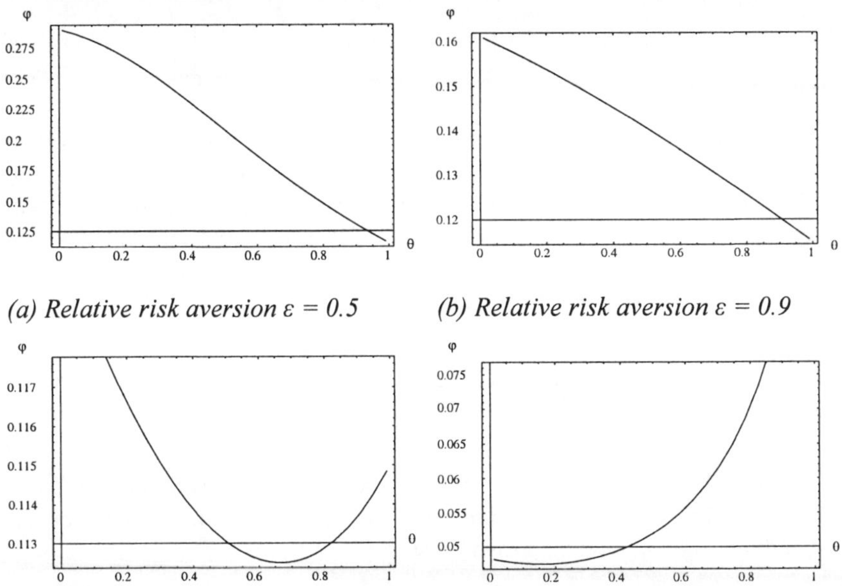

(a) Relative risk aversion ε = 0.5 *(b) Relative risk aversion ε = 0.9*

(c) Relative risk aversion ε = 1.2 *(d) Relative risk aversion ε = 3*

Figure 8.1 Growth impact of perceived pollution

Within the shown interval of relative risk aversion ($0.5 \leq \varepsilon \leq 3$), the growth impact of perceived pollution changes significantly. For all risk aversions less than 0.5, the growth effect is qualitatively the same as in Figure 8.1a and for risk aversions greater than three the curve remains qualitatively the same as in Figure 8.1d. The magnitude of the environmental growth effect gets larger with increasing deviation of relative risk aversion from unity.

4. ENVIRONMENTAL POLICY

To derive optimal environmental policy, maximum intertemporal lifetime utility has to be determined. Because of the assumptions about the productivity shock, capital at time t follows a geometric Wiener process and is lognormally distributed. Therefore, it is possible to determine an explicit solution for lifetime utility (8.4). Given the initial values of capital k_0 and the stochastic process z_0 at time 0, capital evolves according to:

$$k(t) = k_0 \exp\left\{\left(\varphi - \frac{1}{2}\alpha^2\sigma^2\right)t + \alpha\sigma[z(t) - z_0]\right\}. \tag{8.18}$$

Since population size is normalized to unity, aggregate and individual economic variables are equal in equilibrium. Therefore, relevant pollution without informational asymmetries is given by $P = \eta^{-\alpha}$ independently from perception. Using the properties of the steady state (constant consumption and abatement ratios) and the goods market-clearing condition $\mu^* = A - \varphi^* - \eta^*$, maximal expected lifetime utility results in:

$$U = \frac{(A - \varphi^* - \eta^*)^{1-\varepsilon} \eta^{*\alpha\gamma(1-\varepsilon)} k_0^{1-\varepsilon}}{(1-\varepsilon)\left[\rho - (1-\varepsilon)(\varphi^* - \frac{1}{2}\varepsilon A^2\sigma^2)\right]}. \tag{8.19}$$

To develop Pareto-optimal growth and abatement activity, expected lifetime utility (8.19) is maximized with respect to the environmental expenditure rate, η^*, and the growth rate, φ^*:

$$\eta^* = \frac{\alpha\gamma}{\varepsilon(1+\alpha\gamma) - \alpha\gamma}\left[\rho + (\varepsilon - 1)A + \varepsilon\frac{(1-\varepsilon)}{2}A^2\sigma^2\right] \tag{8.20}$$

$$\varphi^* = \frac{1+\alpha\gamma}{\varepsilon(1+\alpha\gamma) - \alpha\gamma}\left(\frac{A}{1+\alpha\gamma} - \rho + \varepsilon\frac{\varepsilon - 1}{2}A^2\sigma^2\right). \tag{8.21}$$

Pareto-optimal pollution control as determined by equation (8.20) differs from the corresponding deterministic model with respect to the second term. That is, optimal environmental care increases (decreases) with uncertainty if risk aversion is less (higher) than unity.

Hence, in general the outcome of the deterministic model cannot be applied to the case of uncertainty. If risk aversion is sufficiently high ($\varepsilon > 1$), optimal pollution control is overestimated by the setting without risk (and vice versa). This deviation is due to the motive of precautionary savings. With sufficiently risk-averse individuals, optimal savings increase with rising uncertainty. This increase in capital accumulation is accompanied by a reduction not only of instantaneous consumption but also of current environmental expenditures. The opposite applies for an economy where risk aversion is below unity.

The impact of environmental decay, denoted by $\alpha\gamma$, on Pareto-optimal growth (8.21) is ambiguous and depends on the degree of relative risk aversion and the intertemporal elasticity of substitution, respectively. Again, there are counteracting income and substitution effects.[6] The substitution effect of accelerated environmental degradation (increasing $\alpha\gamma$) leads to a decrease in optimal capital accumulation and hence in the growth rate. In contrast, the income effect induces an increase in capital accumulation, because a rise in environmental decay induces more need for future abatement activities. On the other hand, equation (8.20) shows that optimal abatement unambiguously increases when environmental degradation gets more serious.

Optimal environmental policy can now be determined. The government fosters individual abatement activities through the ratio between abatement subsidy rate τ_e and consumption tax rate τ_c and adjusts capital accumulation through the income tax at rate τ_y. More simply, optimal taxation equalizes marginal expected utility of consumption and marginal expected disutility of pollution. The government budget is balanced by a growth-neutral consumption tax. Hence, optimal fiscal and environmental policy can be decomposed into two steps. First, optimal income taxation ensures the equality of equilibrium expected growth, φ, according to (8.17) and Pareto-optimal expected growth, φ^*, as given by (8.21). Second, the government has to adjust individual pollution control, η, determined in (8.16) to the corresponding optimal value, η^*, derived in (8.20).

The impact of income taxation on expected equilibrium growth (8.17) results in the well-known ambiguous growth effect of income taxation in a stochastic growth model. It can be decomposed into a growth-diminishing distortionary effect which is associated with the reduction in expected capital return and an ambiguous growth effect which is associated with the decline in capital risk. As already explained above, the individual response on a decrease in risk depends on the degree of relative risk aversion and may end up in a tendency to increase or decrease savings. For a detailed discussion of the counteracting effects of taxation within stochastic models of endogenous growth, see for example, Eaton (1981), Turnovsky (1995), Smith (1996), Corsetti (1997) or Clemens and Soretz (1997). In the model considered here, the growth effect of a change in the income tax rate is given by:

$$\frac{\partial\varphi}{\partial\tau_y} = -\frac{A}{\varepsilon(1-\theta^2)+\theta^2}\left\{1+(1-\theta^2)(\varepsilon-1)\left[\varepsilon(1-\theta)+\theta\right](1-\tau_y)A\sigma^2\right\}. \quad (8.22)$$

If risk aversion is higher than unity, individuals have a motive for precautionary savings which are reduced by income taxation. Hence, growth diminishes unambiguously with an increase in the income tax rate. If risk aversion is below unity, income taxation leads to an increase in precautionary savings. Nevertheless, it can be shown that a positive certainty equivalent of capital return is a sufficient condition for the domination of the negative distortionary growth impact of income taxation.[7] This condition can be interpreted in the following way: with a positive certainty equivalent risk does not dominate the model. The technology is 'certain enough' to ensure that the effects of the underlying deterministic structure prevail. A negative certainty equivalent would describe a situation where the uncertain capital income flow yields the same utility as a certain interest rate which is negative. With this argument, it becomes immediately obvious that a positive certainty equivalent is a necessary condition for feasible solutions. To conclude, income taxation unambiguously reduces equilibrium expected growth, independently from the degree of relative risk aversion.

Since income taxation influences capital risk, equating equilibrium growth (8.17) and optimal growth (8.21) leads to a quadratic function in the optimal income tax rate, τ_y^*,

$$\begin{aligned}&[\varepsilon(1+\alpha\gamma)-\alpha\gamma]\\&\left\{(1-\theta^2)\frac{(\varepsilon-1)}{2}[\varepsilon(1-\theta)+\theta]A^2\sigma^2(1-\tau_y^*)^2+A(1-\tau_y^*)\right\}\\&-(1+\alpha\gamma)[\varepsilon(1-\theta^2)+\theta^2]\left(\frac{A}{1+\alpha\gamma}+\frac{\varepsilon-1}{2}\varepsilon A^2\sigma^2\right)\\&+\{\theta(1-\theta)[\varepsilon(1+\alpha\gamma)-\alpha\gamma]-\alpha\gamma\}\rho=0.\end{aligned} \tag{8.23}$$

The solution will be analyzed numerically, as the impact of perceived pollution again is quite complex. Figure 8.2 illustrates the effect of perceived environmental degradation, again measured by θ, on the optimal income tax rate. The parameter values are the same as in Figure 8.1 ($A = 0.25$, $\sigma = 0.01$, $\rho = 0.03$). It can be seen that optimal income taxation depends crucially on the degree of relative risk aversion. This reflects the sensitivity of the environmental growth effect with respect to the degree of relative risk aversion which was shown in Figure 8.1.

Figures 8.2c and 8.2d show the positive impact of pollution on the optimal income tax rate one would have expected. With an increase in environmental degradation, $\alpha\gamma$, or in misperception, $1 - \delta$, the negative external effect of capital accumulation increases. Therefore, the need for internalizing income taxation rises. Nevertheless, Figures 8.2a and 8.2b demonstrate that the relation is reversed if risk aversion is sufficiently low. In that case, uncertainty leads to a decrease in accumulation which in turn decreases the optimal income tax rate.

The influence of the perception parameter is isolated in Figure 8.2 as two functions are given in each diagram. The solid line shows the case of high individual sense of responsibility ($\delta = 0.1$) and the dashed line is associated with low individual sense of responsibility ($\delta = 0.9$). Figures 8.2a and 8.2b demonstrate that with modest relative risk aversion ($\varepsilon < 1$) the isolated impact of perception is too small to become visible. Nevertheless, the perceived environmental degradation, θ, contains the perception parameter δ, so any *ceteris paribus* change in δ also affects perceived environmental importance θ and through this channel in fact influences optimal income taxation considerably.

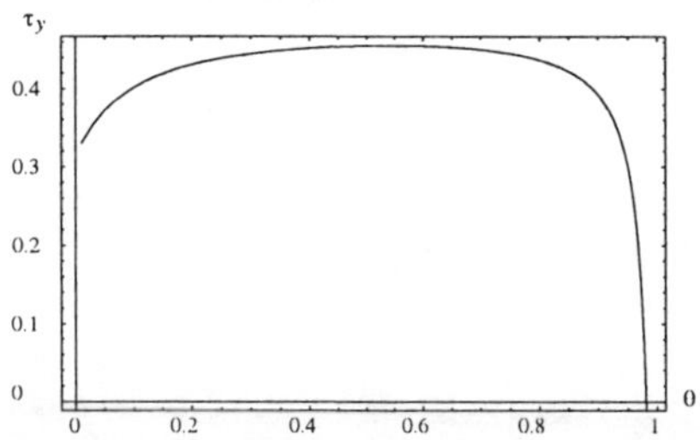

(a) Relative risk aversion $\varepsilon = 0.1$

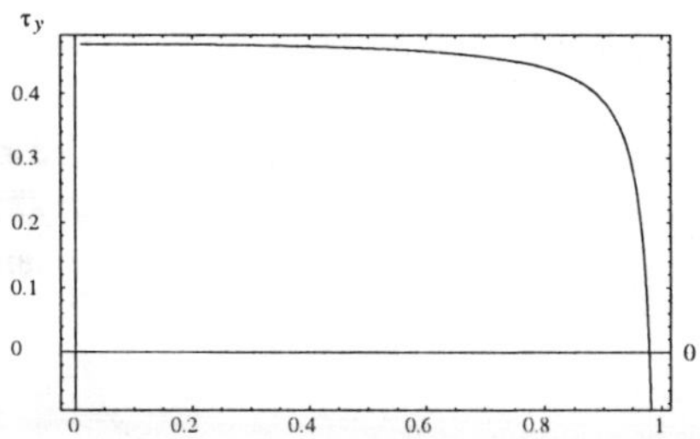

(b) Relative risk aversion $\varepsilon = 0.9$

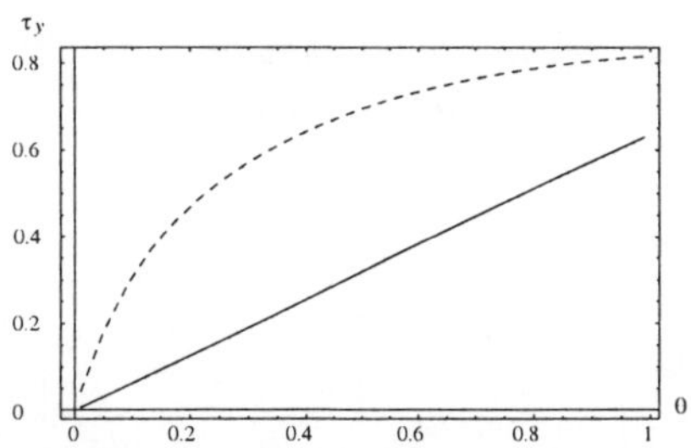

(c) Relative risk aversion $\varepsilon = 2$

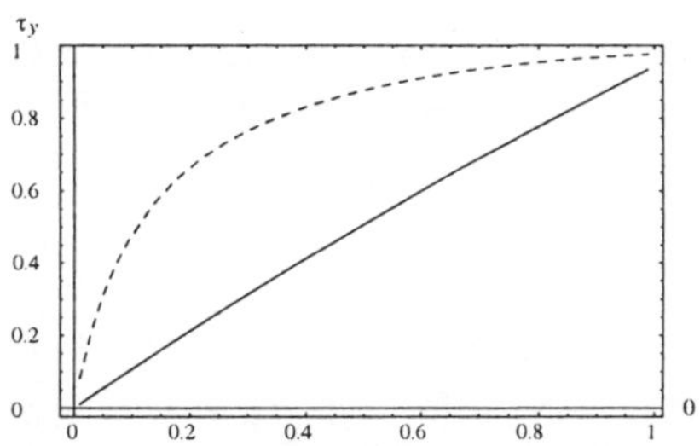

(d) Relative risk aversion $\varepsilon = 10$

Figure 8.2 Optimal income tax rate

To define optimal fiscal policy completely, the subsidy rate on individual abatement activity, τ_e, has to be determined. It results residually from equating equilibrium pollution control (8.16) and optimal abatement ratio (8.20) using equilibrium consumption according to (8.15). The sensitivity of the optimal abatement subsidy rate to perceived environmental decay and to relative risk aversion is clarified by the arguments given above and illustrated in Figure 8.3. Figure 8.3a combines low relative risk aversion ($\varepsilon = 0.8$) with high sense of responsibility for environmental aspects ($\delta = 0.1$). The counterpart for low responsibility ($\delta = 0.7$) is given in Figure 8.3b. The case of high relative risk aversion ($\varepsilon = 3$) together with strong versus modest consciousness ($\delta = 0.1$ versus $\delta = 0.7$) is illustrated in the Figures 8.3c and 8.3d.

Again, one would expect a positive relation between the degree of pollution and the optimal subsidy rate on abatement as given in Figure 8.3. Nevertheless, Figures 8.3a, 8.3b and 8.3d show that perceived pollution also may induce a decrease in the optimal subsidy rate on abatement, depending on the degree of risk aversion. Comparing Figure 8.3a with 8.3b, or 8.3c with 8.3d, respectively, shows that an increase in misperception alone indeed leads to the expected increase in the subsidy rate.

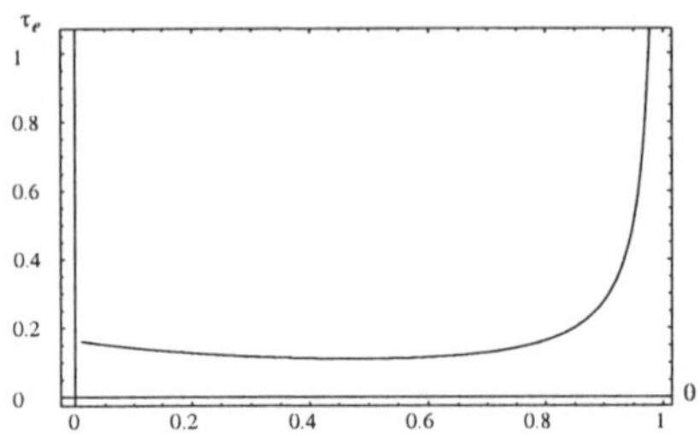

(a) Relative risk aversion ε = 0.8, perception parameter δ = 0.1

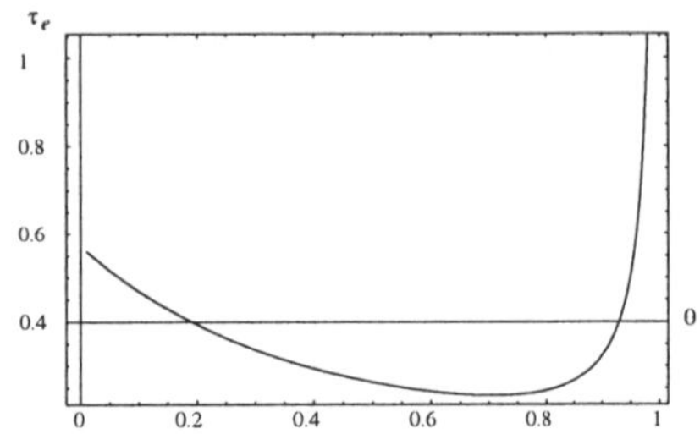

(b) Relative risk aversion ε = 0.9, perception parameter δ = 0.7

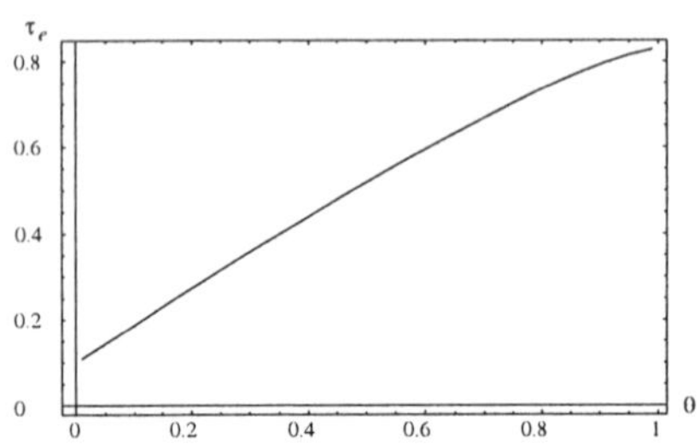

(c) Relative risk aversion ε = 3, perception parameter δ = 0.1

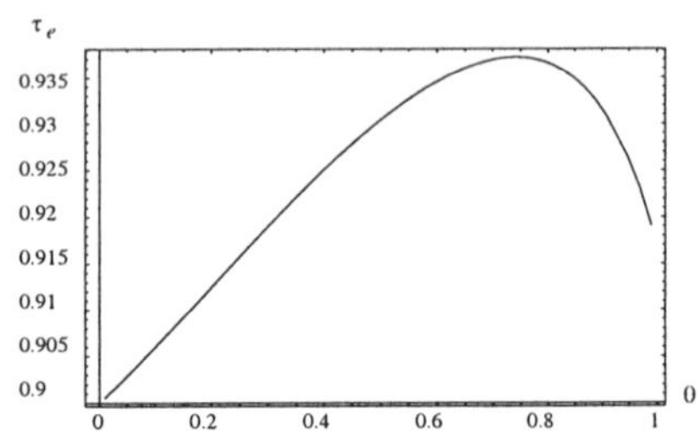

(d) Relative risk aversion ε = 3, perception parameter δ = 0.7

Figure 8.3 Optimal subsidy rate

With respect to optimal governmental policy, it can be stated that optimal fiscal variables are highly sensitive to environmental and preference parameters. Optimal pollution control depends on relative risk aversion and intertemporal elasticity of substitution, respectively, as there are counteracting income and substitution effects. Considering additionally the second-order effects of partial individual responsibility for environmental decay, the ambiguous growth effect of pollution is reflected in highly sensitive policy implications.

5. CONCLUSIONS

In this chapter pollution and abatement are analyzed in a stochastic model of endogenous growth. Partial perception of the individual influence on environmental degradation is taken into account and can alternatively be interpreted as a parameterized sense of responsibility for the environment or as parameterized rivalry in the 'production' of pollution. Due to the partial responsibility for environmental aspects, equilibrium growth is affected in an ambiguous way by an increasing (perceived) pollution. The impact of environmental degradation on growth is highly sensitive to the degree of relative risk aversion.

Optimal growth as well as optimal abatement activity depend ambiguously on risk and on the strength of environmental decay. Risk affects the optimal intertemporal allocation through the motive for precautionary savings. If the degree of relative risk aversion is higher (lower) than unity, increasing risk induces a rise (fall) in precautionary savings and therefore reduces (increases) the optimal abatement ratio. An acceleration of environmental decay or stronger preferences for a clean environment unambiguously increase Pareto-optimal abatement, but lead to counteracting income and substitution effects on optimal expected growth.

The set of fiscal instruments which is considered includes income taxation, consumption taxation and a subsidy on abatement activity. These three governmental parameters are sufficient to achieve the Pareto optimum. The sensitivity of equilibrium growth with respect to environmental and preference parameters leads to a great variety of optimal fiscal policies, depending on the underlying parameter values.

NOTES

1. In contrast, for example, Forster (1973), van der Ploeg and Withagen (1991), Stokey (1998) or Jones and Manuelli (2001) define output to be the source of pollution and, for example,

Luptacik and Schubert (1982) and van der Ploeg and Withagen (1991) consider a stock variable. It is straightforward that with the linear production technology assumed here, the outcomes are independent of the source of pollution. Furthermore, with the usual additional assumptions the results remain unchanged for a stock pollutant.
2. The underlying formulation of perceived pollution is based on the discussion of the earlier version $\eta_p = E/(K^{\delta}k^{1-\delta})$ presented at the Conference on Risk and Uncertainty in Environmental and Resource Economics 2002 in Wageningen. I am grateful to Ana Balcao Reis for this suggestion.
3. With the assumption of constant return to scale, the equilibrium number of firms is indeterminate. Hence, there may arise a conflict with the assumption of perfect competition. Nevertheless, to keep the model as simple as possible, I refrain from the usual assumption of spillovers (see Romer 1986) to combine decreasing individual returns with constant aggregate returns.
4. See, for example, Malliaris and Brock (1982, pp. 81 and 110).
5. In order to maintain feasible solutions for $\theta \to 0$, for example, the government would have to provide pollution control.
6. For the ambiguous impact of 'greener preference' on optimal growth in the deterministic setting, see Smulders and Gradus (1996).
7. A positive certainty equivalent requires $[\varepsilon(1-\theta)+\theta]A\sigma^2 < 1$, see Merton (1992, p. 45).

REFERENCES

Aghion, P. and P. Howitt (1998), *Endogenous Growth Theory*, Cambridge, MA: MIT Press.

Baranzini, A. and F. Bourguignon (1995), 'Is sustainable growth optimal?', *International Tax and Public Finance*, **2**, 341–56.

Beltratti, A., G. Chichilnisky and G.M. Heal (1998), 'Uncertain future preferences and conservation', in G. Chichilnisky, G.M. Heal and A. Vercelli (eds), *Sustainability: Dynamics and Uncertainty*, Dordrecht: Kluwer Academic Publishers, pp. 257–75.

Bovenberg, A.L. and S. Smulders (1995), 'Environmental quality and pollution-augmenting technological change in a two-sector endogenous growth model', *Journal of Public Economics*, **57**, 369–91.

Byrne, M.M. (1997), 'Is growth a dirty word? Pollution, abatement and endogenous growth', *Journal of Development Economics*, **54**, 261–84.

Chichilnisky, G. and G.M. Heal (1998), 'Financial markets for unknown risks', in G. Chichilnisky, G.M. Heal and A. Vercelli (eds), *Sustainability: Dynamics and Uncertainty*, Dordrecht: Kluwer Academic Publishers, pp. 277–94.

Clarke, H.R. and W.J. Reed (1994), 'Consumption/pollution tradeoffs in an environment vulnerable to pollution-related catastrophic collapse', *Journal of Economic Dynamics and Control*, **18**, 991–1010.

Clemens, C. and S. Soretz (1997), 'Macroeconomic effects of income taxation in a model of stochastic growth', *Finanzarchiv*, **54**, 471–93.

Corsetti, G. (1997), 'A portfolio approach to endogenous growth: equilibrium and optimal policy', *Journal of Economic Dynamics and Control*, **21**, 1627–44.

Eaton, J. (1981), 'Fiscal policy, inflation and the accumulation of risky capital', *Review of Economic Studies*, **48**, 435–45.

Edwards, J.H.Y. (1990), 'Congestion function specification and the "publicness" of local public goods', *Journal of Urban Economics*, **27**, 80–96.

Forster, B.A. (1973), 'Optimal capital accumulation in a polluted environment', *Southern Economic Journal*, **39**, 544–7.

Glomm, G. and B. Ravikumar (1994), 'Public investment in infrastructure in a simple growth model', *Journal of Economic Dynamics and Control*, **18**, 1173–87.

Gradus, R. and S. Smulders (1993), 'The trade-off between environmental care and long-term growth – pollution in three prototype growth models', *Journal of Economics*, **58**, 25–51.

Gruver, G. (1976), 'Optimal investment and pollution control in a neoclassical growth context', *Journal of Environmental Economics and Management*, **5**, 165–77.

Jones, L.E. and R.E. Manuelli (1995), 'A positive model of growth and pollution controls', NBER Working Paper Series 5205, Cambridge, MA: National Bureau of Economic Research.

Jones, L.E. and R.E. Manuelli (2001), 'Endogenous policy choice: the case of pollution and growth', *Review of Economic Dynamics*, **4**, 369–405.

Leland, H.E (1968), 'Saving and uncertainty: the precautionary demand for saving', *Quarterly Journal of Economics*, **82**, 465–73.

Ligthart, J.E. and F. van der Ploeg (1994), 'Pollution, the cost of public funds and endogenous growth', *Economics Letters*, **46**, 351–61.

Luptacik, M. and U. Schubert (1982), *Optimal Economic Growth and the Environment, Economic Theory of Natural Resources*, Vienna: Physica.

Malliaris, A.G. and W.A. Brock (1982), *Stochastic Methods in Economics and Finance*, Amsterdam: North-Holland.

Merton, R.C. (1969), 'Lifetime portfolio selection under uncertainty: the continuous time case', *Review of Economics and Statistics*, **51**, 247–57.

Merton, R.C. (1992), *Continuous-time Finance*, Cambridge, MA: Blackwell.

Mohtadi, H. (1996), 'Environment, growth, and optimal policy design', *Journal of Public Economics*, **63**, 119–40.

Rebelo, S. (1991), 'Long-run policy analysis and long-run growth', *Journal of Political Economy*, **99**, 500–521.

Reis, A.B. (2001), 'Endogenous growth and the possibility of eliminating pollution', *Journal of Environmental Economics and Management*, **42**, 360–73.

Romer, P.M. (1986), 'Increasing returns and long-run growth', *Journal of Political Economy*, **94**, 1002–37.

Sandmo, A. (1970), 'The effect of uncertainty on savings decisions', *Review of Economic Studies*, **37**, 353–60.

Smith, W.T. (1996), 'Taxes, uncertainty, and long-term growth', *European Economic Review*, **40**, 1647–64.

Smulders, S. and R. Gradus (1996), 'Pollution abatement and long-term growth', *European Journal of Political Economy*, **12**, 505–32.

Stokey, N.L. (1998), 'Are there limits to growth?', *International Economic Review*, **39**, 1–31.

Turnovsky, S.J. (1993), 'Macroeconomic policies, growth, and welfare in a stochastic economy', *International Economic Review*, **34**, 953–81.

Turnovsky, S.J. (1995), 'Tax policy in a stochastically growing economy', *Japanese Economic Review*, **46**, 125–47.

Turnovsky, S.J. (2000), 'Fiscal policy, elastic labor supply, and endogenous growth', *Journal of Monetary Economics*, **45**, 185–210.

Turnovsky, S.J. and W.H. Fisher (1998), 'Public investment, congestion, and private capital accumulation', *Economic Journal*, **108**, 399–413.

van der Ploeg, F. and E. Withagen (1991), 'Pollution control and the Ramsey problem', *Environmental and Resource Economics*, **1**, 215–30.
van Marrewijk, C., F. van der Ploeg and J. Verbeek (1993), 'Is growth bad for the environment? Pollution, abatement and endogenous growth', Working paper 1151, World Bank, Policy Research (Environment).

9. Securitizing the Environment: A Property Rights Approach to Managing Climate Change

Stephen C. Peck and Thomas J. Teisberg

1. INTRODUCTION

For many years, economists have proposed using market-based systems as efficient alternatives to command and control methods of reducing environmental pollution. At first the use of corrective taxes was suggested (Pigou 1920). The use of tradable emission permits has its intellectual roots in much later work (Coase 1960) and was subsequently formalized (Montgomery 1972). Later still, the conditions were clarified under which emission taxes and emission permits would produce the same economic outcome (Weitzman 1974).

The exhortations of economists have had an impact on the policy process, most notably in the establishment of a sulfur dioxide allowance trading program under the Clean Air Act amendments of 1990. Largely because of the success of this program, market based approaches are now routinely thought of as reasonable policies for a whole range of environmental problems (Stavins 1998).

Emissions trading systems have been widely proposed as a mechanism to deal with the greenhouse gas emissions problem. An overview is provided of the full range of policy instruments, including emissions trading systems that might be applied to this problem (Fisher et al. 1996).

Most of the analysis of emissions trading in the context of the climate change problem has been directed at a system that would limit the emissions rate of greenhouse gases, rather than allocate the overall capacity of the atmosphere to accept greenhouse gases. A prominent exception to this is the work of Kosobud et al. (1994), which analyzes a system of tradable emission permits in which the accumulation of emissions over several decades is limited, but the timing of emissions may be determined by private decision makers. Analysts at the Brookings Institution made a significant later contribution along these lines (McKibbin and Wilcoxen 1997).

This chapter can be viewed as a general endorsement of the Kosobud et al. approach, motivated by the attention now being given to stabilizing greenhouse gas concentrations, as opposed to limiting annual greenhouse gas emissions. Our theoretical development of this approach modifies that of the Kosobud et al. paper by incorporating the natural depreciation of CO_2 in the emission permit system. Also, we address some of the practical difficulties in implementing this kind of system, and suggest an approach that we feel might work.

The UN Framework Convention on Climate Change set an objective of stabilizing 'greenhouse gas concentrations in the atmosphere at a level that would prevent dangerous anthropogenic interference with the climate system' (UN 1992). A major worldwide research program is underway to determine an appropriate set of target concentration levels for the various greenhouse gases. Because many of these gases have long lives in the atmosphere, their concentrations are driven by cumulative emissions over decades or centuries. Consequently, once a set of target concentration levels is determined, emission reduction efforts must be appropriately balanced over both space and time if they are to stabilize greenhouse gas concentrations at lowest cost. In this chapter, attention is focused on CO_2, which is the most important of the greenhouse gases; however, the same concepts would apply with appropriate modifications to any of the other long-lived greenhouse gases.

Our view is that issuing a stock of long-lived emission permits is an appealing policy for minimizing the cost of achieving whatever CO_2 concentration target is ultimately agreed upon. Such permits would be usable at any time during the period before concentrations reach the target level. By thus making permits transferable over time as well as through space, decentralized private decision making can be relied upon to induce CO_2 emission reductions where and when they can be achieved at least cost.

We begin, in Section 2, with a brief review of the theoretical principles characterizing a cost-minimizing approach to stabilizing CO_2 concentrations at any given level. There would be two phases in such an approach. In the first phase, during which CO_2 concentrations are rising, a least-cost policy to reduce emissions must provide for equal marginal cost of emissions reduction anywhere in the world at each point in time, and a marginal cost that rises over time at a rate equal to the sum of the real interest rate and the rate of natural removal of CO_2 from the atmosphere. In the second phase when a stable level of CO_2 concentration has been achieved, marginal cost must be set at a level sufficient to produce only enough emissions to balance the natural removal of CO_2 from the atmosphere. The principle of balancing emissions reductions over both space and time, known as 'where and when' flexibility, has been extensively investigated (Richels et al. 1996).

In Section 3, we present the theory supporting use of a market-based approach for achieving 'where and when' flexibility in reducing CO_2 emissions. This market-based approach also has two phases. In the first phase, a stock of long-lived permits would be issued (in one or more stages). Each permit would entitle the holder to emit CO_2 at any time until a terminal year, at which the target CO_2 concentration will have been reached. To reflect the natural removal of CO_2 from the atmosphere, any permit allows for the emission of more carbon dioxide the further in time from the terminal year that it is used. Any emitter of CO_2 would undertake emission reduction efforts until the marginal cost of emission reductions equaled the value of the permits saved. We show that the establishment of a market for these permits will give rise to exactly the same behavior over time of the marginal cost of emissions reductions as that required for a cost-minimizing approach. And, since permits could, in principle, be traded across different nations, the marginal cost of emissions reductions would be equalized in space. In the second phase, after the terminal year, an annual quantity of emission permits would be issued just sufficient to balance the natural loss of CO_2 from the atmosphere. Trading in these permits would ensure that marginal costs would be equalized in space. The implication is that a two-phased market-based approach could be used to manage the climate issue in a cost-effective manner.

In Section 4, we turn from theory to consideration of the practical issues related to implementation of this kind of market-based approach to limiting concentrations. Our discussion of implementation issues is selective, and omits many of the institutional and scientific issues identified by Heydlauff (1997). Our basic proposal is that about 20 years of permits be outstanding at any one time, that *international* trading in permits be restricted to government-to-government transfers which only occur when interregional marginal costs are seriously different. This approach may sacrifice some of the efficiencies attainable (in theory) from a pure market trading system, but it also responds to some practical problems that might otherwise doom a pure market approach to failure. Section 5 describes some possible extensions of this kind of approach and Section 6 provides a brief conclusion.

2. COST-EFFECTIVE POLICIES

If the marginal cost of reducing a ton of carbon as CO_2 was \$50 in country A and \$20 in country B, then, by switching one ton of emissions reductions from country A to country B, the two countries could save \$30.[1] It follows that a least-cost CO_2 emission reduction policy will equalize the marginal cost of emission reductions everywhere in the world at a given point in time. In addition, a least-cost policy to stabilize atmospheric concentrations must satisfy intertemporal efficiency conditions, as follows.

A least-cost emission reduction policy for stabilizing atmospheric concentrations will have two phases over time; the first while the target atmospheric concentration is being approached, and the second after it has been reached. In the first phase, a particular relationship, dependent on the time value of money and the rate of removal of CO_2 from the atmosphere, will obtain between the marginal cost of emission reductions in adjacent time periods.

To a first approximation, the removal of CO_2 from the atmosphere by physical and biological processes can be represented by a simple decay rate, referred to as δ; thus, in terms of future concentration, one unit of CO_2 emitted in year t is equivalent to $(1 - \delta)$ units of CO_2 emitted in year $t + 1$. Representing the marginal cost of reducing emissions in year t as MC_t, the cost of reducing emissions by $(1 - \delta)$ units in year $t + 1$ is:

$$(1 - \delta)\, MC_{t+1}.$$

Letting r be the market rate of interest, the above cost in year t present value is

$$(1 - \delta)\, MC_{t+1} / (1 + r).$$

In a cost-effective program, this present value marginal cost of $(1 - \delta)$ units in period $t + 1$ must be equal to the marginal cost of one unit in period t; thus the intertemporal efficiency condition is:

$$MC_t = (1 - \delta)\, MC_{t+1} / (1 + r).$$

Since δ is small, this condition can be rewritten as:

$$MC_{t+1} = MC_t\,(1 + r + \delta).$$

The above condition says that the marginal cost of emission reduction should rise at a rate equal to the sum of the interest rate and the decay rate. Equivalently, one could say that the present-value marginal cost should rise at the decay rate, reflecting the fact that earlier emissions are less of a problem since there is more time for early emissions to be removed from the atmosphere by natural processes.

Once the target concentration is reached, the marginal cost of emissions reduction is set at a level such that emissions just balance the natural decay of CO_2 from the atmosphere, thereby maintaining the target concentration.

We can illustrate the implications of the above intertemporal efficiency conditions by using some recent experiments undertaken with the CETA (carbon emissions trajectory assessment) model. CETA is an energy economy model with simple representations of: (i) the world economy including the fundamental determinants of its growth; population, technical change and capital deepening; (ii) the energy sector including technologies and their costs for reducing carbon dioxide emissions; (iii) the carbon cycle (Maier-Reimer and Hasselmann 1987); (iv) exogenous emissions of other major greenhouse gases; (v) the determinants of global temperature increase; and (vi) modules to represent the damages associated with global temperature increase. Generally CETA is used for investigations of carbon dioxide and associated energy sector trajectories, which optimize the intertemporal tradeoffs between the costs of reducing carbon dioxide emissions and the benefits from reduced damage caused by temperature rise. For our purposes here, however, CETA's temperature increase and damage modules are not used. Instead, the CETA model is used to identify the marginal costs of emission reduction and intertemporal least-cost strategies for achieving a given concentration target (Peck and Teisberg 1992).

In these CETA model experiments, uncontrolled emissions in 2010 are 8 billion tons per year, while in 2070 and 2100 they are 15.7 and 28.1 billion tons per year, respectively. The increase in uncontrolled emissions between 2010 and 2070 is due to economic growth, only partially offset by increases in energy efficiency and reductions in carbon intensity of energy production. The large jump between 2070 and 2100 is due to the advent of a CO_2 emissions-intensive coal-based synthetic fuel industry replacing the declining production of oil and gas.

Suppose that the ongoing worldwide research program indicates that it is appropriate to aim for a stabilized atmospheric concentration of CO_2 of 550 parts per million (PPM). The CETA model indicates that a 550 PPM concentration target would be reached in 2070, with a carbon shadow price of $226/ton. At this time, CO_2 emissions would be about 5.3 billion tons of carbon per year, and thus emissions reductions would be about 10.4 billion tons per year. Subsequently, as constraints on the introduction rate of certain carbon-free energy technologies become non-binding, the carbon shadow price would drop back to $125/ton. At this level, emissions would be about 4 billion tons per year, or roughly the amount of carbon naturally removed from the atmosphere on an annual basis.

If the interest rate is 5 per cent per year and the CO_2 decay rate is 0.9 per cent per year, then extrapolating backwards from 2070's price of $226/ton to

2010 at a rate of 5.9 per cent a year implies that the efficient marginal cost of emission reduction in 2010 is about \$6.5/ton. This is a relatively low marginal cost, and the corresponding optimal emission reduction in 2010 is small. However, the optimal emissions reduction begins to rise until it is very substantial toward the latter part of the twenty-first century. This postponement of the largest emissions reductions is a common feature of models like CETA, and it has been explained as due to: (a) positive productivity of capital (interest rate of 5 per cent per annum in our example); (b) the expense that would result from early obsolescence of long-lived capital stock; (c) the increased availability and lower cost of low carbon substitutes in the future (for example, in CETA, the substitution of a carbon-free non-electric energy supply technology at a marginal cost of \$125/ton of carbon reduced); and (d) the greater time for earlier emissions of carbon dioxide to be removed from the atmosphere by natural processes (depreciation rate of 0.9 per cent per annum in our example).

If the shadow price of carbon in 2010 is \$6.50/ton of carbon, the effect of this shadow price on the cost of most common fuels would be modest, as shown in Table 9.1. The cost increase for a gallon of gasoline, for example, is only 2 cents.

Table 9.1 Cost increase in 2010 due to \$6.50/ton shadow price of carbon

Fuel	Cost increase in 2010
Crude oil	0.79 (\$/bbl)
Gasoline	0.02 (\$/gal)
Heating oil	0.02 (\$/gal)
Natural gas	0.10 (\$/mcf)
Coal	3.60 (\$/short ton)
Electricity	0.11 (cents/kWh)

As the foregoing suggests, a cost-effective carbon emission reduction policy is likely to involve low marginal costs and small emission reductions for the next few decades. Such a pattern of emission reductions is at variance with many prescriptions that we should stabilize emissions more or less immediately, and then reduce emissions by some amount after a few years. Does it make much difference whether emission reductions follow this kind of path rather than the efficient path? Richels et al. examine this issue and concludes that it makes a great deal of difference – the cost of meeting a given concentration target, using policies with 'where and when' flexibility, could be 80–90 per cent lower (Richels et al. 1996).

In the prior example, it was assumed that the atmospheric concentration of CO_2 is to be stabilized at 550 PPM. If the worldwide research program indicated that a different concentration target was appropriate, then the numbers would be different. Table 9.2 shows the estimated carbon shadow prices in 2010 and their implications for the cost of gasoline, coal, and natural gas for CO_2 concentration targets ranging from 550 PPM to 750 PPM.

Table 9.2 Cost implications in 2010 of alternative concentration targets

Concentration target (PPM)	550	650	750
Carbon shadow price ($/ton)	6.50	1.270	0.390
Gasoline cost increase ($/gal)	0.02	0.003	0.001
Coal cost increase ($/short ton)	3.60	0.703	0.216
Natural gas increase ($/mcf)	0.10	0.019	0.006

3. IMPLEMENTING LEAST-COST EMISSION REDUCTIONS WITH A MARKET MECHANISM

In principle, there are several ways to implement an efficient emission reduction policy that incorporates 'where and when' flexibility. The policy could be implemented by command and control, by carbon taxes, or through marketable permits. Here a marketable permits-based scheme is described to ensure 'where' *and* 'when' flexibility. With the exception of Kosobud et al. (1994), and McKibbin and Wilcoxen (1997) whose approach shares common elements with this chapter,[2] existing discussions have focused predominately on 'where' flexibility (Fisher et al. 1996).

Suppose, in the spirit of Ronald Coase, that some authority created property rights to use up the remaining capacity of the atmosphere to receive CO_2 during the period to 2070 in which the carbon dioxide concentration was increasing in the atmosphere. For the moment, we put aside questions about how these rights are distributed, in order to concentrate on showing how a system based on such rights could make use of decentralized private decision making to achieve a concentration target at least cost. In later sections, we will turn to a consideration of practical implementation issues, including how permits might be distributed and traded.

If the concentration target were to be 550 PPM, and the property rights program were to start in 2010, the nominal capacity of the atmosphere to receive additional carbon by 2070 would be approximately 425 billion tons.[3] However, because of the natural decay of CO_2 in the atmosphere, actual emissions between 2010 and 2070 could total considerably more than 425 billion tons, while still ensuring that the atmosphere stayed within the 550 PPM concentration target. A natural way to take this into account would be to issue carbon emission permits with a face value of 425 billion tons. Then, to emit a ton of carbon, one would be required to surrender a certain specified number of permits, depending on the time of emission.[4] For a ton of carbon emitted in 2070, one permit would be required. For a ton emitted in 2069, only $(1 - \delta)$ permits would be required; for a ton emitted in 2068, only $(1 - \delta)^2$ permits would be required, and so on. This surrender rule effectively provides a 'credit' for emissions that occur earlier in time, since these emissions use less of the 425 billion tons capacity of the atmosphere in 2070.[5]

How would CO_2 emitters respond to this system? They will compare the cost of reducing emissions by one unit with the value of the permits saved by this emission reduction. Whenever the cost of emission reduction is less than the value of permits saved, the emitters will choose to reduce emissions. In fact, they will reduce emissions up to the point where the marginal cost of emission reduction is just equal to the value of the permits saved. Because the market for these emission permits would be global, permit traders would ensure a uniform price of permits worldwide. This would mean that the marginal cost of control would also be uniform worldwide, implying that emission reduction would be efficient along the spatial dimension.

What might be the price of the permits? First, in order to induce holding of permits for the future, the price of permits would need to rise (in expected value) at the rate of interest. Second, since one permit is needed to emit 1 ton in 2070, the price of the permit in 2070, denoted P_{2070}, must be equal to the marginal cost of control, MC_{2070}, in that year:

$$MC_{2070} = P_{2070}.$$

It is also possible to relate the price of the permits and the marginal cost of emissions reduction in any other year. For instance, in 2069, the permit price, P_{2069}, would be:

$$P_{2069} = P_{2070} / (1 + r),$$

where r is the rate of interest. However, in 2069 only $(1 - \delta)$ permits would be required to emit a ton of carbon. Since the marginal cost of emission reduction in year 2069, MC_{2069}, would again be equated to the value of the permits saved,

$$
\begin{aligned}
MC_{2069} &= P_{2069} * (1 - \delta) \\
&= [MC_{2070} / (1 + r)] * (1 - \delta) \\
&= MC_{2070} / (1 + r + \delta).
\end{aligned}
$$

Alternatively stated,

$$MC_{2070} = MC_{2069} * (1 + r + \delta).$$

Thus, marginal cost of control grows by a rate of $(r + \delta)$ from 2069 to 2070. By a similar argument, it can be shown that marginal cost increases by this rate between any pair of time periods.[6] Since this is exactly the condition derived earlier for efficiently meeting a concentration target, the above permit system would provide the proper incentive for efficiently meeting such a target and the price of a permit in 2070 would be the same as the marginal cost of control in 2070 – that is, \$226.

With a permit price, in 2070, of \$226/ton and a real rate of interest for this asset of 5 per cent, the price of a permit in 2010 would be about \$11.25. Note that if atmospheric CO_2 decays at a rate of 0.9 per cent per year, only about 0.58 permits would be required for a ton of emissions in 2010; thus the marginal cost of control in 2010 would be 0.58 permits/ton multiplied by \$11.25/permit or \$6.5/ton, the same as the marginal cost of control in the optimal program.

The foregoing example assumed that the atmospheric concentration of CO_2 is to be stabilized at 550 PPM. For a different concentration target, the numbers would be different. Table 9.3 summarizes some key numbers for possible concentration targets of 550 PPM to 750 PPM. Note that the permit value in 2010 rises monotonically as the target concentration falls from 750 PPM to 550 PPM, reflecting the fact that there is a more rapid rise in the permit price than the fall in the number of issued permits.

Subsequent to 2070 the permit regime would develop from the cumulative form into a more familiar annual form. Every year (or whatever multi-year averaging period is deemed appropriate) sufficient permits would be issued to maintain the stable atmospheric concentration of CO_2. Worldwide permit trading would again equalize the price of the permits and hence the marginal cost of emissions reduction.

Table 9.3 Permit value implications in 2010 of alternative concentration targets

Concentration target (PPM)	550	650	750
Date target is reached	2070	2110	2130
Mgl. cost at target date ($/ton)	226	465	465
Permit price in 2010 ($)	11.25	3.13	1.15
Permits in 2010 (billions)	425	682	911
Permit value in 2010 ($trillion)	4.8	2.1	1.1

4. PRACTICAL IMPLEMENTATION OF AN EMISSION PERMIT SYSTEM

The example we presented in the preceding section suggested that if permits were all issued in 2010, permits covering 425 billion tons would be issued and each permit would have a price of $11.25. This would imply that the total value of permits issued in 2010 would be just under $4.8 trillion. Over time, the value of permits that remained outstanding would change. The value would tend to rise because the price of permits rises at 5 per cent per year, while it would tend to fall at about 1/60 or 1.6 per cent annually because fewer permits would be outstanding as time passed. For the example in the preceding section, the value of permits outstanding would peak in 2050 at a little more than $12 trillion, and then fall to zero in 2070.[7]

To get a rough idea of the interregional distribution of permits, we ran a parallel analysis using a two-region version of the CETA model. In this analysis, we found that the Organization for Economic Cooperation and Development (OECD) would use approximately 35 per cent of total permits for its emissions, while the rest of the world (ROW) would use the remaining 65 per cent, after both regions had implemented optimal emission reductions for a 550 PPM target.

Approximately $5 trillion is a lot of wealth to distribute among the nations of the world. Moreover, 65 per cent of this would go the non-OECD countries, which would need to set aside a large fraction of these permits for use in later decades when their emissions are projected to be much larger than OECD emissions.

If all these permits were issued and such permits were freely marketable, there would be great temptation for some nations to sell their permits early, and then later default on their obligations to reduce emissions. Moreover, at the present time only the OECD countries appear even close to ready to make any binding commitments to reduce CO_2 emissions. These considerations imply that an immediate issuance of all permits is inadvisable.

Instead, permits should be issued according to a timetable consistent with entry points of blocs of countries into a control agreement. Under such a timetable countries would be responsible for issuing the efficient number of their own permits but not until they had committed to enter the agreement, and would subsequently issue about 20 years' worth of permits and maintain that inventory outstanding by issuing about one year's additional permits per year. The choice of 20 years is the result of our subjective tradeoff to provide enough stability in the permit price trajectory to enable companies to make confident investments in capital-intensive greenhouse gas reducing technologies while not allowing uncooperative permit-holders to unload too many permits.

Note that issuing permits is attractive for governments because if the permits can be auctioned they are a green tax. Being able to issue 20 years' worth of permits at one time can generate large government revenues. If the permits are specified to be buyer liability, then only if the government enforces the carbon dioxide emissions permit scheme, will it maximize its permit income from subsequent one year auctions at progressively higher permit prices – so the system is self-reinforcing.

To see how this might actually work, suppose we divide the world into four blocs: (1) the United States (US), (2) the other members of the OECD (OOECD), (3) the nations of the Former Soviet Union (FSU), and (4) the rest of the world (ROW) focusing initially on Brazil, China and India with their large and rapidly growing populations. Then, suppose the US announces in 2003 that it will commit to emit no more than 17.5 per cent of the total allowable emissions of carbon dioxide from 2010 to 2070.[8] Thus it will use less than 0.175 * 150 or 26 billion permits by 2020 and 0.175 * 435 or 76 billion permits by 2070. We assume that the OOECD, with its strong commitment to climate change mitigation, will make the same type of commitment starting in 2010. Then both the US and the OOECD being within the 'zone of law' can be expected to enforce on their citizens the rule that if carbon dioxide is emitted, the appropriate quantity of permits should be surrendered to the government.

In our opinion, the amount of permits allocated to the US and the OOECD should be determined to minimize the likelihood that any interregional trading will be needed. The notion here is to allocate permits in a way that will *not* create permit-related income transfers among participants in the agreement. Since this notion is contrary to what is often intended, it is worth some further discussion.

Consider the following hypothetical example. Suppose that two nations' electricity industries have one company each; country A has 33,000 MW of coal capacity and country B has 33,000 MW of natural gas capacity. Natural gas is assumed to be cheap, so the operating costs of coal and natural gas are the same. There is also unlimited geothermal capacity that produces no carbon dioxide but is slightly more expensive than coal or gas generation. Since coal emits about twice as much carbon dioxide as gas, the output of carbon dioxide is 100 units (33 * 2 for coal and 33 * 1 for gas). Suppose that the governments of A and B decide to cut back emissions of carbon in the cheapest possible way by 17 per cent to 83 units.

To achieve this with permits but *without inter-country trading*, country B should receive 33 permits for its gas plants and country A should receive 50 permits for its coal plants. The industry composition after the permits have been allocated is 25,000 MW of coal capacity, 33,000 MW of gas capacity and 8000 MW of geothermal capacity. *Note that this allocation has nothing to do with equity but only with efficiency*. If persuasion is needed for country A with its coal company, then agricultural surplus, for instance, from country B could be provided – or some income generated from auctioning permits in B. The fundamental point is that permits themselves need not be used for equity purposes.

However, *as a safety valve*, if the price of permits in one region is consistently and significantly higher than the price in the other, then a government-to-government agreement could be made to transfer some permits at a price to be negotiated. This would have to be based on a convincing case being made by the recipient governments that they had made an adequate effort to invest in CO_2-reducing technology. Thus flexibility in space would be achieved, though only approximately.

Since the US and the OOECD both have strong rules of law, it might even be that the permits could be traded within a unified US–OOECD permit market. In that case it would not be so important to get the initial allocation of permits between the US and the OOECD so precisely on target because an efficient allocation of emissions reductions would be achieved due to the fact that the permit price in both markets would be the same.

Returning to the international CO_2 permits problem, after 2010, the US and the OOECD state that they expect the FSU to commit to an efficient share of permits, to enter the climate stabilization program around 2015, and to enforce on its citizens the obligation to surrender permits for carbon dioxide emissions. If the FSU requires persuasion to conform, then the US, and presumably the OOECD, can provide additional foreign aid support to the FSU. If the FSU gives no indication of joining the agreement by 2015, then the US and the OOECD can for instance issue a larger number of permits than they originally intended which would keep down their own permit prices but also commit the world to a higher CO_2 target concentration level (in addition to the fact that the target concentration would rise because of the non-participation of the FSU).

But suppose that the FSU does join the agreement in 2015. Permits to allow the FSU to meet its least-cost target are then issued so 20 years' worth of permits are available to the FSU. In addition, the US, the OOECD and the FSU state that they expect the ROW, particularly Brazil, China and India to enter the agreement by 2020.

By means of persuasion and training for emission monitoring they work to bring the ROW into the agreement. If unsuccessful, they have the same option of increasing their own permits and again allowing CO_2 concentration to rise. If successful, the ROW enters the agreement, 20 years of permits are made available on a continuous basis to that bloc and the world aims for a given concentration level.

It is less likely, although possible, that a unified emissions permit market could be created between the US, the OOECD and the FSU because respect for property rights is not so well established in the FSU as in the first two regions. This is even more so as one adds Brazil, China and India. Thus particular attention needs to be paid to giving these newly joining regions about the right number of permits they would need in an intertemporally efficient world. Attention also needs to be focused on a design that transfers some permits from regions that turn out to have low permit prices to those with high permit prices due to a mistake in initial allocations, without undercutting the incentive of regions to invest in carbon dioxide emissions reduction technologies and approaches.

After 2070, each bloc is issued with the number of permits needed for efficient maintenance of the atmospheric concentration at 550 parts per million by volume (PPMV) of carbon dioxide.

In the example described above, the ultimate concentration could actually be higher than 550 PPMV because some major players are not reducing emissions for some part of the period from 2010 to 2070. To prevent exceeding 550 PPMV, the number of permits to be allocated to the early participants could be reduced from those levels suggested above.

In the scenario described above, we have assumed that each bloc implements the carbon dioxide cumulative constraint in the same way. But what is most important, of course, is the commitment by each bloc not to exceed the use of a given cumulative number of permits. The United States has strong institutions and a preference for market solutions and should, we believe, adopt the long-term market-based approach that we described. The OOECD also has strong institutions but is more inclined to command and control and may prefer a shorter stock of outstanding permits than for 20 years; we believe such an approach is likely to be overly expensive but if the

OOECD prefers that approach, it is their decision to make. The same applies to the FSU and the ROW when their turn comes. So long as they meet their cumulative commitment, it is a matter of secondary importance to the US, how they do so. In making their decision, they will presumably consider the fact that both 'command and control' and the 'market approach' require strong institutions.

5. EXTENSIONS

In this section, we discuss some possible extensions of this kind of permit system. We consider the implications of delayed commitment to the agreement, more complicated models of the carbon cycle, and incorporating the costs of climate change.

5.1 Delayed Commitment to the Agreement

As discussed above, it is most likely that participation in an agreement would occur later in time for some regions of the world. When this is the case, the optimal time path of marginal cost of control still rises smoothly at the rate of interest plus the rate of removal of the CO_2 from the atmosphere (that is $r + \delta$). Regions which participate from the beginning will face this marginal cost immediately.

Regions whose participation is delayed will have zero marginal cost of controlling emissions initially. Once they join, however, their marginal cost will jump to the then-current marginal cost of control in the regions already participating.

The initial marginal cost of control for regions participating from the beginning is determined by the constraint that concentration never exceeds the ceiling level. When participation by one or more regions is delayed, this initial marginal cost will need to be higher to compensate for the period of time during which some regions will have done nothing to reduce emissions.

5.2 More Complicated Models of the Carbon Cycle

The carbon cycle is often represented mathematically by assuming that emitted CO_2 is deposited into several different 'pools' in fixed proportions. Carbon is then removed from each pool at a different rate. This is easily handled for our purposes by defining a different initial marginal cost for each pool and then having that marginal cost rise at the rate of interest plus the pool-specific rate of removal of CO_2. Then, the optimal marginal cost of CO_2 emissions reduction is the weighted average of these pool-specific costs, where the weights are the proportions of emitted CO_2 entering each of the pools.[9]

If a permit system were used in this context, several different permits would be issued, one for each pool. When a ton of carbon is emitted, some permits of each type would need to be surrendered. The amounts of each type surrendered would be determined by the fractions of emitted CO_2 entering the respective pools as well as the pool-specific CO_2 removal rates and time remaining before concentration reaches the ceiling level.

5.3 Incorporating the Costs of Climate Change

There are also costs of climate change induced by CO_2 emissions – otherwise there would be no point in controlling emissions. If climate change costs are considered in determining emission rates, CO_2 concentration should increase at a slower rate, which reduces climate damage costs, albeit at the expense of somewhat higher emission control initial costs.

The permit system described above can be modified to produce an optimal path of emissions, taking account both of the costs of climate change and the costs of emissions control. The modification required involves paying a subsidy to permit owners who have not yet used their permits to emit CO_2. This subsidy is effectively a 'dividend' paid on permits that are still outstanding at various points in time. The appropriate dividend is related to the marginal damage from the discharge stock. The existence of such a dividend induces permit holders to use up their permits at a somewhat slower rate. As a result the initial market determined price starts somewhat higher and rises more slowly particularly as the marginal damage increases as atmospheric concentration increases. See Appendix 9A1 for a mathematical development of this idea.

If benefit/cost balancing were to be done in practice, the administering authorities might compute the marginal damage every half-decade or so, and change the dividend payments accordingly. Proceeds from auctioning some of the permits could be used to finance the dividends.

6. CONCLUSION

In recent years, the climate change policy debate has become focused on concentration limits as the fundamental objective of policy. This raises two policy questions. First, what should be the concentration target? Second, what is the least-cost program to achieve a given target? This chapter has focused on the second question. We have shown how a concentration target can be achieved at least cost using a system of marketable permits that appropriately accounts for the natural removal of CO_2 from the atmosphere.

We have also made a proposal for implementation of an international system of marketable permits designed to achieve a concentration target. The essence of this proposal is that permits should be issued according to a timetable consistent with actual entry points of blocs of countries into a control agreement. Such a timetable would not issue permits to countries until they had committed to enter the agreement. Finally, it would in some cases restrict international trading of permits to avoid creating an incentive for rogue or weakly committed countries to cash in their permits and then exit the agreement.

Obviously the number of permits received by each nation (or bloc if there are common working legal systems in each nation) should be determined by negotiation. We suggest that the number of permits be determined by efficiency considerations so that the permit markets should primarily be contained within each nation or bloc. Side-payments can be made in many ways including cash received from auction permitting.

ACKNOWLEDGEMENTS

We are grateful to Jesse Ausubel, Hung-Po Chao, Richard Chastain, Darius Gaskins, Richard Richels, Michael Toman and Arnold Zellner for many helpful suggestions. However the views in this chapter and any errors are the authors'.

NOTES

1. This result deals with efficiency and carries no distributional implication that the emissions reductions of each country should be paid for by its citizens.
2. The approach of Kosobud et al. (1994) is similar to that in this chapter, but they do not specify permits that enable the user to emit more, the further removed in time from the terminal year. Accordingly they do not make a distinction between the rate at which marginal cost rises and the rate at which the permit price rises. This may be due to the fact that their carbon cycle model is a mixture of an atmospheric fraction model and a decay model with, consequently, a very low rate of decay.
3. The calculation is as follows. In 2010, CO_2 concentrations are expected to exceed the pre-industrial level (280 PPM) by 120 PPM. We assume that only the excess over the pre-industrial level (that is, 120 PPM) decays, because natural processes replace the CO_2 lost due to decay of the 280 PPM pre-industrial stock. Thus, over the 60 years from 2010 to 2070, the 120 PPM excess over pre-industrial stock would decay to about 70 PPM at a 0.9 per cent annual decay rate. This would leave 350 PPM in the atmosphere if there were no additional emissions. Thus to have 550 PPM in 2070 an additional 200 PPM would need to be added to the atmosphere; 200 PPM translates into 425 billion tons of additional carbon using the standard IPCC conversion factor from concentration at the surface in PPMV to atmospheric

mass loading of 2.123. This calculation is close to the sum of decadal depreciated emissions from the relevant CETA solution.

4. Carbon sequestration projects might be treated in an analogous way by issuing additional permits when it could be shown credibly that actions to sequester carbon emissions were reducing the flow of CO_2 to the atmosphere. If sequestered CO_2 later flowed back into the atmosphere, the sequesteror would be required to purchase emissions permits and to return them to the permitting authority. In principle, providing market incentives for carbon sequestration would further reduce costs of meeting a concentration target.
5. In principle, the use of permits could be so 'front-loaded' that concentration would exceed 550 PPM for a time, before falling back to 550. But this seems unlikely to be a significant problem in practice.
6. A more general argument is as follows. Marginal cost in any time period t is set equal to the value of permits saved in that time period as follows:

$$MC_t = P_t*(1-\delta)^{(2070-t)}.$$

Since the permit price grows at the rate r we have:

$$MC_t = P_{2070}*(1+r)^{(t-2070)}*(1-\delta)^{(2070-t)}$$

Substituting MC_{2070} for P_{2070} and simplifying we get:

$$MC_t = MC_{2070}*(1+r+\delta)^{(t-2070)}$$

or

$$MC_t*(1+r+\delta)^{(2070-t)} = MC_{2070},$$

which says that the marginal cost of control grows at the rate $(r+\delta)$.

7. In order not to interfere with the first phase of Kyoto, the permits might be issued in 2012 not 2010. Subsequent to 2070 the permit regime would make the transition from the cumulative form to a more familiar annual form. The value of the permits issued annually would be about 4 billion tons per year times \$125/ton or \$500 billion per year.
8. We split the OECD total in half because in 1990 the US annual emissions of carbon dioxide approximately equaled those of the OOECD.
9. Suppose that the carbon cycle can be represented by two carbon 'pools', denoted A and B. When a ton of carbon dioxide enters the atmosphere, a fraction w enters pool A with a rate of depreciation δ_A and the remainder, $(1-w)$, enters pool B with a rate of depreciation δ_B. Let MC be overall marginal cost for the world as a whole, and C^A and C^B represent costs for pools A and B. Then overall marginal cost is:

$$MC_t = w* C^A_0*\{\exp[(r+\delta_A)*t]\} + (1-w)* C^B_0*\{\exp[(r+\delta_B)*t]\}, \text{ for } 0 < t < T.$$

The costs at time zero, C^A_0 and C^B_0 may be determined by the fact that the amount of carbon in the atmosphere should not exceed some level and the two pools must reach equilibrium simultaneously.

REFERENCES

Coase, R.H (1960), 'The problem of social cost', *Journal of Law and Economics*, **3**, 1–44.

Fisher, B., S. Barrett, P. Bohm, J.K.E. Mubazi, A. Shah and R.N. Stavins (1996), 'An economic assessment of policy instruments to combat climate change', in J.P.

Bruce, H. Lee and E.F. Haites (eds), *Climate Change 1995: Economic and Social Dimensions of Climate Change*, Cambridge: Cambridge University Press, pp. 397–439.

Heydlauff, D.E. (1997), 'International greenhouse gas emissions trading: institutional and scientific issues', Working Paper, American Electric Power, Columbus, Ohio.

Kosobud, R.F., T.A. Daly, D.W. South and K.G. Quinn (1994), 'Tradable cumulative CO_2 permits and global warming control', *Energy Journal*, **15** (2), 213–32.

Maier-Reimer, E. and K. Hasselmann (1987), 'Transport and storage of carbon dioxide in the ocean and an organic ocean-circulation carbon cycle model', *Climate Dynamics*, **2**, 63–90.

McKibbin, W.J. and P.J. Wilcoxen (1997), 'A better way to slow global climate change', *Brookings Policy Brief 17*, Washington DC: Brookings Institution.

Montgomery, W.D. (1972), 'Markets in licenses and efficient pollution control programs', *Journal of Economic Theory*, **5**, 395–418.

Peck, S.C. and T.J. Teisberg (1992), 'CETA: a model for carbon emissions trajectory assessment,' *Energy Journal*, **13** (1), 55–77.

Pigou, A.C. (1920), *The Economics of Welfare*, London: Macmillan.

Richels, R.G., J.A. Edmonds, H. Gruenspecht and T.M.L. Wigley (1996), 'The Berlin Mandate: the design of cost-effective mitigation strategies', in N. Nakicenovic, W.D. Nordhaus, R. Richels and F.L. Toth (eds), *Climate Change: Integrating Science, Economics, and Policies*, Laxenburg, Austria: International Institute for Applied Systems Analysis (IIASA), pp. 229–48.

Stavins, R.N. (1998), 'What can we learn from the grand policy experiment? Positive and normative lessons from SO_2 allowance trading', *Journal of Economic Perspectives*, **12** (3), 69–88.

UN (1992), United Nations Conference on Environment and Development (UNCED), 3–14 June, Rio de Janeiro, Brazil.

Weitzman, M.L. (1974), 'Prices vs. quantities', *Review of Economic Studies*, **XLI**, 477–91.

APPENDIX 9A1 REFLECTING CLIMATE DAMAGE COSTS IN A PERMIT SYSTEM

A permit system that minimizes the cost of meeting a given CO_2 concentration ceiling takes no account of the damage costs that would occur during the time that CO_2 is rising to the ceiling level. However, it is possible to modify a permit system to take account of such damages, thereby achieving an optimal path to the ceiling concentration (which presumably was chosen to achieve the optimal long-run tradeoff between emission control costs and climate change costs). The modification required is to pay 'dividends' on permits that have not yet been used to emit CO_2. The dividend rate would depend on the marginal damage from climate change and the rate of removal of CO_2 from the atmosphere. This appendix describes how such a system would be designed.

Assume that the costs of climate change can be represented as a function, $h(D_t)$, of the discharge stock, D_t. Then we formulate this problem as one of minimizing, by choice of the emissions reduction X_t, the present value sum of control costs, $C(X_t, t)$, and climate change costs, $h(D_t)$.

Minimize with respect to x:

$$PV = \int_{\tau}^{\infty} \{[C(X,t) + h(D)] * \exp(-r*t)\}\, dt$$

$$dD/dt = U - X - \delta D,$$

U is uncontrolled emissions at time t. The solution to the above problem is a condition derived from the Hamiltonian on the marginal cost of control, MC:

$$d(MC)/dt = (r + \delta) * MC - d[h(D)]/dD$$

$$\frac{d(MC)/dt}{MC} = (r+\delta) - \frac{d[h(D)]/dD}{MC}.$$

This is a relationship which holds for marginal cost (\$/ton). It suggests that marginal cost rises more slowly than $(r + \delta)$ by the marginal damage divided by the marginal cost, which is presumably positive and becomes larger with D.

We convert this relationship into one involving permit price. Since:

$$P = MC * \exp[\delta * (T - t - 1)]$$

$$\frac{d(P)/dt}{P} = \frac{d(MC)/dt - \delta}{MC}$$

$$\frac{d(P)/dt + \delta}{P} = (r + \delta) - \frac{d[H(D)]/dD}{MC}$$

$$\frac{d(P)/dt}{P} = r - \frac{d[h(D)]/dD}{MC}.$$

Now substituting for *MC* from above:

$$\frac{d(P)/dt}{P} = r - \frac{d[H(D)]/dD}{P\exp[-\delta*(T-t-1)]}.$$

The units of the last expression are as follows:

$$\frac{\text{(Damage per ton)}}{\text{(Price per permit)} * \text{(Permits per ton)}}.$$

This expression is dimensionless, thus representing a dividend rate per permit. Thus the permit price appreciation rate is the real interest rate minus the dividend yield of the permit.

10. Risk Aversion in Economic Decision Making: Pragmatic Guides for Consistent Choice by Natural Resource Managers

Jock R. Anderson and J. Brian Hardaker

1. INTRODUCTION

Risk in agriculture and natural resource management (NRM), as in life, is everywhere. But dealing with it systematically, whether for farmers, other natural resource managers, researchers or anyone, is difficult. The difficulty comes from the complexity of risky choice and so cannot be avoided. In this chapter we deal with only one aspect of that complexity, namely risk aversion. We review the capture of risk aversion in economic decision making through consistent application of the subjective expected utility (SEU) hypothesis, and examine how some of the inherent challenges in applications to NRM might best be handled. We do not here take up some of the modern alternatives to SEU such as reviewed by Chambers and Quiggin (2000).

2. THEORETICAL BACKGROUND

2.1 The SEU Hypothesis

Risk assessment requires coming to grips with both probabilities and preferences for outcomes held by a decision maker (DM). Chances of bad versus good outcomes can only be evaluated and compared knowing the DM's relative preferences for such outcomes. According to the widely but not universally accepted SEU hypothesis (Savage 1954; Anderson et al. 1977, pp. 66–9) the DM's utility function for outcomes is needed to assess risky prospects. The SEU hypothesis states that the utility, or index of relative preference, of a risky prospect is the DM's expected utility for that prospect, meaning the weighted average of the utilities of outcomes. This index is computed using the DM's personal or subjective probabilities for outcomes as weights and using the DM's utility function to encode preferences for outcomes.[1] Faced with a choice among alternative risky prospects, the hypothesis is that the prospect with the highest expected utility is preferred.

2.2 Definition and Measurement of Risk

The concept of risk is a difficult one to define unambiguously because the term means different things to different people. If there is no universally accepted definition of risk, we obviously face difficulty in measuring it. For our purposes, following Hardaker et al. (1997, p. 5), we define risk as 'uncertain consequences, particularly exposure to unfavorable consequences'.

The SEU hypothesis implies that risk can only be assessed in terms of the whole distribution of the uncertain outcome measure X.[2] Complete specification requires the probability density function $f(X)$, or equivalently and often more conveniently, the cumulative distribution function $F(X)$. Either way, there is evidently no single statistic to measure risk. However, it is generally accepted that a mean-preserving increase in the dispersion of X implies an increase in risk and contrariwise for a decrease in dispersion. Hence it is often found convenient to summarize risky outcomes in terms of the mean of X, $E[X]$, and a measure of dispersion such as the variance $V[X]$ or the standard deviation $S[X]$. Note that, although frequently done, defining and measuring risk in terms of either of these statistics of dispersion on their own may be misleading unless the mean is held constant. Partly for this reason, some authors, such as Newbery and Stiglitz (1981), have found it convenient to reflect risk using the coefficient of variation of X, $C[X] = S[X]/E[X]$. Here too, however, there is ambiguity because a reduction in $C[X]$ does not *always* imply an increase in utility for a risk-averse DM.

2.3 Certainty Equivalents and Risk Premiums

The SEU hypothesis implies that the utility of any risky prospect is its expected utility. This utility value can be converted through the inverse utility function into a certainty equivalent (*CE*). Ranking prospects by *CE* will be the same as ranking them by expected utility, that is, in the order preferred by the DM. Moreover, the difference between the *CE* and the expected value of a risky prospect, known as the risk premium (*RP*), is a measure of the cost of risk aversion:

$$RP = E - CE. \tag{10.1}$$

For a risk-averse DM, *RP* will be positive and its magnitude will depend on both the distribution of outcomes and the DM's attitude to risk. It is sometimes convenient to compute the proportional risk premium, *PRP*, defined as:

$$PRP = RP/E, \tag{10.2}$$

that is, the proportion of the expected value of the risky project absorbed by the risk premium in computing the *CE*. The more risk averse is the DM or the more uncertain the risky prospect, the higher will be the *PRP*.

In relation to the earlier discussion of the problems of defining and measuring risk, the *CE* may be taken to be a measure of risk-adjusted performance, meaning that a risky prospect with a higher *CE* will be preferred to one with a lower *CE*. On the other hand, while *RP* and *PRP* measure the actual and proportional costs of risk aversion, respectively, they should not be taken to measure risk *per se*; since *CE* depends on both *E* and *RP*, considering only the latter term can lead to similar confusion as can arise in treating *V* alone as a measure of risk. Moreover, as we shall see, risk aversion itself is an elusive concept that depends on the context, especially on the measure of outcome being used.

3. OPERATIONAL PROBLEMS IN ASSESSING RISK AVERSION

The above discussion shows that risk cannot be assessed without accounting for the risk attitude of the DM. According to the SEU hypothesis, risk preference is reflected in the DM's utility function for consequences. The shape of such a utility function specifies an individual's attitude to risk. Several attempts have been made, therefore, to elicit such utility functions from relevant DMs in order to put the SEU hypothesis to work in the analysis of risky prospects in agriculture and other natural resource industries. Usually the results have been rather unconvincing, even to the respective authors. There is evidence that the functions obtained are vulnerable to interviewer bias and to bias from the way questions are framed.

Some of the difficulties in utility function elicitation may be reduced by wise choice of the measure of outcome. It is clear, for example, that people assess losses and gains differently from how they view, say, income or wealth. This seemingly irrational behavior is sometimes called 'failure in asset integration'.

As Rabin (2000) and Rabin and Thaler (2001) argue, people tend to exhibit more risk aversion for risky prospects with small losses and gains than large. Indeed, Rabin convincingly showed that the degree of risk aversion for small payoffs (of the order of plus or minus $100) commonly exhibited (usually for hypothetical choices) is inconsistent with the proposition, widely accepted by economists, that risk aversion is a reflection of the diminishing marginal utility of wealth. In other words, in situations where there are roughly equal chances of winning or losing around $100, many people exhibit 'loss aversion', meaning that they are apparently extremely risk averse about such decisions. They apparently do not view such small lotteries as changes in wealth for if they did many of them would recognize that they could easily afford to risk a relatively small stake for a better than fair chance of winning. Curiously, the same people will often exhibit risk preference for small-stake risky prospects with low probabilities of very large gains, such as buying lottery tickets. (Risk preference means people will accept prospects with less than fair odds.) On the face of it, such behavior is inconsistent with the SEU hypothesis to the extent that Rabin and Thaler claimed the theory to be as dead as the parrot in a famous Monty Python sketch!

However, there is another explanation, which we prefer. Most of the people who exhibit either risk preference or behavior inconsistent with asset integration reconsider their choice and act more 'rationally' for low-cost risky prospects if they have the chance to play the same 'game' repeatedly. Thus, for example, a 50:50 chance of winning $110 versus losing $100 will often be rejected, but the same people often say they would accept the prospect if able to play several times. Similarly, except for addicted gamblers, most people who gamble will limit the amount they stake; they may buy a $10 lottery ticket, but will not buy 100 or 1000 such tickets.

For a prescriptive theory of choice it is clear that both risk preference and extreme risk aversion are not sensible general behavioral rules. Over many 'small' risky decisions, risk preference will almost certainly lead to net losses and extreme risk aversion will almost certainly mean forgone opportunities to gain with little or no risk of loss. Moreover, it is clear that in practice farmers or other NRM DMs do not persistently act in these irrational ways in their day-to-day business decision making; if they did they would go broke. In what follows, therefore, we assume that rational NRM DMs will generally view losses and gains as changes in wealth and will evaluate them in those terms, in almost all cases being slightly to moderately risk averse.

4. SOLVING OR CIRCUMVENTING THE PROBLEMS

In light of the above, it is not surprising that plausible utility functions are most often obtained from elicitation of the utility of wealth, and that utility functions for income are often more convincing than those for losses and gains. The truth is, however, that few people are able to articulate their risk preferences consistently. Some efforts have been made to circumvent the elicitation difficulties by estimating risk aversion from observed behavior, usually using cross-sectional data (reviewed, for example, by Hardaker et al. 1997, pp. 101–2). While these methods certainly cannot be dismissed, given the lack of success of more direct methods, they all suffer from the fundamental weakness of being based on the assumption that the manager and the analyst share the same probabilities about the risky phenomena at issue. In so far as this assumption is invalid, the results will be biased. Also, errors in model specification tend to be rolled into the estimated risk-aversion coefficient, possibly causing further bias.

4.1 Measures of Risk Aversion

Because of perceived difficulties in getting empirical measures of risk aversion, it may be necessary to make some strong assumptions about the degree of risk aversion of DMs if any analysis of risk is to be performed. To this end we need to define a quantitative measure of risk aversion. However, measuring degree of risk aversion is not simple for two reasons. First, a utility function is defined only up to a positive linear transformation. Any measure of risk aversion, which is essentially a measure of curvature of the utility function, must remain constant for such a transformation. Second, as noted above, we need to be clear about what is the argument of the utility function.

For simplicity, we start by assuming that we are assessing risk aversion in respect of the DM's wealth, that is, that there is an actual or implicit utility function $U = U(W)$. Later we consider the implications of utility expressed in terms of other measures such as income or losses and gains.

The simplest measure of risk aversion that is constant for a positive linear transformation of the utility function is the absolute risk aversion function:

$$r_a(W) = -U''(W)/U'(W) \tag{10.3}$$

where $U''(W)$ and $U'(W)$ represent the second and first derivatives of the utility function, respectively (Pratt 1964; Arrow 1965, p. 33). It is generally accepted that $r_a(W)$ will decrease with increases in W.

Absolute risk aversion is a much used and abused concept. First, note that it is a function, not a constant, as is often implied. Moreover, although robust enough to be unaffected by a positive linear transformation of the utility function, absolute risk aversion as measured by $r_a(W)$ depends on the monetary units of W. Thus, risk-aversion coefficients derived in different currency units are not comparable. It is not valid to transport a coefficient estimated for US farmers in US dollars to an analysis of a non-US farm management problem where outcomes are expressed in local currency units or worse, perhaps thousands of them.

The currency units problem is overcome using the concept of relative risk aversion, defined as:

$$r_r(W) = Wr_a(W). \tag{10.4}$$

This relative measure of risk aversion is unit-free and so can be used in international comparisons of risk aversion, only remembering that both $r_r(W)$ and $r_a(W)$ are in general functions, not constants, though either, and especially $r_r(W)$, may often reasonably be assumed to be constant, at least for relatively small changes in W.

While there is general agreement that $r_a(W)$ declines as wealth increases, there is less agreement on how $r_r(W)$ is likely to be affected by increases in wealth. Arrow (1965, p. 36) argues on theoretical and empirical grounds that it would generally be an increasing function of W. Although he noted that some fluctuations are possible, he suggested that the actual value should hover around 1, being, if anything, somewhat less for low wealth and somewhat higher for high wealth. Similarly, Eeckhoudt and Gollier (1996, p. 46) hypothesized that, if wealth increases, relative risk aversion does not decrease. On the other hand, Hamal and Anderson (1982) found that, in extremely resource-poor farming situations, relative risk aversion could reach values as extreme as four or more – quite contrary to what Arrow had hypothesized. While such lack of full agreement implies the need for more study, it nevertheless seems that $r_r(W)$ is likely to be more constant than $r_a(W)$ as W changes.

Constant relative risk aversion (CRRA) means that preferences among risky prospects are unchanged if all payoffs are multiplied by a positive constant. Constant absolute risk aversion (CARA) means that preferences are unchanged if a constant amount is added to or subtracted from all payoffs.

Obviously, the choice of any particular form of utility function has implications for $r_a(W)$ and $r_r(W)$. For example, the widely used negative exponential function $U = 1 - \exp(-cW)$ has the properties that $r_a(W)$ is equal to the constant c (CARA) while relative risk aversion increases with W. On the other hand, the power function $U = W^c$, $0 < c < 1$ has decreasing absolute risk aversion (DARA) and constant relative risk aversion (CRRA). The power function reduces to $U = \ln(W)$ when $r_r(W) = 1$. A special form of the CRRA power function that has operational advantage on occasion is $U = [1/(1 - r)]W^{(1-r)}$, where r is the constant relative risk-aversion coefficient ($r \neq 1$).

4.2 Assumptions about Degrees of Risk Aversion

In the past, it has been common to assume, often implicitly, that all NRM DMs are indifferent to risk. Such an assumption is necessary to justify the many farm and NRM budgets that are formulated with no accounting at all for risk. Such an assumption seems to be a second-best option when we know that risk aversion is widespread. A course that seems more sensible to us, if there is no other information at all, would be to assume a relative risk-aversion coefficient of 1.0. The constant relative risk-averse function for $r = 1$ is $U = \ln(W)$, the so-called 'everyone's utility function' postulated by Daniel Bernoulli as long ago as 1738. But this approach has seemingly not yet been widely adopted by advisers assisting DMs in decision analysis.

If this seems to be too strong an assumption, Anderson and Dillon (1992) have proposed a rough and ready classification of degree of risk aversion, based on the magnitude of the relative risk-aversion coefficient, that some might find plausible. Their classification is:

$r_r(W) = 0.5$, hardly risk averse at all;
$r_r(W) = 1.0$, somewhat risk averse (normal);
$r_r(W) = 2.0$, rather risk averse;
$r_r(W) = 3.0$, very risk averse;
$r_r(W) = 4.0$, extremely risk averse.

The estimates of risk aversion might be validated to some extent by constructing a representative risky prospect, computing its CE using the CRRA function with r_r equal to the tentatively chosen value, and then asking the DM whether the implied indifference between the risky prospect and the sure thing seems reasonable.

If $r_a(W)$ is needed, and if it is assumed that $r_r(W)$ is more or less constant for local variation in wealth at r_r, $r_a(W)$ may be derived using the formula $r_a(W) = r_r/W$. In the work of research stations and extension agencies estimates of the ranges of r_r and W might be made for some target group of natural resource managers such as farmers, leading to an estimate of the range of r_a that might be plausible. This range can be used in risk analysis in applied work. Whether such estimates if used in normative fashion make much difference to the decisions indicated as optimal is a purely empirical issue about which there is far too little experience documented. A similar situation prevails as to whether risk aversion of this type has greater or lesser influence on optimal behavior than option value representations of those investment decisions with environmental implications, although other contributions to this volume may shed light on this uncertainty.

4.3 The Effect of Choice of Payoff Measure

So far, we have considered utility and risk aversion only in terms of wealth. What are the implications of our assumptions when we move to outcomes measured in other ways, such as in terms of income or losses and gains? Consider the latter first. Under the assumption of asset integration, a loss or gain is simply a change in the wealth of the person experiencing that loss or gain. We can write:

$$W_t = W_0 + X \qquad (10.5)$$

where W_t is terminal wealth after the event, W_0 is initial wealth and X is the loss or gain. If we assume (for the moment) that either W_0 is known for sure or that X and W_0 are stochastically independent (not correlated), then we should expect a rational person to make the same choice whether the risky outcomes are expressed in terms of wealth or gains/losses.

Recall that constant absolute risk aversion means that preferences are unchanged if a constant is added to or subtracted from all payoffs – the exact situation we have here. Therefore, if we do not want preference to change whether we express outcomes in terms of W or X, and assuming X is small relative to W so that $W_0 \cong W_t \cong W$, we can specify that $r_a(W) = r_a(X)$, equivalent to saying that absolute risk aversion is the same whether viewed from a wealth or gains perspective. As before, $r_r(W) = Wr_a(W)$ so $r_a(W) = r_r(W)/W$. Moreover, $r_r(X) = Xr_a(X)$ by definition, but $r_a(X) = r_a(W)$ so:

$$r_r(X) = Xr_a(W) = (X/W)r_r(W). \qquad (10.6)$$

In other words, in assessing risky choices expressed in terms of losses and gains, it is not correct to apply the same relative risk-aversion coefficient as for wealth. Moreover, the smaller is X relative to W, the smaller is the applicable relative risk-aversion coefficient. The relative risk-aversion function $r_r(X)$ in equation (10.6) is also sometimes called the partial risk-aversion function since it refers to only part of the payoff, as shown in equation (10.5).

Now let us consider risky choice where payoffs are expressed in terms of income. At least two types of risky choices affecting farm income can be imagined. One is where the income next year (or in some single year in the future) is uncertain. This is the typical situation when doing, say, annual farm planning. The uncertainty in the outcomes stems largely from the year-to-year unpredictability of yields, prices and costs that affect farmers' incomes. This type of uncertainty contrasts with longer-term uncertainty as when a resource manager may be contemplating a major investment, perhaps associated with a dramatic change to the managed system. Here the uncertainty is about the long-run level of income. The distinction between the two is similar to the distinction Friedman (1957) drew between *permanent income* and *transitory income* in his work on the consumption function.

Drawing further on Friedman's ideas, it seems clear that transitory income can be treated in decision analysis rather like losses and gains. We could write:

$$W_t = W_0 + y - c_p \tag{10.7}$$

where y is transitory income and c_p is Friedman's permanent consumption, assumed constant. Defining $X = y - c_p$ converts equation (10.7) into equation (10.5), so the matter will not be pursued further since identical conclusions apply as for risk aversion with payoffs as losses and gains. Now consider what happens when it is long-run or permanent income that is risky and the focus of attention. It seems reasonable to assume that a rational person will view his or her wealth as equal to the capitalized value of future (permanent) income flows with the capitalization factor calculated over the relevant future time horizon.[3] In that case we can write:

$$W = kY \tag{10.8}$$

where W is current wealth, Y is the annual permanent income and k is the appropriate capitalization factor, $k > 1$. Then, since wealth is viewed (ignoring for simplicity terminal asset valuation issues) as a fixed multiple of income (and vice versa), a rational individual will assign the same proportional risk premium to a given risky prospect whether the payoffs are expressed in wealth or in terms of the equivalent permanent income. This is equivalent to the proposition that:

$$r_r(W) = r_r(kY) = r_r(Y). \tag{10.9}$$

Since $r_a(W) = r_r(W)/W$ and $r_a(Y) = r_r(Y)/Y$, then $r_a(Y) = r_r(W)/Y$ or:

$$r_a(Y) = (W/Y)\, r_a(W). \tag{10.10}$$

Finally, since $k = W/Y$ from equation (10.8), then $r_a(Y) = kr_a(W)$. In other words, $r_a(Y)$ is k times as large as $r_a(W)$ where k is the relevant capitalization factor.

By way of a postscript to the above discussion of the effect of choice of argument of a utility function on risk aversion, it should have become apparent that there are likely to be very substantial difficulties in inferring anything about the appropriate degree of risk aversion if payoffs are expressed in other ways than those canvassed above. It becomes difficult indeed to see how an appropriate degree of risk aversion can be derived for such measures as gross margin per hectare of crop, per kilogram of milk produced or per dollar invested. Still worse are attempts to derive an appropriate degree of risk aversion for comparing distributions of, say, crop yield per hectare or biodiversity. Yet it is not unusual to come across examples of results expressed and analyzed in just such partial terms!

5. THE IMPORTANCE OF RISK AVERSION

An indication of the implications for risky choice of different degrees of risk aversion can be obtained from the approximation (Freund 1956):[4]

$$CE = E - 0.5r_aV, \tag{10.11}$$

where CE is certainty equivalent, E is expected payoff, r_a is the appropriate absolute risk aversion coefficient (assumed constant) and V is variance of payoff. Then the approximate risk premium, RP, is given by

$$RP = E - CE = 0.5r_aV. \tag{10.12}$$

Multiplying through by E/E^2 gives the proportional risk premium PRP, representing the proportion of the expected payoff of a risky prospect that a DM would be willing to pay to trade away all the risk for a sure thing:

$$PRP = RP/E = 0.5r_aE(V/E^2) = 0.5r_rC^2 \tag{10.13}$$

where C is the coefficient of variation of the risky prospect, equal to the standard deviation divided by the mean. For example, if $r_r = 2$ and $C = 0.2$, $PRP = 0.04$ or 4 per cent. Similarly, if $r_r = 4$ and $C = 0.3$, $PRP = 0.18$. Note, however, that, for reasons explored above, magnitudes of r_r such as 2 or 4 are only likely to apply for risky prospects expressed in terms of permanent income or total wealth.

The impact of risk aversion will be different from the above for DMs assessing a *marginal* additional risky prospect (Anderson 1989). If such a marginal risky prospect is evaluated in terms of gains and losses, X, relative to initial wealth W_0, now treated as uncertain, the relevant risk premium is:

$$RP[X] = 0.5 r_a \Delta V, \tag{10.14}$$

where:

$$\begin{aligned} \Delta V &= V[X] + V[W_0] + 2\mathrm{Cov}[X, W_0] - V[W_0] \\ &= V[X] + 2\rho S[X] S[W_0], \end{aligned} \tag{10.15}$$

where Cov is covariance, ρ is the relevant correlation coefficient and S is standard deviation. (In equation (10.14) we assume that $r_a(X) = r_a(W_0) = r_a(W) = r_a$, that is, a constant, as in equation (10.11).) Thus the risk deduction as a proportion of $E[X]$ is:

$$\begin{aligned} PRP_X &= 0.5 r_a E[X]\{V[X]/E[X]^2 + 2\rho S[X] S[W_0]/E[X]^2\} \\ &= 0.5 r_p(X) C[X]^2 + r_p(X)\rho C[X] S[W_0]/E[X], \end{aligned} \tag{10.16}$$

where r_p is the partial risk aversion function for gains or losses defined as:

$$r_p(X) = r_a(W_0)X = E[X]/E[W_0]\, rr(W_0) = Z r_r(W_0), \tag{10.17}$$

with $Z = E[X]/E[W_0]$. However, since $E[X] = ZE[W_0]$, the proportional risk deduction for X can be written as:

$$\begin{aligned} PRP_X &= 0.5\, r_p(X) C[X]^2 + r_p(X)\rho C[X] C[W_0]/Z \\ &= 0.5 r_r(W_0) Z C[X]^2 + r_r(W_0)\rho C[X] C[W_0] \\ &= r_r(W_0) C[X]\{0.5 Z C[X] + \rho C[W_0]\}. \end{aligned} \tag{10.18}$$

By way of illustration, Hardaker et al. (1997) give the case for $r_r(W_0) = 1.0$, $C[X] = 0.3$, $Z = 0.1$, $\rho = 0.5$ and $C[W_0] = 0.2$, yielding a value for PRP_X of 0.0345. In other words, for the values indicated the DM would be willing to sacrifice only 3.45 per cent of $E[X]$ to avoid the associated additional variance. The same authors show the value of PRP_X for a range of other plausible values of the variables, mostly indicating that the additional risk-aversion effects are relatively small.

5.1 The Cost of Ignoring Risk Aversion

As shown by equation (10.18) and illustrated above, the cost of risk aversion may be a small proportion of the expected value for some transiently risky prospect that constitutes only a part of the risk faced by, say, a farm household. While it is an empirical matter, many such marginal risks in diversified capitalist agricultural systems may have near-zero values of *PRP*, so that choices can be based on expected values alone. Even when *PRP* values are somewhat larger, the ranking of alternatives based on expected payoffs may be the same as that based on expected utility.

To assess the costs of ignoring risk aversion we need to compare the indicated optimal choice in some risky decision when accounting for risk aversion with the choice indicated when assuming risk indifference. In other words, we need to compare the choice under the SEU maximization rule with that under the maximization of expected money value. These two decisions can conveniently be compared in terms of their CEs. We can then define the cost of ignoring risk aversion, *CIRA*, as:

$$CIRA = CE_{U*} - CE_{E*}. \tag{10.19}$$

Then, somewhat analogously with our treatment of the risk premium, and assuming that both CEs are positive (which will normally be the case if the payoffs are measured in terms of terminal wealth), we can define the proportional cost of ignoring risk aversion, *PCIRA*, as:

$$PCIRA = CIRA \,/\, CE_{U*}. \tag{10.20}$$

It is apparent that *CIRA* and *PCIRA* will depend on the particular decision context, including the choice options and the degree of risk aversion of the DM. However, we can illustrate the relationships involved in an E,V context as shown in Figure 10.1. We assume a portfolio selection problem such as the choice of a cropping and stocking plan for a farm. Thus, the set of feasible plans is effectively infinite, with near perfect divisibility of activity levels. We also assume an indirect utility function of the form:

$$U = E - 0.5r_aV. \tag{10.21}$$

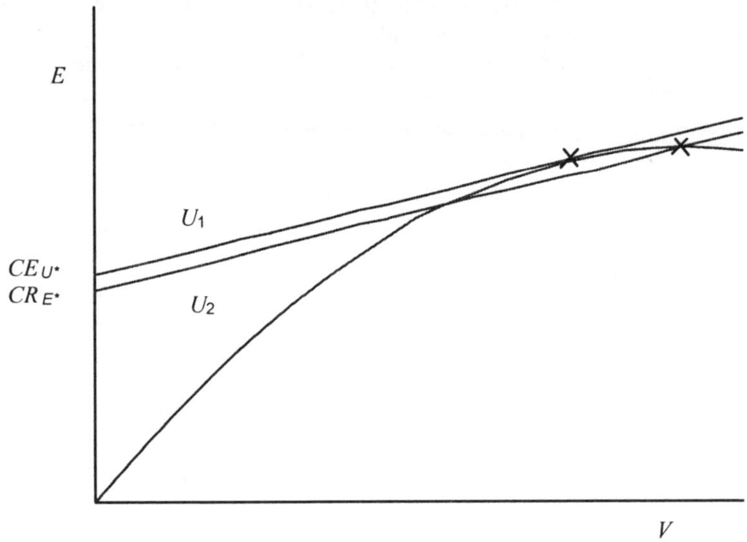

Figure 10.1 Graphical representation of the cost of ignoring risk aversion

From this construction it is evident that *PCIRA* will be smaller the 'flatter' are the gradients of the *E*,*V*-indifference lines U_1 and U_2. The gradient of these lines is $0.5r_a$, which declines as risk aversion diminishes. *PCIRA* also depends on the shape of the *E*,*V*-efficient frontier, particularly on its gradient in the region of the two optima as well as on the location of the frontier as it affects CE_{U^*}. These are all empirical matters, making generalization impossible. However, experience shows that, at least for some Australian farm planning applications, *PCIRA* is typically very small (Pannell et al. 2000).

Given the added degree of difficulty and complexity in assessing risk aversion and incorporating it into the analysis, the problem for analysts, of course, is to distinguish *ex ante* those cases where risk aversion really matters from the bulk of everyday decisions for which it can safely be ignored. While it may be easy to distinguish cases that lie firmly in one category or the other by informed guesswork, more marginal cases are difficult to deal with at present. As more experience is gained in evaluating *PCIRA* for a range of situations, it may be possible to make better-informed guesses in future.

If empirical testing shows the costs of risk to be small for a range of operational NRM situations, it is good news for scientists who can focus more intently on developing technologies that improve expected returns without worrying too much about stability.

More generally, because in many practical choice situations the cost of risk aversion may be relatively small, it can be argued that agricultural and resource economists have paid too much attention to risk aversion, at least relative to efforts to get good specifications and cogent updates of the probability distributions of outcomes (Perrings 1991; Hardaker 2000). If these distributions are mis-specified or incompletely estimated, the estimate of E will be biased, which may matter far more than an error in calculating RP through using the wrong risk-aversion coefficient. Moreover, the focus on risk aversion and its cost may have been a source of confusion in that attention has been directed to reducing variability of outcomes such as yields, rather than on finding the most risk-efficient option (erroneously minimizing V rather than maximizing CE).

Such mistaken emphasis on variability reduction may come from analyses of risk from a policy perspective where risk can be viewed as a friction to resource allocation. Risk aversion may lead managers to use resources less intensively than would be the case if they were indifferent to risk, at least for decisions important to them. Yet, from a social welfare perspective, most risks faced by individual managers or groups of managers are rather unimportant. This is evident from equation (10.18) applied to farm-level risk in a social setting; in that case Z will be small since the uncertain returns for an individual farm or an aggregation of (perhaps even all) farms (the numerator in Z) will typically be small relative to the usually much larger national wealth from other sources, and the relevant correlation will be small because of the diversified nature of the rest of the economy. DMs acting in a public capacity would thus be right to act in close to a risk-neutral manner, as cogently set out by Fisher (1981, p. 137). It therefore becomes a potentially legitimate role of public policy to consider the scope for reducing the cost of risk to farmers in order to reduce the social welfare loss from farm-level risk aversion. It is, of course, quite another matter to decide whether interventions to reduce such welfare losses are justified. Given the high information needs and the likely difficulty and high cost of devising appropriate interventions, the chances are that, in many cases, governments should leave well alone. This view is reinforced by the point argued earlier in this section that, for many local-level decisions, the risk friction might well be less than seems to be widely believed.

The breadth of possible government interventions under the umbrella of addressing the implications of risk aversion is beyond the scope of this chapter, but has been tackled recently for rural areas in general (including 'reputational risk' faced by public institutions) by, for example, Anderson (2003), and in the context of genetic manipulation by various commentators, including Anderson (2001) and Paarlberg (2001). Whether the question be dealing with the specific risks of policy making on use of genetically modified organisms, on biodiversity conservation, or the consequences of natural disasters, for example, public institutions are obliged to deal in some way with the issues, we hope sensibly. However, we feel that the institutions should put their emphasis on understanding, as best they can afford to, the nature of the risks faced. They should adopt a stance toward risk that is intrinsically at most only modestly averse to risk *per se*, while recognizing that important irreversibilities surely oblige considerations that go beyond pure risk aversion.

6. CONCLUSION

Accounting for risk in the analysis of NRM systems is much harder than pretending it doesn't exist. In the past, the difficulties have been compounded by confusion over just what risk is and how it can be measured. It seems that risk is generally best formalized as the whole distribution of outcomes, if only to ensure reliable estimation of expected values that are so central to most good analyses. Risk analysis in NRM has stumbled in the past because of difficulties in assessing and categorizing managers' attitudes to risk. While no easy solutions to these problems are offered in this chapter, it is argued that risk aversion may not be as important for many choices as is commonly believed. Moreover, as described above, there are some rough and ready ways to estimate a range of risk aversion likely to be relevant for a designated target group.

Some risk analyses that have been based on brave assumptions about the degree of risk aversion have overlooked aspects of the complexity in making the move from utility of wealth to utility of gains and losses or the utility of income. Moreover, very few such analyses have recognized that risk aversion for permanent income is likely to be much more important than is risk aversion for transitory income.

Risk analysis has also been avoided in the past because so many would-be analysts were afraid to tackle the evaluation of risky choices when too few hard data were available to work out the required probability distributions 'objectively'. Too many of those who braved the waters of risk analysis left untold or underemphasized the dubious relevance to the problem at hand of the data they used to represent uncertainty. It seems that the task of finding better ways to deduce the probability distributions that describe the risks that managers face has been relatively neglected by analysts.

Risk analysis is, and will remain, the art of the possible. But successful artistry needs to be founded on a good knowledge of principles and technique. Clearly there is much more work to be done, especially given the challenges inherent in the other topic areas of this volume. As Drèze observed in an address in 1970 about the state of formal analysis of economic decision problems under uncertainty then (and we think also still today): 'we are a long way from operational routines for a formal analysis … but the goal is in sight, and the task is challenging' (Drèze 1987, p. 417).

ACKNOWLEDGEMENTS

Without implicating him in remaining shortcomings, the authors are grateful to our friend Sushil Pandey, from the International Rice Research Institute (IRRI), Los Baños, Philippines, for interaction on earlier drafts.

NOTES

1. Depending on the decision context, the utility function might encode the DM's 'personal' preferences for personal outcomes or her/his 'corporate' preferences when acting in the capacity of manager of a business or other organizational entity.
2. We assume for simplicity that X is a single measure of worth, although some of what follows can be extended to cases where outcomes have multiple attributes.
3. The income stream may also include a terminal value of assets or could be extended to an infinite horizon, if appropriate, one or other of these usually being appropriate in social decision making.
4. The relationship is exact for the negative exponential utility function (with CARA) if the returns are normally distributed (Freund 1956). For other cases the approximation may be derived as a truncated Taylor series expansion omitting terms after the second. The omitted terms incorporate products of successive derivatives of the utility function and successively higher-order moments of the utility function.

REFERENCES

Anderson, J.R. (1989), 'Reconsiderations on risk deductions in public project appraisal', *Australian Journal of Agricultural Economics*, **28** (1), 1–14.

Anderson, J.R. (2001), 'Rural R&D technology policy', in P.G. Pardey (ed.), *The Future of Food: Biotechnology Markets and Policies in an International Setting*, Washington DC: International Food Policy Research Institute, pp. 293–7.

Anderson, J.R. (2003), 'Risk in rural development: challenges for managers and policy makers', *Agricultural Systems*, **75** (2–3), 161–97.

Anderson, J.R. and J.L. Dillon (1992), 'Risk analysis in dryland farming systems', Farming Systems Management Series No. 2, Food and Agricultural Organization, Rome.

Anderson, J.R., J.L. Dillon and J.B. Hardaker (1977), *Agricultural Decision Analysis*, Ames, IA: Iowa State University Press.

Arrow, K.J. (1965), *Aspects of the Theory of Risk-Bearing*, Helsinki: Yrjö Jahnssonin Säätiö, Academic Bookstore.

Bernoulli, D. (1738), 'Exposition of a new theory on the measurement of risk', English translation from the Latin by L. Sommer (1954), *Econometrica*, **12**, 23–36.

Chambers, R.G. and J. Quiggin (2000), *Uncertainty, Production, Choice, and Agency: The State-Contingent Approach*, Cambridge: Cambridge University Press.

Drèze, J.H. (1987), *Essays on Economic Decisions under Uncertainty*, Cambridge: Cambridge University Press.

Eeckhoudt, L. and C. Gollier (1996), *Risk: Evaluation, Management and Sharing*, Hemel Hempstead, UK: Harvester Wheatsheaf.

Fisher, A.C. (1981), *Resource and Environmental Economics*, Cambridge: Cambridge University Press.

Friedman, M. (1957), *A Theory of the Consumption Function*, Princeton, NJ: Princeton University Press.

Freund, R.J. (1956), 'The introduction of risk into a programming model', *Econometrica*, **24**, 253–61.

Hamal, K.B. and J.R. Anderson (1982), 'A note on decreasing absolute risk aversion among farmers in Nepal', *Australian Journal of Agricultural Economics*, **26** (3), 220–25.

Hardaker, J.B. (2000), 'Some issues in dealing with risk in agriculture', Working Paper Series in Agricultural and Resource Economics No. 2000-3, March, 18pp. Available at: http://www.une.edu.au/febl/EconStud/wps.htm.

Hardaker, J.B., R.B.M. Huirne and J.R. Anderson (1997), *Coping with Risk in Agriculture*, Wallingford, UK: CAB International.

Newbery, D.M.G. and J.E. Stiglitz (1981), *The Theory of Commodity Price Stabilization*, Oxford, UK: Clarendon Press.

Paarlberg, R.L. (2001), *The Politics of Precaution: Genetically Modified Crops in Developing Countries*, Baltimore, MD: Johns Hopkins University Press.

Pannell, D.J., B. Malcolm and R.J. Kingwell (2000), 'Are we risking too much? Perspectives on risk in farm modelling', *Agricultural Economics*, **23**, 69–78.

Perrings, C. (1991), 'Reserved rationality and the precautionary principle: technological change, time and uncertainty in environmental decision making', in R. Constanza (ed.), *Ecological Economics: The Science and Management of Sustainability*, New York: Columbia University Press, pp. 153–66.

Pratt, J.W. (1964), 'Risk aversion in the small and in the large', *Econometrica*, **32**, 122–36.

Rabin, M. (2000), 'Risk aversion and expected utility theory: a calibration theorem', *Econometrica*, **68**, 1281–92.

Rabin, M. and R.H. Thaler (2001), 'Anomalies: risk aversion', *Journal of Economic Perspectives*, **15**, 219–32.

Savage, L.J. (1954), *The Foundations of Statistics*, New York: Wiley.

11. Uncertainty Analysis in Integrated Assessment Models for Acidification

Silke Gabbert and Carolien Kroeze

1. INTRODUCTION

Integrated assessment models (IAMs) aim at providing tools to analyze complex real-world problems and to portray their social, economic, environmental and institutional dimensions. They may serve as an interface between science on the one hand, and the decision makers and stakeholders on the other. IAMs can have several functions. They can serve as early-warning systems, policy evaluation tools, and as tools for public decision making.

According to the multi-dimensionality of the problems addressed, IAMs are subject to various uncertainties due to, for example, variability of parameters, inaccuracy of model specification or lack of knowledge with regard to model boundaries. Although the existence of uncertainties has been recognized early in the process of developing IAMs, in many of them uncertainty analysis is included only partially or still not at all. This has caused increasing dissatisfaction both among scientists and policy makers. Furthermore, the comparability of studies dealing with uncertainty analysis in IAMs is complicated by terminological inconsistencies, in particular with regard to the typology of uncertainties used. Motivated by the awareness of the inadequacy of deterministic models for problems such as climate change or air pollution, and by the wish to improve confidence in model results it has repeatedly been pointed out that frameworks for a more systematic treatment of uncertainties in IAMs are necessary. Responding to this need, several approaches have been proposed during the past five years in order to fill this gap. Among these, the most important are developed by van der Sluijs (1997), van Asselt (2000) and van Aardenne (2002). However, each of these frameworks has been developed for and applied to a specific problem context. Given the heterogeneity of IAMs the question arises if, and to what extent, they can be generalized and applied to integrated assessment problems other than those for which they have been constructed.

The aim of this chapter is threefold. Our first objective is to conduct a comparative review of uncertainty analysis in IAMs. Second, we summarize the frameworks mentioned above for a more systematic uncertainty analysis in IAMs and critically discuss their strengths and weaknesses. Finally, we provide some general comments with regard to the applicability of these frameworks to IAMs for acidification from a research economics perspective. We argue that uncertainty analysis in IAMs should be done efficiently: since IAMs are usually complex models, the potential benefits of uncertainty analysis, for example, increased confidence in model results, have to be weighed against the costs of uncertainty analysis, arising mainly through increased research time needed. Thus, frameworks for uncertainty analysis in IAMs should allow for selecting most relevant uncertainties according to pre-defined criteria.

The chapter is organized as follows. In the following section, we present a classification of IAMs. In Section 3 we provide an overview of the past work on uncertainty analysis in IAMs for acidification. We also summarize different strands of critique with regard to the treatment of uncertainties in these IAMs. Section 4 surveys the frameworks proposed by van der Sluijs, van Asselt and van Aardenne. Section 5 concludes.

2. CLASSIFYING INTEGRATED ASSESSMENT MODELS

2.1 'Integrated Assessments' and 'Integrated Assessment Models'

At least a dozen different definitions or descriptions of 'integrated assessments' (IAs) have been published over the last decade. In fact, definitions are still under discussion and many different interpretations exist. Analyzing the literature, we must conclude that a commonly accepted definition for IA does not exist. However, several authors agree that it is important to distinguish between IA as a process, and IAMs as a tool in this process (Hordijk 1995; Timmerman and Munn 1997).

There seems to be general agreement that IA is aimed at serving (political) decision making (Hordijk 1995; Parson and Fisher-Vanden 1996; Schneider 1997; Rotmans 1998), and that it involves integration of knowledge from multiple scientific disciplines (Parson 1995; Rothman and Robinson 1997; Gough et al. 1998; Kolstad 1998; Rotmans and van Asselt 2001; Agrawala 2002). Several authors stress the importance of participatory approaches in which scientists, stakeholders and policy makers interact (for example, UNEP/SCOPE 1995; Parker et al. 2002; van der Sluijs 2002).

The development of IAMs has a history of more than three decades. Early IAMs were not specifically developed for environmental issues but focused on sustainable development and the interrelations between social, economic and physical components of the world system (Risbey et al. 1996; Timmerman and Munn 1997; Rotmans and van Asselt 2001).[1] During the 1970s, first models dealing with environmental issues such as energy consumption emerged in the United States. Among these, the National Coal Model (NCM) was one of the first IAMs addressing air pollution problems. As a result of the increasing international concern about air pollution, the next generation of IAMs developed in the 1980s had a clear focus on acidification. Prominent examples are the IA studies worked out within the National Acid Precipitation Assessment Program (NAPAP) in the United States and the Regional Acidification Information and Simulation model (RAINS) developed in 1983 by the International Institute for Applied Systems Analysis (IIASA) for Europe (Alcamo et al. 1990; Castells and Ravetz 2001).[2] In the late 1980s and early 1990s, climate change became an additional issue addressed by IAMs such as IMAGE (Rotmans 1990; Alcamo 1994). The most recent IAMs developed during the 1990s deal with sustainable management of global water resources, for example the AQUA model (Hoekstra 1998).[3]

IAMs make use of many different types of other models, which can be classified in different ways. According to the conceptual structure of the model, Parker et al. (2002) distinguish between (i) data models, (ii) qualitative conceptual models, (iii) quantitative numerical models that are formalizations of the conceptual models, (iv) mathematical methods and models to analyze the numeric models and their results, and (v) decision-making models that transform value and knowledge into actions. A specific IAM may include some or all of these types. Kann and Weyant (2000), on the contrary, focus on the objectives for which an IAM is used and distinguish between (i) policy evaluation models and (ii) optimization models. Whereas policy evaluation models aim at evaluating certain policy scenarios and are therefore very complex, the latter type of models concentrates on the optimization of key decision variables (cost minimization, welfare maximization). Since this requires large computational resources, the structure of optimization models is usually less detailed than that of policy evaluation models. Most IAMs usually combine quantitative and qualitative information. Nevertheless, their results are often based on qualitative descriptions of possible futures (storylines) (Alcamo 2001).

2.2 Characterizing Environmental IAMs

Environmental IAMs typically integrate information from different scientific disciplines, environmental compartments (water, air, soil) and economic sectors.[4] This allows for analyzing interrelations between the disciplines addressed, such as human activities, their environmental impact and policies to reduce these impacts. Environmental IAMs usually consist of different components modelling economic processes causing environmental damage (for example, the emission of acidifying substances or greenhouse gases), the dispersion and deposition of harmful substances, and potential environmental impacts (for example, exceedance of critical loads for acidification). Furthermore, most environmental IAMs also include components examining the costs of emission and/or deposition control and the benefits of control policies, expressed through avoided damage costs (see Table 11.1).

The purposes for which environmental IAMs can be used are threefold. First, the models can be used for scenario analysis, where model runs are performed for different combinations of assumptions and parameters. Another common way to use environmental IAMs is optimization analysis, where the models are used to analyze how certain environmental targets can be met at minimum cost.[5] Third, with environmental goals increasingly entering the policy agenda of governments during the past years, IAMs have become frameworks for evaluating policy strategies. By defining different scenarios for human activities, the models explore a variety of possible future developments, thus assisting decision makers in choosing between alternative strategies.

In general, a distinction can be made between deterministic and stochastic modelling approaches. Stochastic models explicitly account for uncertainties in model components, usually in terms of probability frequencies. However, the stochastic components were usually limited to a few parameters. The majority of environmental IAMs are deterministic, implicitly assuming that variables used to model a certain process are known with certainty. The uncertainties in deterministic models may be assessed by sensitivity analysis or quantitative uncertainty analysis for which different techniques are available.[6]

In this chapter, we focus on a specific subgroup of environmental IAMs, namely IAMs for acidification, for two reasons. First, IAMs for acidification belong to the 'early generation' of environmental IAMs. Second, this subgroup gained much more policy relevance than, for example, IAMs for climate change. Of some 60 existing environmental IAMs, about 20 models deal with acidification problems.[7] Among these, four particular models (two models for Europe, that is, ASAM and RAINS, and two for North America, that is, Canada IAM-RAISON and Ellis) have been used by policy makers and are still under development. These models are summarized in Table 11.1. In the table the models are characterized according to the regional domain, the model components selected, the methodology on which the model is based, the spatial and the temporal resolution of the model, and the area for which the model has been used in practice. They all include some kind of uncertainty analysis, which is explained in more detail in the following section (see Table 11.3, below). Of the models selected, only RAINS is used on a regular basis for policy purposes at present.

3. UNCERTAINTY ANALYSIS IN IAMS FOR ACIDIFICATION: AN OVERVIEW

According to Gardner et al. (1988) the usefulness of any given model depends on the accuracy and reliability of the prediction. Accuracy and reliability are dependent on knowledge, information on the process being studied and the translation of processes in mathematical formulation. Because of the complexity of IAMs for acidification the knowledge and information on the processes of concern is, in general, limited and to a large extent uncertain. In order to determine the usefulness of IAMs as assessment and decision-making tools, an analysis of these uncertainties is inevitable. Within this chapter, we define any method exploring the impact of input variance on variance in model output as uncertainty analysis. Thus, sensitivity analysis is explicitly included in methodologies used for uncertainty analysis.[8] In contrast to many scientists (see, for example, Morgan and Henrion 1990; Scott et al. 1999; Syri et al. 2000) we not only focus on quantitative methods but also include techniques for qualitative analysis in our definition (see Section 3.2 for further details).

Uncertainty analysis in IAMs has different objectives. First, uncertainties need to be identified in order to gain insight into the functioning of an IAM, its analytical potential and its boundaries. Second, once uncertainties have been identified, their impact on model output has to be examined. This allows for an evaluation of the quality of model results guiding further work to reduce uncertainty where possible and where most relevant. For those models used by policy makers, the impact of model uncertainties on the whole policy process has to be examined. Furthermore, uncertainty analysis can help to improve the decision-making process. This is the case if uncertainty analysis helps to determine most relevant uncertainties (according to predefined criteria), which is a key condition for deriving policy strategies.

Table 11.1 Overview of selected IAMs for acidification

Name	Developers	Model description
ASAM (Abatement Strategy Assessment Model)	Imperial College, UK	*Domain*: Europe *Model components*: S, A, E, C, B* *Method*: Scenario analysis, stepwise ranking of reduction strategies *Spatial resolution*: 150 × 150 km grid *Temporal resolution*: Simulation period 1980–2010, time steps of 10 years *Model use*: International negotiations on the Long Range Transboundary Air Pollution Convention (UN/ECE) *Uncertainty analysis*: Yes
Canada IAM-RAISON (Integrated Assessment Model – Regional Analysis by Intelligent Systems ON microcomputers)	Environment Canada	*Domain*: North America *Model components*: S, A, E, C* *Method*: Scenario analysis, Optimization analysis, decision theory *Spatial resolution*: 40 source regions, model output at various resolutions *Temporal resolution*: Simulation period 1980–post-2000 *Model use*: Environment Canada *Uncertainty analysis*: Yes

Name	Developers	Model description
Ellis	Johns Hopkins University, USA	*Domain*: Europe *Model components*: S, A, E, C* *Method*: Optimization analysis *Spatial resolution*: European countries (input), 150 × 150 km grid (output) *Temporal resolution*: Simulation period 1980–2030, time steps of 1 year *Model use*: US National Acid Precipitation Assessment Program *Uncertainty Analysis*: Yes
RAINS (Regional Acidification INformation System)	IIASA, Austria	*Domain*: Europe *Model components*: S, A, E, C* *Method*: Scenario analysis, Optimization analysis *Spatial resolution*: European countries (input), 150 × 150 km grid (output) *Temporal resolution*: Simulation period 1980–2030, time steps of 1 year *Model use*: For international negotiations on the Long Range Transboundary Air Pollution Convention (UN/ECE) and within the Clean Air for Europe (CAFÉ) programme of the European Union *Uncertainty analysis*: Yes

Notes: * S = Sources of emissions, A = Atmosphere, E = Environmental effects, C = Costs of control, B = Benefits (avoided damage costs).

Source: Modified from Hordijk and Kroeze (1997).

3.1 Classifying Uncertainties: The Problem of Terminological Consistency

To facilitate a systematic identification of uncertainties and to compare results of uncertainty analyses in IAMs for acidification, a consistent classification system is required. In the literature on IA modelling a large number of different typologies have been used in recent years. They can generally be divided into two groups. On the one hand, we find several examples where the classification of uncertainties directly refers to a specific problem of concern (Table 11.2). While in some studies the classifications proposed seem to be terminologically similar (compare, for example, Beck 1987; Alcamo and Bartnicki 1990), most of them show large differences with regard to the typologies used, which complicates their comparability considerably.

On the other hand, there have been attempts to generalize the classification of uncertainties by grouping them into 'types' or 'sources' and to further divide these classes into appropriate subcategories. However, for the purpose of uncertainty analysis such a categorization is only useful if the terminology is explicitly defined. A look into the literature using these categories reveals that this is far from being trivial. Only van Asselt (2000, p. 84) provides a definition of types and sources by denoting a 'source' to be the origin of uncertainty, whereas 'types' refer to 'the way in which uncertainty manifests in a particular context'.[9] Funtowicz and Ravetz (1990), for instance, give a similar description for types but do not clearly explain their understanding of sources.[10] Furthermore, the terms 'types' and 'sources' have sometimes been used interchangeably, denoting certain subcategories in one case as types of uncertainties and in the other as sources.[11]

Van der Sluijs (1995) first proposed a two-dimensional classification scheme consisting of both types and sources of uncertainties. He assumed that any type of uncertainty could be associated with different sources. Combining types with sources allows defining 'areas to be addressed in uncertainty management in IAMs' (van der Sluijs 1997, p. 205–6). In a modified form, such two-dimensional taxonomies have also been used by van Asselt (2000) and van Aardenne (2002). Again, the comparability of these three classification systems is complicated considerably by different specifications and delimitations of the subcategories used.[12]

Given our objectives, we need a classification system that allows in the first instance for identification of relevant types of uncertainties occurring in the models. One conclusion that can be drawn from the literature reviewed in this section is that uncertainty analysis in IAMs can refer to different aspects of the problem, that is, (i) technical model specification, (ii) model quality

Table 11.2 Problem-specific classification systems of uncertainties in IA modelling

Author	Topic of paper	Classification
Beck (1987)	Uncertainty in water quality modelling	Uncertainty about model structure Uncertainty about parameter values Uncertainty about the future behaviour of the system Uncertainty about the design of experiments
Alcamo and Bartnicki (1990)	Uncertainty of atmospheric source–receptor relationships	Transport wind uncertainty Meteorological uncertainty Parameter uncertainty Emissions uncertainty
Lam et al. (1996)	Acid rain assessment	Uncertainty about model input Uncertainty about model coefficients Uncertainty about model structures Uncertainty in observed data Uncertainties over model choice
Casman et al. (1999)	Uncertainty in complex policy models	Variability of parameters Lack of knowledge
Kann and Weyant (2000)	Uncertainty in large-scale energy/policy models	Uncertainty about model structure Parametric uncertainty Stochasticity Uncertainty about values
Aaheim and Bretteville (2001)	Climate policy	Parametric uncertainty Uncertainty about occurrence of a particular damage Uncertainty about estimated results of abatement efforts

and (iii) model boundaries. Based on these, we specify three types of uncertainties as follows:

1. Technical uncertainty:
   (a) uncertainty about quantification, including specification errors, aggregation errors, simplification and approximation errors, and
   (b) uncertainty about model form, addressing uncertainties about model structure and the choice of mathematical algorithms.
2. Model quality uncertainty, addressing the scientific quality of the parameters and the extent to which value-laden knowledge is used.
3. Ignorance, including all information that has not been included in the model, either because of lacking data or an incomplete understanding of the process of concern.

Note that this classification principally follows the one suggested by Funtowicz and Ravetz (1990) and used by van der Sluijs (1997). But also note that uncertainties subsumed particularly under the category 'model quality uncertainty' and 'ignorance' have been specified differently.[13]

3.2 Uncertainty Analysis in Policy-relevant IAMs for Acidification: The State of the Art

As indicated in Section 2.1, the group of IAMs for acidification comprises about 20 different models. Of these only a few, that is, two models for Europe and two for North America, have been used by policy makers and are still under development. The techniques used in each model for uncertainty analysis are listed in Table 11.3. Only Ellis developed a stochastic model, ASAM, IAM-RAISON, and RAINS are deterministic IAMs, where uncertainty analysis has been applied to the results of the modelling process.

However, using our classification scheme of uncertainties introduced in the previous section it turns out that in IAMs for acidification exclusively technical uncertainties have been addressed so far. Most of the studies were concerned with uncertainties about quantification, that is the assessment of uncertainties due to variability of specific parameters (analysis of individual uncertainties) or combinations of them (composite uncertainty analysis). Only in the model developed by Ellis (1990) and Watanabe and Ellis (1993, 1994), uncertainties about model form were addressed (see Table 11.3). Furthermore, we have to state that uncertainty analysis has been constrained to a few mathematical and numerical techniques such as sensitivity analysis, Monte Carlo simulation and stochastic programming. No analysis has been prepared addressing unreliability and ignorance in these models. There may be different reasons for this. First, quantitative methods are often still associated with producing 'objective' results, whereas judgements about model quality or about model boundaries are assumed to be highly value-laden. As van Asselt (2000) points out, this view ignores the fact that quantitative uncertainty analysis also includes many subjective judgements, for example with regard to how scientists design their analysis. Second, appropriate techniques to address ignorance, in particular, are still missing. And third, resulting from the first two reasons, uncertainties due to unreliability and ignorance might be more difficult to communicate than quantifiable uncertainties. However, despite these arguments that might explain the lack of analytical approaches, it remains surprising that the problem of tackling unreliability and ignorance within IAMs for acidification has not been addressed even verbally.

In recent years the lack of attention towards types of uncertainties other than technical uncertainty has repeatedly been criticized (Hordijk and Kroeze 1997; Cocks et al. 1998; Rotmans 1998). One of the key arguments raised is that quantitative methods for uncertainty analysis such as Monte Carlo techniques and sensitivity analyses capture only parts of a multidimensional problem. Thus, these techniques can provide only limited information about uncertainties in IAMs. Furthermore, quantitative techniques can be of limited applicability. For example, a Monte Carlo-based analysis of uncertainty for each input parameter in IAMs is often not possible because of constraints in time and computational resources (Kann and Weyant 2000). This holds particularly for optimization models, which tend to be computationally more demanding than policy evaluation models. In order to conduct such analysis, a number of assumptions, for example with regard to the distribution of parameters, have to be made which can introduce additional uncertainties. Looking at the studies mentioned in Table 11.3 (see above) the choice of a certain methodology for uncertainty analysis is often poorly motivated. For instance Suutari et al. (2001) estimated coefficients of variation for individual model parameters within the RAINS model. They considered previous attempts to assess uncertainty in RAINS 'to provide only partial answers' to uncertainty. However, it remains unclear what comparative advantages their method has in comparison to the previous ones.

Summing up, we conclude that uncertainties not only have been insufficiently addressed in the past but it also seems that existing work on this topic has been conducted unsystematically. Given the fact that uncertainty has become a key issue in IAMs, the development of a framework for a more systematic and comprehensive analysis of uncertainty is necessary. In recent years, different attempts have been made in order to respond to this need. The approaches developed will be discussed in the following section.

Table 11.3 Methods used for uncertainty analysis in selected IAMs for acidification

Model acronym	Method used	Objective of analysis
	Stochastic models	
Ellis[a]	• Two-stage stochastic programming • Chance-constrained stochastic programming	Assessment of model robustness with regard to uncertainty in transport prediction of pollutants
	Deterministic models	
ASAM[b]	• Sensitivity analysis	Assessment of model robustness with regard to uncertainties in data on critical loads, meteorological data and cost curves
IAM-Raison[c]	• Monte Carlo analysis	Estimation of parameter distributions for regionalization of data sets
	• Sensitivity analysis	Analysis of influence of parameter variability on Monte Carlo analysis results
	• Bayesian probability calculus	Uncertainty propagation from input sources, spatial interpolation and intervariable processes to selected receptor sites

RAINS[d]	• Sensitivity analysis	Assessment of the influence of parameter variability on cost calculation and emission ceilings
	• Monte Carlo simulation	Identification of most influential parameters for pH variability
	• Stochastic simulation	Assessment of uncertainty in source–receptor combinations for sulphur
		Analysis of probability of critical loads exceedance due to uncertain emissions, atmospheric transport and critical loads
	• Stochastic programming	Determination of effective solutions for SO_2 emission reduction under cost uncertainty
	• Error propagation	Analysis of variability of specific model terms

Notes:

a. Cf. Ellis (1990); Watanabe and Ellis (1993, 1994).

b. Cf. ApSimon et al. (1994); Warren and ApSimon (1999).

c. Cf. Lam et al. (1989, 1996, 1998).

d. Cf. Alcamo and Bartnicki (1990); Hettelingh (1990); Altman et al. (1996); Bak and Tybrik (1998); Syri et al. (2000); Suutari et al. (2001).

4. TOWARDS IMPROVING UNCERTAINTY ANALYSIS IN IAMS

Recognizing the limited knowledge about uncertainties in IAMs on the one hand and the growing importance of uncertainty analysis for evaluating the practical usefulness of these models on the other, several suggestions have been made in recent years about how to deal with uncertainties in a more systematic and comprehensive way. They are based on the assumption that knowledge about uncertainties in IAMs is a goal of its own, independent of the objectives for which this knowledge is used. Thus, it is argued that uncertainty analysis should be endogenized into the IA modelling process in order to identify uncertainties as completely as possible. These are:

1. a framework for uncertainty management based on the NUSAP method,[14] developed by van der Sluijs (1997),
2. the 'Pluralistic fRamework for Integrated uncertainty Management and risk Analysis' (PRIMA), developed by van Asselt (2000), and
3. the 'FRamework for the Assessment of Uncertainties in Large-scale Emission INventories' (FRAULEIN), developed by van Aardenne (2002).

A common element of these studies is that they are based on a two-dimensional classification system of uncertainties. However, the studies differ with respect to the definition of subcategories (see Section 3.1) and the objectives stated for uncertainty assessment, resulting in different approaches to reach these objectives.

Van der Sluijs's aim is to provide tools for a systematic assessment of uncertainties in IAMs of anthropogenic climate change. By combining the sources and types of uncertainty he defines different areas for uncertainty assessment (van der Sluijs 1995 and 1997). Looking at the tools that have in fact been applied for uncertainty analysis in IAMs, he concludes that research activities have concentrated mainly on uncertainty due to inexactness in input data and model parameters whereas all the other areas have received much less attention so far (van der Sluijs 1997). In order to reduce this mismatch, van der Sluijs states that uncertainty assessment should be embedded in a more comprehensive analysis of the quality of model output. For this purpose he applied the NUSAP method developed by Funtowicz and Ravetz (1990).

The core element of the NUSAP method is to assess the quality of any model parameter by means of a diagnostic diagram. This allows a certain quality level (ranging from poor to high) to be assigned to each model parameter (see Figure 11.1). The quality level depends on the parameter's relative contribution to the spread in model output (Y-axis score, determined by means of sensitivity and Monte Carlo analysis) and its strength, that is, its qualitative underpinning (X-axis score). The latter can be obtained by asking experts in a panel to attach scores to defined evaluation criteria of model parameters. For each parameter, the scores obtained are then summarized in a so-called 'pedigree matrix', from which finally its overall average strength can be derived by applying certain aggregation procedures.[15] For the construction of a diagnostic diagram, van der Sluijs (1997) has developed a 10-step iterative framework. The procedure starts with the selection of experts to form a panel. Further steps include the selection of model constituents and the choice of appropriate evaluation criteria. As a final step, the Y- and X-axis scores obtained for each parameter are mapped in the

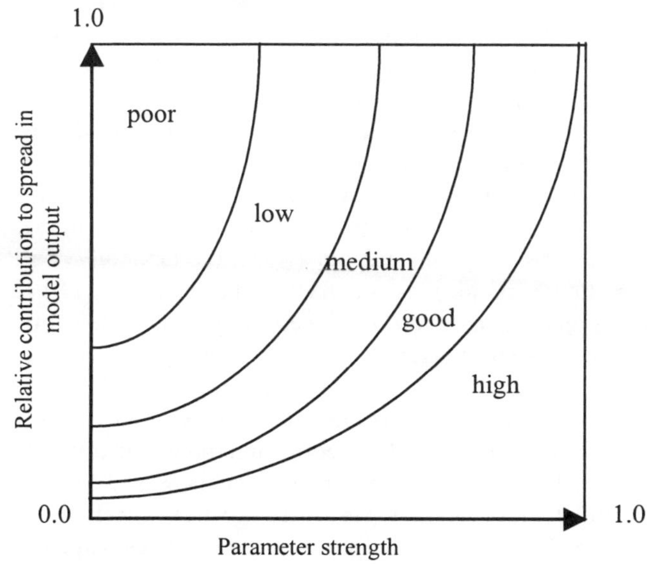

Source: Funtowicz and Ravetz 1990.

Figure 11.1 Diagnostic diagram to assess the quality of a model parameter

diagnostic diagram. Apart from evaluating overall model performance, the framework also allows for an identification of the most uncertain parts in an IAM which should therefore be given priority when examining possibilities for model improvements. It is also assumed to be a useful tool in order to distinguish between solvable and unsolvable uncertainties. With some modifications the NUSAP method has been applied to identify and assess key uncertainties in the so-called TARGETS-IMAGE Energy Regional (TIMER) model, which is part of the IMAGE model, an IAM for analyzing climate change (van der Sluijs et al. 2002).[16] In another application NUSAP was used for the assessment of the quality and uncertainty of volatile organic compounds emission figures (van der Sluijs et al. 2001).

Rotmans and van Asselt (2001) argue similarly to van der Sluijs that uncertainty analysis in IA modelling has failed to cover the whole range of uncertainties. Since research has been focusing mainly on technical uncertainties, no methods have been developed for examining certain aspects of variability (for example, technological surprise) and uncertainties in model structure. Furthermore, the use of qualitative methods for uncertainty analysis has largely been neglected. Thus, methods currently available provide only very limited knowledge about uncertainty in IAMs and even ignore those which the authors consider to be most fundamental. Given the multidimensionality of uncertainties they propose a 'Pluralistic fRamework for Integrated uncertainty Management and risk Analysis' (PRIMA). PRIMA is defined as 'a participatory assessment process in which the salient uncertainties are interpreted according to different perspectives and structured into multiple risk judgements in such a way that robust insights can be deducted' (van Asselt 2000, p. 228). The objective of PRIMA is to provide tools that allow for an examination of uncertainties from a number of different directions. Thus, the authors assume the flexibility of PRIMA with respect to future projections of IAMs, the focus of PRIMA on key uncertainties and the inclusion of formerly neglected uncertainties to be the main comparative advantages of this approach (Rotmans and van Asselt 2001).

The choice of key uncertainties in IAMs depends on the view from which the world (including nature and society) is interpreted (that is, the choice of a 'perspective'). Based on Cultural Theory, Rotmans and van Asselt (2001) suggest using four different types of perspective (hierarchist, egalitarian, individualist and fatalist). The selection of uncertainties will differ according to the choice of one of these perspectives. The next step within the PRIMA framework is to specify 'model routes', that is, to create model formulations for each of these perspectives and the perspective-based selection of uncertainties (van Asselt and Rotmans 1996). Experimenting with the model routes is assumed to lead to multiple model scenarios, which can then be assessed by, for example, comparing them with previous IAM results. In order to test the PRIMA framework in a practical context, the implementation of perspectives has first been applied to the TARGETS model (Rotmans et al. 1994; van Asselt and Rotmans 2002).[17] A later study has examined how uncertainties were treated in the 'Environmental Outlooks', a scientific series published by the National Institute of Public Health and the Environment in the Netherlands (RIVM). In addition, the first two steps of PRIMA (definition of a 'perspective on pluralism' and definition of a 'perspective on uncertainties') have been applied in a RIVM workgroup (van Asselt 2000).

The third framework to be discussed has been developed by van Aardenne (2002). In contrast to van der Sluijs and van Asselt, he focuses on a very specific topic, that is, uncertainties in large-scale emission inventories. Such inventories provide information about the quantities of certain pollutants emitted into the atmosphere. They are used both as instruments for monitoring progress of environmental policies as well as inputs into atmospheric dispersion models, which themselves are part of several IAMs for air pollution (for example, the RAINS model). In emission inventories, uncertainties can arise because of inaccurate representation of 'true' emissions of pollutants. The reason for this is that emissions usually cannot be measured at each individual source but have to be quantified or even estimated at higher aggregation levels. Uncertainties in emission inventories can also arise because of lack of knowledge of the degree to which the inventory is meeting user-specific quality criteria. This is called 'unreliability' (van Aardenne 2002). Inaccuracy and unreliability of emission inventories depend on each other in the sense that lack of reliability can be caused by inaccuracy.

Based on this typology, the aim of van Aardenne's study is to develop an approach for systematically assessing uncertainties in emission inventories in order to evaluate potential improvements with respect to reliability and accuracy. This includes first identifying sources of inaccuracy and unreliability. The sources of unreliability depend on the specific quality criteria set by the users of emission inventories. Since they can differ across inventories they have to be identified for each inventory. Sources of inaccuracy, on the contrary, can be generalized better and grouped into structural inaccuracy and input value inaccuracy.

The FRAULEIN framework suggested by van Aardenne to assess the different sources of uncertainties consists of two paths. Path A focuses on the analysis of uncertainties due to unreliability which checks whether or not the quality criteria specified for a certain inventory have in fact been met. Path B refers to the analysis of uncertainties due to inaccuracy. Here, van Aardenne presents an overview of tools available for external (that is, by using other independent information) and internal assessment of uncertainties. For the latter a large number of techniques is available ranging from qualitative discussion and expert judgement to error propagation (including, for example, Monte Carlo analysis). In contrast to NUSAP and PRIMA, the FRAULEIN approach includes a complete overview of the tools and techniques available for the analysis of uncertainties. Based on the purpose of the uncertainty analysis at stake, researchers may select one or more of these tools to analyze uncertainties in emission inventories. It should be noted that FRAULEIN does not indicate priorities within the group of methodologies described for uncertainty analysis. So far, FRAULEIN has not been applied in practical contexts.

5. CONCLUSIONS AND DISCUSSION OF NEEDS FOR FURTHER RESEARCH

The treatment of uncertainty in IAMs has gained increasing attention during the past years. Motivated by dissatisfaction concerning the way uncertainties have been addressed in IAMs, substantial progress has been made in developing frameworks in order to identify and analyze uncertainties more systematically. Looking at the frameworks proposed, we can conclude the following.

The three approaches described in the previous section have been developed from different research perspectives. NUSAP and PRIMA both have a philosophical foundation, which van der Sluijs (1997) describes as 'post-normal science'. The main characteristics of this way of doing research are the multi-perspectivity of approaches used, the treatment of uncertainties as endogenous elements and the involvement of stakeholders at any level of the analysis. In contrast to this, van Aardenne's work focuses exclusively on the technical and statistical dimension of uncertainty assessment.

According to the research perspectives taken, the (expected) outcomes of the frameworks differ considerably: the framework suggested by van der Sluijs allows for a *quality assessment* of model parameters. The aim is to identify most uncertain parameters and to set priorities among them guiding further work for improving the model of concern. PRIMA focuses on uncertainty *management* rather than assessment. The main innovative element is to filter key uncertainties according to an initial choice of a 'perspective' on uncertainties. Given the selection of uncertainties a range of different model outcomes can be produced, which have then to be further interpreted and analyzed. Van Aardenne systematizes the range of possibilities for uncertainty analysis in emission inventories. This can facilitate the *choice* of an appropriate methodology for uncertainty analysis, given an initial decision on what type and source of uncertainty should be examined.

NUSAP and FRAULEIN have been developed for specific problem contexts (IA of anthropogenic climate change and large-scale emission inventories, respectively). PRIMA does not explicitly focus on a certain type of IA activity, but its application in IAMs has so far been confined to those of global change and sustainable development (TARGETS). We can therefore conclude that an approach for the type of IAMs we are focusing on in this chapter, that is, policy-relevant IAMs for acidification, still does not exist.

However, the NUSAP and the PRIMA approaches, in particular, are not restricted to the problem context for which they have been initially developed and applied. On the contrary, the authors underline the general usefulness of their frameworks for any type of IA problem (van Asselt 2000; van der Sluijs et al. 2001; van Asselt and Rotmans 2002). Although FRAULEIN is explicitly focused on emission inventories, the structure of this approach might also be transferable to other IA problems. It is therefore worth discussing if, and to what extent, these frameworks could be applied to IAMs of acidification. Here we would like to stimulate the discussion about uncertainty analysis in IAMs through the following principal considerations.

The key motivation for the design of IAMs of acidification such as RAINS, ASAM and CASM (Coordinated Abatement Strategy Model) was to provide scientific backing to the political negotiation process for emission reduction under the Convention on Long Range Transboundary Air Pollution (CLRTAP).[18] One of the main functions of such models is, therefore, to provide decision support to policy makers in order to identify the 'best' abatement strategy subject to, for example, national budget constraints. Thus, making uncertainty analysis an integral part of such models requires policy makers to participate in this process. The need for a better involvement of policy actors in the design and use of IAMs has repeatedly been pointed out in the literature (Schneider 1997). One way of doing this is to make policy makers become integrated assessors by asking them to express their preferences for uncertainty analysis in IAMs.[19] Among the frameworks for uncertainty analysis considered in this chapter, NUSAP and PRIMA implicitly account for this need. However, looking at the case studies where these approaches have been applied, policy makers have in fact not been included in the analysis. Since FRAULEIN is designed as a purely technical approach, it does not consider the inclusion of stakeholders.

The IAMs for acidification shown in Table 11.1, above, are fairly complex models. Uncertainty analysis can help to improve the quality of and the confidence in the models, but these benefits have to be weighed against the costs of uncertainty analysis, arising mainly through increased research time needed. Thus, uncertainty analysis has clear economic dimensions. We therefore propose to focus attention on the question how uncertainty analysis can be done efficiently. In this context none of the three approaches described seems to be directly applicable. Van der Sluijs and van Asselt explicitly mention the high requirement of time for application as one of the main shortcomings of their approaches (van der Sluijs et al. 2001; van Asselt

2000). Looking at NUSAP, particularly the assessment of parameter strength is very time-consuming because it is the part of the scheme that is less computerized. In the case of applying NUSAP to the IMAGE/TIMER model it turned out that parameter strength could only be assessed for selected parameters in order to keep the whole process manageable (van der Sluijs et al. 2002). Applying PRIMA to IAMs for acidification would mean defining for each uncertain parameter (and for each combination of uncertain parameters) different values and computing the model for each of these specifications. Bearing in mind that of the models mentioned in Table 11.1 many (for example, the RAINS model) include several hundreds of parameters, this procedure can easily create work for years. Such an approach might be very informative, but it is questionable whether it is in fact supportive for decision-making purposes. Similar doubts can be stated with regard to FRAULEIN: since IAMs for acidification are much more complex than emission inventories, a complete statistical analysis of uncertainties in IAMs based on the methodologies suggested by van Aardenne would prove immensely time-consuming.

Because of the resource constraints explained above, one of the main challenges for an efficient uncertainty analysis in IAMs for acidification is to define reasonable criteria in order to select the most relevant (types and sources of) uncertainties. NUSAP and PRIMA both suggest methodologies of how this problem can be solved. Within PRIMA, the selection of uncertainties depends on the initial choice of a perspective on uncertainty. However, it remains unclear how priorities among uncertainties chosen within a given perspective can be set. By means of the diagnostic diagram, the NUSAP approach provides – at least for uncertainties in model parameters – a clear guidance for prioritization of uncertainties: the parameters shown in a diagnostic diagram cannot only be ranked according to their quality, it is also possible to identify which quality aspect of a parameter has to be improved in order to strengthen its overall quality. The FRAULEIN approach, on the contrary, is not intended to give a solution. Before this framework can be used, the analyst has to decide what type of uncertainty (unreliability or inaccuracy) should be examined. Given this decision, the further selection of methodologies depends in turn on the judgement of the analyst. Thus, listing methodologies available for the analysis of different types of uncertainties, FRAULEIN addresses the analytical step following the selection of uncertainties.

From a research economics perspective (costs and benefits of uncertainty analysis in IAMs) the NUSAP approach seems to be the most promising since it allows for the inclusion of stakeholders and attempts a prioritization of parameters. We regard both aspects to be essential requirements for a more systematic analysis of uncertainty in IAMs for acidification and for improving their practical usefulness.

ACKNOWLEDGEMENTS

Comments from two anonymous referees and the editors are gratefully acknowledged.

NOTES

1. An example for these early IAMs is the 'limits to growth' model developed in 1972.The model tried to capture the impact of population growth and the resulting increasing consumption and resource depletion on human well-being.
2. For a detailed review of IAMs about acidification, see Hordijk and Kroeze (1997) and Hordijk et al. (1999).
3. AQUA is not an acronym but the name for a modelling framework for an integrated analysis of hydrology, water quality, water demand and water supply in relation to land use changes, soil degradation, element cycles and climate change, as well as in relation to food and energy supply, human development and economics. AQUA is part of the more extensive integrated assessment model TARGETS (Tool to Assess Regional and Global Environmental and health Targets for Sustainability) developed by RIVM.
4 For instance, most IAMs for acidification model emissions, atmospheric transport as well as environmental impact (Hordijk and Kroeze 1997).
5. For instance, the RAINS model is used to calculate the national emission reductions needed to realize predefined environmental targets in the most cost-effective way (Alcamo et al. 1990).
6. There may be several reasons for IAMs to be largely deterministic. The most important is probably that most IAMs are too complex to include a lot of stochasticity. Another reason may be that not all users of the models are interested in the uncertainties involved.
7. See Hordijk and Kroeze (1997) for a review of IAMs for acid rain. In their overview they include only models that cover at least three of the following five components (i) sources of emissions, (ii) atmospheric transport and transformations, (iii) environmental effects, (iv) abatement and mitigation options and (v) monetary evaluation.
8. Kleijnen (1994, p. 322) defines sensitivity analysis as 'the systematic investigation of the reaction of model outputs to extreme values of the model inputs and to drastic changes of the model structure'. Uncertainty analysis, on the contrary, is characterized as a method where 'model inputs are sampled from certain distributions, to quantify the consequences of the uncertainties in the model inputs for the model outputs. In the empirical literature, however, there is often no clear distinction between sensitivity and uncertainty analysis (Hettelingh 1990).
9. According to van Asselt (2000), a classification of uncertainties into sources should be universally valid, whereas types of uncertainties always refer to a specific context or method.
10. A 'type' denotes a certain sort of uncertainty within a model. The authors suggest further dividing the types of uncertainties into inexactness, unreliability and bordering on ignorance, the last denoting any information about the process of concern, which is not known at a certain point in time and therefore not included in the model.

11. Alcamo and Bartnicki (1987), for example, refer to 'model structure' as a type of uncertainty, whereas van der Sluijs (1997) and Syri et al. (2000) call it a source of uncertainty.
12. For example, 'inexactness' as a type of uncertainty proposed by van der Sluijs (1997) explicitly includes technical and conceptual model structure, which is referred to as a separate type ('methodological uncertainty') in van Asselt (2000).
13. For example, we argue that model confidence is a technical matter and should therefore be subsumed under category (a) instead of (b) as in van der Sluijs (1997). Furthermore, in our understanding 'ignorance' should include not only the information that model builders are in fact not aware of when developing their model, but also knowledge that could not be included because of missing or insufficient data.
14. Assuming that uncertainty in quantitative information is mainly a matter of its quality, NUSAP is considered a notational scheme for assessing the quality of scientific information. The NUSAP system consists of five different assessment categories, that is: (i) Numeral (denoting ordinary numbers, intervals or finite sets of integers), (ii) Unit (for example kilograms or dollars), (iii) Spread (expressing the inexactness of scientific information in a traditional statistical way, for example via sensitivity analysis), (iv) Assessment (referring to qualitative aspects of scientific information, for example through significance or confidence levels or simply the qualitative judgements such as 'optimistic' or 'pessimistic'), and (v) Pedigree (denoting the mode of production of the information, usually by means of a matrix) (Ravetz and Funtowicz 2002).
15. It would be beyond the scope of this chapter to describe the aggregation process in detail. For further information about this, see, for example, van der Sluijs et al. (2002).
16. The IMAGE model (Integrated Model to Assess the Global Environment) has been developed by the National Institute of Public Health and the Environment (RIVM, the Netherlands). The model has mainly been used for the development of emission scenarios for policy decision making, for example within the Intergovernmental Panel on Climate Change (IPCC) (van der Sluijs 2002).
17. The TARGETS model (Tool to Assess Regional and Global Environmental and health Targets) is an IAM focusing on global change and sustainable development. It has also been developed by RIVM.
18. The CLRTAP was signed in 1979 in Geneva by 34 governments and the European Community.
19. One step in this direction is a study conducted by Gough (1999) where representatives from several Directorates of the European Commission were interviewed. One of the results stated is that the most frequently noted uncertainties recognized by policy makers are lack of data, lack of knowledge regarding cause–effect links in IAMs, and institutional uncertainties (incomplete or inappropriate understanding of the institutional context in which a policy will be applied).

REFERENCES

Aaheim, H.A. and C. Bretteville (2001), 'Decision-making frameworks for climate policy under uncertainty', CICERO Working Paper 2001:2, Centre for International Climate Research (CICERO), Oslo, Norway.

Agrawala, S. (2002), 'Use of integrated assessment models in policy making', available at http://sedac.ciesin.org/mva/MVAUG/ugpolicy.html (accessed February 2002).

Alcamo, J. (1994), *IMAGE 2.0: Integrated Modeling of Global Climate Change*, Dordrecht: Kluwer Academic Publishers.

Alcamo, J. (2001), 'Scenarios as tools for international environmental assessments', Environmental Issue Report No. 24, European Environmental Agency, Copenhagen, Denmark.

Alcamo, J. and J. Bartnicki (1987), 'A framework for error analysis of a long-range transport model with emphasis on parameter uncertainty', *Atmospheric Environment*, **21** (10), 2121–31.

Alcamo, J. and J. Bartnicki (1990), 'The uncertainty of atmospheric source–receptor relationships in Europe', *Atmospheric Environment*, **24A**, 2169–89.

Alcamo, J., R. Shaw and L. Hordijk (1990), *The Rains Model of Acidification. Science and Strategies in Europe*, Dordrecht: Kluwer Academic Publishers.

Altman, A., M. Amann, G. Klaassen, A. Ruszcynski and W. Schoepp (1996), 'Cost-effective sulphur emission reduction under uncertainty', *European Journal of Operational Research*, **90**, 395–412.

ApSimon, H.M., R.F. Warren and J.J.N. Wilson (1994), 'The Abatement Strategies Assessment Model – ASAM: applications to reductions of sulphur dioxide emissions across Europe', *Atmospheric Environment*, **28** (4), 649–63.

Bak, J. and K. Tybrik (1998), 'The EU acidification strategy: sensitivity of calculated emission ceilings for nitrogen and sulphur for Denmark', *Environmental Pollution*, **102** (S1), 625–33.

Beck, M.B. (1987), 'Water quality modeling: a review of the analysis of uncertainty', *Water Resources Research*, **23** (8), 1393–442.

Casman, E.A., M.G. Morgan and H. Dowlatabadi (1999), 'Mixed levels of uncertainty in complex policy models', *Risk Analysis*, **19** (1), 33–42.

Castells, N. and J. Ravetz (2001), 'Science and policy in international environmental agreements. Lessons from the European experience on transboundary air pollution', *International Environmental Agreements: Politics, Law and Economics*, **1**, 405–25.

Cocks, A.T., I.R. Rodgers, R.A. Skeffington and A.H. Webb (1998), 'The limitations of integrated assessment modelling in developing air pollution control policies', *Environmental Pollution*, **102** (S1), 635–9.

Ellis, J.H. (1990), 'Integrating multiple-long-range transport models into optimisation methodologies for acid rain policy analysis', *European Journal of Operational Research*, **46**, 313–21.

Funtowicz, S.O. and J.R. Ravetz (1990), *Uncertainty and Quality in Science for Policy*, Dordrecht: Kluwer Academic Publishers.

Gardner, R.H., V.H. Dale and R.V. O'Neill (1988), 'Error propagation and uncertainty in process modelling', *Proceedings of Conference on Forest Growth: Process Modelling of Response to Environmental Stress*, Gulf Shores conference, 19–22 April 1988, Auburn University, AL: Timber Press.

Gough, C.A. (1999), 'Quality and practice in integrated assessment: some users' perspective', *International Journal of Environment and Pollution*, **11** (4), 462–78.

Gough, C.A., N. Castells and S.O. Funtowicz (1998), 'Integrated assessment: an emerging methodology for complex issues', *Environmental Modelling and Assessment*, **3**, 19–29.

Hettelingh, J.-P. (1990), *Uncertainty in Modeling Regional Environmental Systems: The generalization of a watershed acidification model for predicting broad scale effects*, RR-90-3, Laxenburg: International Institute for Applied Systems Analysis.

Hoekstra, A.Y. (1998), *Perspectives on Water. An Integrated Model-based Exploration of the Future*, Utrecht: International Books.

Hordijk, L. (1995), 'Integrated assessment models as a basis for air pollution negotiations', *Water, Air and Soil Pollution*, **85**, 249–60.

Hordijk, L. and C. Kroeze (1997), 'Integrated assessment models for acid rain', *European Journal of Operational Research*, **102**, 405–17.

Hordijk, L., J. van Aardenne and C. Kroeze (1999), 'Integrated assessment models and uncertainty analysis', Paper presented at the European Forum on Integrated Environmental Assessment (EFIEA) Workshop on Uncertainty, Baden, Austria, 10–18 July 1999.

Kann, A. and J.P. Weyant (2000), 'Approaches for performing uncertainty analysis in large-scale energy/economic policy models', *Environmental Modeling and Assessment*, **5**, 29–46.

Kleijnen, J.P. (1994), 'Sensitivity analysis versus uncertainty analysis: When to use what?', in J. Grasman and G. van Straten (eds), *Predictability and Nonlinear Modelling in Natural Sciences and Economics*, Dordrecht: Kluwer Academic Publishers, pp. 322–33.

Kolstad, C.D. (1998), 'Integrated assessment modeling of climate change', in W.D. Nordhaus (ed.), *Economics and Policy Issues in Climate Change*, Washington DC: Resources for the Future, pp. 263–86.

Lam, D.C.L., G. Howell, D.A. Swayne, A.S. Fraser, J. Storey and I. Wong (1989), 'A knowledge-based approach to regional acidification modelling: a case study of New Brunswick, Canada', in J. Kaemaeri, D.F. Brakke and A. Jenkins (eds), *Regional Acidification Models: Geographic Extent and Time Development*, Berlin: Springer-Verlag, pp. 213–25.

Lam, D.C.L., K.J. Puckett, I. Wong, M.D. Moran, G. Fenech, D.S. Jeffries, M.P. Olson, D.M. Whelpdale, D. McNicol, Y.K.G. Miriam and C.K. Minns (1996), 'An integrated acid rain assessment model for Canada using the RAISON for Windows System', Paper presented at the ASAAQ Conference 1996, Seattle.

Lam, D.C.L., K.J. Puckett, I. Wong, M.D. Moran, G. Fenech, D.S. Jeffries, M.P. Olson, D.M. Whelpdale, D. McNicol, Y.K.G. Miriam and C.K. Minns (1998), 'An integrated acid rain assessment model for Canada: from source emission to ecological impact', *Water Quality Resources Journal Canada*, **33** (1), 1–17.

Morgan, M.G. and M. Henrion (1990), *Uncertainty – A Guide to Dealing with Uncertainty in Quantitative Risk and Policy Analysis*, Cambridge: Cambridge University Press.

Parker, P., R. Letcher, A. Jakeman, M.B. Beck, G. Harris, R.M. Argent, M. Hare, C. Pahl-Wostl, A. Voinov, M. Janssen, P. Sullivan, M. Scoccimaro, A. Friend, M. Sonnenshein, D. Barker, L. Metejicek, D. Odulaja, P. Deadman, K. Lim, G. Laroque, P. Tarikhi, C. Fletcher, A. Put, T. Maxwell, A. Charles, H. Breeze, N. Nakatani, S. Mudgal, W. Naito, O. Osidele, I. Eriksson, U. Kautsky, E. Kautsky, B. Naeslund, L. Kumblad, R. Park, S. Maltagliati, P. Giradin, A. Rizzoli, D. Mauriello, R. Hoch, D. Pelletier, J. Reilly, R. Olafsdottir and S. Bin (2002), 'Progress in integrated assessment and modelling', *Environmental Modelling & Software*, **17**, 209-217.

Parson, E.E. (1995), 'Integrated assessment and environmental policy making: in pursuit of usefulness', *Energy Policy*, **23** (4/5), 463–75.

Parson, E.E. and K. Fisher-Vanden (1996), 'In search of integrated assessment – thematic guide to integrated assessment modeling', available at http://sedac.ciesin.org/mva/iamcc.tg/insearchof.html (accessed June 2002).

Ravetz, J. and S.O. Funtowicz (2002), 'NUSAP: The management of uncertainty and quality in quantitative information', available at http://www.nusap.net/sections.php?op=viewarticle&artid=14 (accessed September 2002).

Risbey, J., M. Kandlikar and A. Patwardhan (1996), 'Assessing integrated assessments', *Climatic Change*, **34**, 369–95.

Rothman, D.S. and J.B. Robinson (1997), 'Growing pains: a conceptual framework for considering integrated assessments', *Environmental Modelling and Assessment*, **46**, 23–43.

Rotmans, J. (1990), *IMAGE: An Integrated Model to Assess the Greenhouse Effect*, Dordrecht: Kluwer Academic Publishers.

Rotmans, J. (1998), 'Methods for IA: the challenges and the opportunities ahead', *Environmental Modelling and Assessment*, **3**, 155–79.

Rotmans, J. and M.B.A. van Asselt (2001), 'Uncertainty in assessment modelling: a labyrinthic path', *Integrated Assessment*, **2**, 34–55.

Rotmans, J., M.B.A. van Asselt, A.J. de Bruin, M.G.J. den Elzen, J. de Greef, H. Hilderink, A.Y. Hoekstra, M.A. Janssen, H.W. Koester, W.J.M. Martens, L.W. Niesse and H.J.M. de Vries (1994), *Global Change and Sustainable Development – a modelling perspective for the next decade*, GLOBO Report Series No. 4, RIVM, Bilthoven.

Schneider, S.H. (1997), 'Integrated assessment modeling of global climate change: transparent rational tool for policy making or opaque screen hiding value-laden assumptions?', *Environmental Modelling and Assessment*, **2**, 229–49.

Scott, M.J., R.D. Sands, J. Edmonds, A.M. Liebetreu and D.W. Engel (1999), 'Uncertainty in integrated assessment models: modeling with MiniCAM 1.0', *Energy Policy*, **27**, 855–79.

Suutari, R., M. Amann, J. Cofalfa, Z. Klimont, M. Posch and W. Schoepp (2001), *From Economic Activities to Ecosystem Protection in Europe. An Uncertainty Analysis of Two Scenarios of the RAINS Integrated Assessment Model*, CIAMS/CCE Report 1/2001, International Institute for Applied Systems Analysis, Laxenburg, Austria.

Syri, S., R. Suutari and M. Posch (2000), 'From emissions in Europe to critical load exceedances in Finland – uncertainty analysis of acidification integrated assessment', *Environmental Science and Policy*, **3**, 263–76.

Timmerman, P. and R.E. Munn (1997), 'The tiger in the dining room: designing and evaluating integrated assessments of atmospheric change', *Environmental Monitoring and Assessment*, **46**, 45–58.

UNEP/SCOPE (1995), 'Panatal Regional Workshop: Project on Integrated Adaptive Ecological/Economic Modelling and Assessment', Draft Report.

van Aardenne, J.A. (2002), *Uncertainties in Emission Inventories*, The Hague: CIF-Gegevens Koninklijke Bibliotheek.

van Asselt, M.B.A. (2000), *Perspectives on Uncertainty and Risk. The PRIMA Approach to Decision Support*, Boston: Kluwer Academic Publishers.

van Asselt, M.B.A. and J. Rotmans (1996), 'Uncertainty in perspective', *Global Environmental Change*, **6** (2), 121–57.

van Asselt, M.B.A and J. Rotmans (2002), 'Uncertainty in integrated assessment modelling', *Climatic Change*, **54**, 75–105.

van der Sluijs, J.P. (1995), 'Integrated assessment models and the management of uncertainties', WP-96-119, Laxenburg: International Institute for Applied Systems Analysis.

van der Sluijs, J.P. (1997), *Anchoring Amid Uncertainty. On the Management of Uncertainties in Risk Assessment of Anthropogenic Climate Change*, The Hague: CIF-Gegevens Koninklijke Bibliotheek.
van der Sluijs, J.P. (2002), 'A way out of the credibility crisis of models used in integrated environmental assessment', *Futures*, **34** (1), 133–46.
van der Sluijs, J.P., J. Potting, J. Risbey, D. van Vuuren, B. de Vries, A. Beusen, P. Heuberger, S.C. Quintana, S.O. Funtowicz, P. Kloprogge, D. Nuijen, A. Petersen and J. Ravetz (2002), *Uncertainty Assessment of the IMAGE/TIMER B1 CO2 Emission Scenario, Using the NUSAP Method*, Report no. 410 200 104 (2002), Dutch National Research Programme on Global Air Pollution and Climate Change.
van der Sluijs, J.P., J.S. Risbey and J. Ravetz (2001), *Uncertainty Assessment of VOC Emissions from Paint in the Netherlands*, Copernicus Institute for Sustainable Development and Innovation, Department of Science Technology and Society, Utrecht University, the Netherlands.
Warren, R.F. and H.M. ApSimon (1999), 'Uncertainties in integrated assessment modelling of abatement strategies: illustration with the ASAM model', *Environmental Science and Policy*, **2**, 439–56.
Watanabe, T. and J.H. Ellis (1993), 'Robustness in stochastic programming models', *Applied Mathematical Modelling*, **17**, 547–54.
Watanabe, T. and J.H. Ellis (1994), 'A joint chance-constrained programming model with row dependence', *European Journal of Operational Research*, **77**, 325–43.

PART III

Impact on Private Sector Response

12. Stochastic Dominance Portfolio Analysis of Forestry Assets

Veli-Pekka Heikkinen and Timo Kuosmanen

1. INTRODUCTION

During recent decades there has been increasing research interest in forestry decision making under risk. A frequent approach is to consider forest as one investment alternative among other assets in a financial portfolio, the primary source of risk being the fluctuations in the stumpage prices (for example, Thomson 1991; and Reeves and Haight 2000). This perspective allows forest owners to hedge the uncertain logging income by diversifying a proportion of their wealth to other assets such as financial assets traded in the stock market. Conventional tool for portfolio choice is the classic Mean-Variance (MV) model by Markowitz (1952). The MV model requires the asset returns to be normally distributed or the decision maker's utility function to be of quadratic form. In many circumstances, however, these assumptions appear to be questionable, not least in the case of forestry and other natural resource assets. For example, there is empirical evidence that forestry returns (first differences of log prices) are not normally distributed (Toppinen and Toivonen 1998; Heikkinen and Kanto 2000).

When the assumptions of MV do not hold, Stochastic Dominance (SD) efficiency criteria offer the most immediate extension (see, for example, Bawa 1982; or Levy 1992 for a survey of SD). SD accounts for the entire probability distribution and applies for the general classes of non-satiated and/or risk-averse preference functions. In the SD approach, the question is whether the current forest stands form an efficient portfolio strategy *as such*, or should some of them be harvested to generate logging income which can be invested in the stock markets? It is a well-known fact that decision makers' utility functions are not easy to specify. Decision makers are often not willing or able to answer precise questions regarding their preferences. The SD approach involves only minimal assumptions concerning decision makers' preferences. The second-order SD (SSD) only assumes that the decision maker is risk averse and non-satiated. These assumptions usually hold for the majority of the decision makers.

While it is relatively simple to identify the MV-efficient set of portfolios, until now there has been no method for testing whether a given portfolio is SD efficient or not, let alone for computing all SD-efficient portfolios (that is, the SD-efficient set). This also explains why theoretically appealing SD criteria are so rarely employed in finance and related fields. The recent work of Kuosmanen (2001, 2002) and the subsequent developments by Post (2001) have eliminated this handicap of SD. It turns out that the SD-efficient set exhibits a relatively simple polyhedral structure, which can be analyzed by standard techniques and algorithms. In fact, one can test for SD efficiency by solving a simple Linear Programming problem, while MV analysis requires more complex Quadratic Programming.

This chapter considers the forest owner's portfolio problem from the SD perspective. Focusing on the short-term forest management by means of harvesting, we show how the SD approach can be adapted and applied in this area, and discuss the strengths and weaknesses of that approach compared to alternative tools. To this end, we re-examine the forest portfolio problem of Heikkinen (1999) from the SD perspective.[1] The main empirical question concerns the influence of the side-constraints on the portfolio efficiency in terms of the more general SD criteria. Furthermore, results of the MV model are compared with and contrasted to the results of two alternative SD approaches.

The rest of the chapter is structured as follows. Section 2 introduces the forest owner's portfolio problem and motivates the use of the SD approach. Section 3 briefly reviews the diversification analysis proposed by Kuosmanen (2001, 2002) and the two alternative test procedures. This is followed by a description of the empirical forest management problem and the data set. In Section 4, the SD method is applied to the present data, and the results are discussed. The concluding section suggests some interesting routes for future research.

2. HARVESTING DECISION AS A PORTFOLIO STRATEGY

Consider the following forest owner's short-term portfolio problem outlined by Heikkinen (1999). Suppose the wealth of the forest owner consists mainly of a forest estate, including different-aged growing timber stock. Forest management is implemented at the level of forest stands, which are defined according to geographic location. Each stand is assumed to have a unique mixture of timber species and assortments, as well as physical growth, and hence the stands are managed as independent assets. Suppose further the rotation interval of the forest (according to the Faustmann rule) is relatively long (as in the case of boreal forests), and the stumpage prices are highly volatile over time.

Each period, a number of stands mature and become liquid assets. Mature stands can be harvested, and the logging income can be invested in new assets such as equities traded in the stock market or new timber stock. Harvesting immature stands is not allowed.[2] The land owner's investment problem is to reallocate his or her liquid timber assets in the most productive way. Two basic short-term strategies are considered, which both involve risk. The first is to harvest the timber immediately, and invest the logging income in equities traded in the stock market. The second alternative is to postpone harvesting to the next period. If harvesting is postponed, the timber stock yields additional physical growth, which is considered to be deterministic. Postponing the harvest also has an option value as the stumpage prices may increase in the future.[3] It also involves an opportunity cost: if cuttings are implemented at the beginning of the planning period, some rate of return for the next tree generation is generated during the planning period. If cuttings are not implemented, this return naturally does not exist. According to Heikkinen (1999), the rate of return on the next tree generation is so minimal that it can be ignored in a short-run model of long rotation forests assumed in the present study.[4]

Besides the two pure strategies discussed above, a full continuum of 'mixed' diversified strategies is considered. Since we focus on timber harvesting, the liquid timber asset can be considered perfectly divisible. For example, it is possible to harvest $100 \cdot b$ per cent ($0 \leq b \leq 1$) of the liquid timber and invest it in the stock market, and hedge the risk by leaving the remaining $100 \cdot (1 - b)$ percent of timber to be harvested in the future. Moreover, the risk profile of the total portfolio can be influenced by targeting fellings in specific stands. In other words, it is not necessary to harvest all stands to the same degree. However, attention is restricted to final felling in the sense that it is not possible (or cost effective) to the target harvest to specific species within any given stand to change the composition (and hence the risk profile) of the stand. By this simplification, the historical rates of return of each forest stand can be computed as the physical growth plus the change in the stumpage price index (calculated for each forest stand separately, taking into account the composition of timber species and thickness).

In the setting outlined above, the forest owner's short-term portfolio problem can be formally presented as the following optimization problem

$$\max_{\lambda \geq 0} \left\{ E\left[u(\underline{\rho})\right] \middle| \underline{\rho} = \sum_{i=1}^{N} \lambda_i \underline{r}_i ; \sum_{i=1}^{N} \lambda_i = 1; \underline{r}_i \sim \Upsilon_i \right\} \tag{12.1}$$

where u, is the Von Neumann–Morgenstern utility function of the forest owner, $\underline{\rho}$ is the rate of return of the portfolio, $\underline{r}_i$ is the (risky) rate of return from asset i, $\lambda = (\lambda_1 ... \lambda_N) \geq 0$ is the vector of portfolio weights, and Υ_i is the associated probability distribution. The investment universe consists of N assets, which include all harvestable forest stands (as separate assets) together with alternative investment opportunities such as stocks and bonds.

The portfolio weights λ associated with forest stands can be interpreted as the proportion of timber stock in the stand to be held in the portfolio during the planning period. Let λ^0 denote the present portfolio weights. The optimal solution $\lambda_i^* = \lambda_i^0$ for stand i means that harvesting should be postponed at least until the next period, $\lambda_i^* < \lambda_i^0$ means that $100 \cdot \lambda_i^* / \lambda_i^0$ per cent of stand i should be harvested, whereas $\lambda_i^* > \lambda_i^0$ implies new growing timber stock should be purchased which is similar in species and assortment to that of stand i. If acquiring new growing stock of desired quality is not possible in the short run (that is, only harvesting is being considered, as is often the case), problem (12.1) should be refined by adding a side-constraint $\lambda_i \leq \lambda_i^0$ for portfolio weights, so the decision problem becomes

$$\max_{\lambda \geq 0} \left\{ E\left[u(\underline{\rho})\right] \middle| \underline{\rho} = \sum_{i=1}^{N} \lambda_i \underline{r}_i ; \sum_{i=1}^{N} \lambda_i = 1; \lambda \leq \lambda^0; \underline{r}_i \sim \Upsilon_i \right\} \tag{12.2}$$

Problem (12.1) will henceforth be referred to as the 'unconstrained case' and problem (12.2) represents the 'constrained case'.

Finding a unique numerical solution to these portfolio problems requires knowledge of the utility function u and the probability distribution functions Υ_i for each asset i. Needless to say, this information is typically not available. The classic approach to portfolio choice solves this problem by identifying an entire range of *efficient portfolios*, which can be viewed as possible candidate solutions for all risk-averse and non-satiated investors (with $u' \geq 0, u'' \leq 0$) (for example, Dybvig and Ross 1982). By limiting the number of alternatives, the efficient set can help the forest owner to solve his/her portfolio choice problem. It can also provide the researchers with insight on how a rational forest owner would behave.

However, the unknown probability distributions Υ_i have to be estimated from the empirical data (typically historical time series). Hence, a finite (and therefore discrete) sample of observed rates of return of the N assets from T time periods indexed as $\nu \equiv \{1,2,...,N\}$ and $\tau \equiv \{1,2,...,T\}$ is assumed. This gives a panel data of observed historical rates of return representable in the form of matrix $R \equiv (r_1 ... r_N)^T$ with $r_j \equiv (r_{j1} ... r_{jT})$.

To estimate the distribution, it is assumed that all elements of r_j are drawn from the same distribution Υ_j. The MV approach makes a simplifying assumption that the distributions Υ_i belong to the family of normal (that is, Gaussian) distributions.[5] In principle, normality is an empirically testable hypothesis, but most studies impose it as a maintained assumption. If the normality hypothesis fails to hold, then there is no guarantee that the optimal solution to (12.1) or (12.2) is found in the MV-efficient set, and hence a more general approach is needed.

Instead of characterizing the distribution functions by means of the first two moments (that is, mean and variance), we can make use of all the information available in the historical time series. The *empirical distribution function* (EDF), defined as:

$$\hat{\Upsilon}_i(x) \equiv card\{t \in \tau | x \geq r_{it}\}/T, \tag{12.3}$$

is an unbiased, minimum-variance estimator of the unknown distribution function Υ_i. Characterizing the efficient set of portfolios using the EDF (12.3) instead of the MV calibrated normal distributions is called the second-order Stochastic Dominance (SSD) approach (see, for example, Bawa 1982; or Levy 1992). Unfortunately, characterizing the SSD-efficient set, or even determining whether some given portfolio is efficient, has been an unsolved problem. Only very recently, Kuosmanen (2001) derived the explicit characterizations of the SSD dominating sets for an arbitrary evaluated portfolio y_0, the results of which are next briefly reviewed.

3. EMPIRICAL SSD EFFICIENCY TESTS

The standard definition of SSD can be expressed in terms of EDFs as follows: portfolio j dominates portfolio k by *SSD* (denoted henceforth as $r_j D_2 r_k$) if and only if:

$$\int_{-\infty}^{x}\left[\hat{\Upsilon}_k(t)-\hat{\Upsilon}_j(t)\right]dt \geq 0 \quad \forall x \in \mathbb{R} \text{ and}$$

$$\int_{-\infty}^{x}\left[\hat{\Upsilon}_k(t)-\hat{\Upsilon}_j(t)\right]dt > 0 \text{ for some } x \in \mathbb{R}. \tag{12.4}$$

Assuming away shortsales, the set of feasible portfolios can be characterized in terms of weights as $\Lambda \equiv \left\{\lambda \in \mathbb{R}_+^N \middle| \sum_{i=1}^{N} \lambda_i = 1\right\}$, or in terms of state-specific return vectors as $\Psi \equiv \left\{r \in \mathbb{R}^T \middle| r = \lambda R; \lambda \in \Lambda\right\}$. Focusing on the portfolio set Ψ, SD efficiency is characterized by the following definitions. Consider portfolios j and k: $r_k \in \Psi$. Portfolio k is *SSD efficient* in Ψ, if and only if $r_j D_2 r_k \Rightarrow r_j \notin \Psi$, otherwise k is SSD inefficient. The set $\Delta(r_0) \equiv \left\{r \in \mathbb{R}^T \middle| r D_2 r_0\right\}$, is called the SSD *dominating set of* the evaluated portfolio r_0. It follows directly from these definitions that portfolio r_0 is SSD efficient if and only if the dominating set of r_0 does not include any feasible portfolio, that is $\Psi \cap \Delta(r_0) = \varnothing$. As an immediate corollary, if the dominating set can be identified, the SD efficiency of the portfolio can be tested by checking whether the intersection of the dominating set and the portfolio set is empty. This is the key to the tests that follow.

Matrix $W = \left[W_{ij}\right]_{T \times T}$ is called *doubly stochastic* if its elements are non-negative real numbers and all its rows and columns sum up to unity. Formally, the set of doubly stochastic matrices is henceforth denoted by

$$\Xi \equiv \left\{\left[W_{ij}\right]_{T\times T} \middle| 0 \leq W_{ij} \leq 1; \sum_{i=1}^{T} W_{ij} = \sum_{j=1}^{T} W_{ij} = 1 \ \forall i, j \in \tau\right\}.$$

Note that the set of *permutation matrices*:

$$\Pi \equiv \left\{\left[P_{ij}\right]_{T\times T} \middle| P_{ij} \in \{0,1\}; \sum_{i=1}^{T} P_{ij} = \sum_{j=1}^{T} P_{ij} = 1 \ \forall i, j \in \tau\right\}$$

is a subset of Ξ, but the converse is not true. Utilizing the theorem of doubly stochastic matrices by Hardy et al. (1934), Kuosmanen (2001, 2002) derived the following analytical characterization of the dominating set:

$$\Delta(r_0) = \left\{ r \in \mathbb{R}^T \middle| \exists W \in \Xi : r \geq r_0 W; r \neq r_0 P \ \forall P \in \Pi \right\}. \tag{12.5}$$

This set is closed, monotonous, and symmetric with respect to the diagonal ray of risk-free assets. In addition, it is a convex set, which is very convenient from the operational point of view.

The SD efficiency of any given portfolio y_0 can be tested by checking whether the dominating set Δ and the portfolio set Ψ share common portfolios, in other words, whether any dominating portfolio is feasible. Thus, consider the test statistic $\theta_2^n(r_0)$ obtained as the optimal solution to the following Linear Programming (LP) problem.[6]

$$\theta_2^n(r_0) = \max_{\lambda^0, W} \left(\sum_{t=1}^{T} \sum_{i=1}^{N+1} R_{it}^0 \lambda_i^0 - \sum_{t=1}^{T} r_{0t} \right) / T \tag{12.6}$$

s.t.

$$\sum_{i=1}^{N+1} R_{ti}^0 \lambda_i^0 \geq \sum_{j=1}^{T} W_{tj} r_{0j} \quad \forall t \in \tau$$

$$\sum_{i=1}^{T} W_{ij} = \sum_{j=1}^{T} W_{ij} = 1 \ \forall i, j \in \tau$$

$$\sum_{k=1}^{N+1} \lambda_k^0 = 1$$

$$W_{ij}, \lambda_k^0 \geq 0 \ \forall i, j \in \tau, k \in \nu$$

where $R^0 = \begin{pmatrix} r_0 & R \end{pmatrix}^T$ and $\lambda^0 = \begin{pmatrix} \lambda_0 & \lambda \end{pmatrix}^T$. Since all elements of r_0 and R^0 are assumed to be finite numbers, the optimal solution to (12.6) always exists.

The test statistic θ_2^n has a natural interpretation as the 'inefficiency premium' of the evaluated portfolio: $\theta_2^n(r_0)$ indicates the difference of the mean return between the evaluated portfolio and the dominating portfolio with the highest mean return. In other words, even a most risk-averse investor could gain at least $\theta_2^n(r_0)$ by following the portfolio strategy $\lambda^* \equiv \arg\max \theta_2^n(r_0)$, which does not involve more risk compared to the present situation. Intuitively, the objective function maximizes the inefficiency premium, while the first constraint guarantees SSD dominance. The remaining constraints simply ensure that W is a doubly stochastic matrix and λ is a vector of portfolio weights of the benchmark portfolio.

Following Kuosmanen (2002), $\theta_2^n(r_0) = 0$ is a necessary condition for SSD efficiency of portfolio r_0. However, $\theta_2^n(r_0) = 0$ is not yet a sufficient condition. In particular, it is easy to verify that any equal-mean portfolio r_0W, $W \in \Xi - \Pi$ dominates the original portfolio y_0 by SSD but the previous test cannot identify that. To test whether any of those dominating portfolios might be feasible, the following test statistic can be calculated:

$$\theta_2^s(r_0) = \min_{W,\lambda^0,s^+,s^-} \sum_{j=1}^{T}\sum_{i=1}^{T}(s_{ij}^+ + s_{ij}^-) \tag{12.7}$$

s.t.

$$\sum_{i=1}^{N+1} R_{ti}^0 \lambda_i^0 = \sum_{j=1}^{T} W_{tj} r_{0j} \ \forall t \in \tau$$

$$\sum_{i=1}^{T} W_{ij} = \sum_{j=1}^{T} W_{ij} = 1 \ \forall i, j \in \tau$$

$$W_{ij} = \tfrac{1}{2} + s_{ij}^+ - s_{ij}^-$$

$$\sum_{k=1}^{N+1} \lambda_k^0 = 1$$

$$W_{ij}, s_{ij}^+, s_{ij}^-, \lambda_k^0 \geq 0 \ \forall i, j \in \tau, k \in \nu.$$

This test essentially checks whether it is possible to find a portfolio r_0W, $W \in \Xi - \Pi$. If such a portfolio is feasible, it dominates r_0. Variables s_{ij}^+, s_{ij}^- are here used analogous to the 'slack' variables of the additive Data Envelopment Analysis model of Charnes et al. (1985). Utilizing both test statistics, we have a necessary and sufficient condition for SSD efficiency of portfolio y_0 as $\theta_2^n(r_0) = 0$ and $\theta_2^s(r_0) = T^2/2$.

There is also a more straightforward way of testing SSD efficiency, which utilizes results of Dybvig and Ross (1982). Consider the following alternative test statistic:

$$\widehat{\theta}_2(r_0) = \max_{w} \sum_{t=1}^{T} r_{t0} w_t \tag{12.8}$$

s.t.

$$\sum_{t=1}^{T} R_{tj} w_t \leq 1 \ \forall j \in N$$

$$w_t < w_s \ \forall t, s \in \tau : r_{t0} > r_{s0}$$
$$w_t > 0 \ \forall t \in \tau.$$

This offers an alternative necessary and sufficient condition for SSD efficiency as $\widehat{\theta}_2(r_0) \geq 1$.

The test statistic $\widehat{\theta}_2$ is in all essential parts identical to that proposed by Post (2001), derived from the Expected Utility interpretation of SSD. The only difference of problem (12.8) compared to Post's original formulation is that (12.8) imposes two strict inequality constraints, while Post uses weak inequalities. In the present framework, the strict inequalities are required for a genuine necessary and sufficient test, to take into account the fact that portfolio $r_0 W$, $W \in \Xi - \Pi$, is generally 'less risky' than the original portfolio r_0. The basic LP algorithms do not allow for strict inequalities. Still, the standard trick may be employed, thereby using an arbitrarily small sensitivity parameter ε to convert the strict inequalities into the standard LP form:

$$\begin{aligned} &w_l \leq w_k + \varepsilon \ \forall l, k \in \tau : r_{0l} > r_{0k} \\ &w \geq \varepsilon \cdot 1^T \end{aligned} \qquad (12.9)$$

Replacing the strict inequality constraints of (12.8) with constraints (12.9) enables derivation of a necessary and sufficient test as the limiting case $\varepsilon \to 0$. For any real-valued $\varepsilon > 0$, a *sufficient* test results: $\theta_2(r_0) \geq 1$ implies efficiency, but $\theta_2(r_0) < 1$ does not imply inefficiency. For $\varepsilon = 0$, however, there is a *necessary* test: $\theta_2(r_0) \geq 1$ does not verify efficiency, but $\theta_2(r_0) < 1$ does confirm inefficiency. To obtain a necessary and sufficient efficiency diagnosis, a pair of test statistics can be solved with $\varepsilon = 0$ and some small $\varepsilon > 0$, to check whether the conclusions are mutually consistent. If not, the value of the sensitivity parameter ε can be decreased for the sufficiency test until diagnoses become unisonous, or until the test is declared inconclusive.

The infinitesimally thin line between the efficient and the inefficient sets highlights a possible disadvantage of the test statistic (12.8): if r_0 is efficient, a long (potentially infinite) series of iterations may be required to find sufficiently small $\varepsilon > 0$ that confirms efficiency. On the other hand, the advantage of the latter test is its simplicity: problem (12.6) involves $3T^2 + N$ variables in contrast to the T variables of problem (12.6), and hence the latter can be solved much faster. While the computation time of (12.6) is measured in minutes or hours depending on the data size, the time of solving problem (12.8) is measured in seconds. (See Table 12.4 below for evidence.) However, there are some attractive features in the computationally more demanding test statistic θ_2^n which deserve consideration. First, the test statistic itself has an intuitive interpretation as a cardinal 'inefficiency' measure, which allows for comparing the inefficiency premiums of various inefficient portfolios, for example. By contrast, Post's test statistic is merely an arbitrary dummy. Second, in case of inefficiency diagnosis, the optimal solution to (12.6) always identifies a dominating portfolio as a benchmark, while (12.8) does not. This feature may have significance in portfolio management applications. Third, perhaps most importantly, in (12.6) additional constraints can be imposed on the feasible set of portfolio weights λ. This is not possible in formulation (12.8). This proves a pivotal advantage for the Kuosmanen approach in the forest management application to follow.

4. APPLICATION

This section re-examines the harvesting problem of a real forest holding in Eastern Finland which has been earlier studied in the MV framework by Heikkinen (1999, 2003). In this case, final felling is allowed in only four forest stands, aged between 70 and 90 years. Therefore, only the timber stock on those specific four stands can be considered as liquid assets. Table 12.1 presents descriptive statistics concerning timber species and assortments, growth, monetary value, weight in the original portfolio, and land area of the four stands considered. Two stands consisted mainly of spruce sawlogs and pulpwood, the other two mainly of pine sawlogs and pulpwood. The annual growth of stands varied between 3.2 and 4.1 per cent. The total timber volume of these four stands was 628 m^3 and their value was € 18,210, at December 1996 prices.

For simplicity, the general stock market index of the Helsinki Stock Exchange (HEX) represents equities as an alternative investment possibility. The monthly arithmetic averages of the daily closing values of HEX were calculated to make data comparable to stumpage prices, which are reported on a monthly basis. Historical data range from October 1985 to December 1996. During this period, the Helsinki stock market offered a mean return of 16 per cent, with a standard deviation of 21 per cent. The forest stands offered a much more modest growth, with a mean return of approximately 6 per cent.[7] On the other hand, the growth was also more stable: The standard deviation of the rates of return varied approximately between 7 and 10 per cent for all four forest stands. (For more detailed statistics and discussion, see Heikkinen 1999.)

Table 12.1 Characteristics of the four harvestable stands

	Stand #162	Stand #163	Stand #165	Stand #173	Total	Prices € /m^3 1996:12
Pine sawlogs (m^3)		16	17			41.73
Spruce sawlogs (m^3)	67	1		267		34.66
Birch sawlogs						16.50
Pine pulpwood (m^3)		9	16			20.82
Spruce pulpwood (m^3)	25	2		191		41.53
Birch pulpwood (m^3)		3	14			15.84
Total (m^3)	92	31	47	485	628	
Growth (%)	3.20	4.10	4.10	3.70		
Value (€)	2,843	940	1,195	13,232	18,210	
Portfolio weight (%)	0.16	0.05	0.07	0.72		
Area (ha)	0.70	0.50	0.60	2.20	4	
Mean return (%)	5.56	5.51	5.81	6.01		
Std deviation (%)	6.74	8.48	9.82	7.08		

Most earlier studies applying portfolio optimization techniques have simply assumed that forest stands can be traded like financial assets. Heikkinen (1999) was the first to explicitly model the constraints for acquiring additional timber stock with desired characteristics (compare the unconstrained model (12.1) and the constrained model (12.2)). Given the original portfolio weights $\lambda_{162} = 0.16$, $\lambda_{163} = 0.05$, $\lambda_{165} = 0.07$, $\lambda_{173} = 0.73$, and $\lambda_{HEX} = 0.00$, Heikkinen imposed the linear constraints $\lambda_{162} \le 0.16$, $\lambda_{163} \le 0.05, \lambda_{165} \le 0.07$, $\lambda_{173} \le 0.73$ in the standard MV quadratic optimization problem to rule out purchases of additional timber stock. This specifies the model to be a pure harvesting model. This is especially relevant in the present Finnish case, where the timber is a reasonably liquid asset, whereas the forest land is not. Interestingly, the constraints did not make any significant difference to the efficient portfolio strategies or efficiency status of the original portfolio. The purpose of the present application is to re-examine this result without imposing the normality assumption underlying the MV model.

As the first step, the normality assumption required by MV was tested to check whether the MV approach would suffice or whether there is indeed a case for SD analysis. There are several statistical tests for testing normality hypotheses, including corrected Kolmogorov–Smirnov tests, the Anderson–Darling test, and the chi-squared test. Since there are no a priori hypotheses of the mean and the variance of the theoretical distribution, the most basic test procedures do not apply. We therefore employed the Shapiro–Wilks W-test, a standard approach that has performed well in comparisons (for example, Royston 1992). Table 12.2 reports the results.

Table 12.2 Shapiro–Wilks normality test statistics and the associated significance levels (n = 135)

	HEX	Stand #162	Stand #163	Stand #165	Stand #173
Test statistic	0.792	0.862	0.82	0.902	0.793
p-value	< 0.0001	< 0.0001	< 0.0001	< 0.0001	< 0.0001

The interpretation of the W-tests is clear: in all cases of all assets the null hypothesis of normality is rejected at the 99 per cent significance level or higher. By visual inspection, all five assets appear to follow a bell-shaped distribution, symmetric around the mean. Normality is violated mainly because of the high kurtosis, not because of any notable skewness. Figure 12.1 illustrates how the cumulative return distribution of Stand #165 deviates from the CDF of a normal distribution with the equal mean and variance levels.

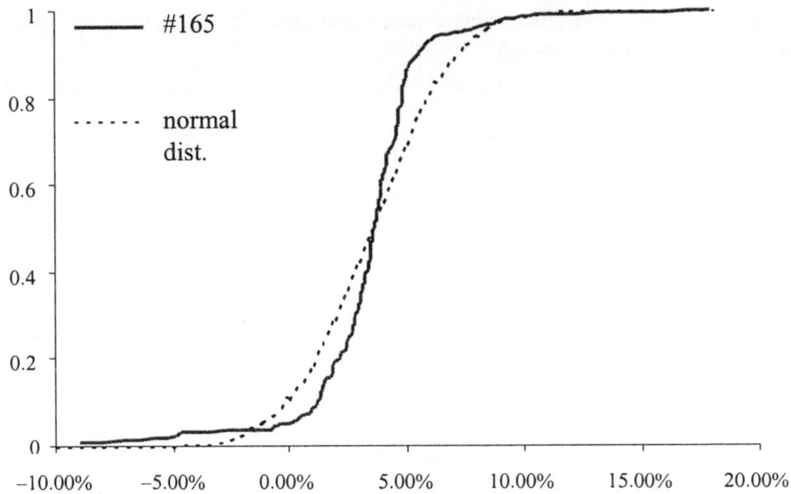

Figure 12.1 *Cumulative return distribution of Stand #165 (solid curve), compared to the normal distribution with the equal mean and variance (dashed curve)*

The SSD tests were next applied to the data described above to investigate the influence of the purchasing constraints on SSD efficiency. The GAMS software, powered by the CONOPT2 solver and a 1.7 GHz processor with 256 MB of physical memory, was used for solving the test statistics θ_2^n, θ_2^s, and $\widehat{\theta}_2$ for the original portfolio $\lambda_{162} = 0.16$, $\lambda_{163} = 0.05$, $\lambda_{165} = 0.07$, $\lambda_{173} = 0.73$, and $\lambda_{HEX} = 0.00$. Table 12.3 reports the values of the test statistics.

Table 12.3 *SSD efficiency test statistics*

	θ_2^n	θ_2^s	$\widehat{\theta}_2$
Unconstrained case	0.0008	–	0.4920
Constrained case	0.0000	8978.00	n.a.

In the unconstrained case, both the Kuosmanen and the Post approaches diagnose the present forest portfolio as inefficient. The Kuosmanen statistic reveals that the mean return could be increased only by the minimal 0.08 percentage points without altering the risk profile. The Post statistic confirms the inefficiency diagnosis, but does not provide any additional information.

(As the necessary condition was already violated, the sufficient θ_2^s statistic was omitted as meaningless.)

The optimal solution of (12.6) involves the optimal weights: $\lambda_{162}^* = 0.906$ and $\lambda_{HEX}^* = 0.094$. That is, the maximum rate of return with the current risk profile would be obtained by harvesting all other stands, but acquiring almost equal amounts of additional timber stock similar to Stand #162. That is, mature spruce forest with over 70 per cent of the timber suitable for sawlogs. In this respect, the result is well in line with the recent trends in forestry practices in Finland. In the short run, however, this would require trading the forest land. Moreover, it is highly unlikely that the present land ownership could be instantaneously traded for large areas of old spruce forests. The result supports our view that additional constraints are needed for making the model realistic enough for short-run planning. It should be further noted that the expected gains of 0.08 percentage points are very minimal. This should be balanced against the transaction costs of making radical changes of the investment strategy, the environmental and the aesthetic losses due to increased homogeneity of the tree species, which have not been duly accounted for in the present analysis.

Consider next the constrained case (pure harvesting case) where increasing the timber stock is not allowed in the short run. As discussed above, additional constraints on the portfolio weights cannot be incorporated into Post's approach, so the Kuosmanen tests are the only alternative. Interestingly, the original portfolio turns out to be efficient if the buying constraint is imposed. That is, the current forest portfolio is the optimal, expected utility-maximizing choice for at least some non-satiated risk-averse investors. In other words, the observed portfolio choice can be rationalized applying the SSD criteria when the action is restricted to timber harvesting only. Of course, this does not imply that the risk profile of the current portfolio optimally matches the preferences of the forest owner. It merely underlines that it is not possible to find a preferable alternative portfolio without learning more about the forest owner's preferences.

These results are now compared with those of Heikkinen's MV analysis. The MV approach minimizes the variance of the portfolio, given an exogenously specified target mean return. From the scenarios considered by Heikkinen, the case of 6 per cent mean return target is closest to the original mean return of 5.9 per cent. In the unconstrained case, the MV approach also finds the original portfolio inefficient. Interestingly, the efficient portfolio also involved a similar buying and harvesting strategy, concentrating as much as 43.5 per cent of the total wealth in the forest similar to Stand #162. The MV analysis indicated that the optimal diversification strategy would decrease the portfolio variance by roughly 5.9 per cent.

In the constrained case, the SD and MV approaches yielded different qualitative results. While the original portfolio was diagnosed to be efficient under SD criteria, the MV criteria suggest inefficiency. However, the MV efficient benchmark portfolio at the target mean return of 6 per cent does not deviate substantially from the original forest portfolio. In fact, only 2 per cent of the total wealth is reallocated from the timber assets to the stock market. This would yield a rather marginal 1.8 per cent decrease in the portfolio variance.

In conclusion, most risk-averse forest managers would probably postpone harvesting and preserve the present composition of the portfolio in the light of these results. Indeed, both SD- and MV-approaches fail to demonstrate any significant gains from further diversification of the portfolio to stocks, either in terms of higher mean return or lower variance. Less risk-averse forest owners could scan the SD or the MV efficient subsets of the portfolio set Ψ to identify preferable diversification strategies. Since this would involve more active interaction with the forest managers, and effective methodologies for identifying and representing the efficient subsets remain to be developed, we refrain from further operational recommendations.

As a final technical note, evidence of the relative computational burden of the different tests was also obtained, as reported in Table 12.4. As expected, Post's test statistic proved the quickest to solve, requiring only two seconds for complete execution, whereas the Kuosmanen version took over 10 minutes in the unconstrained case, and almost 8 minutes in the constrained one. Furthermore, confirming the efficiency status took over 2 hours of computation time in the constrained case. Still, there are many situations where this may be an affordable price to pay for a meaningful efficiency score, and for the identity of the dominating portfolio yielding the highest mean return. Most notably, in the constrained case the Kuosmanen approach is the only option.

Table 12.4 Total computation times of different SD statistics (seconds)

	θ_2^n	θ_2^s	θ_2
Unconstrained case	628.4	–	2.3
Constrained case	461.9	7290.9	n.a.

5. CONCLUDING REMARKS

The SD approach offers useful tools for portfolio analysis involving forest and/or other natural resource assets with non-normally distributed rates of return. Portfolio analysis can be made using a minimum number of assumptions if compared with MV or some other portfolio optimization tools that require highly specific information about decision-maker preferences. A review was made of the theoretical framework and the operational tests recently outlined in Kuosmanen (2001) and the subsequent work of Post (2001). The forestry portfolio management case of Heikkinen (1999) was re-examined to shed further light on some important practical aspects of the SD tests. The main focus was to study the impact of the possibility of purchasing additional quantities of timber-land with the desired species and quality characteristics. This is an important factor in the Finnish forestry environment where the liquidity of the timber harvested is much higher than the liquidity of the land. If additional timber stock cannot be purchased, the problem is a pure harvesting one from the forest point of view. This is the problem that land owners face most often.

Interestingly, the constraints on the acquisition of new timber stock were found to make a big difference in the SD efficiency of the portfolio. If the desired type of timber stock could be bought, it would pay to trade the present forest holdings for homogeneous spruce forest in the short run. This strategy would yield 11 percentage points higher mean return without changing the present risk exposure or profile in any way. In the short run, however, it is not so simple to trade with forest land. Therefore, in short-run planning it is relevant to impose the constraint that the share of timber assets cannot be increased in the portfolio.

From a methodological perspective, the present application proved an interesting case for comparing the two alternative test approaches proposed by Kuosmanen and Post, respectively. The application confirmed the theoretical fact that Post's test requires less time and fewer computational resources. However, Post's test cannot accommodate additional restrictions for the portfolio weights, so the Kuosmanen approach was the only option in the more short-term planning problem.

The present application focused on the new SD tools, ignoring the possible intertemporal dynamics in the rates of return, as well as the possible sampling errors. Future research could pay further attention to integrating these aspects into the SD framework. This chapter also focused exclusively on portfolio optimization in the short run, ignoring the influence of the present decisions on the alternatives available in the future. In long-term planning, profiles of the forest stands which mature and are harvestable in the following periods should be taken into account. The present one-period model could be extended to a multi-period model where new stands mature in each period, but this falls beyond the scope of the present chapter.

The SD approach might also prove a useful analytical framework for dealing with 'catastrophic' events. For example, forestry risks also include such threats as fire, tornados, heavy snow, floods and pests, which shape the left tail of the return distribution. However, there are at least two major difficulties in application of SD to assets exposed to catastrophic events. First, since the catastrophic events are relatively rare, the observed time-series data may fail to adequately account for these risks. Second, the SD criteria are sensitive to sampling error, especially in the left tail of the distribution. To circumvent the problems with the left tail, the empirical distribution might be enriched by a combination of a theoretical catastrophe model and/or the bootstrapping technique. Although this chapter did not extend the analysis in these directions, it could serve as a useful starting point for future investigations and extensions which address specifically these two difficulties.

ACKNOWLEDGEMENTS

We thank Arnaud Reynaud, Gilles Lafforgue, Laurens Cherchye, Hans-Peter Weikard, Justus Wesseler, and two anonymous referees for perceptive comments. This research is part of the NOMEPRE research program on nonparametric methods see: http://www.sls.wageningen-ur.nl/enr/staff/kuos-manen/program1/.

The financial support from the Emil Aaltonen Foundation is gratefully acknowledged.

NOTES

1. Heikkinen's (1999) forest owner's decision problem is taken here as given (for example, investment alternatives), that is, it was beyond the scope of this chapter to remodel the investment problem.
2. In Finland, for example, forestry legislation forbids final felling of young stands. Harvesting requires permission from a regional forestry center.
3. Postponing the harvest can also enable the forest owner to learn more about the return distribution of the risky assets and so make a better-informed decision. In the present short-term model, however, the information value of a single additional price observation is omitted as negligible.
4. Reeves and Haight (2000) drew similar conclusions by assuming that the land is sold immediately after the harvest.
5. The normality assumption can be relaxed in the special case where the utility function u has a quadratic form.
6. Note that the basic structure of problem (12.6) is similar to basic models of non-parametric efficiency analysis, also known as Data Envelopment Analysis (DEA) (for example, Färe et al. 1994). The observed returns of assets are here treated analogously to the way that efficiency analysis treats outputs and inputs (= negative outputs).
7. The rates of return of forest stands were calculated as the sum of the (deterministic) physical growth and the change of the (stochastic) stumpage price index. Stand-specific stumpage price indices were calculated to take into account the differences in species and assortment composition.

REFERENCES

Bawa, V.S. (1982), 'Stochastic Dominance: a research bibliography', *Management Science*, **28**, 698–712.

Charnes, A., W.W. Cooper, B. Golany, L. Seiford and J. Stutz (1985), 'Foundations of Data Envelopment Analysis for Pareto–Koopmans efficient empirical production functions', *Journal of Econometrics*, **30** (1), 91–107.

Dybvig, P.H. and S.A. Ross (1982), 'Portfolio efficient sets', *Econometrica*, **50** (6), 1525–46.

Färe, R., S. Grosskopf and C.A.K. Lovell (1994), *Production Frontiers*, Cambridge: Cambridge University Press.

Hardy, G.H., J.E. Littlewood and G. Polya (1934), *Inequalities*, Cambridge: Cambridge University Press.

Heikkinen, V.-P. (1999), 'Cutting rules for final fellings: a Mean-Variance portfolio analysis', *Journal of Forest Economics*, **5** (2), 269–84.

Heikkinen, V.-P. (2003), 'Timber harvesting as a part of the portfolio management: a multiperiod stochastic optimisation approach', *Management Science*, **49** (1), 131–42.

Heikkinen, V.-P. and A. Kanto (2000), 'Market model with long-term effects – empirical evidence from Finnish forestry returns', *Silva Fennica*, **34** (1), 61–9.

Kuosmanen, T. (2001), 'Stochastic Dominance efficiency tests under diversification', Helsinki School of Economics and Business Administration, Working Paper W-283, Helsinki.

Kuosmanen, T. (2002), 'Efficient diversification according to the Stochastic Dominance criteria', unpublished manuscript.

Levy, H. (1992), 'Stochastic Dominance and Expected Utility: survey and analysis', *Management Science*, **38** (4), 555–93.

Markowitz, H.M. (1952), 'Portfolio selection', *Journal of Finance*, **12**, 77–91.

Post, G.T. (2001), 'Testing for Stochastic Dominance with diversification possibilities', Erasmus Research Institute of Management (ERIM), Discussion Paper 117, forthcoming in *Journal of Finance*.

Reeves, L.H. and R.G. Haight (2000), 'Timber harvest scheduling with price uncertainty using Markowitz portfolio optimization', *Annals of Operations Research*, **95**, 229–50.

Royston, P. (1992), 'Approximating the Shapiro–Wilk W-test for non-normality', *Statistics and Computing*, **2**, 117–19.

Thomson, T.A. (1991), 'Efficient combinations of timber and financial market investments in single-period and multi-period portfolios', *Forest Science*, **37** (2), 461–80.

Toppinen, A. and R. Toivonen (1998), 'Roundwood market integration in Finland: a multivariate co-integration analysis', *Journal of Forest Economics*, **4** (3), 241–66.

13. Weather-based Index Insurance to Hedge Temperature Exposure of Greenhouse Horticultural Firms

Marcel A.P.M. van Asseldonk and Alfons G.J.M. Oude Lansink

1. INTRODUCTION

In this chapter the viability of a weather derivative contract to hedge heating energy demand in greenhouse horticultural firms is studied. A normalized quadratic profit function was used to estimate the effect of heating degree-days (HDD). Then Monte Carlo simulation was used to estimate the effectiveness of a non-linear weather derivative contract. Stochastic elements in the model were HDD as well as the residuals from the profit function.

Many economic activities are highly dependent on the prevailing temperature. Energy demand for heating and cooling, for example, shows a significant correlation with the ambient temperature (Quayle and Diaz 1979; Colombo et al. 1999). Moreover, consumer demand for retail goods is sensitive to temperature conditions (Agnew and Palutikof 1999) and temperature conditions have an important impact on aspects of agricultural production such as pest management, planting date and ultimately harvesting date (Kadioğlu et al. 1999). To safeguard against adverse consequences of excessive weather conditions, specific insurance-related financial instruments such as weather derivatives have been developed.

These risk-transfer instruments are linked to specific weather events; contracts are written against defined weather outcomes (Skees and Barnett 1999). Weather derivatives are a means to hedge risks (Müller and Grandi 2000) that result from weather-related changes in the demand for or supply of products. In most cases a hedge is sought for a severe decline in business turnover.

The market came into existence in the United States in the energy sector. Power companies realize high turnovers in cold winters (high number of heating degree-days) and hot summers (high number of cooling degree-days), but turnovers are low in mild winters and cool summers. In order to cover themselves against the risks of loss of sales due to 'unfavourable' temperatures, the companies can use weather derivatives based on the number of degree-days (Müller and Grandi 2000). Derivative contracts can also be based on, for example, the number of millimetres of precipitation, the number of days of frost in a year, or the number of hours of sunshine in the summer.

The derivative contract could be specified in different formats, that is, swap, cap (or floor) and collar. In a swap format, counterparts agree to exchange payments conditional on the outcome of the agreed weather event with no fixed premium. Payments are triggered when the actual weather index is different from the strike level, and are based on the unit payment. As shown in Appendix 13A1, a company (for example, greenhouse grower) for which heating costs increase when the heating degree-days are high, and thus profit decreases, enters into a swap to reduce its exposure above a predetermined level. In comparison to the swap format, the cap format permits the purchaser of the weather derivative to buy protection at a fixed premium. Caps provide protection against adverse outcome weather conditions while allowing the buyer to retain the full potential of unusually favourable outcomes (such as a warm winter for a greenhouse grower). If the climatic variable remains within some agreed range, as defined by a zero-cost collar, no payments occur. However, if the climatic variable falls outside the collar's upper limit, an indemnification is provided in return for a premium if the climatic variable falls outside the collar's lower limit, or vice versa. For the three types of contracts, a maximum indemnity can be agreed upon by setting an upper bound.

The main advantage of ceding risks by means of objective indices is to overcome problems of asymmetric information and systemic risks. Asymmetric information manifests itself in moral hazard and adverse selection. Moral hazard occurs when an individual purchases an insurance policy and as a result of having purchased that policy, alters his/her behaviour thereby increasing the potential magnitude of a loss and/or the probability of a loss. Insurance can control this problem only partially by careful underwriting and by various policy provisions (for example, deductibles and waiting periods, exclusions). Adverse selection arises when potential insurance purchasers have more or better information about their potential magnitude of loss and/or probability of loss than does the insurer (Rejda 1998). With systemic (that is, correlated) risks, multiple insureds can suffer losses at the same time (Skees et al. 1997). As a result insurance companies have problems pooling such risks themselves. By means of derivatives, systemic risks can be hedged that cannot really be hedged in another way because it is easier to tap into bigger insurance capacities via the capital market.

Because a derivative pays out automatically, rather than in response to an actual loss as is the case with traditional insurance, considerable care must be taken in the design of the derivative contract. The derivative should be based on an index that is highly correlated (ideally perfectly correlated) with the risk to be hedged, that is, there is little basis risk (Miranda 1991; Skees and Barnett 1999; Turvey 2001).

The objective of the current study is to present a framework for analysing the viability of weather derivatives to hedge heating energy demand in Dutch greenhouse horticultural firms. Insurance to indemnify losses as a result of extra energy use is not available, partially as a result of problems with respect to asymmetric information and systemic risk. The weather derivative under research can be seen as a complementary risk management tool enabling farmers to cope with such adverse weather conditions. Without the hedging alternative, adverse temperature conditions will increase heating energy demand (non-linear) or reduce output, or both. Hedging may reduce heating energy demand and thus output in extreme cold winters, but losses are indemnified by means of the weather derivative contract. An annual profit function and three netput equations (energy, materials and services) are estimated. Fixed inputs are structures, machinery and installations, and labour. In addition a weather variable is included based on heating degree-days. A time trend is included in the empirical model to account for technical change in the estimation period (Oude Lansink 2000). Including a weather variable in the profit function allows for quantifying the effect of a weather derivative contract on profit and netput quantities. Subsequently, the hedging effectiveness, that is the relative reduction in volatility as measured by using the coefficient of variation (Miranda 1991) is derived by means of Monte Carlo simulation.

The chapter is organized as follows: first the empirical model used is explained, then the analysed data and estimation procedure are described. Subsequently, the normative model is described. The model is parameterized with the results obtained from the empirical model and simulates the impact of a weather derivative on profit volatility. The simulation approach provides additional information on more theoretical extreme events which may be absent from the actual data because of the relatively short time horizon. Finally, the results and conclusions are presented.

2. METHOD

Econometric estimates of temperature risks are derived from a model of profit-maximizing firms. The restricted normalized[1] profit function is defined for firm *h* as:

$$\pi_h(w, z_h, t, H) = \max_{y_h, x_h} \{y_h - w' \cdot x_h \mid z_h, t, H\} \tag{13.1}$$
$$\text{s.t. } y_h = F_h(x_h, z_h, t, H)$$

where π and w_i are normalized profit and normalized input prices, using the price of output as numeraire; z_h is a vector of fixed input quantities, t denotes technological progress, H reflects heating degree-days, x_h is a vector of quantities of variable inputs, and $F_h(\cdot)$ represents the firm-specific production function. Applying Hotelling's Lemma yields a system of input demand equations:

$$\frac{\partial \pi_h(w, z_h, t, H)}{\partial w} = -x_h(w, z_h, t, H) \tag{13.2}$$

whereas the (numeraire) output supply equation is derived using the definition of normalized profit:

$$y_h(w, z_h, t, H) = \pi_h(w, z_h, t, H) + w \cdot x_h(w, z_h, t, H). \tag{13.3}$$

2.1 Empirical Model

This section starts by specifying the profit function that is to parameterize the model simulating the impact of a weather derivative on profit volatility in a subsequent stage. The normalized quadratic is used here because it is a flexible and self-dual functional form. Also, it has a hessian of constants implying that convexity in prices can be tested and/or imposed globally. A further advantage of the normalized quadratic that is relevant in this study is its empirical simplicity. The normalized quadratic profit function for firm h takes the form:

$$\pi_h = \alpha_h + \sum_{i=1}^{3} \alpha_{hi} w_i + \sum_{j=1}^{5} \beta_j z_{hj} + 0.5 \sum_{i=1}^{3} \sum_{j=1}^{3} \alpha_{ij} w_i w_j$$
$$+ 0.5 \sum_{i=1}^{5} \sum_{j=1}^{5} \beta_{ij} z_{hi} z_{hj} + \sum_{i=1}^{3} \sum_{j=1}^{5} \gamma_{ij} w_i z_j \tag{13.4}$$

where π and w_i are normalized profit and normalized input prices, using the price of output as numeraire; z_{hj} are quantities of fixed inputs, technological change and a weather indicator; all α, β and γ are parameters to be estimated. Note that α_h and α_{hi} are firm-specific parameters, whereas it is assumed that all slope parameters of the estimated equations are equal across firms. This assumption is made since panel data estimation methods based on Least Squares or Maximum Likelihood estimation allow for estimating firm-specific intercepts in panel data with a large number of firms. Estimating firm-specific slope parameters using Least Squares or Maximum Likelihood methods may rapidly decrease the number of degrees of freedom and leads to computationally intractable models.[2] Netput equations can be derived by applying Hotelling's Lemma :

$$-x_{hi} = \alpha_{hi} + \sum_{j=1}^{3} \alpha_{ij} w_j + \sum_{j=1}^{5} \gamma_{ij} z_j . \tag{13.5}$$

The (numeraire) output supply equation is obtained by using the definition of normalized profit:

$$\pi_h = y_h + \sum_{i=1}^{3} w_i x_{hi}$$

$$y_h = \alpha_h + \sum_{i=1}^{5} \beta_i z_i - 0.5 \sum_{i=1}^{3} \sum_{j=1}^{3} \alpha_{ij} w_i w_j + 0.5 \sum_{i=1}^{5} \sum_{j=1}^{5} \beta_{ij} z_i z_j . \tag{13.6}$$

For a more detailed description of the empirical model we refer to Oude Lansink (2000) who used a similar model but without the temperature variable, which is a prerequisite to account for temperature exposure for the current research. The proposed profit function allows for the fact that the relationship between ambient temperature and energy demand is highly non-linear. Theoretical arguments from thermodynamics state that heat loss through a barrier is proportional to the fourth power of the temperature differential. However, a practical observation is that the heating capacity is limited and thus no further effect of more severe weather on energy demand can be expected (Engle et al. 1986). In addition, managerial practices may also affect the relationship between ambient temperature and energy demand.

2.2 Data and Estimation

Data on specialized potplant firms covering the period from 1975 to 1995 come from a stratified sample of Dutch glasshouse firms keeping accounts for the LEI-DLO accounting system.[3] The firms typically remain in the panel for a maximum of eight years, so the panel is incomplete. The data set used for estimation contains 985 observations on 207 firms.

One output and three variable inputs (energy, materials and services) are distinguished. Output consists mainly of potted plants. Other outputs included are fruit, vegetables and flowers. Energy consists of gas, oil and electricity, as well as delivery of thermal energy by electricity plants. Materials consist of seeds and planting materials, pesticides, fertilizers and so on. Services are those provided by contract workers and from storage and delivery of outputs.

Fixed inputs are structures (z_1) including buildings, glasshouses, land and paving, machinery and installations (z_2), and labour (z_3). Labour is measured in quality-corrected man-years, and includes family as well as hired labour. Labour is assumed to be a fixed input because a large share of total labour consists of family labour. Flexibility of hired labour is further restricted by the presence of permanent contracts and by the fact that hiring additional labour involves search costs for the firm operator. Capital in structures, machinery and installations is measured at constant 1985 prices.[4]

Tornqvist price indices are calculated for output and the three composite variable inputs with prices obtained from the LEI-DLO/CBS. The price indices vary over the years but not over the firms, implying that differences in the composition of inputs and output or quality differences are reflected in the quantity measures (Cox and Wohlgenant 1986). Implicit quantity indices are generated as the ratio of value to the price index.

Other variables included in the empirical model are a time trend to account for technological change (z_4), and an indicator for weather (z_5), that is, heating degree-days (HDD). HDD are calculated as the absolute difference between a reference or base temperature (T_{ref}) and the daily average temperature (T_{avg}), defined as the average of the maximum and minimum temperatures for each day. If the daily average temperature exceeds the reference temperature, HDD is zero. Subsequently the daily (t) HDD values are summed over the specified period to be hedged (n):

$$HDD = \sum_{t=1}^{n} \max\left\{0; T_{ref} - T_{avg,t}\right\}. \tag{13.7}$$

The reference temperature and the time horizon, in the current application, are 18°C and a whole year, respectively. The sample temperature data originate from the principal meteorology station in the closest proximity to the greenhouse so as to reduce spatial basis risk (van Asseldonk 2003).

Table 13.1 provides a description of the mean and variability of the data that have been used in this research. As a measure of volatility the table also gives the average intra-firm coefficient of variations that are calculated using the firm-specific mean and standard deviation.

Equations (13.5) and (13.6) represent the system of equations to be estimated. Before estimation, error terms are added to (13.5) and (13.6) in order to account for omitted variables that are peculiar to the individual firm and the time period. The error term of the ith equation is assumed to be identically and

Table 13.1 Description of data and variability

Variable	Dimension	Mean	SD	CV_h
Quantities				
Output	1985 euro × 1000	603.34	569.09	16.27
Energy	1985 euro × 1000	–110.18	103.11	–19.79
Materials	1985 euro × 1000	–139.35	159.72	–23.80
Services	1985 euro × 1000	–52.17	55.94	–25.05
Structures	1985 euro × 1000	341.77	361.44	19.80
Machinery and installations	1985 euro × 1000	175.55	208.66	22.23
Labour	Man-years	6.82	4.85	12.29
Trend	1975 = 0	10.37	5.71	29.64
HDD	Heating degree-days	3803.24	250.24	3.88
Prices				
Energy	Base year 1985	0.70	0.21	17.81
Materials	Base year 1985	1.12	0.16	4.82
Services	Base year 1985	1.07	0.05	4.32

independently distributed with a zero mean and variance σ_i^2. The system of equations, (13.5)–(13.6), is estimated by seemingly unrelated regressions to account for possible correlation of error terms across equations. In order to account for heterogeneity of the firms in the sample, it is assumed that each firm has a firm-specific intercept (fixed effects assumption) in each equation of the system. Estimation is enabled by transforming the data prior to estimation to overcome numerical problems. The transformation has the effect of expressing each variable in terms of its deviation from the mean of the firm (see Judge et al. 1988; pp. 470–72).[5] The regression has been performed by the PROC MODEL routine in SAS.

2.3 Simulation

From the empirical model the effect of HDD on annual profit function and three netput equations (energy, materials and services) are estimated. Subsequently these estimates are included in a Monte Carlo simulation model to determine the effectiveness of a weather derivative contract. Given a perfect setting, simulated outcomes should be similar to those obtained from historical outcomes. But there is an element of randomness, so exact replication is not to be expected; the observed past is only one sample from the infinite set of possible pasts. Moreover, simulation can provide information on more theoretical extreme events which may be absent from the actual data because of the relatively short time horizon. A number of iterations have to be executed before the accumulated output represents a reliable overview of the most likely and possibly extreme outcomes. As more iterations are run the outcome becomes more stable as the statistics describing each distribution change less and less until they converge. The results presented here are based on a convergence criterion that is set at a threshold of 1.5 per cent change of the variance.

The intra-firm volatility of profit is simulated by including the effect of HDD as a stochastic element. It is assumed that the cumulative distribution of degree-days on an annual basis is approximately a Gaussian (that is, normal) probability density function $N(0, \sigma_{HDD})$ and thus only the mean and the variance are required (Seginer and Jenkins 1987; Şen and Kadioğlu 1998). The normal distribution extends over the entire range of real numbers (that is, from –infinity to +infinity). HDD is defined to be zero or positive and therefore the use of the normal distribution in such cases is inappropriate. However, HDD are aggregated over a long period extending over a whole year, thereby approximating a non-censored distribution.

For a given firm h without a weather derivative contract profit volatility ($\Delta\pi_h$) is simulated as:

$$\Delta\pi_h = N(0,\sigma(\varepsilon_y)) + \sum_{i=1}^{3} N(0,\sigma(\varepsilon_i))w_i + (\beta_5 + \sum_{i=1}^{4}\beta_{i5}z_i)N(0,\sigma_{HDD})$$

$$+ 0.5\beta_{55}N(0,\sigma_{HDD})^2 + (\sum_{i=1}^{3}\gamma_{i5})N(0,\sigma_{HDD}). \qquad (13.8)$$

The error terms of equations (13.5) and (13.6) are added to account for omitted variables that reveal residual volatility not explained by the equations. The error terms are assumed to be normally distributed with a zero mean and variance σ^2 $\{N[0, \sigma(\varepsilon_y)] - N[0, \sigma(\varepsilon_i)]\}$. The covariance structure of the error terms is included since the system of equations is estimated by seemingly unrelated regressions to account for possible correlation of error terms across equations. Correlation between HDD and the error terms are assumed to be absent because HDD was included in the estimation procedure as an independent variable.

Subsequently the effect of a weather derivative can be determined. The maximum reduction of profit volatility, as a result of relative cold years, can be achieved if the unit payment equals the estimated HDD effect. In the contract under study the strike level is set at mean HDD. Because a quadratic profit function is estimated, a non-linear weather derivative contract was applied. A swap contract is used in order to balance indemnities and premiums. As a result of these payments the adjusted profit for a given firm *h* differs with π_h because the stochastic effect of $N(0, \sigma_{HDD})$ in equation (13.8) is cancelled out.

Pricing is based on the pure premium and thus excluding loading for administrative expenses, profit and a margin for contingencies. The weather derivative market is currently often seen as one-sided: there would appear to be more demand than supply. Therefore, rather than the weather derivative market intermediating a net exchange of risk between end users exposed in opposite directions, the market is rather a mechanism by which institutions seeking diversification of risks are matched with hedgers. This would suggest that the premium of the derivative will be consistently below fair value, the spread to fair value reflecting the risk premium necessary for institutions to enter the market to insure those who are exposed. However, the risk premiums to be paid on the derivative market are expected to be below those for insurance for similar risks. The type of contract modelled was chosen for analysis because it provides the maximum possible variance reduction.

The hedge effectiveness (*HE*) is the reduction in the normalized risk by using the coefficient of variation (Miranda 1991), whereby:

$$HE = \frac{\sigma_h/\mu_h - \sigma_{h'}/\mu_{h'}}{\sigma_h/\mu_h} * 100, \qquad (13.9)$$

where $\sigma_{h'}$ and $\mu_{h'}$ result from the weather derivative contract (σ's are based on equation (13.8), μ's are based on equation (13.4)).

3. RESULTS

Estimates of the slope parameters and their estimated *t*-values are given in Table 13.2. Fifty-eight per cent of the slope parameters are significant at the 5 per cent significance level (24 out of 41). In the output supply equation neither the main effect of HDD (β_5) nor the quadratic effect of HDD (β_{55}) were significant at the 10 per cent significance level. The negative signs for both parameters show that a positive value of HDD (thus colder than an average year) will decrease output. Two out of four interaction parameters with HDD in the output supply equation are significant at the 5 per cent significance level (β_{15} and β_{25}). In the energy demand equation the HDD parameter was highly significant (γ_{15}) and quantified that a relatively cold year will increase energy demand. The opposite holds for materials and services demand since the slope parameters γ_{25} and γ_{35} were both positive: in a relatively cold year materials and services demand decreased.

The variance-covariance structure of the error terms (ε_y, ε_1, ε_2, ε_3) is presented in Table 13.3. The largest dispersion was observed for the output, followed by the variable input materials. The model generated three significant correlation coefficients at the 0.1 per cent level. Variable inputs materials and services were positively correlated and both have a reverse relationship with output. The energy error component was independent from the other variable inputs as well as the output.

Subsequently, by means of Monte Carlo simulation, the coefficient of variation of profit is derived per firm given a situation with and without a weather derivative contract. Only those firms that are in the panel data in the most recent year (1995) were included in the analyses. The results obtained from 36 firms are provided in Table 13.4. The coefficient of variation demonstrated a substantial heterogeneity among firms. The mean CV for the sample without and with a derivative contract was 36.33 and 28.67, respectively. Note that CV is calculated for the difference between output and variable inputs (that is, gross margin). Using net farm income instead would increase CV substantially. However, fixed costs were not registered in the analysed accountancy database. The mean relative effectiveness of the derivative contract was 20.41 per cent. Thus, the derivative contract reduced profit volatility, but a substantial heterogeneity among firms existed.

The simulated heterogeneity between firms stemmed from the three fixed inputs – structures, machinery and installations, and labour – that jointly deter-

Table 13.2 Results of estimation profit function

Parameter	Estimate	*t*-value	Parameter	Estimate	*t*-value
β_1	0.688456	6.58	β_{33}	−1.075898	−1.71
β_2	−0.357643	−2.00	β_{34}	0.313126	0.84
β_3	44.043411	6.60	β_{35}	−0.00770132	1.54
β_4	13.455964	2.53	β_{44}	−0.294326	−0.70
β_5	−0.042078	−0.56	β_{45}	−0.00491229	−0.81
α_{11}	56.059077	11.00	β_{55}	−0.00022567	−1.37
α_{12}	−9.401219	−1.06	γ_{11}	−0.060590	−6.30
α_{13}	0.763631	0.23	γ_{12}	−0.078137	−5.48
α_{22}	83.953603	2.14	γ_{13}	−3.794807	−5.30
α_{23}	−6.086550	−0.46	γ_{14}	0.099520	0.20
α_{33}	60.325201	6.48	γ_{15}	−0.023540	−4.52
β_{11}	−0.00047042	−4.30	γ_{21}	−0.145127	−8.35
β_{12}	0.00010561	0.71	γ_{22}	0.120645	4.70
β_{13}	0.038952	5.10	γ_{23}	−17.509993	−13.56
β_{14}	−0.022754	−4.03	γ_{24}	0.841051	0.73
β_{15}	−0.00024091	−2.91	γ_{25}	0.017303	1.61
β_{22}	−0.00026277	−0.80	γ_{31}	−0.039197	−5.93
β_{23}	0.00189098	0.19	γ_{32}	−0.016557	−1.69
β_{24}	0.027947	2.75	γ_{33}	−6.106483	−12.43
β_{25}	0.00029033	2.27	γ_{34}	−3.289254	−7.87
			γ_{35}	0.012436	3.09

Table 13.3 Error terms in estimated functions

	SD	Correlation coefficients			
		ε_y	ε_1	ε_2	ε_3
ε_y	94.48		–0.04	–0.59*	–0.68*
ε_1	22.19			–0.03	–0.06
ε_2	40.04				0.38*
ε_3	15.06				

Note: * $P < 0.001$.

Table 13.4 Simulated coefficient of variation per firm without and with a derivative contract and the maximum effectiveness of a derivative contract

	Mean	SD	Min	Max
CV	36.33	33.62	5.70	186.27
CV_{WD}	28.67	26.87	5.32	150.12
Effectiveness (HE)	20.41	6.48	1.59	33.39

mined netputs and thus profit. The time effect that accounted for technological change was set at the most recent year in the data set, while the weather exposure was identical for all firms. The implication is that, for example, given a firm with a relatively substantial energy demand (determined by the combination of fixed inputs) the effect of HDD on a firm's profit, and thus the hedging effectiveness, will be substantial too. The reverse holds for the variable inputs materials and services since both estimated slope parameters were positive.

4. DISCUSSION AND CONCLUSION

This chapter has presented a framework to study the viability of a weather derivative contract. A normalized quadratic profit function was used to estimate the weather effect. Then the effectiveness of a non-linear weather derivative contract was estimated by means of Monte Carlo simulation. Stochastic elements in the model were based on estimated weather effect as well as the residuals from the profit function.

The method was applied to estimate the effectiveness of a non-linear weather derivative contract to hedge heating energy demand in greenhouse horticultural firms. The derivative contract reduces profit volatility, but a substantial heterogeneity among firms exists.

In the current study the hedging effectiveness was derived on the basis of individual firm data, while at the same time technological change was estimated on the basis of the panel as a whole. This former feature has an advantage because it determines the heterogeneity between firms in contrast to aggregated data, such as commonly used county yields. Since firms under study are divers with respect to firm structure and management this approach is an enhancement. However, a firm-specific slope parameter to account for firm-specific weather exposure is absent in the present framework. Therefore the potential variance reduction is underestimated. Including such a firm-specific slope parameter within the current framework would overcome this limitation. An alternative is to estimate the optimal hedging effectiveness solely on individual firm records, but the change in production technology and the scope of fixed inputs need to be accounted for.

In the current study weather derivatives were applied as a complementary risk management tool enabling farmers to cope with adverse temperature conditions. This hedging alternative expanded the environment of energy input and output decisions. But the approach can also be applied to other weather-related input or output risks such as pesticide and fertilizer use.

NOTES

1. Normalized profit is used here, because the empirical model uses a normalized quadratic profit function, using the price of output as numeraire.
2. Alternatively, generalized maximum entropy estimation can be used to estimate a profit function that is firm specific in intercepts and slope parameters (see, for example, Paris and Howitt 1998; Oude Lansink 1999).
3. Agricultural Economics Research Institute and Netherlands Central Bureau of Statistics
4. The deflators for capital in structures and machinery and installations are calculated from the data supplied by the LEI-DLO accounting system. Comparison of the balance value in year t and the balance value in year $t-1$ gives the yearly price correction used by the LEI-DLO. This price correction is used to construct a price index for capital and a price index for machinery and installations. These price indices are used as a deflator.
5. The within transformation can also be applied to incomplete panels (Wansbeek and Kapteyn 1989). Firm-specific intercepts can be recovered after estimating the transformed system (see Judge et al. 1988).

REFERENCES

Agnew, M.D. and J.P. Palutikof (1999), 'The impacts of climate on retailing in the UK with particular reference to the anomalously hot summer of 1995', *International Journal of Climatology*, **19**, 1496–507.

Agricultural Economics Research Institute and Netherlands Central Bureau of Statistics (1975–1995), *Landbouwcijfers*, The Hague: LEI-DLO/CBS.

Colombo, A.F., D. Etkin and B.W. Karney (1999), 'Climate variability and the frequency of extreme temperature events for nine sites across Canada: implications for power usage', *Journal of Climate*, **12**, 2490–502.

Cox, T.L. and M.K. Wohlgenant (1986), 'Prices and quality effects in cross-sectional demand analysis', *American Journal of Agricultural Economics*, **68**, 908–19.

Engle, R.F., C.W.J. Granger, J. Rice and A. Weiss (1986), 'Semiparametric estimates of the relation between weather and electricity sales', *Journal of the American Statistical Association*, **81**, 310–20.

Judge, G.R., C. Hill, W. Griffiths, G. Lutkepohl and L. Tsoung-Chao (1988), *Introduction to the Theory and Practice of Econometrics*, New York: Wiley.

Kadioğlu, M., Z. Şen and L. Gültekin (1999), 'Spatial heating monthly degree-day features and climatologic patterns in Turkey', *Theoretical and Applied Climatology*, **64**, 263–9.

Miranda, M.J. (1991), 'Area yield insurance reconsidered', *American Journal of Agricultural Economics*, **73**, 233–42.

Müller, A. and M. Grandi (2000), 'Weather derivatives: a risk management tool for weather-sensitive industries', *Geneva Papers on Risk and Insurance*, **25**, 273–87.

Oude Lansink, A.G.J.M. (1999), 'Generalised maximum entropy and heterogeneous technologies', *European Review of Agricultural Economics*, **26**, 101–15.

Oude Lansink, A.G.J.M. (2000), 'Productivity growth and efficiency measurement: a dual approach', *European Review of Agricultural Economics*, **27**, 59–73.

Paris, Q. and R.E. Howitt (1998), 'An analysis of ill-posed production problems using maximum entropy', *American Journal of Agricultural Economics*, **80**, 124–38.

Quayle, R.G. and H.F. Diaz (1979), 'Heating degree-day data applied to residential heating energy consumption', *Journal of Applied Meteorology*, **19**, 241–6.

Rejda, G.E. (1998), *Principles of Risk Management and Insurance*, New York: Addison-Wesley.

Seginer, I. and B.M. Jenkins (1987), 'Temperature exposure of greenhouses from monthly means of daily maximum and minimum temperatures', *Journal of Agricultural Engineering*, **37**, 191–208.

Şen, Z. and M. Kadioğlu (1998), 'Theoretical risk formulation for degree-day calculation', *Theoretical and Applied Climatology*, **61**, 121–6.

Skees, J.R. and B.J. Barnett (1999), 'Conceptual and practical considerations for sharing catastrophic/systemic risks', *Review of Agricultural Economics*, **21**, 424–41.

Skees, J.R., J.R. Black and B.J. Barnett (1997), 'Designing and rating an area yield crop insurance contract', *American Journal of Agricultural Economics*, **79**, 430–8.

Turvey, C.G. (2001), 'Weather derivatives for specific event risks in agriculture', *Review of Agricultural Economics*, **23**, 333–51.

Van Asseldonk, M.A.P.M. (2003), 'Insurance against weather risk: use of heating degree-days from non-local stations for weather derivatives', *Theoretical and Applied Climatology*, **74**, 137–44.

Wansbeek, T. and A. Kapteyn (1989), 'Estimation of the error components model with incomplete panels', *Journal of Econometrics*, **41**, 341–61.

APPENDIX 13A1

Swap

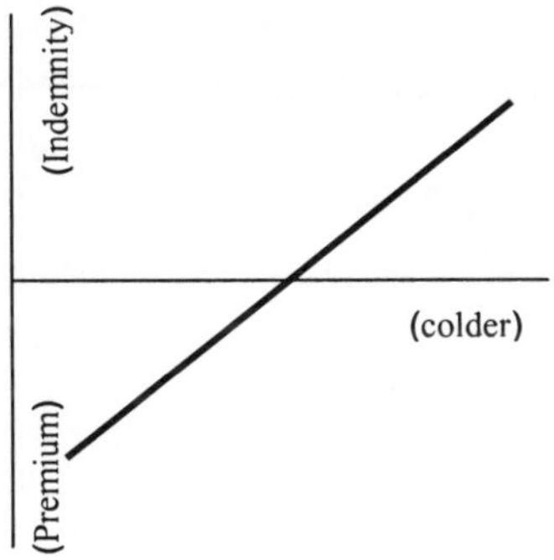

Cap

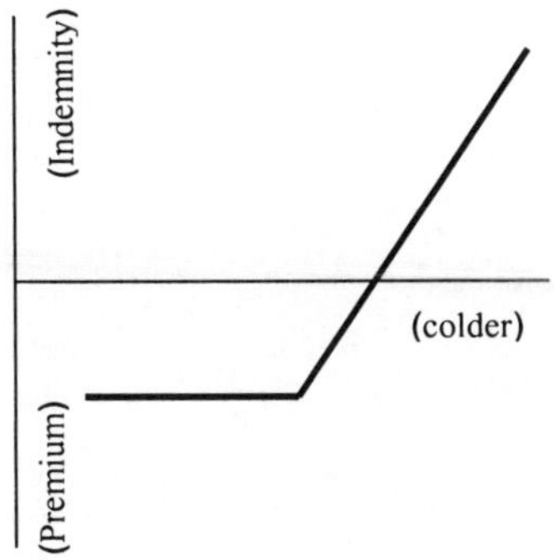

Collar

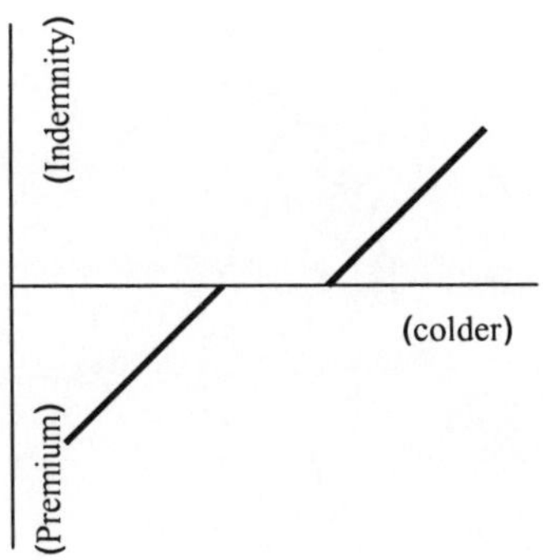

Figure 13A1.1 Alternative contract formats of weather derivatives

14. Parents' Valuation of Latent Health Risks to their Children

Mark Dickie and Shelby Gerking

1. INTRODUCTION

A key aspect of environmental policy in the United States involves reducing hazards faced by children. Children frequently are at greater risk than adults from environmental hazards such as lead poisoning, pesticides, drinking water contaminants, and exposure to solar radiation (USEPA 1996). Additionally, President Bill Clinton's Executive Order #13045 (1997) directed federal agencies to address environmental health and safety risks that disproportionately affect children. Appropriate policy aimed at reducing these risks will differ depending on the hazard considered; yet all such policies operate at least partly through adult caregivers who are responsible for children's behavior. For example, parents can be encouraged to take protective actions that will reduce exposure to environmental hazards. Effectiveness of this approach, however, rests on parents' beliefs about risks to their children's health, as well as how they make choices between their children's health, their own health and other goods.

This chapter extends previous work by Dickie and Gerking (1996, 1997) to look at decisions parents make for themselves and their children to reduce risk of skin cancer from solar radiation exposure. Skin cancer is the most common type of cancer occurring in the United States (Scotto et al. 1982; MacKie et al. 1989; Finkel 1998; American Cancer Society 2001) and solar radiation exposure during childhood is an important determinant of lifetime skin cancer risk (Reynolds et al. 1996; Robinson et al. 1997; Creech and Mayer 1998). In fact, as much as 80 per cent of a person's lifetime accumulation of solar radiation exposure occurs before the age of 18 (American Academy of Dermatology 2001). Two questions are addressed using data from a survey of 160 parents of children aged 3–12. (i) What determines parents' (*ex ante*) subjective beliefs about their own and their children's risk of getting skin cancer? (ii) How do parents' tradeoff changes in skin cancer risk to themselves against changes in skin cancer risk to their children? Estimation of this tradeoff is important because it can be interpreted as a measure of parents' altruism toward their children. In general, greater altruism inspires greater confidence that informed parents will take action to protect their children from environmental hazards.

These issues have seldom been directly examined in prior research on children's health, although a few studies have estimated parents' willingness to pay to improve the health of children (for a survey of this literature, see Dickie and Nestor 1998). For example, Agee and Crocker (1996), using a similar approach to that developed by Dickie and Gerking (1991), estimate a production function for risk perceived by parents that their child will develop chronic, lead-induced health impairments. Their analysis, however, does not consider how risk perceptions are formed. Risk perceptions have been extensively studied in previous work (Kunreuther 1976; Lichtenstein et al. 1978; Grether and Plott 1979; Arrow 1982; Kahneman and Tversky 1982; Slovic et al. 1985; Tversky et al. 1990), but not in cases where parents form beliefs about risks to a child.

The remainder of the chapter is divided into five sections. Section 2 develops the theoretical model to be applied. Section 3 describes the survey data collected. Section 4 presents evidence on the determinants of beliefs held by parents about skin cancer risks to themselves and their children. Section 5 estimates an indifference map for parents to support calculation of the tradeoff between skin cancer risks to themselves and their children. Section 6 concludes.

2. THE MODEL

This section develops a simple, one-period household production function model to guide the empirical analysis. The model focuses on a parent and child who might get skin cancer at some point in their lifetimes. A multi-period framework would be an attractive extension for modeling timing of occurrence of skin cancer, but the length of time (or latency period) until the onset of this disease was not explicitly addressed in the survey and, thus, is not considered here. For ease of exposition, the model deals only with perception and valuation of skin cancer risks within a family and altruism of parents toward their children. The issue of altruism toward persons outside the family would not be difficult to incorporate, but would draw attention away from the family decision-making issues that are the main focus here. In any case, the model described below is familiar so the discussion is kept brief.

A parent's lifetime utility (U) function is:

$$U = U(X, R^*_{PN}, R^*_{PM}, R^*_{CN}, R^*_{CM}), \tag{14.1}$$

where X denotes a composite good, R^*_{ij} denotes perception of lifetime risk of getting skin cancer, P denotes the parent, C denotes the child, M denotes melanoma skin cancer, and N denotes non-melanoma skin cancer. Thus, for example, R^*_{CM} denotes perceived risk of the child developing melanoma skin cancer at some point during his/her life. This formulation abstracts from consequences of sunlight exposure such as suntanning/sunburning and aging/wrinkling of skin and draws attention to two types of risk comparisons: (i) between illnesses of different severity (melanoma versus non-melanoma) faced by either the parent or child and (ii) between the parent and child for a particular type of illness. The model assumes that family resources are allocated to maximize utility of an altruistic parent (or the consensus utility function of two altruistic parents), a working hypothesis adopted in most research on economics of the family (Becker 1991; Behrman et al. 1995). The possibility of divergent interests of family members is ignored, although recently it has been applied to value environmental risks in a household production framework (see Smith and van Houtven 1998). Also, the intragenerational issue of unequal treatment of siblings, a common theme when analyzing parents' investment in their children (Rosenzweig and Schultz 1982; Pitt et al. 1990), is ignored and only one child is included in the model. This simplification allows later analysis to focus more directly on how parents make tradeoffs in health risks between themselves and their children.

Parents' perceived risk about their own chances of getting skin cancer are formed according to:

$$R^*_{Pj} = R^*_{Pj}(R_{Pj}, \theta, \gamma), \tag{14.2}$$

where R_{Pj} denotes actual risk of skin cancer ($j = N,M$), θ denotes the parent's attitude toward and awareness of effects of sunlight exposure, and γ denotes family characteristics such as the number of children present in the household and whether a spouse is present. Actual skin cancer risks to parents, in turn, are determined by:

$$R_{Pj} = R_{Pj}(G, \Omega_P), \tag{14.3}$$

where G denotes a purchased good that both parent and child may use to reduce harmful effects of sunlight exposure, such as a sun protection product, and Ω_P denotes aspects of the parents' genetic endowment and history of exposure to solar radiation. Genetic factors such as skin type and complexion and, for example, a history of bad sunburn are important to consider in the context of skin cancer.

Additionally, a parent's perception about the child's risk of skin cancer is given by:

$$R^*_{Cj} = R^*_{Cj}(R^*_{Pj}, R_{Cj}, \theta, \gamma), \tag{14.4}$$

where R_{Cj} is the actual risk of skin cancer faced by the child and is determined similarly to equation (14.3) as shown in equation (14.5):

$$R_{Cj} = R_{Cj}(G, \Omega_C) \tag{14.5}$$

and where Ω_C denotes genetic endowment and exposure history of the child. Thus, parents are assumed to see risk to their children as a function of perceived risk to themselves, actual risk to their children, attitudes and family history. This formulation allows for the extreme view that parents form risk beliefs about risks to their children using only their own risk as a reference point. Alternatively, it allows for parents to form beliefs about risks to their children by disregarding beliefs about their own risk and considering only risk factors facing their children. These two possibilities are considered in Section 4, which looks at empirical evidence on how parents form beliefs about risks faced by their children.

Parents maximize utility subject to the budget constraint:

$$I = X + q_G G, \tag{14.6}$$

where I denotes income, q_G denotes the price per unit of G and where the price of X has been normalized to unity. Under standard assumptions, the utility-maximizing choice of G can be expressed as a function of the exogenous variables in the model (I, q_G, θ, γ, Ω_P, Ω_C). Appropriate substitutions show that R^*_{Pj} and R^*_{Cj} can be expressed in terms of these variables as well as shown in equation (14.7).

$$R^*_{ij} = f(I, q_G, \theta, \gamma, \Omega_P, \Omega_C). \tag{14.7}$$

Thus, in this model, beliefs about skin cancer risk can be expressed as the outcome of utility-maximizing consumption choices. In an earlier study, Dickie and Gerking (1996) examined how adults form perceptions about their own chances of getting skin cancer. This study develops additional evidence on this point; but the main focus is on parents' perceptions of the likelihood that one of their children will get skin cancer.

Additionally, an indifference map can be developed by solving for the change in expenditure on G that holds parents' utility constant:

$$d(q_G G) = \Sigma_{ij}[(q_x U_{R*ij} / U_x)dR^*_{ij}] - WdT. \tag{14.8}$$

Equation (14.8) can be used to calculate the *ex ante* willingness to pay or option price of reductions in different types of skin cancer risk faced by the parent and the child. These option prices are the coefficients of dR^*_{pj} and dR^*_{cj} ($j = M, N$) which are monetized marginal rates of substitution between perceived risk and the composite good. Also, by setting $d(q_G G) = 0$, the perceived risk–risk tradeoff between the child's health and the parent's health can be calculated as the ratio of the coefficients of dR^*_{pj} and dR^*_{cj}. Risk–risk tradeoffs have been calculated in other studies in the context of one person facing two (or more) hazards (Viscusi et al. 1991). The analysis presented here reformulates this concept in the context of parents trading off risk to themselves against a similar risk to a child. Moreover, note that the desired risk–risk tradeoff (the ratio of monetized marginal rates of substitution) reduces to U_{R*pj} / U_{R*cj}. In the timeless world considered here, this ratio reflects the parent's strength of preference at the margin for reducing his or her own skin cancer risk versus reducing risks faced by the child. Thus, it measures altruism of parents toward their children in the context of an environmental hazard, extending work by Viscusi et al. (1988).

A key aspect of the survey design involves defining a good G so that the four risk changes in equation (14.8) can be varied independently. This feature is important so as to avoid joint production problems that can complicate both estimation of option prices and development of risk–risk tradeoffs (see Hori 1975 and Bockstael and McConnell 1983 for additional details). In the context of the model at hand, the approach taken involves: (i) defining a hypothetical sunscreen lotion as a bundle of attributes offering different levels of melanoma and non-melanoma skin cancer protection for adults and children and (ii) varying these attributes independently. Product labels would convey information about attributes of the sunscreen products to survey respondents. Thus, this approach builds on earlier studies that have used labels to convey risk information and to elicit preferences for risk reduction (see, for example, Viscusi et al. 1986 and Dickie and Gerking 1996).

3. DATA

To implement the model, data were collected during summer of 2000 in an in-person survey of 160 parents of children aged 3–12. All survey respondents lived in the Hattiesburg, MS metropolitan statistical area. The location, climate and racial composition of this community make it a desirable setting for a study of risk beliefs about skin cancer. Hattiesburg lies near the coast of the Gulf of Mexico and has a subtropical climate with a great deal of sunshine. Also, African-Americans comprise 26 per cent of the population; thus, risk beliefs between groups with widely divergent skin cancer rates can be examined. Melanoma incidence among whites is about 16 times the incidence among blacks (Ries et al. 1999). Approximately 70 per cent of respondents had participated in a survey focused on acute respiratory illness experienced by adults and children. These respondents had originally been recruited by dialing telephone numbers in the Hattiesburg area at random during daytime and evening hours on both weekdays and weekends. At the conclusion of the earlier survey, conducted at the University of Southern Mississippi during June–July 2000, respondents indicated whether they were willing to participate in a second survey to be conducted later that summer. Those who indicated a willingness to participate were contacted by telephone during the recruitment of subjects for the skin cancer survey. A fresh round of random digit dialing was used to recruit the remaining 30 per cent of the sample. As telephone calls were made, those contacted were given a brief introduction in which the general idea of the survey was explained, and people were added to the sample if they agreed to participate and if they had at least one biological child between the ages of 3–12 living at their home. Respondents were told that they would receive $30 for participating and were asked to choose a convenient time to come to the University of Southern Mississippi for the interview.

The interview began by ascertaining the race and age of the respondent, the age and gender of all biological children living in the respondent's home, and the number of the respondent's other children who may live elsewhere. Of the 160 sample parents, 51 (32 per cent) were African-American, 110 (69 per cent) were women, and 84 per cent had either one or two biological children living with them. From among the children between the ages of 3 and 12, one child was randomly selected (if there was more than one) and designated the sample child. The remainder of the survey then obtained information about the parent/respondent and the sample child. Information was not obtained about other children to limit the length of the interview, to avoid repetitive questioning, and because in the model described above, parents treat each child equally. The interview then turned to a brief series of general questions about experiences with skin cancer, such as whether the respondent had ever been diagnosed with this disease or had known of anyone (relatives, friends, or public figures) who had it and/or died from it. Respondents were also asked if they ever had thought about the possibility of getting skin cancer as well as the possibility that their children might get it.

After these preliminary questions, respondents were shown two posters (one for melanoma and another for non-melanoma). As shown in the example in Figure 14.1, each poster had two risk ladders. The ladder on the left-hand side had 51 numbered steps going from zero to 100 in increments of two and the risk ladder on the right-hand side broke down the interval between the first and second rung (that is between zero and two chances in 100) into 10 smaller steps. Interviewers explained the concept of chances in 100, pointed out the reference risks shown beside some of the steps on the two ladders, and then showed respondents how to use the two ladders to represent a risk estimate. They then asked respondents to place a pin on the steps that best reflected their own chances of getting both melanoma and non-melanoma skin cancer at some point later in life (or getting it again if the respondent had already had it). After respondents completed this task, attention was directed to the sample child. Interviewers first asked whether the respondent believed that the other natural parent's future risk of skin cancer was higher, lower or about the same as their own and reminded respondents that there may be other factors causing the sample child's risk to be different as well. Then respondents were asked to estimate the lifetime risk of melanoma and non-melanoma skin cancer faced by the sample child using two risk ladders that were identical to the one shown in Figure 14.1. In answering for both themselves and the sample child, respondents were instructed not to consider the severity of the diseases and to focus only on the chances of occurrence. Interviewers also emphasized that the ladders were to help respondents collect their thoughts about skin cancer risk and did not represent 'quiz questions' with right or wrong answers.

Table 14.1 shows means of initial risk assessments for both types of skin cancer risk made by white and black parents for themselves and their sample children. On average, white parents placed their own lifetime risk of getting melanoma and non-melanoma skin cancer at steps 17.3 and 27.7, respectively, while black parents placed the corresponding risk estimates at steps 6.2 and 7.6. These estimates are larger than actual lifetime skin cancer risks estimates reported in Ries et al. (1999), which place lifetime melanoma and non-melanoma risks for whites at about steps 1.5 and 20, and for blacks at about steps 0.2 and 0.3. Thus, people in the lowest risk categories appear to have overestimated their own risk by the greatest amount. This outcome is consistent with observations by other investigators that people tend to overestimate small risks. Or, it may imply that some respondents did not understand the difference between the two types of skin cancer as melanoma risks were overestimated by a greater amount than non-melanoma risks. Yet, 16 per cent of respondents represented their risk of non-melanoma skin cancer on the small (right-hand) ladder (see Figure 14.1) and 32 per cent of respondents did the same to represent their risk of melanoma skin cancer.

Additionally, the fact that the survey introduced the possibility of getting skin cancer again if the respondent had already had it does not appear to be a significant complicating factor. Sample members were relatively young (recall that all were parents of a child aged between 3 and 12); their average

age was 36 years, 96 per cent were less than 50 years old, and only one reported personal experience with either form of this disease.

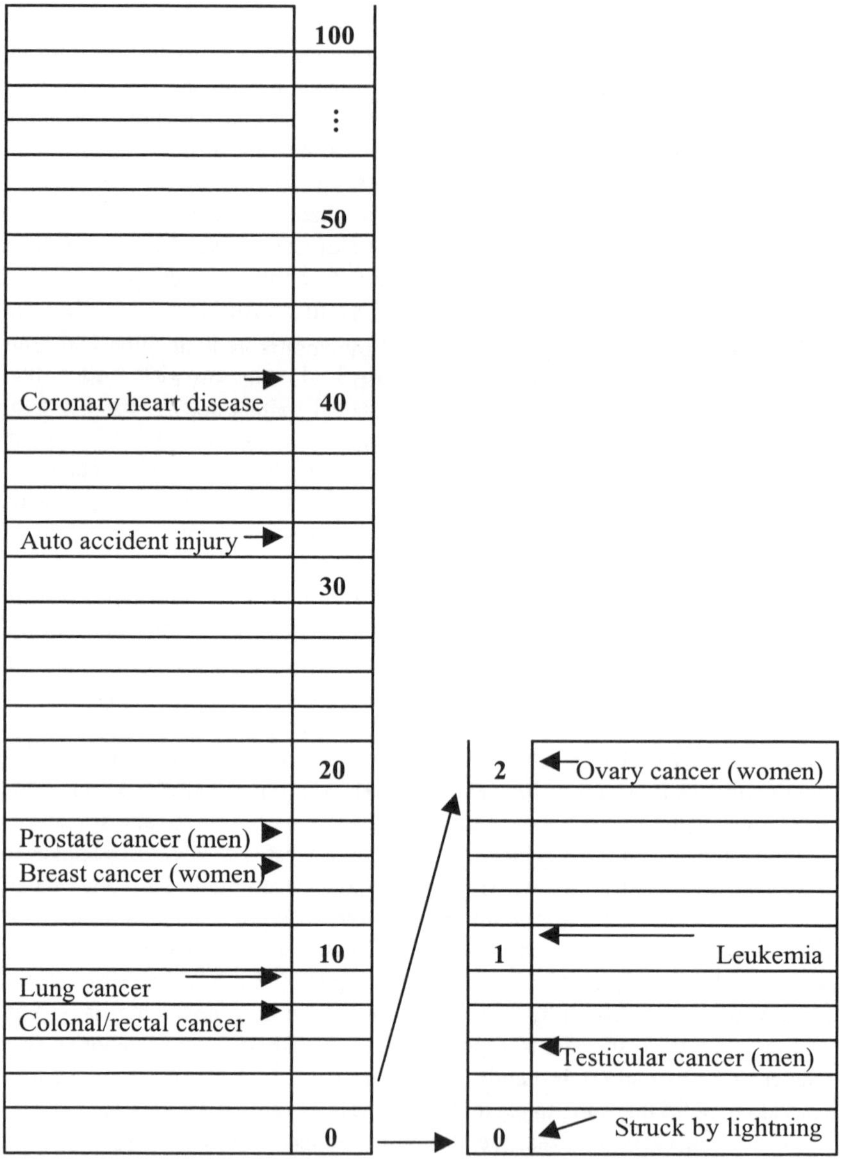

Figure 14.1 Parent's lifetime chance of melanoma skin cancer

Table 14.1 Mean values of perceived risk

	Parent				Child			
	Non-melanoma		Melanoma		Non-melanoma		Melanoma	
	Initial risk	Revised risk	Initial risk	Revised risk	Initial risk	Revised risk	Initial risk	Revised risk
White	27.67	21.85	17.28	10.09	21.90	15.23	13.93	5.87
Black	7.64	4.33	6.18	3.45	6.78	3.67	6.58	2.51

Also, Table 14.1 shows that risk estimates for sample children tended to be lower than those provided for the parent/respondents. For example, white parents placed their sample child's non-melanoma risk at step 21.9 (on average), while placing their own risk at step 27.7. The only exception in this regard is that African-American parents placed melanoma skin cancer risk faced by their children at step 6.6, while placing their own risk at step 6.2. This outcome conflicts with the possible hypothesis that parents will estimate higher risks for their children than for themselves because children have more years of life remaining in which to get skin cancer. However, it may reflect parents' beliefs that they take greater precautions regarding skin cancer risks with their own children than their parents did in an era when less information was available about the consequences of solar radiation exposure. Also, it may reflect: (i) a broader desire on the part of some parents to see harm come to themselves before coming to their children, (ii) an expectation that medical science will find ways to reduce future risks below the levels faced today and/or (iii) a recognition that it will take longer for skin cancer to develop in children than parents together with the notion that delayed risks are perceived as being smaller. Note that this last explanation implies that a discount rate may exist for risks. In any case, this finding together with the speculative explanations, points to an opportunity for more theoretical work as well as additional empirical estimates to see whether it emerges in related settings.

In the next segment of the survey, interviewers provided information to respondents about skin cancer risks and asked questions about skin cancer risk factors. First, respondents were told that the average person has an 18 per cent chance of getting non-melanoma skin cancer and a 1.4 per cent chance of getting melanoma skin cancer. Interviewers identified these points on the two sets of risk ladders using different colored pins, further indicated that skin cancer risk is higher for some demographic groups than others, and then moved the pins to show the applicable risks for the respondent's and sample child's race/gender group. Lifetime non-melanoma and melanoma risks shown were 28 per cent and 1.8 per cent for white males, 0.4 per cent and 0.2 per cent for black males, 12 per cent and 1.4 per cent for white females, and 0.2 per cent and 0.2 per cent for black females.

Then, interviewers collected information regarding genetic and lifestyle risk factors for both the respondent and the sample child. Data collected about genetic risk factors included natural skin color, sensitivity of skin to direct sunlight, eye color, natural hair color, freckles, and moles as well as whether an immediate relative had ever been diagnosed with skin cancer. Information obtained about lifestyle risk factors included time spent outdoors between 11 a.m. and 3 p.m. in a typical week during the summer months, a judgment as to whether lifetime exposure to sunlight had been more or less time than average, experience with bad sunburn, protective clothing (that is, hats and long-sleeve shirts) worn while in direct sunlight, and use of sun protection products.

After providing (and receiving) information about genetic and lifestyle risk factors, respondents were asked to make a second estimate of lifetime melanoma and non-melanoma skin cancer risk for themselves and their sample children. Respondents made these estimates using the same risk ladders as before, so their own initial estimates and average risk estimates provided by the interviewers were in view. As shown in Table 14.1, mean revised risk estimates are lower than initial risk estimates in all cases considered. Yet, even after receiving information about the two types of skin cancer, African-Americans continued to provide apparent overestimates of risk for themselves as well as their children and all respondents continued to substantially overestimate the lifetime risk of developing melanoma skin cancer. For example, white parents, on average, placed their own risk of melanoma at step 10.1 on the ladder, reflecting a risk estimate about five times higher than the actual risk they were shown. Also, respondents generally continued to estimate greater skin cancer risks for themselves than for their children.

The final part of the survey assessed willingness to pay for a hypothetical sun protection product. Respondents were shown one of four labels describing the hypothetical sunscreen and were given time to read it as if they were thinking of buying the product for the first time. Labels were randomly assigned to respondents and each label was presented to 40 respondents. Each of the labels (see Figure 14.2 for an example) indicated that the new sunscreen would be similar in some respects to currently marketed products (available in a variety of sun protective factors (SPFs), non-comedogenic, oil-free, and unscented) but that it would be more water-resistant and offer greater levels of skin cancer protection. The four labels differed in the amount of skin cancer protection offered. One label (the label shown in Figure 14.2) offered 'clinically proven maximal protection against exposures that increase chances of both melanoma and non-melanoma'. A second label offered limited protection against these exposures, while the third and fourth labels offered maximal protection against one type of skin cancer, but limited protection against the other.

Interviewers reviewed the features of the sunscreen label shown and then asked how much it would reduce both melanoma and non-melanoma skin cancer risks for both respondents and their sample children if they began using it right away according to the directions. Respondents then had an opportunity to make new estimates of lifetime skin cancer risk on each ladder which, when compared to the revised risk estimate discussed previously, reflected the perceived effectiveness of the product. Also, respondents were asked whether they would buy enough of the product to last one year for themselves and their sample children at one of eight prices. Interviewers instructed respondents not to consider buying the sunscreen for other people, such as other household members. Prices were randomly assigned to respondents, did not depend on the label shown, and each price was presented to 20 respondents. If respondents said that they would buy (not buy) at the stated price, they were asked if their decision would be the same at a higher (lower) price. Table 14.2 shows the resulting frequency distribution of initial prices for the sunscreen offered.

Table 14.2 Number of 'yes' and 'no' responses by initial price

	White		Black	
Initial Price	Yes	No	Yes	No
$ 5	14	0	3	3
$10	14	1	1	4
$15	11	1	3	5
$20	15	3	0	2
$30	8	4	2	6
$40	6	6	2	6
$50	5	7	3	5
$60	3	11	1	5
Total	76	33	15	36

Among white respondents, 70 per cent indicated that they would buy the sunscreen at the initial price offered, whereas 29 per cent of blacks chose to buy at the initial price. The survey then concluded by ascertaining marital status, schooling completed, occupation, and household income for each respondent.

(Front of Bottle)

SkinSaver

Sun Protection Lotion

For Adults & Children

Developed with dermatologists to protect skin from harmful effects of sun exposure.

Non-Melanoma Protection

Melanoma Protection

Ultra Waterproof

SPF___

Figure 14.2 Sample of hypothetical sunscreen label

(Back of Bottle)

New SkinSaver® sun protection lotion.

Skin Cancer Protection

Clinically proven maximal protection against long-term skin damage from total exposure to sun	Used regularly, helps reduce chances of Non-Melanoma skin cancer
Clinically proven maximal protection against long-term skin damage from incidents of over-exposure to sun	Used before high exposure, helps reduce chances of Melanoma skin cancer

Parents Note: 80% of lifetime sun exposure occurs before age 18 and even one incident of over-exposure in childhood can increase chances of Melanoma. Protect your child *and* yourself with SkinSaver®.

More Skin Protection

Parsol®1789	Extra protection against premature skin aging
SPF ___	__ times the skin's natural sunburn protection

More Added Features

∗ Ultra long-lasting waterproof formula – One application lasts all day∗

∗ Non-comedogenic–Won't block pores ∗ Oil-free–Won't feel greasy ∗

∗ Gentle enough for faces – even under make-up ∗

∗ Hypoallergenic ∗ PABA-free ∗ Unscented ∗

∗ Contains Aloe and Vitamin E ∗

DIRECTIONS: Apply generously and evenly to all exposed areas of skin at least 15 minutes before sun or water exposure.

ACTIVE INGREDIENTS: Oxybenzone, octocrylene, 2-ethylhexyl salicate, homosalate, avobenzone.

4. DETERMINANTS OF RISK BELIEFS

This section estimates determinants of parents' beliefs about skin cancer risk faced by their sample child. Data described in the previous section are applied to estimate equation (14.4) developed in Section 2. Estimates of this equation are useful in showing the extent to which parents use their own risk as a reference point in assessing a similar risk to their children. To obtain the equation estimated, equation (14.5) was substituted into equation (14.4) to obtain:

$$R^*_{Cj} = g(R^*_{Pj}, G, \Omega_C, \gamma, \theta). \qquad (14.9)$$

Two regressions are estimated, one for melanoma risk and another for non-melanoma risk, and estimation accounts for endogeneity of parent perceptions of their own skin cancer risk (R^*_{Pj}) and use of the sun protection product, G. Also note that equation (14.9) excludes I, q_G, and Ω_P from the complete set of exogenous variables in model (I, q_G, θ, γ, Ω_P, Ω_C). Thus, equation (14.9) is overidentified under the order condition.

Table 14.3 reports results of estimating equation (14.9) along with means and definitions of all variables used. In both regressions shown, the dependent variable is the initial step number from the risk ladder chosen by the parent/respondent to estimate perceived lifetime skin cancer risk to the sample child, measured as chances in 100. Instruments for the parent's own perceived risk of skin cancer (both melanoma and non-melanoma) and for the sample child's use of sun protection products were constructed using predicted values from reduced-form regressions of these variables on measures of (I, q_G, θ, γ, Ω_P, Ω_C), as discussed in connection with equation (14.7) in Section 2. Results of these regressions are reported in the appendix.

Also, in Table 14.3, the regressions reported were jointly estimated because medical and epidemiological evidence suggests that melanoma and non-melanoma risk factors are somewhat different. Whereas particular types of 'dangerous' moles (large, irregularly shaped, with shades of varying colors, and/or having a flat portion) and irregular but intense exposure to solar radiation are thought to be factors leading to greater risk of melanoma, non-melanoma risk has not been associated with these factors.

Results presented in Table 14.3 show that parents appear to have relied heavily on their estimate of skin cancer risk to themselves in making estimates of skin cancer risk to their sample child. In the survey, parents made risk estimates for themselves before being asked to make risk estimates for their sample child. Thus, a possible interpretation of this outcome is that parents recognized genetic similarities between themselves and their children and that some skin cancer risk factors are inherited characteristics. In any case, the coefficients of the parent-perceived risk variable in both the melanoma and non-melanoma equation were positive fractions that differed from zero at conventional significance levels. Both coefficients also were significantly less than unity, reflecting the previously discussed tendency for parents to make lower estimates of skin cancer risk for their children than they made for themselves.

In contrast, parent/respondents appear to have disregarded information about the sample child's skin color and complexion type as well as whether the child had freckles and/or particular types of moles in forming beliefs about both melanoma and non-melanoma skin cancer risk. Effects of these factors on skin cancer risks, however, may already have been picked up in the parent risk variable just discussed if it can be interpreted as a marker for transmission of genetic characteristics from parent to child. In this same vein, the child's gender has no effect on the parent's risk assessment even though females tend to have lower risk than males in the general population. This result also supports the notion that parents form beliefs about the child's risk through the lens of their own risk and do not explicitly assess the child's own risk factors.

Additionally, results from both the melanoma and non-melanoma equations indicate that respondents took account of perceived skin cancer risks faced by the other biological parent in making the risk assessment for the sample child. If parent/respondents believed that the other biological parent's risk was higher (lower) than their own, a higher (lower) risk estimate was made for the sample child. These effects were significant in both regressions at less than the 5 per cent level under a one-tail test. This outcome is not surprising because, as discussed in Section 2, respondents were reminded that the other biological parent's risk should be considered just prior to asking for a risk assessment for the child. Yet, it does reinforce the interpretation above that parents make skin cancer risk assessments for their children partly on the basis of inherited characteristics.

Parents also based their sample child's risk assessment of both melanoma and non-melanoma on prior exposure to solar radiation and ethnicity. On the one hand, if the child had ever used sunscreen, parents lowered their risk estimate by 12.1 percentage points in the case of non-melanoma and 10.6 percentage points in the case of melanoma. On the other hand, if the child had experienced three or more bad sunburns over his/her lifetime, parents increased their risk assessment by about 9.8 percentage points in the case of non-melanoma and 5.7 percentage points in the case of melanoma. Also, African-American respondents provided lower risk assessments for their children by 11.4 percentage points in the case of non-melanoma and by 7.6 percentage points in the case of melanoma. These results are noteworthy in that the survey elicited initial risk assessments *before* focusing on solar radiation exposure history and socioeconomic/demographic measures. Thus, these results again suggest that parents are at least broadly familiar with skin cancer risk factors and take them into account when making risk assessments for their children.

Table 14.3 Parent's perception of children's skin cancer risk, 3 SLS estimates[a]

Explanatory variable	Non-melanoma	Melanoma
Respondent's own perceived risk[b]	0.49	0.645
	(6.026)	(10.796)
Child uses sunscreen[b]	–12.139	–10.602
	(–2.304)	(–2.813)
Child complexion is fair	–0.266	–1.517
	(–0.098)	(0.778)
Child skin is type 1	1.642	0.668
	(0.689)	(0.396)
Child has freckles	2.989	–0.370
	(1.244)	(–0.22)
Respondent thinks other parent has higher risk	3.868	3.35
	(1.824)	(–2.199)
Respondent thinks other parent has lower risk	–4.3013	–3.551
	(–1.863)	(–2.245)
Child has had 3 or more bad sunburns	9.771	5.693
	(2.954)	(2.409)
Child is female	–1.504	–0.515
	(–0.901)	(–0.433)
Respondent is black	–11.395	–7.637
	(–2.959)	(–2.699)
Respondent knows people who have had skin cancer	0.775	0.005
	(0.369)	(–0.003)
Child has a 'dangerous' mole	–[c]	–0.829
		(–0.61)
Child has had irregular exposure	–[c]	–0.886
		(–1.098)
Constant	16.577	12.775
	(3.430)	(3.656)

Notes:

a. *t*-statistics in parentheses.

b. Endogenous variable.

c. Excluded variable.

5. TRADEOFFS BETWEEN PARENT AND CHILD HEALTH

Empirical estimates showing how parents make tradeoffs between their own health and the health of their children are based on equation (14.7) from Section 2 together with data described in Section 3. As previously discussed, equation (14.7) shows how parents vary expenditures on G in the face of perceived skin cancer risk changes to themselves and their children, holding utility constant. Expenditure data were obtained from responses about intentions to buy the hypothetical sun protection product. More specifically, dG is measured as the amount that respondents said they would pay for one year's supply of the sunscreen for themselves and their sample children. Perceived risk changes were measured by the difference between the revised and final steps chosen on the risk ladder, with the expectation that greater differences would be associated with higher intended expenditures.

The intended expenditure data are analyzed using the double-bound model described by Hanemann et al.(1991), Cameron and Quiggen (1994), and Alberini (1995). Four issues warrant further discussion before we examine the results. First, respondents' intended expenditures for the hypothetical sunscreen may have been influenced not only by its perceived effectiveness in reducing skin cancer risk, but also by its perceived effects on sun tanning, premature aging of skin, and possibly other factors. These joint production issues are ignored in developing the estimates presented below because earlier work (Dickie and Gerking 1996) focused extensively on these issues in a similar context, finding that they were relatively unimportant in determining willingness to pay for reducing skin cancer risk. Second, the expenditure data obtained from the survey pertain to a one-year's supply of sunscreen, rather than the lifetime supply envisaged in the theoretical model. This discrepancy is treated as an errors-in-variables problem in which the always non-negative disturbance imparts a downward bias to the estimate of the constant term, but has no effect on other estimates. Third, the analysis allows for probable simultaneity between sunscreen expenditure and perceived risk change. The appendix reports estimates of four equations for perceived risk change (parent and sample child risk of both melanoma and non-melanoma skin cancer) as a function of genetic risk factors, historical behavior, and socioeconomic/demographic characteristics. The estimator for the intended expenditure equation extends the work of Hanemann, Cameron and Quiggin, and Alberini and is adapted from methods developed by Amemiya (1978, 1979) for simultaneous probit and tobit models. Amemiya showed that his estimator was more efficient than the more commonly employed two-stage estimator which uses predicted values of jointly determined variables as regressors. Fourth, the intended expenditure equation was just-identified under the order condition by positing that variables measuring parent and child genetic characteristics (Ω_P and Ω_C), parents' perceptions and awareness of skin cancer (θ) and family characteristics (γ) have no direct impact on sunscreen expenditures and instead affect these expenditures indirectly through their impact on skin cancer risk.

Results from estimating the double-bound model are shown in Table 14.4. Coefficients presented are marginal effects, interpreted as the change in annual willingness to pay for the hypothetical sunscreen for a one-unit change in an explanatory variable. As shown, three of the four risk-change variables have marginal effects that are not significantly different from zero at conventional levels. The marginal effect of risk change for the sample child, however, is positive and significantly different from zero at less than the 5 per cent level using a two-tailed test. This estimate suggests that parents are willing to pay about \$3.18 for a one-percentage point reduction in non-melanoma risk to the child. Table 14.4 also indicates that willingness to pay for the sunscreen is higher for parents who were shown one of the two labels offering maximum protection from melanoma and who said that their sample child would use it.

An illustrative estimate of the marginal rate of substitution between risk to parents and risk to their children can be calculated simply by taking the ratio of the marginal effects of two risk changes reported in Table 14.4 (see discussion of equation (14.8)). This calculation is made for non-melanoma risk; estimated marginal effects for melanoma risk were not significantly different from zero either for children or for adults perhaps because respondents were asked about too many related risks (14.4) in the survey or because they had trouble with the two scales shown on each ladder. In any case, disregarding its low *t*-statistic, the point estimate of parents' willingness to pay to reduce their own non-melanoma risk is \$1.29 and the corresponding point estimate for sample children is \$3.18, as discussed above. Thus, the marginal rate of substitution in this case would be about 2.47, a result suggesting that parents are willing to accept about a 2.5 percentage point increase in non-melanoma skin cancer risk to themselves in return for lowering this risk to their children by one percentage point. Of course, this calculation is only an illustration in light of the fact that the marginal effect of a change in parent risk on willingness to pay for the sunscreen did not differ significantly from zero. Additionally, a Wald test for equality of the marginal effects of parent non-melanoma risk change and children's non-melanoma risk change yields a *p*-value of 0.39. Thus, the null hypothesis that the marginal rate of substitution between risk to children and risk to parents equals unity cannot be rejected at conventional levels of significance.

Table 14.4 Parent's willingness to pay for reductions in skin cancer risk

Explanatory variable	Marginal effect[a]
Parent's non-melanoma risk change[b]	1.294 (1.211)
Children's non-melanoma risk change	3.188 (2.001)
Parent's melanoma risk change	0.473 (0.362)
Children's melanoma risk change	–2.048 (–1.064)
Respondent is black	–5.186 (–0.764)
Respondent uses sunscreen	4.338 (0.426)
Child uses sunscreen	43.285 (3.451)
Maximum non-melanoma protection label	–4.198 (–0.601)
Maximum melanoma protection label	13.524 (2.146)
Constant	–13.044 (–1.342)

Notes:

a. *t*-statistics in parentheses.

b. Endogenous variable.

6. CONCLUSION

This chapter has looked into the way in which parents view their children's health using data collected from a survey of risk beliefs about skin cancer. The survey involved an extensive questionnaire administered to 160 parent/respondents living in Hattiesburg, MS with biological children currently aged 3–12. Evidence was presented suggesting that parents form beliefs about risks to their children largely through the lens of their beliefs about risks to themselves. In estimates presented, parents' own risk beliefs were a key determinant of their beliefs about their children's risk, while the children's genetic risk factors appeared to be relatively unimportant. An implication of this outcome is that public information policies about skin cancer risks to children should make certain that parents understand that they themselves are at risk.

ACKNOWLEDGEMENTS

The US Environmental Protection Agency partially funded the research described here under R-82871701-0. The research has not been subjected to agency review and therefore does not necessarily reflect the views of the agency, and no official endorsement should be inferred. We thank Chris Dockins and Ted Gayer for helpful comments, and Shalawn Clark and Fitzgerald Yaw for assistance with survey administration.

REFERENCES

Agee, M.D. and T.D. Crocker (1996), 'Parental altruism and child lead exposure: inferences from the demand for chelation therapy', *Journal of Human Resources*, **31**, 677–91.

Alberini, A. (1995), 'Efficiency vs. bias of willingness-to-pay estimates: bivariate and interval-data models', *Journal of Environmental Economics and Management*, **29**, 169–80.

Amemiya, T. (1978), 'The estimation of a simultaneous equation generalized probit model', *Econometrica*, **44**, 1193–205.

Amemiya, T. (1979), 'The estimation of a simultaneous equation tobit model', *International Economic Review*, **20**, 169–82.

American Academy of Dermatology (2001), 'Who is most at risk for melanoma?', available at: http://www.derm-infonet.com/melanomanet/risk_factors.htm.

American Cancer Society (2001), 'Cancer Reference Information: All about Skin Cancer', available at: http://www.cancer.org.

Arrow, K.J. (1982), 'Risk perception in psychology and economics', *Economic Inquiry*, **20**, 1–9.

Becker, G. (1991), *A Treatise on the Family*, Cambridge, MA: Harvard University Press.

Behrman, J.R., R.A. Pollak and P. Taubman (1995), *From Parent to Child: Intrahousehold Allocations and Intergenerational Relations in the United States*, Chicago: University of Chicago Press.

Bockstael, N.E. and K.E. McConnell (1983), 'Welfare measurement in the household production framework', *American Economic Review*, **73**, 806–14.

Cameron, T.A. and J. Quiggen (1994), 'Estimation using contingent valuation data from a "dichotomous choice with follow-up" questionnaire', *Journal of Environmental Economics and Management*, **27**, 218–34.

Creech, L.L. and J.A. Mayer (1998), 'Ultraviolet radiation exposure in children: a review of measurement strategies', *Annals of Behavioral Medicine*, **19**, 399–407.

Dickie, M. and S. Gerking (1991), 'Willingness to pay for ozone control: inferences from the demand for medical care', *Journal of Environmental Economics and Management*, **21**, 1–17.

Dickie, M. and S. Gerking (1996), 'Formation of risk beliefs, joint production and willingness to pay to avoid skin cancer', *Review of Economics and Statistics*, **78**, 451–63.

Dickie, M. and S. Gerking (1997), 'Genetic risk factors and offsetting behavior: the case of skin cancer', *Journal of Risk and Uncertainty*, **15**, 81–97.

Dickie, M. and D.V. Nestor (1998), 'Valuation of environmental health risks to children: a survey', presented at the World Congress of Environmental and Resource Economists,Venice, Italy.

Executive Order #13045 (1997), 'Protection of children from environmental health risks and safety risks', *Federal Register*, **62**, FR Doc. 97-10695, 564–6.

Finkel, E. (1998), 'Sorting the hype from the facts in melanoma', *The Lancet*, **351**, 1866.

Grether, D. and C. Plott (1979), 'Economic theory of choice and the preference reversal phenomenon', *American Economic Review*, **69**, 623–38.

Hanemann, W.M., J. Loomis and B. Kanninen (1991), 'Statistical efficiency of double-bounded dichotomous choice contingent valuation', *American Journal of Agricultural Economics*, **73**, 1255–63.

Hori, H. (1975), 'Revealed preferences for public goods', *American Economic Review*, **65**, 978–91.

Kahneman, D. and A. Tversky (1982), 'The psychology of preferences', *Scientific American*, **246**, 160–73.

Kunreuther, H. (1976), 'Limited knowledge and insurance protection', *Public Policy*, **24**, 227–61.

Lichtenstein, S., P. Slovic, B. Fischhoff, M. Layman and B. Combs (1978), 'Judged frequency of lethal events', *Journal of Experimental Psychology*, 4, 551–78.

MacKie, R.M., T. Freudenberger and T.C. Aitchison (1989), 'Personal risk factor chart for cutaneous melanoma', *The Lancet*, **354**, 487–90.

Pitt, M.M., M.R. Rosenzwieg and N. Hassan, M.D (1990), 'Productivity, health, and inequality in the intrahousehold distribution of food in low-income countries', *American Economic Review*, **80**, 1139–58.

Reynolds, K.D., J.M. Blaum, P.M. Jester, H. Weiss, S.J. Soong and R.J. Diclemente (1996), 'Predictors of sun exposure in asdolescents in a Southeastern U.S. population', *Journal of Adolescent Health*, **19**, 409–15.

Ries, L.A.G., C.L. Kosary, B.F. Hankey, B.A. Miller, L. Clegg and B.K. Edwards (eds) (1999), *SEER Cancer Statistics Review, 1973–96*, Bethesda, MD: National Cancer Institute.

Robinson, J.K., D.S. Rigel and R.A. Amonette (1997), 'Trends in sun exposure, attitudes, and behaviors: 1986 to 1996', *Journal of the American Academy of Dermatology*, **37**, 179–86.

Rosenzweig, M.R. and T.P. Schultz (1982), 'Market opportunities, genetic endowments, and intrafamily resource distribution', *American Economic Review*, **72**, 803–15.

Scotto, J., T.R. Fears and J.F. Fraumeni, Jr (1982), 'Solar radiation', in D. Schottenfeld and J.F. Fraumeni (eds), *Cancer Epidemiology and Prevention*, Philadelphia: W.B. Saunders Co., 254–76.

Slovic, P., B. Fischhoff and S. Lichtenstein (1985), 'Regulation of risk: a psychological perspective', in Roger Noll (ed.), *Regulatory Policy and the Social Sciences*, Berkeley, CA: University of California Press, 241–78.

Smith, V.K. and G. van Houtven (1998), 'Non-market valuation and the household', Paper presented at the Allied Social Sciences Association annual meeting.

Tversky, A., P. Slovik and D. Kahneman (1990), 'The causes of preference reversal', *American Economic Review*, **80**, 204–17.

US Environmental Protection Agency (USEPA) (1996), *A National Agenda to Protect Children's Health from Environmental Threats*, Washington DC: USEPA.

Viscusi, W.K., W. Magat and A. Forrest (1988), 'Altruistic and private valuations of risk reduction', *Journal of Policy Analysis and Management*, **7**, 227–45.

Viscusi, W.K., W. Magat and J. Huber (1986), 'Informational regulation of consumer health risks: an empirical evaluation of hazard warnings', *Rand Journal of Economics*, **17**, 351–65.

Viscusi, W.K., W. Magat and J. Huber (1991), 'Pricing environmental health risks: survey assessments of risk–risk and risk–dollar tradeoffs for chronic bronchitis', *Journal of Environmental Economics and Management*, **21**, 32–51.

APPENDIX 14A1

Table 14A1.1 Reduced-form equations, estimated coefficients (t-statistics)

Explanatory variable	Respondent's own initial risk assessment (non-melanoma)	Respondent's own initial risk assessment (melanoma)	Child's use of sun protection products
Respondent complexion is fair	−5.646 (−0.825)	−0.766 (−0.124)	−0.132 (−1.057)
Respondent skin is Type 1	6.841 (1.281)	4.866 (1.010)	0.004 (0.039)
Respondent has freckles	−4.392 (−1.014)	0.457 (0.117)	0.119 (1.509)
Respondent has a 'dangerous' mole	10.308 (2.365)	6.538 (1.662)	0.095 (1.199)
Respondent exposure has been irregular	−1.871 (−0.462)	−0.041 (−0.011)	−0.004 (−0.048)
Respondent has had 3 or more bad sunburns (with peeling/blisters)	6.561 (1.325)	5.975 (1.338)	0.057 (0.631)
Respondent had bad sunburn as child or teenager	−5.900 (−1.225)	−4.843 (−1.115)	0.133 (1.511)
Respondent is female	2.926 (0.689)	2.833 (0.739)	0.088 (1.139)
Respondent age in years	0.022 (0.078)	0.226 (0.872)	0.006 (1.159)
Respondent thinks own lifetime exposure is greater than average	−1.540 (−0.354)	−8.457 (−2.153)	−0.034 (−0.432)
Respondent thinks own lifetime exposure is less than average	−1.732 (−0.399)	−7.870 (−2.012)	−0.049 (−0.617)
Child complexion is fair	4.385 (0.683)	−0.271 (−0.047)	−0.001 (−0.009)
Child skin is Type 1	3.323 (0.606)	−1.951 (−0.394)	−0.064 (−0.640)
Child has freckles	−5.415 (−1.037)	−2.886 (−0.612)	0.033 (0.341)
Child has a 'dangerous' mole	2.026 (0.320)	1.669 (0.292)	0.137 (1.187)
Respondent thinks other parent has higher risk	2.616 (0.593)	1.054 (0.265)	−0.052 (−0.640)

Explanatory variable	Respondent's own initial risk assessment		Child's use of sun protection products
	(non-melanoma)	(melanoma)	
Respondent thinks other parent has lower	8.395	2.669	–0.151
risk	(1.843)	(0.649)	(–1.816)
	0.428	0.597	0.076
Child exposure has been irregular	(0.111)	(0.172)	(1.084)
Child has had 3 or more bad sunburns	10.203	7.830	–0.102
(with peeling/blisters)	(1.570)	(1.336)	(–0.864)
	2.899	–0.926	0.059
Child is female	(0.867)	(–0.307)	(0.964)
	–1.099	–0.270	–0.016
Child age in years	(–1.725)	(–0.470)	(–1.418)
	–13.419	–11.216	–0.527
Race = black	(–2.161)	(–2.002)	(–4.650)
Respondent knows of relative, friend or	3.772	1.350	0.031
public figure diagnosed with skin cancer	(0.898)	(0.356)	(0.411)
	2.362	–1.127	–0.059
Family income	(0.496)	(–0.262)	(–0.682)
	2.776	–1.542	–0.024
Family income	(0.460)	(–0.283)	(–0.220)
	–1.233	0.474	–0.028
Number of children	(–0.649)	(0.276)	(–0.811)
	–2.289	–4.190	–0.063
Respondent is married	(–0.529)	(–1.074)	(–0.795)
	2.578	–0.900	0.051
Respondent is college graduate	(0.630)	(–0.244)	(0.687)
	2.635	2.001	–0.024
Respondent is employed	(0.553)	(0.465)	(–0.274)
	–4.086	0.741	–0.132
Respondent has blue-collar occupation	(–0.987)	(0.198)	(–1.747)
	–2.285	5.461	0.016
Respondent looks better with tan	(–0.436)	(1.155)	(0.168)
	6.865	–5.195	0.026
Child looks better with tan	(1.449)	(–1.215)	(0.299)
	22.146	9.892	0.667
Constant	(1.757)	(0.870)	(2.901)

Explanatory variable	Respondent's own initial risk assessment (non-melanoma)	Respondent's own initial risk assessment (melanoma)	Child's use of sun protection products
R^2	0.37	0.27	0.58
F statistic *p*-value	<0.001	0.07	<0.001
N	160	160	160

Table 14A1.2 Reduced-form equations, changes in perceived risk, estimated coefficients (t-statistics)

	Changes in perceived risk with use of new sunscreen			
	Non-melanoma risk change		Melanoma risk change	
Explanatory variable	Respondent	Child	Respondent	Child
	−3.555	1.425	−5.124	0.328
Respondent complexion is fair	(−1.764)	(1.010)	(−3.074)	(0.345)
	−2.851	−0.455	−0.030	−0.778
Respondent skin is Type 1	(−1.691)	(−0.386)	(−0.021)	(−0.979)
	−0.815	0.371	−0.255	−0.172
Respondent has freckles	(−0.595)	(0.387)	(−0.225)	(−0.266)
	0.335	1.470	0.094	0.385
Respondent has a 'dangerous' mole	(0.256)	(1.603)	(0.087)	(0.623)
	−1.179	−0.809	−0.505	−1.287
Respondent is female	(−0.918)	(−0.900)	(−0.475)	(−2.125)
	−0.076	0.018	−0.099	−0.040
Respondent age in years	(−0.850)	(0.295)	(−1.342)	(−0.940)
Respondent thinks own lifetime exposure is	−0.873	−1.122	−0.547	−0.171
greater than average	(−0.639)	(−1.174)	(−0.484)	(−0.266)
Respondent thinks own lifetime exposure is	1.381	0.643	0.119	0.233
less than average	(1.057)	(0.702)	(0.110)	(0.379)
Respondent thinks inherited risk factors give self greater than average chance of	2.883	−0.145	3.845	0.122
skin cancer	(1.503)	(−0.108)	(2.423)	(0.135)
Respondent thinks inherited risk factors give self lower than average chance of skin	0.515	0.490	−2.318	−0.620
cancer	(0.257)	(0.350)	(−1.400)	(−0.657)
	−0.669	−3.190	2.758	−1.545
Child complexion is fair	(−0.335)	(−2.282)	(1.669)	(−1.641)
	2.529	1.878	−0.648	−0.150
Child skin is Type 1	(1.509)	(1.600)	(−0.467)	(−0.189)
	1.192	1.030	2.039	0.118
Child has freckles	(0.783)	(0.967)	(1.620)	(0.164)
Respondent thinks inherited risk factors give child greater than average chance of	−2.909	−1.822	−1.696	1.068
skin cancer	(−1.455)	(−1.301)	(−1.025)	(1.132)
Respondent thinks inherited risk factors give child lower than average chance of	−1.944	−0.629	1.691	1.178

	Changes in perceived risk with use of new sunscreen			
	Non-melanoma risk change		Melanoma risk change	
Explanatory variable	Respondent	Child	Respondent	Child
skin cancer	(–1.019)	(–0.471)	(1.071)	(1.309)
Respondent thinks other parent has higher	–0.127	0.742	1.950	–0.021
risk	(–0.094)	(0.779)	(1.733)	(–0.033)
Respondent thinks other parent has lower	2.257	0.343	1.165	–0.983
risk	(1.585)	(0.344)	(0.988)	(–1.464)
Child has had 3 or more bad sunburns (with	–0.047	0.866	0.096	1.452
peeling/blisters)	(–0.034)	(0.900)	(0.085)	(2.238)
	–0.197	0.460	–1.351	0.103
Child is female	(–0.174)	(0.582)	(–1.447)	(0.193)
	–0.087	–0.139	0.102	0.029
Child age in years	(–0.458)	(–1.048)	(0.651)	(0.329)
	0.659	0.676	–0.317	0.122
Race = black	(0.366)	(0.536)	(–0.213)	(0.144)
	3.161	0.523	3.341	0.638
Family annual income	(2.150)	(0.508)	(2.747)	(0.920)
	0.517	–0.261	1.459	1.498
Family annual income	(0.276)	(–0.199)	(0.941)	(1.695)
	0.324	–0.538	0.618	–0.243
Number of children	(0.549)	(–1.301)	(1.266)	(–0.872)
	0.001	–1.703	–0.618	–0.487
Respondent is married	(0.001)	(–1.764)	(–0.542)	(–0.749)
	–2.293	–0.171	–2.192	0.361
Respondent is college graduate	(–1.892)	(–0.201)	(–2.187)	(0.631)
	0.480	0.326	–1.250	–0.925
Respondent is employed	(0.329)	(0.319)	(–1.035)	(–1.344)
	0.146	–0.648	1.146	0.326
Respondent has blue-collar occupation	(0.117)	(–0.744)	(1.113)	(0.555)
Respondent would use new sunscreen if	1.750	0.945	0.285	0.647
purchased	(0.948)	(0.731)	(0.187)	(0.743)
Child would use new sunscreen if	1.160	1.103	0.114	–0.278
purchased	(0.572)	(0.777)	(0.068)	(–0.291)
Label indicates maximum non-melanoma	1.109	–0.794	1.067	–0.623
protection	(1.084)	(–1.109)	(1.261)	(–1.291)
Label indicates maximum melanoma	–0.901	0.106	0.639	0.040
protection	(–0.919)	(0.155)	(0.788)	(0.087)
	0.192	–0.002	–0.010	0.007

	Changes in perceived risk with use of new sunscreen			
	Non-melanoma risk change		Melanoma risk change	
Explanatory variable	Respondent	Child	Respondent	Child
Respondent non-melanoma RISK1	(4.272)	(–0.078)	(–0.264)	(0.350)
	–0.170	0.195	–0.263	–0.095
Child non-melanoma RISK1	(–1.992)	(3.261)	(–3.732)	(–2.356)
	–0.049	0.025	0.206	0.136
Respondent melanoma RISK1	(–0.743)	(0.536)	(3.792)	(4.376)
	0.287	0.092	0.304	0.329
Child melanoma RISK1	(2.405)	(1.096)	(3.083)	(5.851)
	2.410	0.814	3.178	2.437
Constant	(0.666)	(0.321)	(1.062)	(1.428)
R^2	0.440	0.530	0.570	0.740
F statistic p-value	0.001	0.001	0.001	0.001
N	153	153	153	153

15. The Effect of Heavy Metal Content on Food Pricing Behaviour: Experimental Assessment

Anne Rozan, Anne Stenger and Marc Willinger

1. INTRODUCTION

In this chapter we present the results of an experiment designed to elicit willingness to pay (WTP) for food safety. This is done by comparing two types of products: 'regular' products for which heavy metal content is unknown, and 'labelled' products for which heavy metal content is controlled. Food safety was implemented by a hypothetical heavy metals control in food before distribution on a market. Three heavy metals were considered: cadmium, mercury and lead. Participants were involved in a series of experimental markets in which they could make real transactions. Three types of food products (bread, apples and potatoes) were offered, each on a separate market. These products are among the most frequently bought food products by French households. Furthermore these products are each representative of a different family of products that are exposed to contamination by heavy metals: vegetables (potatoes), fruit (apples) and cereals (bread). The main factor of contamination by heavy metals is due to the practice of sewage sludge disposal on agricultural soils. Although there is considerable uncertainty about the extent to which these products can be contaminated, there is evidence that these categories of food products are directly exposed to contamination because of sewage sludge disposal on soil. Other food products, such as meat or fish, are only indirectly contaminated, with an even higher degree of uncertainty.

The main objective of our experiment was to understand the process by which subjects revise their valuation of a product when new information about the risk induced by its consumption is provided. First, we elicited their valuation for each product without providing any information about heavy metals. Then we provided public information about heavy metal content for each product, and the long-term potential health consequences for alternative consumption scenarios. The subjects then re-evaluated exactly the same products. In addition we elicited their valuation for a set of 'labelled products' whose heavy metal content was controlled. This was done in two different ways: subjects were asked to state a value for each product, and those who agreed to participate in a market were asked to submit a bid for the product, after being told that transactions would be made according to the BDM (Becker–De Groot–Marschak) procedure (Becker et al. 1964). We tested for differences between *ex post* bids and values and *ex ante* bids and values, for labelled and unlabelled products.

In the next section we provide background on food contamination by heavy metals in order to state more precisely the aims of our study. In Section 3 we present the experimental design and in Section 4 we present our results. Section 5 concludes.

2. CONTEXT AND OBJECTIVES

The determination of heavy metals-related food risk requires an understanding of how heavy metals can contaminate humans via the food chain. Heavy metal contamination can be induced through many sources. Soils naturally contain heavy metals, but their content is increased by atmospheric inputs (generated by industrial and urban activities), fertilizers and pesticides. This soil contamination is to some extent irreversible as it appears impossible to eliminate the heavy metal surplus. This is of particular concern for agricultural soils, because of the risk that heavy metals contaminate the food chain. Unlike other toxic substances, heavy metals accumulate in the edible parts of plants. The risk depends on the mobility and bio-availability of heavy metals and on the nature of the soils and plants involved. Some metals are more or less mobile in soils and may or may not reach the upper parts of the plant. Though some of the mobility and bio-availability factors are easy to measure (for example, pH), determination of the food risk contamination is tricky. Furthermore, the transfer process of heavy metals from the soil to plants is poorly documented, because of the lack of data for bio-availability.

Agricultural practices may involve potential food residual contamination and toxic effects in the long term, indirect and even unknown for human health (fertilizers, pesticides, sewage sludge and so on). It is very difficult to establish a 'dose-response' function for each heavy metal, because the relevant data are missing in many cases: in particular, cohort studies for human long-run exposure do not exist. Animal experiments provide estimations of the carcinogenic effects of some heavy metals (for example, cadmium, beryllium or lead), but epidemiological studies cannot confirm these results, except in the case of certain metals such as nickel for which 'dose-response' functions have been found in the industrial sector (Maximilien and Masse 1994).[1] Moreover, some metallic micropollutants (for example, iron or copper) are in fact essential to life and become toxic for humans only beyond a certain level of concentration. Besides the consumption of plants, humans are also exposed to heavy metals through eating meat and fish and drinking water as well as ingesting and inhalating dust. For example, mercury and its derivatives present in industrial areas produce atmospheric fallout. This is also the case for lead in the atmosphere which enters the organism via the respiratory tract.

The main consequences for human health ought to be measured in terms of life expectancy. The toxicity of metals depends on their concentration in organs, which itself depends on their accumulation process. In general, critical concentration will be attained only in the long run, depending on the combination of various factors, such as agricultural practices, consumption habits, exposure to different sources, and so on. However, the health risk potentially threatens the entire population through the consumption of vegetables, beverages and meat. Animal production would be affected mainly through the use of contaminated pasture land and the feeding of fodder.

The dangers of certain trace elements for human health have been identified through investigations concerning the main sources of contamination. It is estimated that about half of the human ingestion of lead, cadmium and mercury has a plant origin (fruit, vegetables and cereals). Moreover, some population groups seem to be more exposed, especially vegetarians since they absorb 'tolerable daily doses' (Decloître 1998) more frequently. It appears therefore that food contamination is the most important one for heavy metals. Further, vegetables comprise a large part of this contamination. Human exposure to heavy metals through consumption of vegetables depends on several types of factors which can be grouped into three categories. First, there are intrinsic factors such as pH, soil structure and types of cultures more or less favourable to the transmission of metals. Second, the risk of human contamination is naturally dependent on the nature and the quantity of toxic components in the contaminants and in the soil. Third, the risk of contamination is related to the food consumption habits of the individual (type of purchase, eating home produce and so on).

While exposure to heavy metals could be reduced by imposing controls on several heavy metal contaminants, such regulations generally do not exist. For example, in France a few recommendations have been made by the National Council of Public Health, but there are no laws restricting the use of pesticides or nitrates to control heavy metal soil contamination. As epidemiological data are lacking for some heavy metals, there is no 'objective' measure of the health risk induced by soil contamination, through the consumption of vegetables, fruit and cereals. This is partly why we are interested in the consumer's perception of this risk. Since there is no objective measure available, we may have to rely on a subjective evaluation of the risk as perceived by the consumer. To do this, we elicited WTP for various consumption goods, in a controlled laboratory experiment, in which we informed subjects about heavy metal content and its possible health effects.

Several studies (Lin and Milon 1995; Hayes et al. 1995) showed that consumers have a higher WTP for food safety only if they perceive a risk to their own health. Their risk perception depends in particular on their knowledge of health risks and on their confidence in measures taken to inform the public. One may therefore question the use of labels to prevent health risks linked to food safety. The introduction of labelled products in pre-existing markets can have two different effects on consumers' WTP: a decrease in the WTP for unlabelled products and an increase in WTP for labelled products in comparison to unlabelled products. According to Bagnara's study (1996) on the use of pesticides in the production of peaches, the introduction of a label is not sufficient to increase the consumer's WTP for the product. However, products that are not labelled are lower priced.

For most consumers, food security valuation concerned the setting of controls for food pathogens (Hayes et al. 1995), the use of a genetically engineered growth enhancer (Buhr et al. 1993) or the development of irradiation in meat to control *Trichinella* (Fox et al. 1998). Experimental techniques have already been applied to value food security (Shin et al. 1992; Buhr et al. 1993; Hayes et al. 1995; Melton et al. 1996; Fox et al. 1998). Experiments help us to better understand the process by which consumers revise their WTP for various food products when new processes or products are introduced in the market. Furthermore, experimental procedures provide better control over WTP elicitation and are easily replicable. Finally, it has been claimed that experimental data can provide guide-values comparable to contingent valuation data (Shogren 1993). Valuation of food safety with respect to heavy metals was first explored by Stenger (2000).

The present study relies on experimental markets for real food products to assess WTP for food safety. We use the Becker–De Groot–Marschak (BDM) elicitation procedure to assess subjects' willingness to pay for food products. It is well known that the BDM procedure has a unique dominant strategy for which subjects announce their true WTP. In the first stage of the procedure each subject secretly submits a buying price. In stage 2 a selling price is randomly chosen. Subjects whose stated buying price is at least equal to the selling price make a transaction in which they have to pay the selling price. In the experiment the exchange involved cash against a specified quantity of the food item. Subjects whose buying price is lower than the selling price are excluded from the transaction. As shown below, stating a buying price above the value represents taking the risk of making a loss, while stating a buying price below the value excludes the subject from a potentially beneficial transaction. Let us make this point clear.

To see why under the BDM procedure stating a buying price equal to the true value is a dominant strategy, let us define v_i player i's private value for the good. Player i's strategy is to announce a buying price b_i, with $b_i \in [p_m, p^M]$ and $p_m < p^M$. After the potential buyer has announced his/her buying price, the selling price p^s is randomly drawn in the interval $[p_m, p^M]$ with uniform probability. If $b_i \geq p^s$ player i buys the item at the selling price. If $b_i < p^s$ player i cannot buy it. Player i's best strategy is to announce $b_i = v_i$. To see this, first assume that $b_i > v_i$. If $p^s \in [v_i , b_i]$, player i makes a loss equal to $p^s - v_i$. Therefore $b_i > v_i$ cannot be an equilibrium. If $b_i < v_i$ and $p^s \in [b_i, v_i]$ player i makes an opportunity loss equal to $v_i - p^s$. Therefore $b_i = v_i$ is the unique dominant strategy equilibrium. Note that the result extends to a discrete strategy space with $b_i \in \{p_m, \ldots, p^M\}$, as the ones used in our experiment.

By combining real transactions and the BDM procedure, we avoid several important biases that generally affect contingent valuation studies, in particular the hypothetical bias. However, this requires that subjects understand correctly the procedure and are convinced that stating their true valuation is the better strategy for them. To guarantee that this was the case in our experimental sessions, we included a teaching phase before the real assessment phase to check the subjects' understanding and allow them to learn the dominant strategy. More details on this part of the procedure are provided in the next section.

3. EXPERIMENTAL DESIGN

Sixty participants were involved in the experiment and were assigned to one of the five sessions that were organized. In contrast to most experiments set up by economists, we used only non-student subjects. All our participants were therefore recruited by an independent company according to two criteria: age and 'responsible for food shopping for the household'. Table 15.1 provides summary statistics about the sample. Participants were told that they would participate in an experimental session, organized by Université Louis Pasteur, about their food consumption behaviour. They were also told that they would earn a FF 150 participation fee for the experiment. Below, we describe the instructions, given both verbally and also partly handed out in written form, together with answer sheets.

*Table 15.1 Main characteristics of the sample (*n *= 60 participants)*

Variable	*n* (total number)
Women (*1 if woman*)	51
Informed about heavy metals previously (*1 if yes*)	31
Perceived health risk (*1 if yes*)	53
Apple consumption in a week (*1 if yes*)	45
Potato consumption in a week (*1 if yes*)	43
Baguette consumption in a week (*1 if yes*)	53
Age (*in years*)	Average 44.9 Max = 62 Min = 30

After arriving at the experimental room, each participant received a small envelope containing his/her code number (which he/she had to quote on all answer sheets during the experiment) and a participation fee of FF 150 in cash. They were told that this sum was theirs to keep, on condition that they stayed until the end of the experiment. Subjects were also told that they were not obliged to make any transaction if they did not want to. On the other hand, if they wanted to make a transaction, they were told that they would have to use their own money (those who did not bring any money could use their participation fee). Next, oral instructions were provided by the experimenter with the help of overheads. The experiment was divided into the five stages that are detailed below.

In *stage 1* the experimenter gave a general presentation of the objectives and principles of the research. Subjects were told that the objective was to assess their personal valuation of various food products through real transactions in the laboratory. To do this they would have to announce their 'buying price' (bid) which would be defined in the instructions. They were also told that if they were selected to make a transaction then they would have to exchange a real cash amount for the chosen food item. They were told that the general procedure was based on a draw of a selling price at random just after they had stated their buying price. If their buying price was higher than the selected selling price, they would receive the product in exchange for a cash amount equal to the selling price. They were also told that subjects whose buying price was lower than the selling price would not participate in the transaction. A practical example was provided involving four individuals who were asked to state a buying price for a chocolate bar. We checked the correct understanding of the transaction procedure by asking participants to identify the buyers who were selected to buy the chocolate bar once the selling price was revealed to them.

In *stage 2*, a bottle of Chinese aperitif wine was put in front of each subject for inspection. After inspection they were told that they could buy one bottle of this wine. An answer sheet was handed out on which they were asked whether they wanted to buy the bottle of wine, and if 'yes' to indicate their buying price (with a minimum of FF 5 and a maximum of FF 50, in whole amounts). Once the answer sheets were collected, the selling price was randomly drawn in the same interval as the bid and was announced publicly to the subjects. Transactions were implemented immediately afterwards for those whose buying price was higher than the selling price. Twenty of the 60 participants bought Chinese wine at a mean selling price of FF 24.6 (the minimum price was FF 9 and the maximum FF 50). Participants who made a transaction at this stage, had to pay the price for their purchase immediately.

Stage 3 was intended to familiarize the subjects with the BDM procedure. We told them that we would sell a token according to the same rule as for the bottle of Chinese wine. Their valuation of the token was marked on their record sheet for stage 3. Each subject was given a private valuation, v_i, that would be redeemed by the experimenter if he/she participated in the transaction. If the subject's buying price for token b_i was higher than the selling price p^s, then he/she would buy the token and earn the difference $v_i - p^s$. A fictitious example involving four individuals was provided in order to explain that their 'best decision' would be to announce that $b_i = v_i$. The example was presented by the experimenter and the different possible outcomes of the procedure were pointed out. Subjects could ask questions. After the example, a sequence of three markets for buying a token followed. Subjects were told that in the two first markets, tokens would not actually be sold, but that in the third market transactions would be implemented and could lead either to gains or losses. For each market, there were new valuations. Subjects were asked to write down on the answer sheet both their private valuation of the token (v_i) as well as their buying price (b_i). Authorized bids were restricted to whole amounts between FF 2 and FF 13. After participants had handed in their answer sheet, the experimenter selected the selling price for the token by throwing two dice at random. Next, the experimenter wrote all the values and bids on the board and commented on each of the participants' decisions in turn.

Stage 4 corresponds to the real purpose of the experiment, which was to evaluate real food products. Each subject was given a sample of the three products that were sold: one apple, one potato and one baguette. As is the case in most outlets where these products are sold, subjects were allowed only to touch the products, but not to taste them. After inspecting the products they were given an answer sheet on which they had to answer three questions for each product:

1. How much do you value this product?
2. Do you want to buy this product?
3. If you answered yes to question 2, indicate your buying price.

The quantity and price range were different from one product to another: 1 kg and FF 5–30 for apples, 2 kg and FF 5–30 for potatoes and one baguette and FF 1–12.50 for bread. Except in the case of bread participants had to nominate whole amounts. They were told that if they elected to buy several products, they could in fact buy only one of them, which would be randomly selected at the end of the session.

In *stage 5*, subjects were given written information about the heavy metal content (lead, cadmium and mercury) of the products. The information was presented in table format and was also displayed using the overhead projector. The experimenter explained the meaning of the data and the possible long-term consequences of consuming products whose heavy metal content was above the standards displayed in the table. After the information was communicated an additional sample of each product was provided to each subject. This additional sample was tagged with the label 'Controlled for Heavy Metal Content'. The label guaranteed that the heavy metal content was not larger than the figures displayed in the table. Subjects could compare the controlled products on their table with the uncontrolled ones.

After inspecting the products they were given three answer sheets, one for each product. On each answer sheet they had to answer the same questions as in stage 4, for the controlled and the uncontrolled products. The experimenter explained that only one of the two stages, 4 or 5, would be selected at the end of the experiment for making real transactions.

The experiment ended with transactions taking place. Subjects were also asked to fill out a short form with personal data (age, sex, education, and so on). A debriefing session followed, during which subjects could give their impressions and ask questions. In all, each session lasted between an hour and a half and two hours.

4. RESULTS AND DISCUSSION

In our questionnaire subjects were first asked to state a 'value' for the product. The stated value is comparable to an answer to a hypothetical valuation question and therefore does not necessarily correspond to the subjects' true WTP. After these values had been recorded, subjects were asked whether they wanted to buy the product, and in the case of a 'yes' answer they had to state their buying price. With such a questionnaire design we could obtain a valuation for each subject, even for those who did not want to make a transaction. We could therefore rely on a complete data set for testing our hypotheses on the price revision process. We could also analyse buying prices and private values separately, and check for consistency for those participants who wanted to make a transaction. We did not find any significant difference (*t*-test, 5 per cent), for any of the products, between values and bids for those subjects who agreed to buy the product. We therefore concluded that the subjects had correctly implemented the dominant strategy in the BDM procedure.

4.1 Buying Prices

We elicited three different buying prices in the experiment. P1 was the buying price of each unlabelled product before the subject had received information about the heavy metal content, and was taken as the benchmark. The two other prices were elicited after the information about heavy metal content was provided to the subjects: P2 was the revised buying price of each unlabelled product after subjects were informed, and $P2^*$ was the corresponding buying price for the labelled products.

Table 15.2 reports the average buying prices for each product with and without the information. Details of the price distribution can be found in Appendix 15A1 (Table 15A1.1). The last three columns of Table 15.2 present the results of a within-subject comparison (Wilcoxon signed rank test) of our main hypotheses. Only subjects who decided to buy the goods are taken into account for this test. According to hypothesis 1, subjects' buying price for unlabelled goods is lower when they are informed than when they are not informed about heavy metal content (H_0: P2 < P1). Hypothesis 2 states that subjects have a higher buying price for labelled goods than for unlabelled goods when they are informed (H_0: $P2^*$ > P2). Finally, hypothesis 3 states that subjects' buying price for labelled goods (that is, after information is provided) is higher than their buying price for unlabelled goods when they are uninformed.

The results reported in Table 15.2 show that subjects have higher buying prices for labelled products than for unlabelled products both in the informed situation and in the uninformed situation. For the three products, the buying prices are significantly higher for labelled goods than for unlabelled goods when no information is provided ($P_2^* > P_1$). Other price differences are not significant at the 5 per cent level. Note that the buying price for unlabelled products is not significantly affected when information is provided, although it decreases on average. When subjects are informed about the potential risks of heavy metal content, we observe that buying prices for labelled products are higher on average than buying prices for unlabelled products ($P2^* > P2$). However this difference is not significant for any of the products. This is due to the fact that buying prices for labelled products unexpectedly increased slightly after information about heavy metal content was provided.

Table 15.2 Mean buying prices elicited by the BDM procedure

	n_1	P1	n_2	P2	n_3	$P2^*$	P2 < P1	$P2^*$ > P2	$P2^*$ > P1
Apples	35	10.98 (3.06)	14	12.07 (3.08)	36	13.26 (3.72)	NS	NS	5%
Potatoes	25	12.52 (3.45)	14	13.29 (4.48)	25	15.16 (4.65)	NS	10%	5%
Baguettes	30	4.42 (0.8)	17	4.50 (1.57)	31	5.69 (2.85)	NS	10%	5%

Note: n_i: number of subjects; standard deviations in parentheses. NS means not significant.

The reason why the price of unlabelled products increased on average is that most of the subjects who declared that they were willing to make a transaction for an unlabelled good when they were uninformed, rejected the same transaction after information was provided. Therefore the average P_2 price is calculated on a different subset of subjects. The increase in the mean price P_2 with respect to P_1 contrasts with the behaviour of buyers. As shown in Table 15.3, after information was provided many buyers exit the market of the unlabelled good and others entered the market for the labelled good. About 50 per cent of the former buyers in the no-information situation withdrew the offer they had made prior to information communication. For example, of the 35 subjects who were willing to buy the unlabelled apple when uninformed, 21 were no longer willing to do so after being informed. On the other hand, 36 subjects were willing to buy the labelled apple when they were informed. This corresponds to 21 subjects who exit the unlabelled apple market and 6 who entered the labelled market. The within-subject test takes into account only subjects who were present in both markets. Instead of quoting a buying price equal to zero, subjects preferred to stay out of the market. By withdrawing from the transaction, however, they clearly expressed their rejection of the product.

Since the price difference $P_2^* - P_1$ is significantly positive, our data essentially reveals that subjects are willing to pay for food safety, because they probably perceived the risk from heavy metals to their own health.

Table 15.3 Entry and exit behaviour

$P_1 - P_2^* - P_2$	Apples	Potatoes	Baguettes
0–1–0	6	4	4
1–1–0	17	9	11
1–0–0	4	4	2

Note: 0 = absent in the market, 1 = present in the market.
Ex: 0–1–0 = absent for P_1, present for P_2^* and absent for P_2.

4.2 Values

Although expressed values are hypothetical, it is worth analysing how subjects revised their valuations after information was provided, and to compare the results with the revision of the buying price. In contrast to buying prices which were expressed by different subjects depending on the product type and on the available information, all subjects had to state their valuations for each product under each condition. Furthermore, not all participants necessarily understood that their dominant strategy was to announce a buying price equal to their 'true' value. Phase 3 of the questionnaire allowed us to check the subject's understanding of the dominant strategy.[2] Elimination of subjects who did not understand their dominant strategy (that is, their buying price differed by more than 2 points from their valuation) does not alter the test results reported in Table 15.2,[3] but after this elimination some of the price differences become significant at the 5 per cent level. Table 15.4 summarizes our findings for the expressed valuations for the whole sample of subjects. Details of the value distribution can be found in Appendix 15A1 (Table 15A1.2).

Table 15.4 Mean hypothetical value for each product elicited by the BDM procedure

	n	V1	V2	$V2^*$	V2 < V1	$V2^*$ > V2	$V2^*$ > V1
Apples	60	10.04 (3.9)	9.49 (4.08)	11.87 (5.1)	NS	5%	5%
Potatoes	60	12.85 (4.51)	11.10 (5.29)	14.03 (6.38)	10%	5%	5%
Baguettes	60	4.27 (1.52)	4.07 (1.58)	5.33 (2.47)	NS	5%	5%

Note: Standard deviations in parentheses.
NS means not significant.

The valuation of the unlabelled products decreases on average when information is provided, and that of labelled products increases on average with respect to unlabelled products, both with and without information. As for the buying prices, none of the differences is not significant. While the valuation of labelled products is significantly higher than that of unlabelled products – both with and without information – there is no significant downward revision of the valuation of unlabelled products. This result confirms our previous observation about buying prices for unlabelled products, which were not significantly affected when information was provided. Combined with the observation that valuations are not reduced when information is provided, we can conclude that subjects value labelling *per se* because these products provide better food safety. Subjects seem to be more attracted by the guarantee of food safety offered by labelled products rather than distracted by the absence of such a guarantee for unlabelled products whose heavy metal content is unknown.

In contrast to buying prices, the *ex post* difference between valuations for labelled and unlabelled products is significant for all goods, which implies again that subjects put a higher value on labelled goods when they are aware of heavy metal content. Note also that we do not observe a value increase for unlabelled goods when information is provided. This confirms our assumption that the increase in buying price was due to exits and entries in the market after information provision.

To get a clearer picture of the process of value revision, Table 15.5 reports the average rate of variation for each product. Since, both for the price and the value statements, the null hypothesis (no revision) for unlabelled products is always accepted, the first column deserves special attention. This column reveals an effective increase for the labelled product.

Table 15.5 Average rate of value increase/decrease per product (%)

	$(V2^* - V1)/V1$	$(V2 - V1)/V1$	$(V2^* - V2)/V2$
Apples	18	– 5	25
Potatoes	9	– 14	27
Baguettes	25	– 5	31

Moreover, in the last column, which corresponds to a situation of a market where the two products would both be available, the (average) relative increase in value for labelled products ranges from one-quarter to one-third. This can be considered as a strong rate of increase, particularly for common products such as bread. Such magnitudes are comparable to relative price differences between conventional products and biological products (between

15 and 50 per cent in France according to the product, see Sylvander 1999). However, not all the subjects agreed to purchase the labelled product. In this experiment, only half of the subjects declared that they were potential buyers (see Table 15.1).

5. CONCLUSION

Our experimental data exhibit two major results. First, subjects value food safety when they are informed, by estimating a higher value for labelled products and by submitting higher bids for labelled products. Second, we observe that the process of value/bid revision is asymmetric. Our hypothesis was that information about heavy metal content would both decrease the value/bid of unlabelled products and increase the value/bid of labelled products with respect to the stated value/bid in the uninformed case. Instead we observe that the value/price decrease of unlabelled products is not significant, while the value/bid of labelled ones increases significantly. A possible interpretation of this result is that subjects are willing to pay an *insurance premium* for labelled products because such products are perceived as being safer. On the other hand, why is the value/bid of unlabelled products not significantly altered? According to Prospect Theory (see Kahneman and Tversky 1974), people are more sensitive to losses than to gains of the same magnitude. Subjects should therefore be more sensitive to the safety loss of unlabelled goods than to the safety gain of labelled products. Indeed, the information provided in the experiment induced a change of reference point which should have altered subjects' evaluations of the products. Since the price (value) of labelled products increased more than the price (value) of unlabelled products, perhaps subjects perceived that the increase in safety offered by labelled products was much larger than the decrease in safety for unlabelled products. Finally, we observe in our data quite a large relative value change which can be compared to figures for real markets of bio-products. Therefore, our findings seem to be in accordance with real market data, which again raises the question how food prices are affected by information about quality uncertainty.

ACKNOWLEDGEMENT

We would like to thank Alexandra Demangeon, Roseline Bouchon and Kene Boun My for their help with the experimental organization.

NOTES

1. Or in the case where some high contaminations occurred in some populations (that is, cadmium and mercury in Japan, lead (saturnism) on young children and so on).
2. Phase 3 was intended to familiarize the subjects with the BDM procedure. We elicited private values for a token. Then three markets for tokens were organized. The first two markets were for training purposes only, but in the third market the tokens were actually sold. The data collected from the real market were taken as an indicator of the subject's understanding of his/her dominant strategy, that is, announcing a buying price for the token equal to his/her private (induced) value.
3. Ten subjects were excluded.

REFERENCES

Bagnara, G.L. (1996), 'Consumer willingness to pay for food safety: results from a survey on peaches', *Acta Horticulturae*, **429**, 157–64.

Becker, G., M. Degroot and J. Marschak (1964), 'Measuring utility by a single-response sequential method', *Behavioral Science*, **9**, 226–32.

Buhr, B.L., D.J. Hayes, J.F. Shogren and J.B. Kliebenstein (1993), 'Valuing ambiguity: the case of genetically engineered growth enhancer', *Journal of Agricultural and Resource Economics*, **18** (2), 175–84.

Decloître, F. (1998), 'La part des différents aliments dans l'exposition au plomb, au cadmium, et au mercure en France', *Cahiers de Nutrition et Diététique*, **33** (3), 167–75.

Fox, J.A, J.F Shogren, D.J Hayes and J.B Kliebenstein (1998), 'Contingent values with experimental auctions', *American Journal of Agricultural Economics*, **80** (3), 455–65.

Hayes, D.J, J.F Shogren, A.Y Shin and J.B Kliebenstein (1995), 'Valuing food safety in experimental auction markets', *American Journal of Agricultural Economics*, **77**, 40–53.

Kahneman, D. and A. Tversky (1979), 'Prospect Theory: an analysis of decision under risk', *Econometrica*, **47** (2), 263–91.

Lin, C.T.J. and J.W. Milon (1995), 'Contingent Valuation of health risk reductions for shellfish', in J.A. Caswell (ed.), *Valuing Food Safety and Nutrition*, Boulder, San Francisco and Oxford: Westview Press, pp. 83–114.

Maximilien, R. and R. Masse (1994), 'Evolution du risque toxicologiques des métaux non ferreux', *Réalités Industrielles*, February, 56–60.

Melton, B.E., W.E. Huffman and J.F. Shogren (1996), 'Economic values of pork attributes: hedonic price analysis of experimental auction data', *Review of Agricultural Economics*, **18**, 613–27.

Shin, S.Y., J. Kliebenstein, D.J. Hayes and J.F. Shogren (1992), 'Consumer willingness to pay for safer food products', *Journal of Food Safety*, **13**, 51–9.

Shogren, J.F. (1993), 'Experimental markets and environmental policy', *Agricultural and Resource Economics Review*, October, 117–29.

Stenger, A. (2000), 'Experimental valuation of food safety', *Food Policy*, **25** (2), April, 211–18.

Sylvander, B. (1999), 'La demande de produits biologiques: une perception de plus en plus vague et vulnérable', *Echo des MIN*, 144, 1999/03, pp. 74–6.

APPENDIX 15A1

Table 15A1.1 *Prices elicited by the BDM procedure: some indicators*

	P_1			P_2			$P2^*$		
	Median	P_{1min}	P_{1max}	Median	P_{2min}	P_{2max}	Median	P_{2*min}	P_{2*max}
Apples	11	6	18	12	8	20	13	7	20
Potatoes	12	8	20	12.5	7	24	14	8	25
Baguettes	4.5	3	7	4	3	10	5	3	20

Note: The effectives are the same as in Table 15.1: only the individuals who bought the product.

Table 15A1.2 *Values elicited by the BDM procedure: some indicators (60 subjects)*

	V_1			V_2			$V2^*$		
	Median	V_{1min}	V_{1max}	Median	V_{2min}	V_{2max}	Median	V_{2*min}	V_{2*max}
Apples	12	4	18	12.5	6.5	20	13	6	21
Potatoes	12	8	20	13	7	25	15	9	29
Baguettes	4.5	3	10	4	3	10	5	4	20

Index